THE AVALON CHRONICLES

VOLUME TWO

THE GIRL AND THE UNICORN

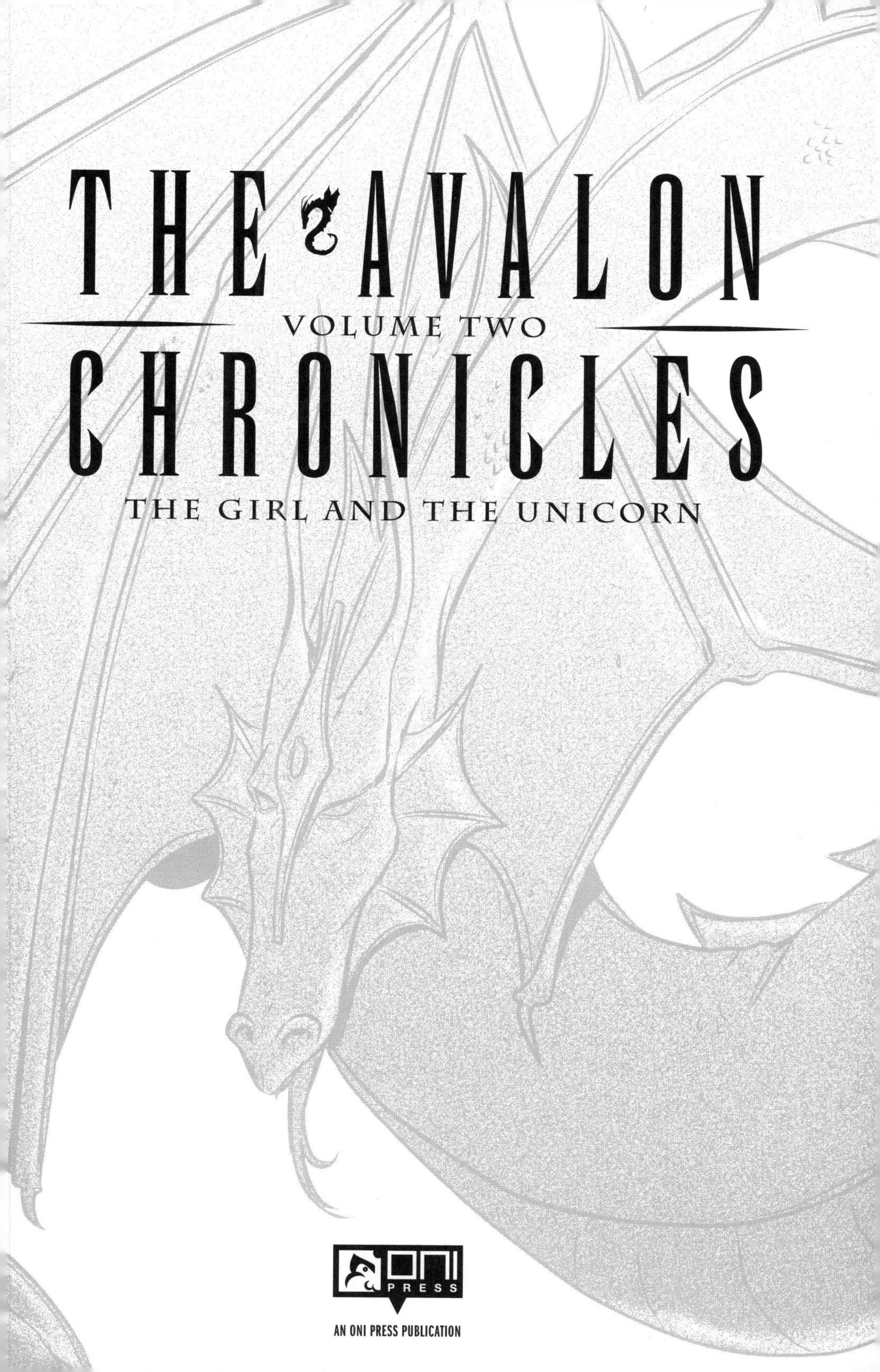

AN ONI PRESS PUBLICATION

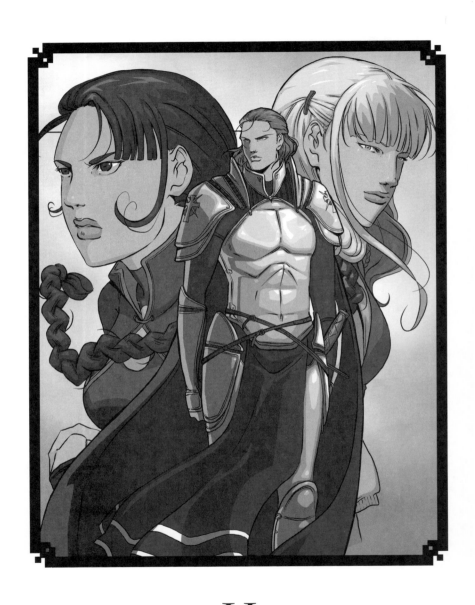

II

THE &AVALON

VOLUME TWO

CHRONICLES

THE GIRL AND THE UNICORN

WRITTEN BY
NUNZIO DEFILIPPIS
& CHRISTINA WEIR

ILLUSTRATED BY
EMMA VIECELI

COVER ILLUSTRATION COLORED BY
DAN JACKSON

LETTERED BY
ED BRISSON

TONED BY
NANA LI

DESIGNED BY
KEITH WOOD

EDITED BY
JILL BEATON

ONI PRESS, INC.

JOE NOZEMACK • PUBLISHER

JAMES LUCAS JONES • EDITOR IN CHIEF

KEITH A. WOOD • ART DIRECTOR

GEORGE ROHAC • DIRECTOR OF BUSINESS DEVELOPMENT

TOM SHIMMIN • DIRECTOR OF SALES AND MARKETING

JILL BEATON • EDITOR

CHARLIE CHU • EDITOR

JASON STOREY • GRAPHIC DESIGNER

TROY LOOK • DIGITAL PREPRESS LEAD

ROBIN HERRERA • ADMINISTRATIVE ASSISTANT

THE AVALON

VOLUME TWO

CHRONICLES

THE GIRL AND THE UNICORN

1305 SE MARTIN LUTHER KING JR. BLVD.
SUITE A
PORTLAND, OR 97214

WWW.ONIPRESS.COM
FACEBOOK.COM/ONIPRESS • TWITTER.COM/ONIPRESS • ONIPRESS.TUMBLR.COM

FIRST EDITION: JUNE 2013
ISBN: 978-1-934964-90-3
eISBN: 978-1-62010-033-2

LIBRARY OF CONGRESS CONTROL NUMBER: 2011933168

1 3 5 7 9 10 8 6 4 2

PRINTED IN CHINA

Chapter 1

SPRING BREAK

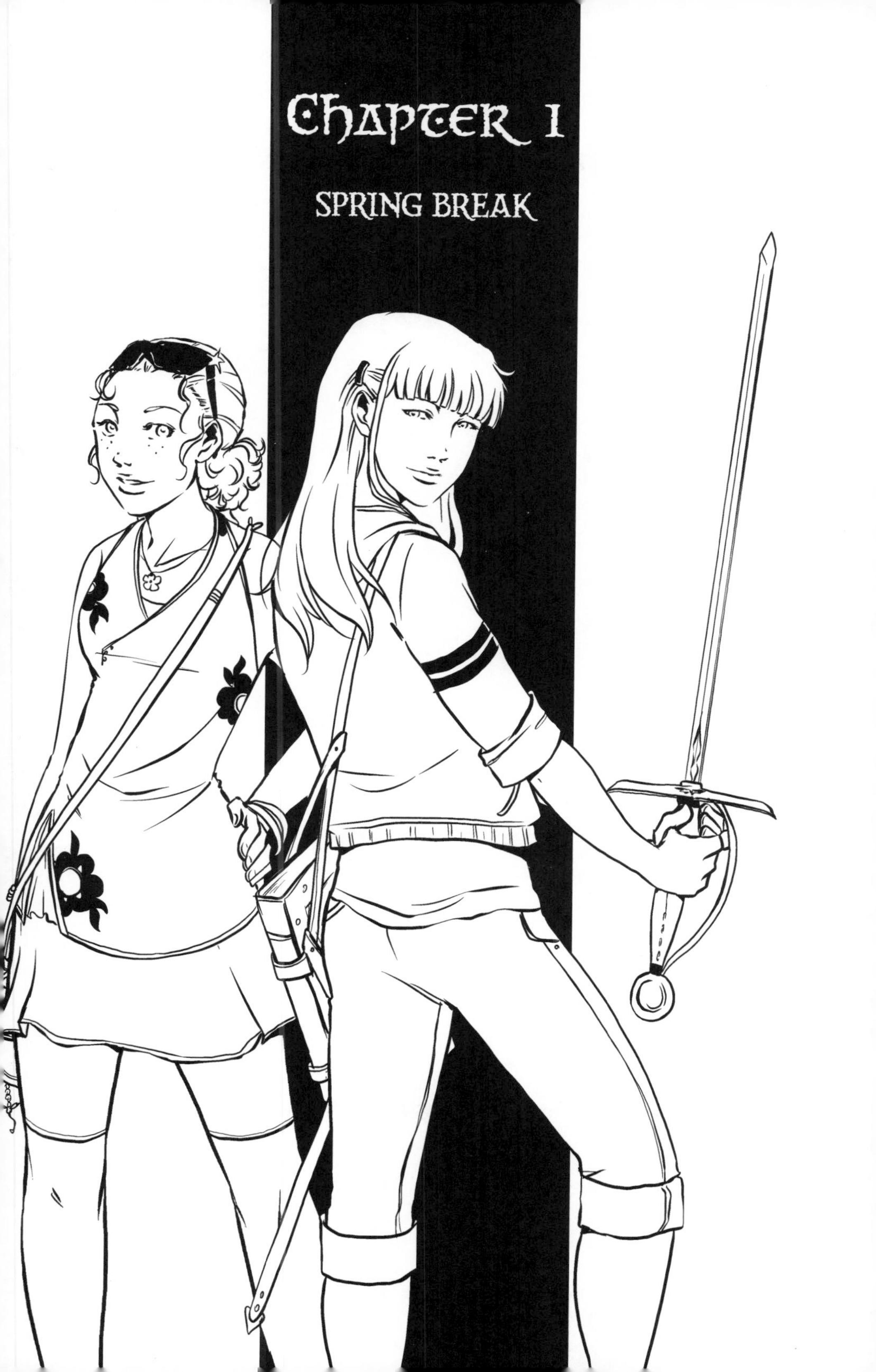

The Kingdom of Avalon was at war. Emperor Khrom's long reign of terror was now finally being challenged. The Keepers Of The Flame, former Royal Knights sworn to return the rightful royal family, the Finns, to power, had emerged from seclusion to challenge the warlord. From Deep Haven in the South, they pushed North and Eastward, capturing several towns along the way.

The Keepers have been roused by the arrival of Aeslin Finn, daughter of the missing King, and the newest Dragon Knight, from the magical world known as Earth.

~~When Aeslin awakened Blue Moon, the last of the Dragons, she stirred the hearts of~~

~~Accompanied by the aspiring knight Cassidy, Aeslin had awakened...~~

Aeslin is magnificent and I can't write.

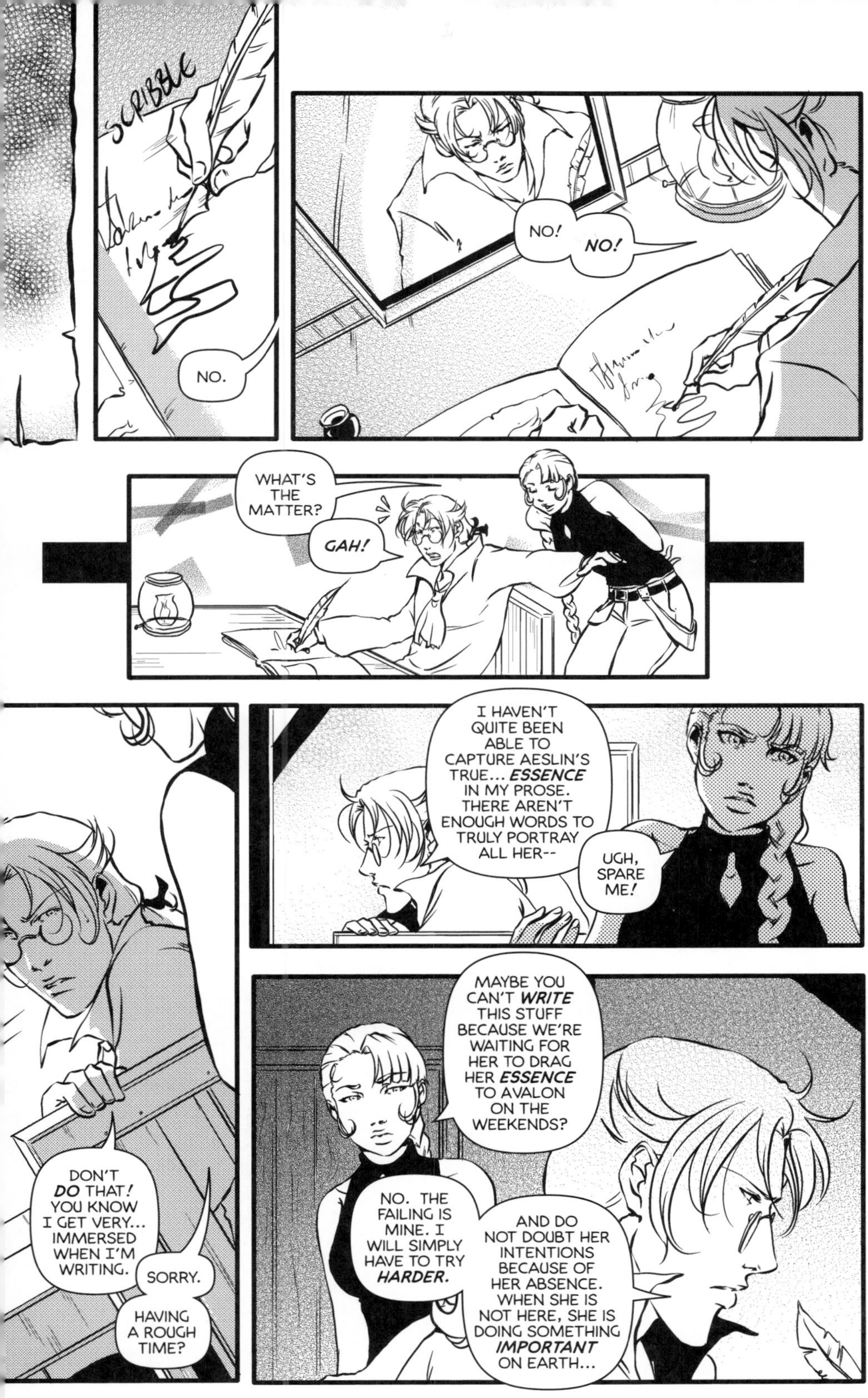
SCRIBBLE
NO.
NO!
NO!
WHAT'S THE MATTER?
GAH!
I HAVEN'T QUITE BEEN ABLE TO CAPTURE AESLIN'S TRUE... ESSENCE IN MY PROSE. THERE AREN'T ENOUGH WORDS TO TRULY PORTRAY ALL HER--
UGH, SPARE ME!
DON'T DO THAT! YOU KNOW I GET VERY... IMMERSED WHEN I'M WRITING.
SORRY.
HAVING A ROUGH TIME?
MAYBE YOU CAN'T WRITE THIS STUFF BECAUSE WE'RE WAITING FOR HER TO DRAG HER ESSENCE TO AVALON ON THE WEEKENDS?
NO. THE FAILING IS MINE. I WILL SIMPLY HAVE TO TRY HARDER.
AND DO NOT DOUBT HER INTENTIONS BECAUSE OF HER ABSENCE. WHEN SHE IS NOT HERE, SHE IS DOING SOMETHING IMPORTANT ON EARTH...

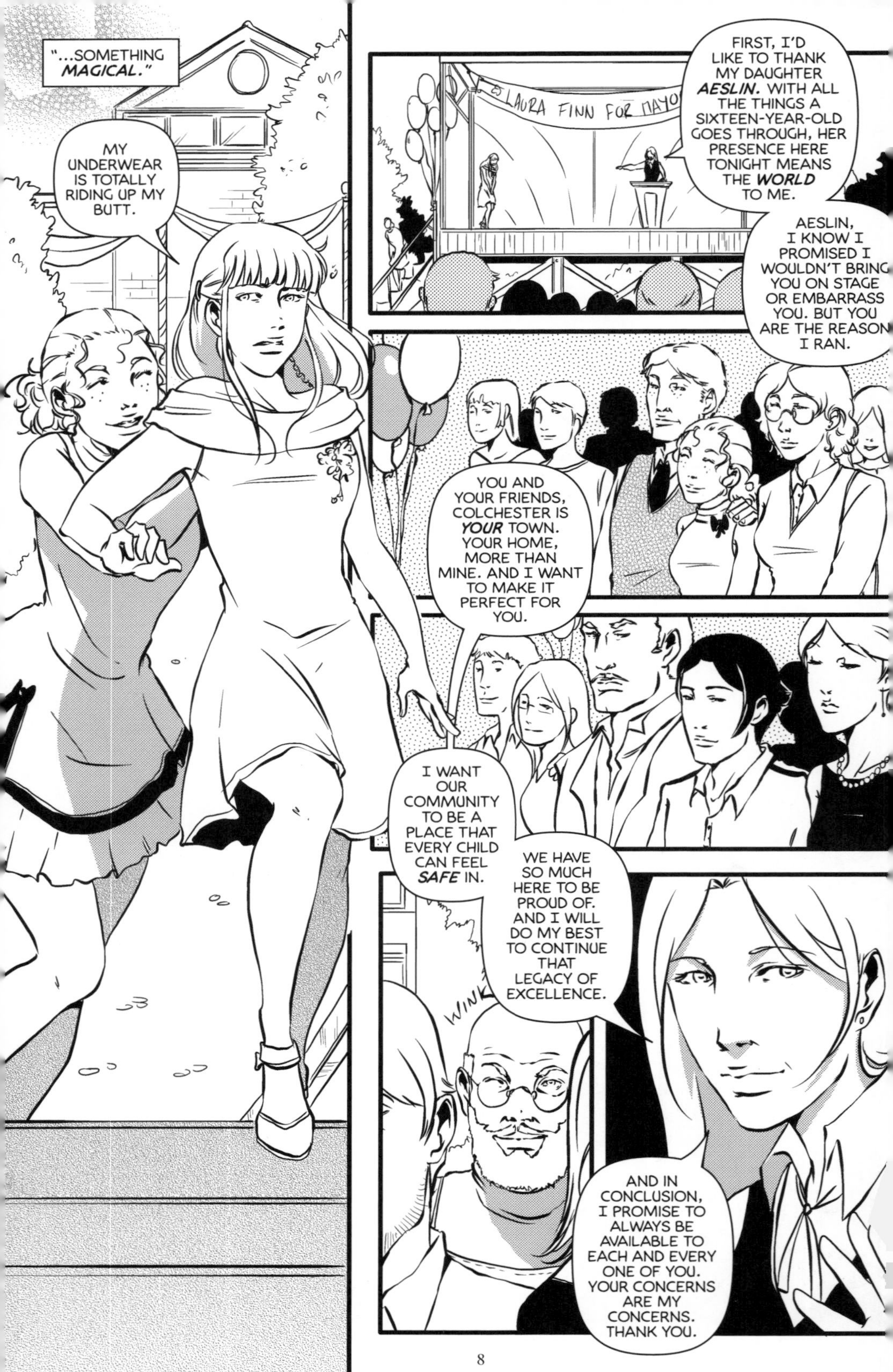
"...SOMETHING MAGICAL."
MY UNDERWEAR IS TOTALLY RIDING UP MY BUTT.
LAURA FINN FOR MAYO
FIRST, I'D LIKE TO THANK MY DAUGHTER AESLIN. WITH ALL THE THINGS A SIXTEEN-YEAR-OLD GOES THROUGH, HER PRESENCE HERE TONIGHT MEANS THE WORLD TO ME.
AESLIN, I KNOW I PROMISED I WOULDN'T BRING YOU ON STAGE OR EMBARRASS YOU. BUT YOU ARE THE REASON I RAN.
YOU AND YOUR FRIENDS, COLCHESTER IS YOUR TOWN. YOUR HOME, MORE THAN MINE. AND I WANT TO MAKE IT PERFECT FOR YOU.
I WANT OUR COMMUNITY TO BE A PLACE THAT EVERY CHILD CAN FEEL SAFE IN.
WE HAVE SO MUCH HERE TO BE PROUD OF. AND I WILL DO MY BEST TO CONTINUE THAT LEGACY OF EXCELLENCE.
WINK
AND IN CONCLUSION, I PROMISE TO ALWAYS BE AVAILABLE TO EACH AND EVERY ONE OF YOU. YOUR CONCERNS ARE MY CONCERNS. THANK YOU.

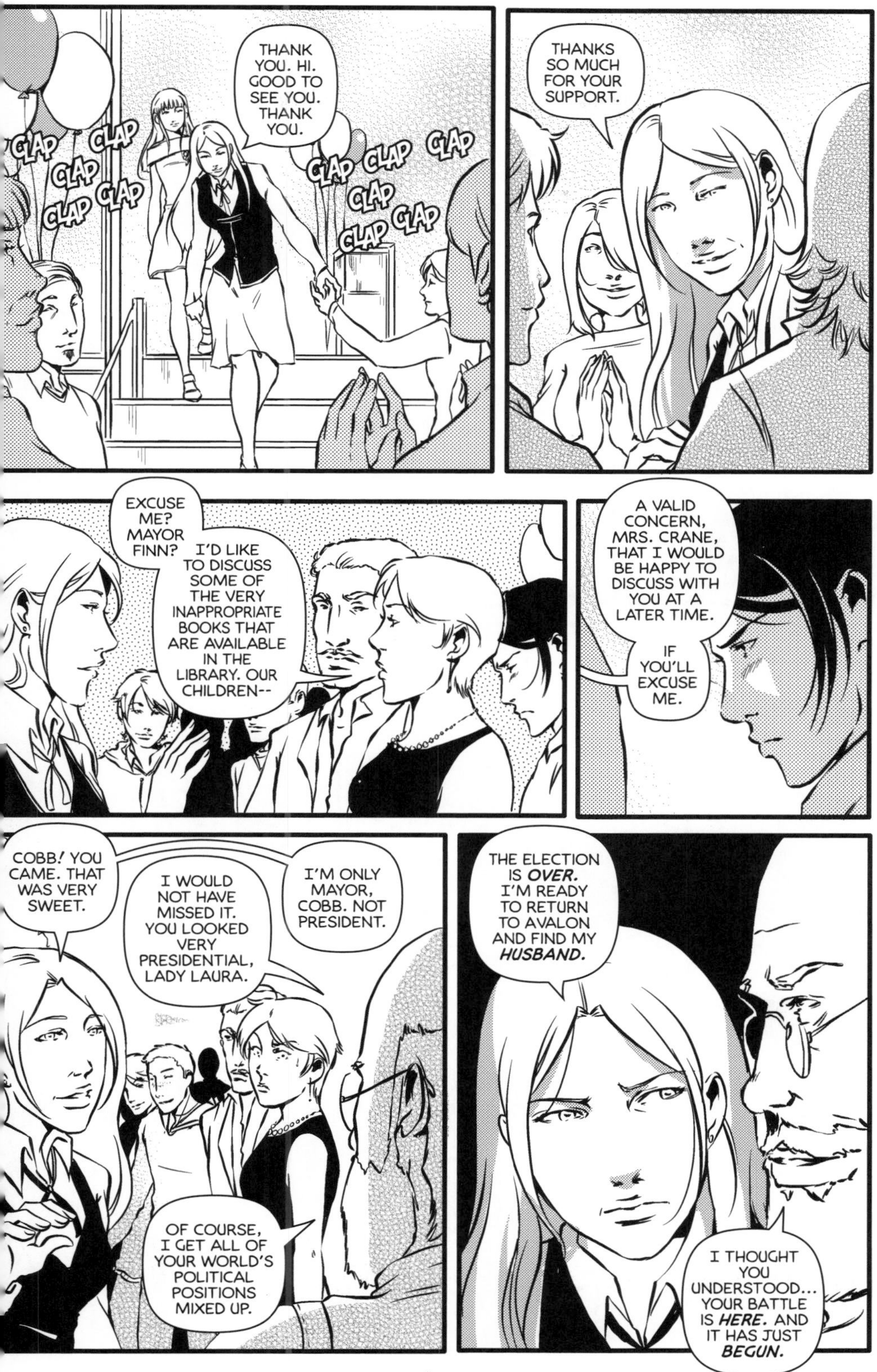
THANK YOU. HI. GOOD TO SEE YOU. THANK YOU.
CLAP CLAP CLAP CLAP CLAP
CLAP CLAP CLAP CLAP CLAP CLAP
THANKS SO MUCH FOR YOUR SUPPORT.
EXCUSE ME? MAYOR FINN?
I'D LIKE TO DISCUSS SOME OF THE VERY INAPPROPRIATE BOOKS THAT ARE AVAILABLE IN THE LIBRARY. OUR CHILDREN--
A VALID CONCERN, MRS. CRANE, THAT I WOULD BE HAPPY TO DISCUSS WITH YOU AT A LATER TIME.
IF YOU'LL EXCUSE ME.
COBB! YOU CAME. THAT WAS VERY SWEET.
I WOULD NOT HAVE MISSED IT. YOU LOOKED VERY PRESIDENTIAL, LADY LAURA.
I'M ONLY MAYOR, COBB. NOT PRESIDENT.
OF COURSE, I GET ALL OF YOUR WORLD'S POLITICAL POSITIONS MIXED UP.
THE ELECTION IS *OVER.* I'M READY TO RETURN TO AVALON AND FIND MY ***HUSBAND.***
I THOUGHT YOU UNDERSTOOD... YOUR BATTLE IS ***HERE.*** AND IT HAS JUST ***BEGUN.***

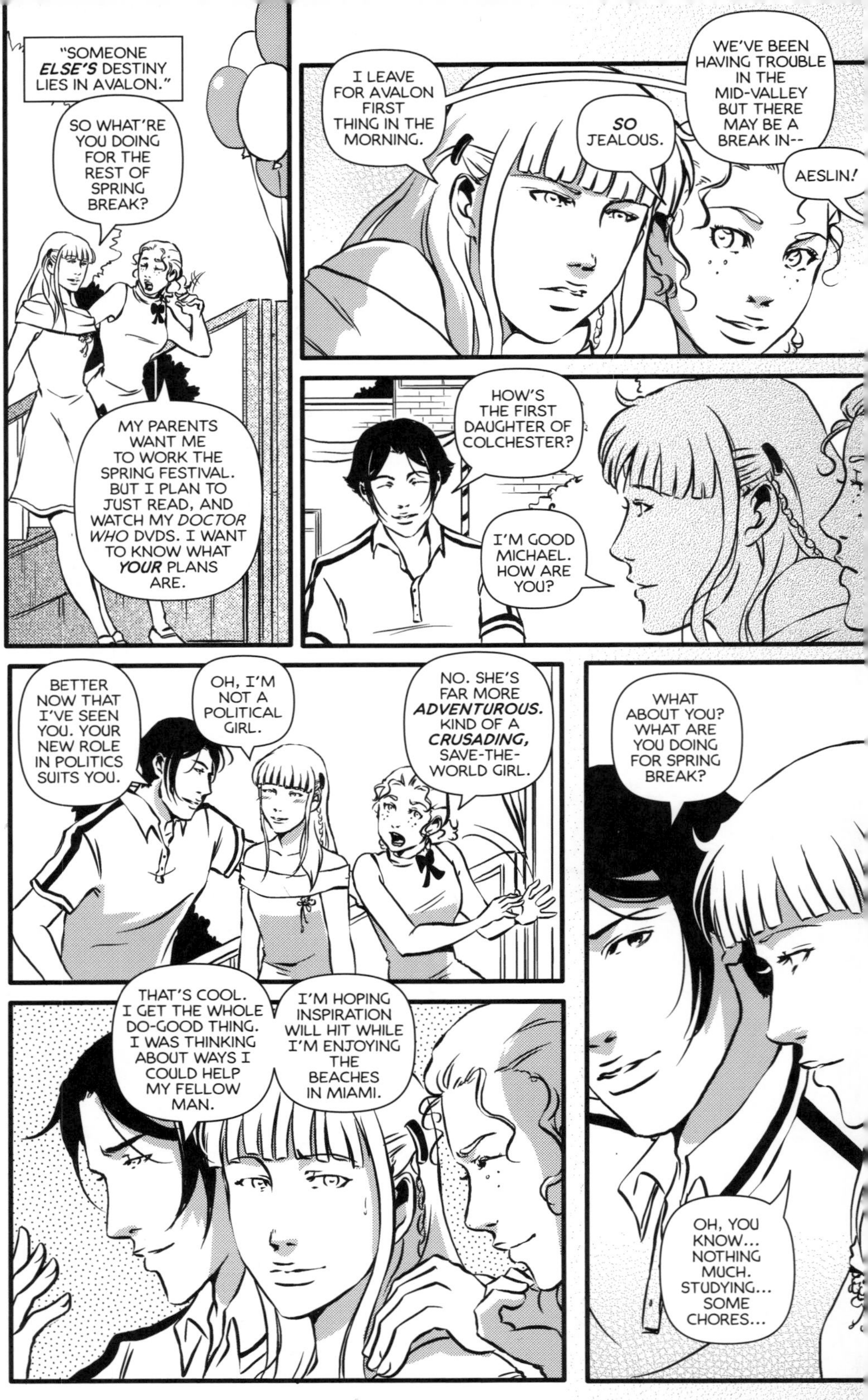
"SOMEONE *ELSE'S* DESTINY LIES IN AVALON."
SO WHAT'RE YOU DOING FOR THE REST OF SPRING BREAK?
MY PARENTS WANT ME TO WORK THE SPRING FESTIVAL. BUT I PLAN TO JUST READ, AND WATCH MY *DOCTOR WHO* DVDS. I WANT TO KNOW WHAT ***YOUR*** PLANS ARE.
I LEAVE FOR AVALON FIRST THING IN THE MORNING.
SO JEALOUS.
WE'VE BEEN HAVING TROUBLE IN THE MID-VALLEY BUT THERE MAY BE A BREAK IN--
AESLIN!
HOW'S THE FIRST DAUGHTER OF COLCHESTER?
I'M GOOD MICHAEL. HOW ARE YOU?
BETTER NOW THAT I'VE SEEN YOU. YOUR NEW ROLE IN POLITICS SUITS YOU.
OH, I'M NOT A POLITICAL GIRL.
NO. SHE'S FAR MORE ***ADVENTUROUS.*** KIND OF A ***CRUSADING,*** SAVE-THE-WORLD GIRL.
WHAT ABOUT YOU? WHAT ARE YOU DOING FOR SPRING BREAK?
THAT'S COOL. I GET THE WHOLE DO-GOOD THING. I WAS THINKING ABOUT WAYS I COULD HELP MY FELLOW MAN.
I'M HOPING INSPIRATION WILL HIT WHILE I'M ENJOYING THE BEACHES IN MIAMI.
OH, YOU KNOW... NOTHING MUCH. STUDYING... SOME CHORES...

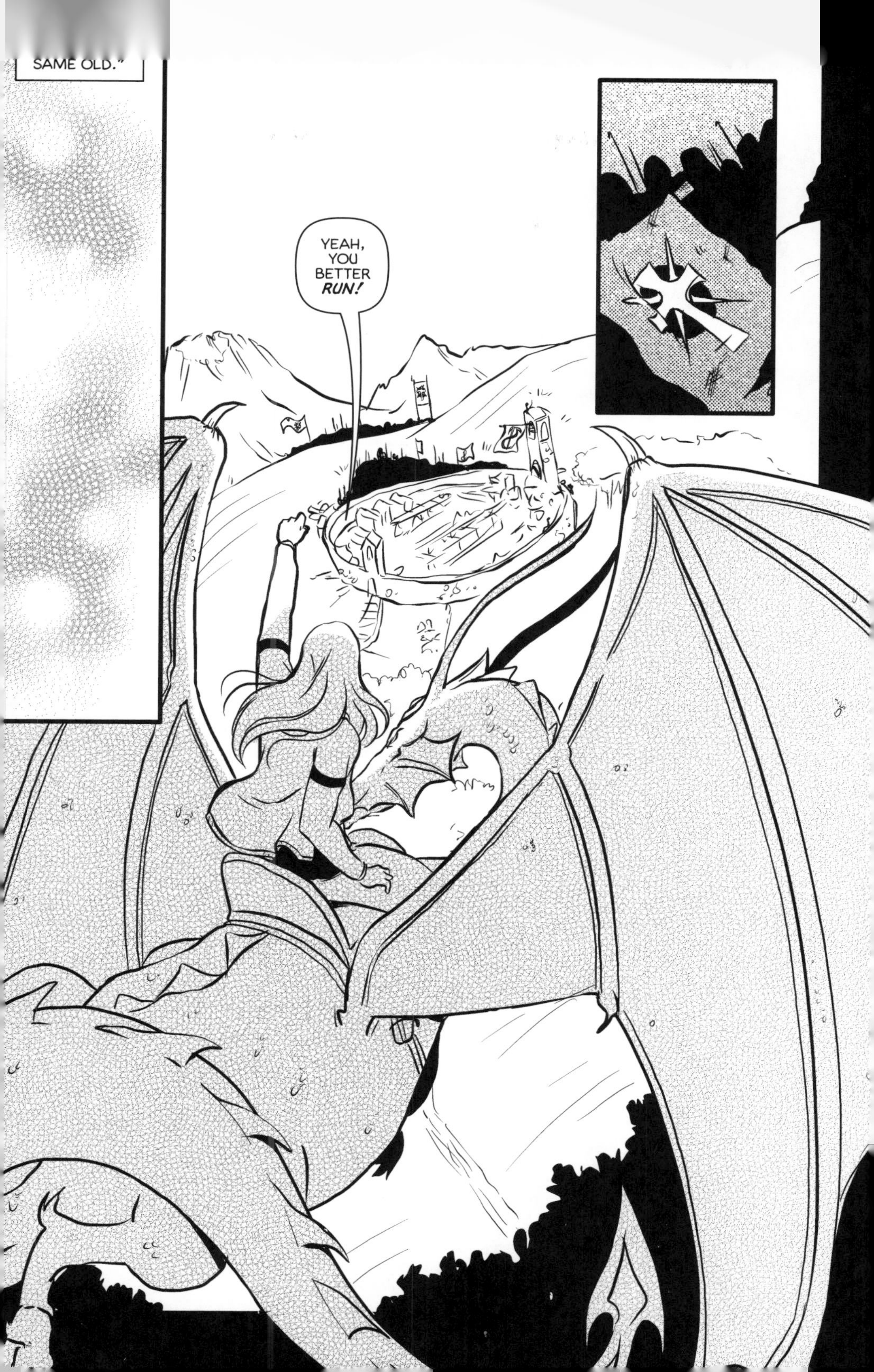
SAME OLD."
YEAH, YOU BETTER RUN!

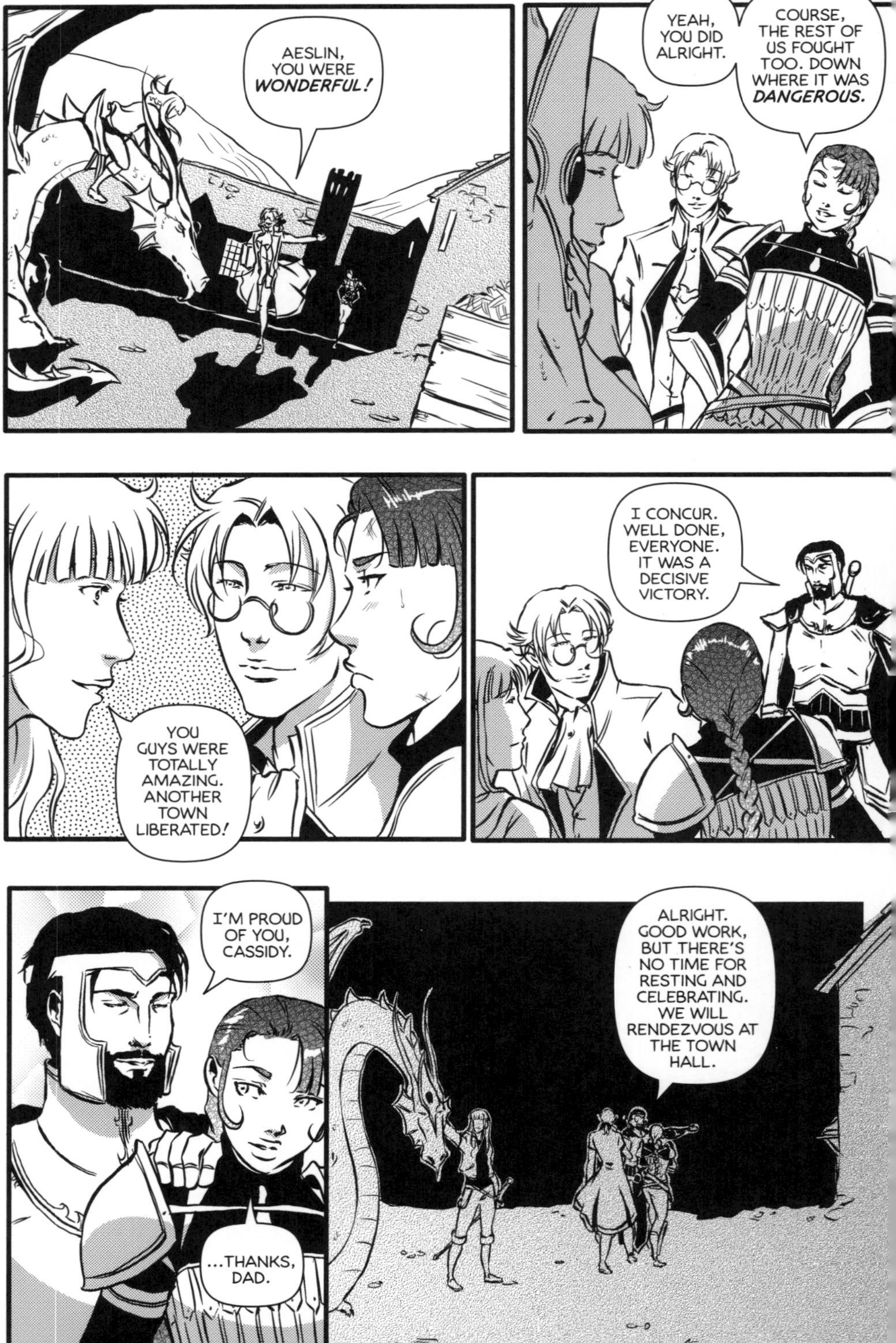

AESLIN, YOU WERE *WONDERFUL!*
YEAH, YOU DID ALRIGHT.
COURSE, THE REST OF US FOUGHT TOO. DOWN WHERE IT WAS *DANGEROUS.*
YOU GUYS WERE TOTALLY AMAZING. ANOTHER TOWN LIBERATED!
I CONCUR. WELL DONE, EVERYONE. IT WAS A DECISIVE VICTORY.
I'M PROUD OF YOU, CASSIDY.
...THANKS, DAD.
ALRIGHT. GOOD WORK, BUT THERE'S NO TIME FOR RESTING AND CELEBRATING. WE WILL RENDEZVOUS AT THE TOWN HALL.

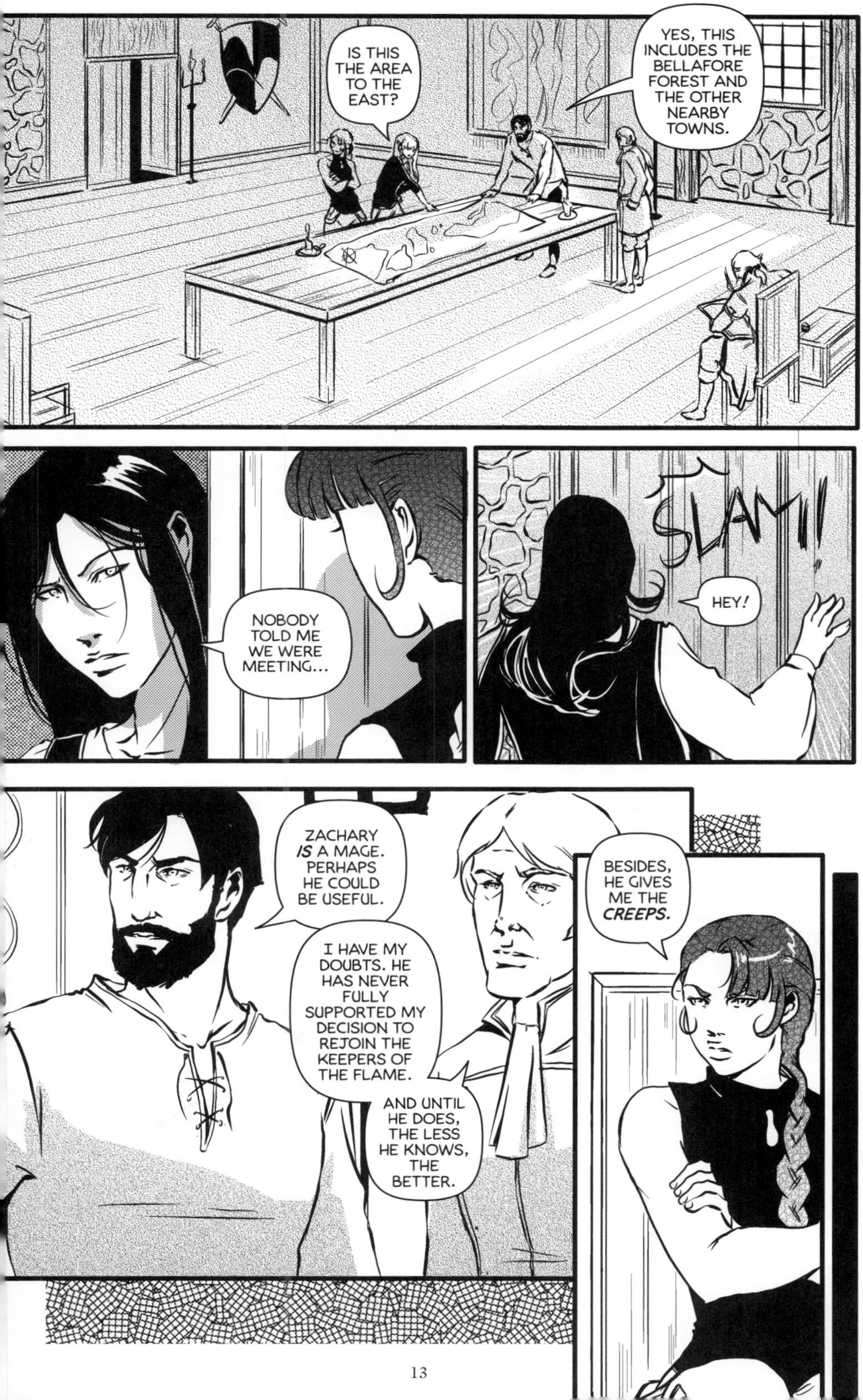
IS THIS THE AREA TO THE EAST?
YES, THIS INCLUDES THE BELLAFORE FOREST AND THE OTHER NEARBY TOWNS.
NOBODY TOLD ME WE WERE MEETING...
SLAM!!
HEY!
ZACHARY *IS* A MAGE. PERHAPS HE COULD BE USEFUL.
I HAVE MY DOUBTS. HE HAS NEVER FULLY SUPPORTED MY DECISION TO REJOIN THE KEEPERS OF THE FLAME.
AND UNTIL HE DOES, THE LESS HE KNOWS, THE BETTER.
BESIDES, HE GIVES ME THE ***CREEPS***.

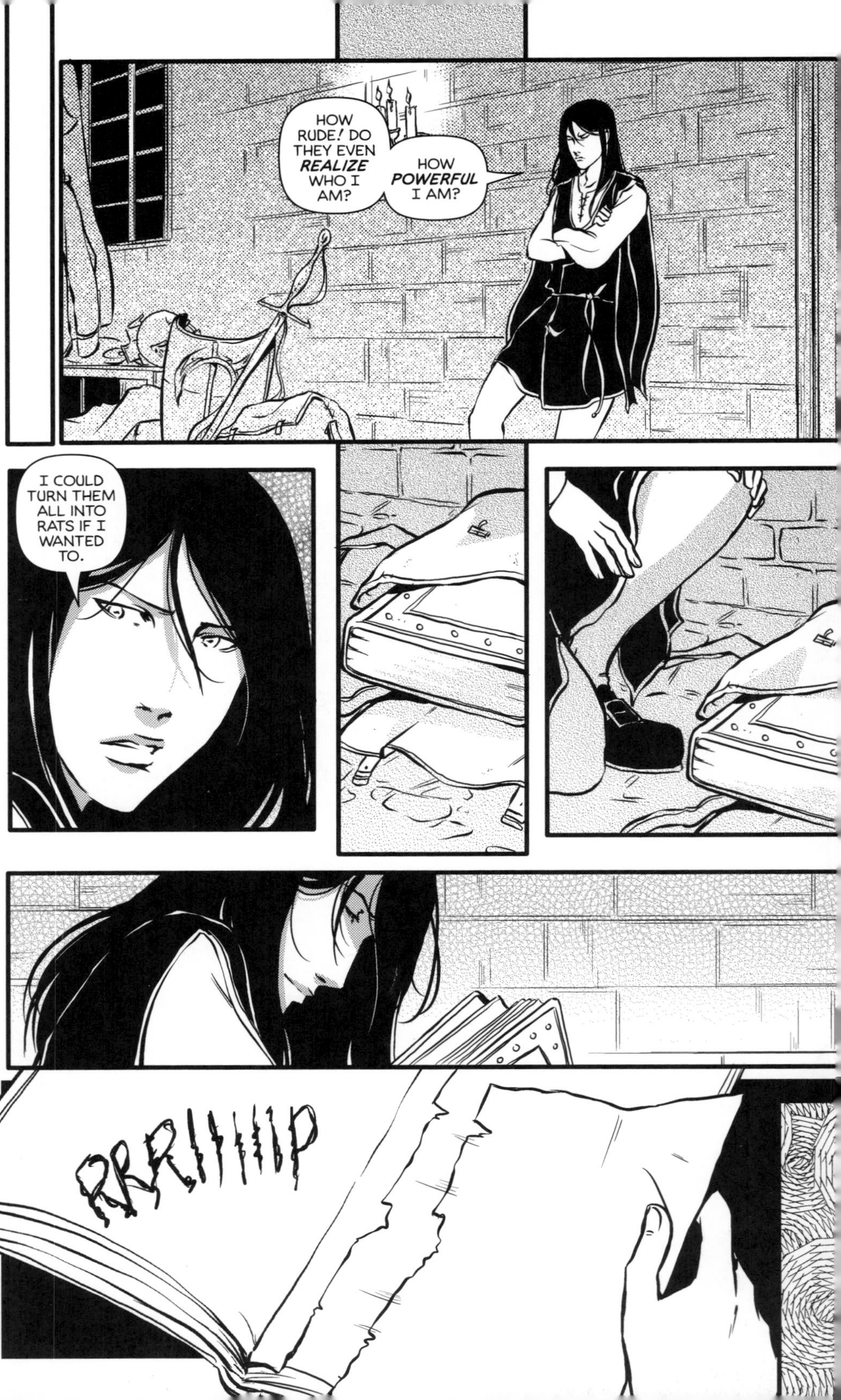
HOW RUDE! DO THEY EVEN REALIZE WHO I AM?
HOW POWERFUL I AM?
I COULD TURN THEM ALL INTO RATS IF I WANTED TO.
RRRIIIIIP

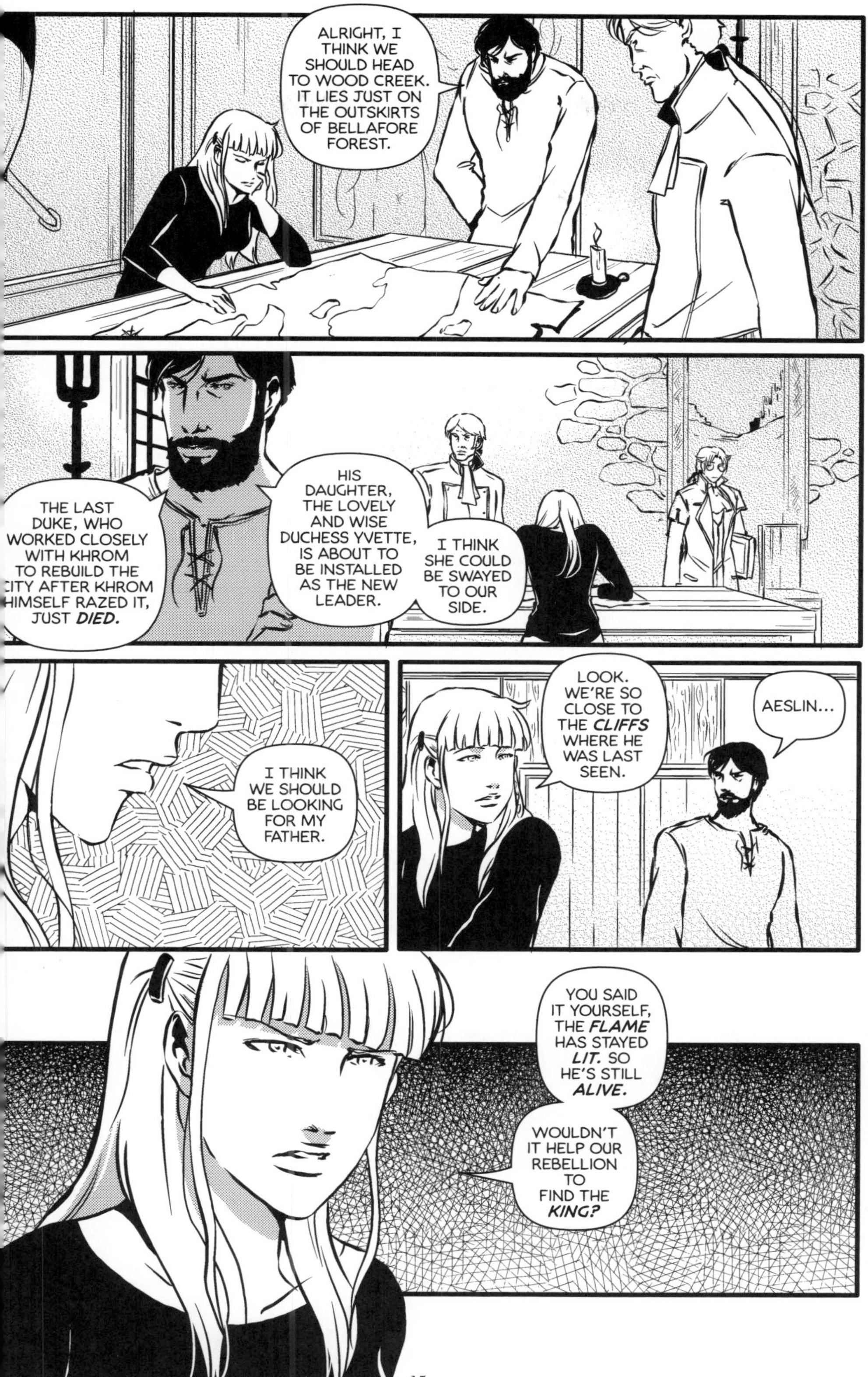

ALRIGHT, I THINK WE SHOULD HEAD TO WOOD CREEK. IT LIES JUST ON THE OUTSKIRTS OF BELLAFORE FOREST.
THE LAST DUKE, WHO WORKED CLOSELY WITH KHROM TO REBUILD THE CITY AFTER KHROM HIMSELF RAZED IT, JUST DIED.
HIS DAUGHTER, THE LOVELY AND WISE DUCHESS YVETTE, IS ABOUT TO BE INSTALLED AS THE NEW LEADER.
I THINK SHE COULD BE SWAYED TO OUR SIDE.
I THINK WE SHOULD BE LOOKING FOR MY FATHER.
LOOK. WE'RE SO CLOSE TO THE CLIFFS WHERE HE WAS LAST SEEN.
AESLIN...
YOU SAID IT YOURSELF, THE FLAME HAS STAYED LIT. SO HE'S STILL ALIVE.
WOULDN'T IT HELP OUR REBELLION TO FIND THE KING?

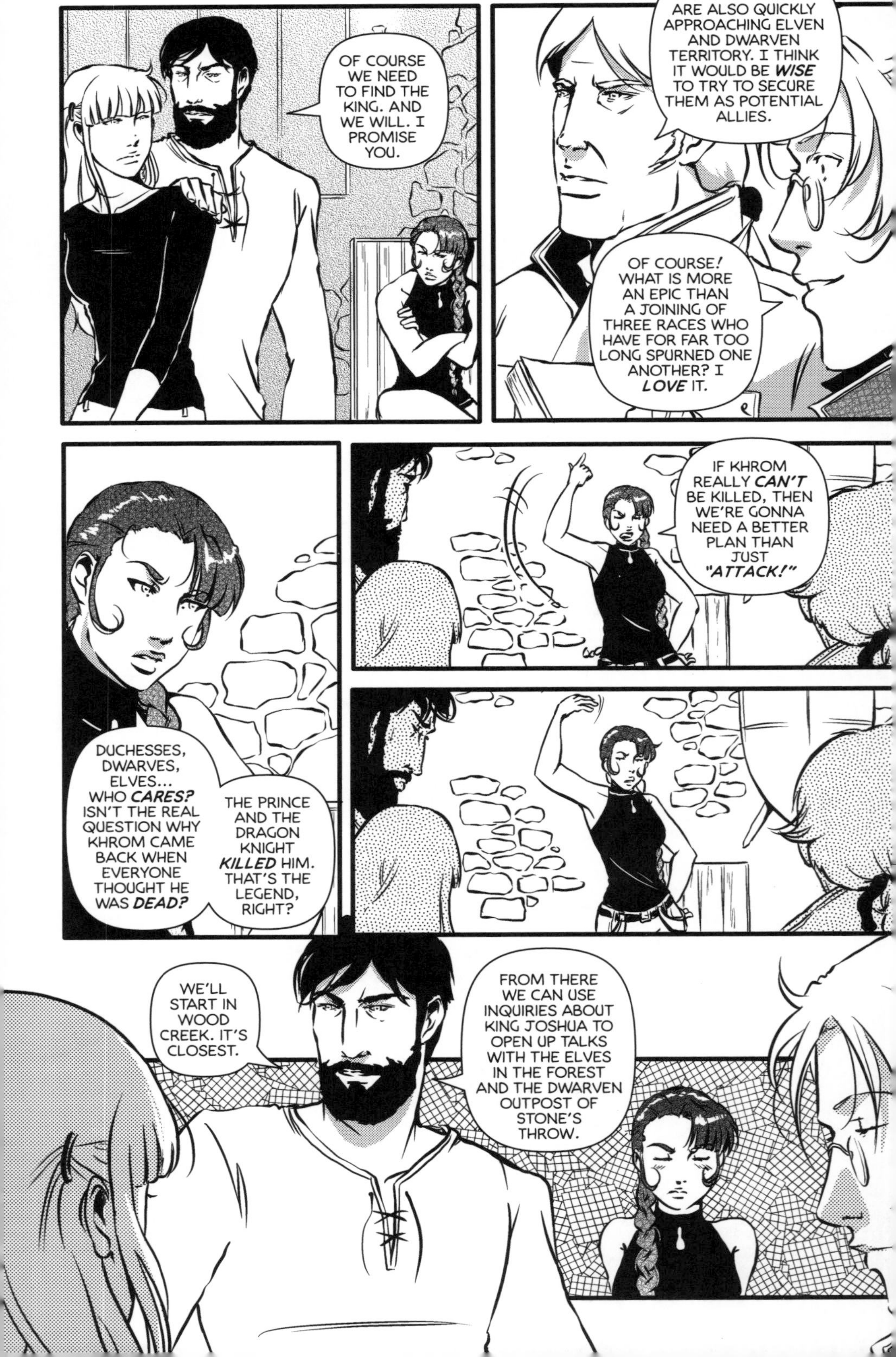

OF COURSE WE NEED TO FIND THE KING. AND WE WILL. I PROMISE YOU.
IF I MAY... WE ARE ALSO QUICKLY APPROACHING ELVEN AND DWARVEN TERRITORY. I THINK IT WOULD BE *WISE* TO TRY TO SECURE THEM AS POTENTIAL ALLIES.
OF COURSE! WHAT IS MORE AN EPIC THAN A JOINING OF THREE RACES WHO HAVE FOR FAR TOO LONG SPURNED ONE ANOTHER? I *LOVE* IT.
DUCHESSES, DWARVES, ELVES... WHO *CARES?* ISN'T THE REAL QUESTION WHY KHROM CAME BACK WHEN EVERYONE THOUGHT HE WAS *DEAD?*
THE PRINCE AND THE DRAGON KNIGHT *KILLED* HIM. THAT'S THE LEGEND, RIGHT?
IF KHROM REALLY *CAN'T* BE KILLED, THEN WE'RE GONNA NEED A BETTER PLAN THAN JUST *"ATTACK!"*
WE'LL START IN WOOD CREEK. IT'S CLOSEST.
FROM THERE WE CAN USE INQUIRIES ABOUT KING JOSHUA TO OPEN UP TALKS WITH THE ELVES IN THE FOREST AND THE DWARVEN OUTPOST OF STONE'S THROW.

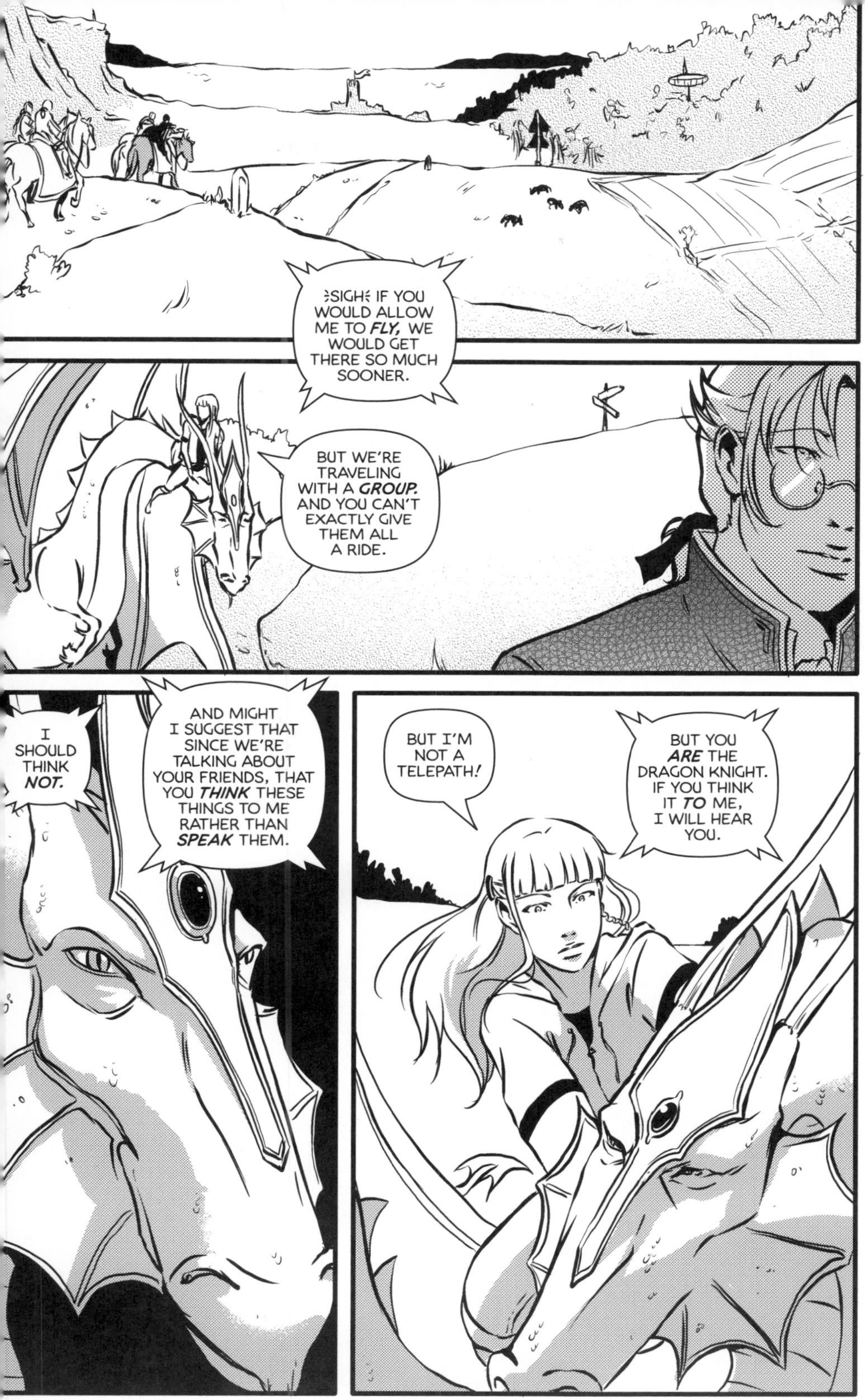
⦚SIGH⦚ IF YOU WOULD ALLOW ME TO *FLY,* WE WOULD GET THERE SO MUCH SOONER.
BUT WE'RE TRAVELING WITH A *GROUP.* AND YOU CAN'T EXACTLY GIVE THEM ALL A RIDE.
I SHOULD THINK *NOT.*
AND MIGHT I SUGGEST THAT SINCE WE'RE TALKING ABOUT YOUR FRIENDS, THAT YOU *THINK* THESE THINGS TO ME RATHER THAN *SPEAK* THEM.
BUT I'M NOT A TELEPATH!
BUT YOU *ARE* THE DRAGON KNIGHT. IF YOU THINK IT *TO* ME, I WILL HEAR YOU.

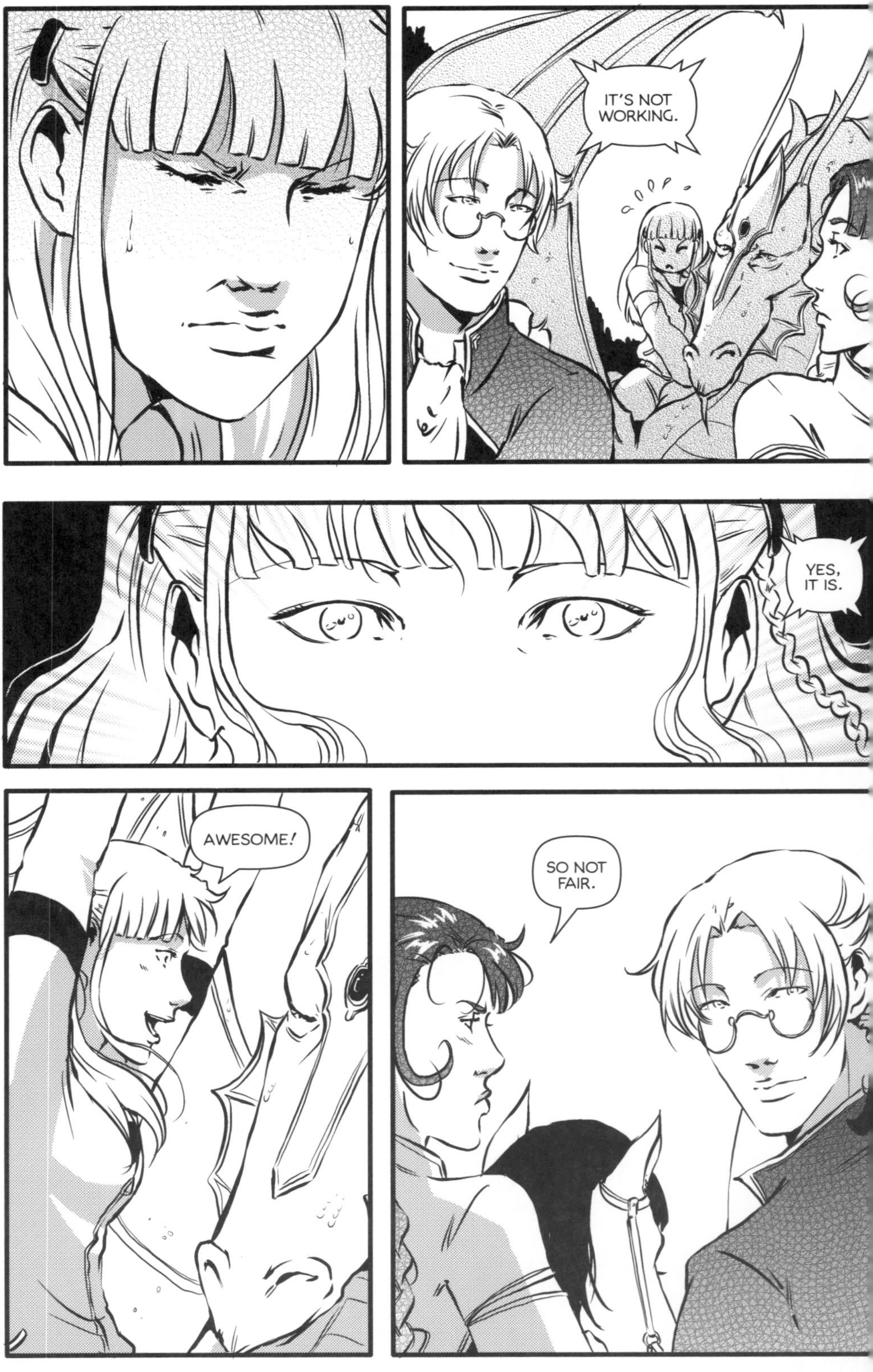
IT'S NOT WORKING.
YES, IT IS.
AWESOME!
SO NOT FAIR.

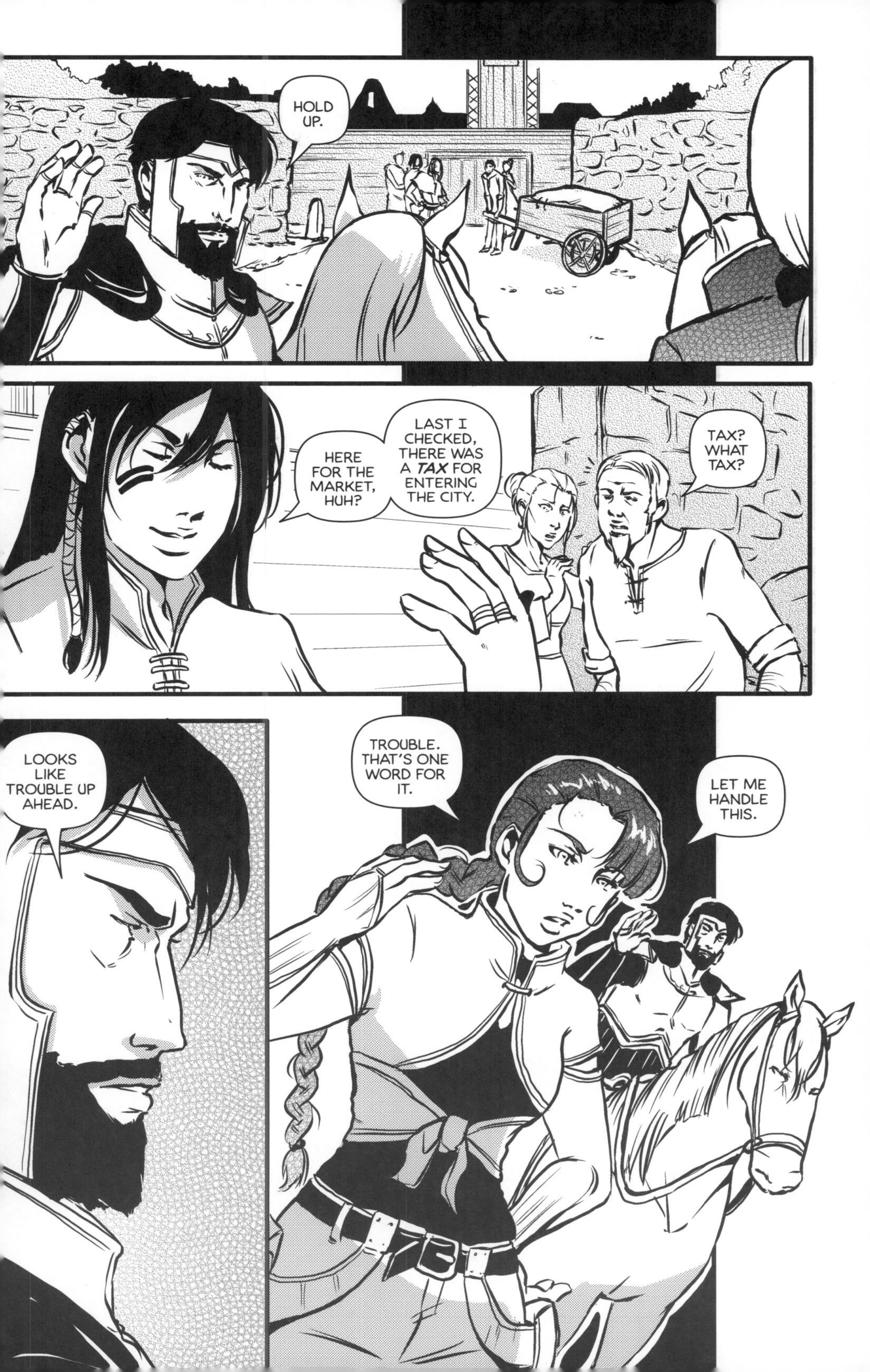
HOLD UP.
HERE FOR THE MARKET, HUH?
LAST I CHECKED, THERE WAS A *TAX* FOR ENTERING THE CITY.
TAX? WHAT TAX?
LOOKS LIKE TROUBLE UP AHEAD.
TROUBLE. THAT'S ONE WORD FOR IT.
LET ME HANDLE THIS.

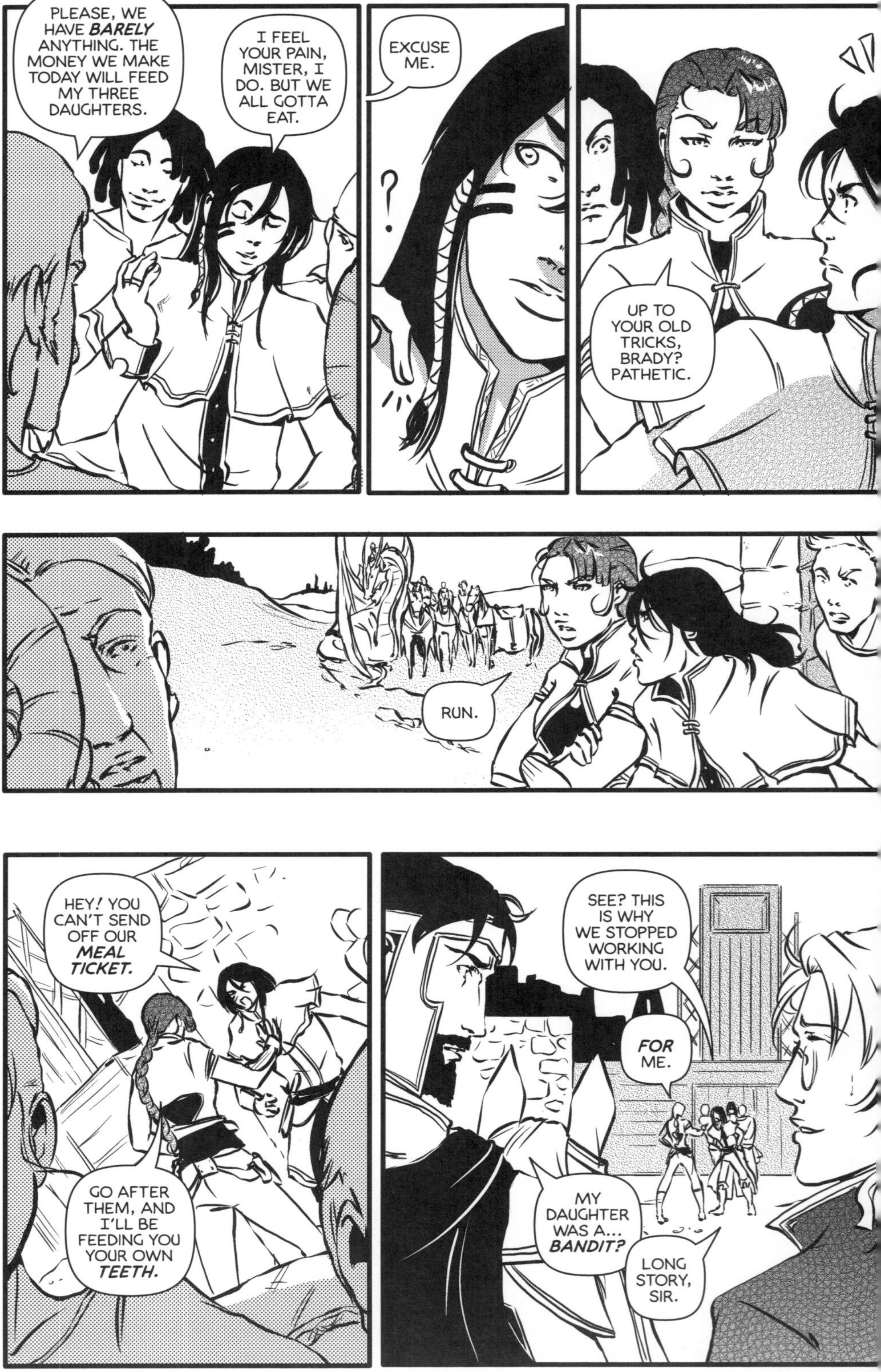
PLEASE, WE HAVE ***BARELY*** ANYTHING. THE MONEY WE MAKE TODAY WILL FEED MY THREE DAUGHTERS.
I FEEL YOUR PAIN, MISTER, I DO. BUT WE ALL GOTTA EAT.
EXCUSE ME.
?
UP TO YOUR OLD TRICKS, BRADY? PATHETIC.
RUN.
HEY! YOU CAN'T SEND OFF OUR ***MEAL TICKET.***
GO AFTER THEM, AND I'LL BE FEEDING YOU YOUR OWN ***TEETH.***
SEE? THIS IS WHY WE STOPPED WORKING WITH YOU.
FOR ME.
MY DAUGHTER WAS A... ***BANDIT?***
LONG STORY, SIR.

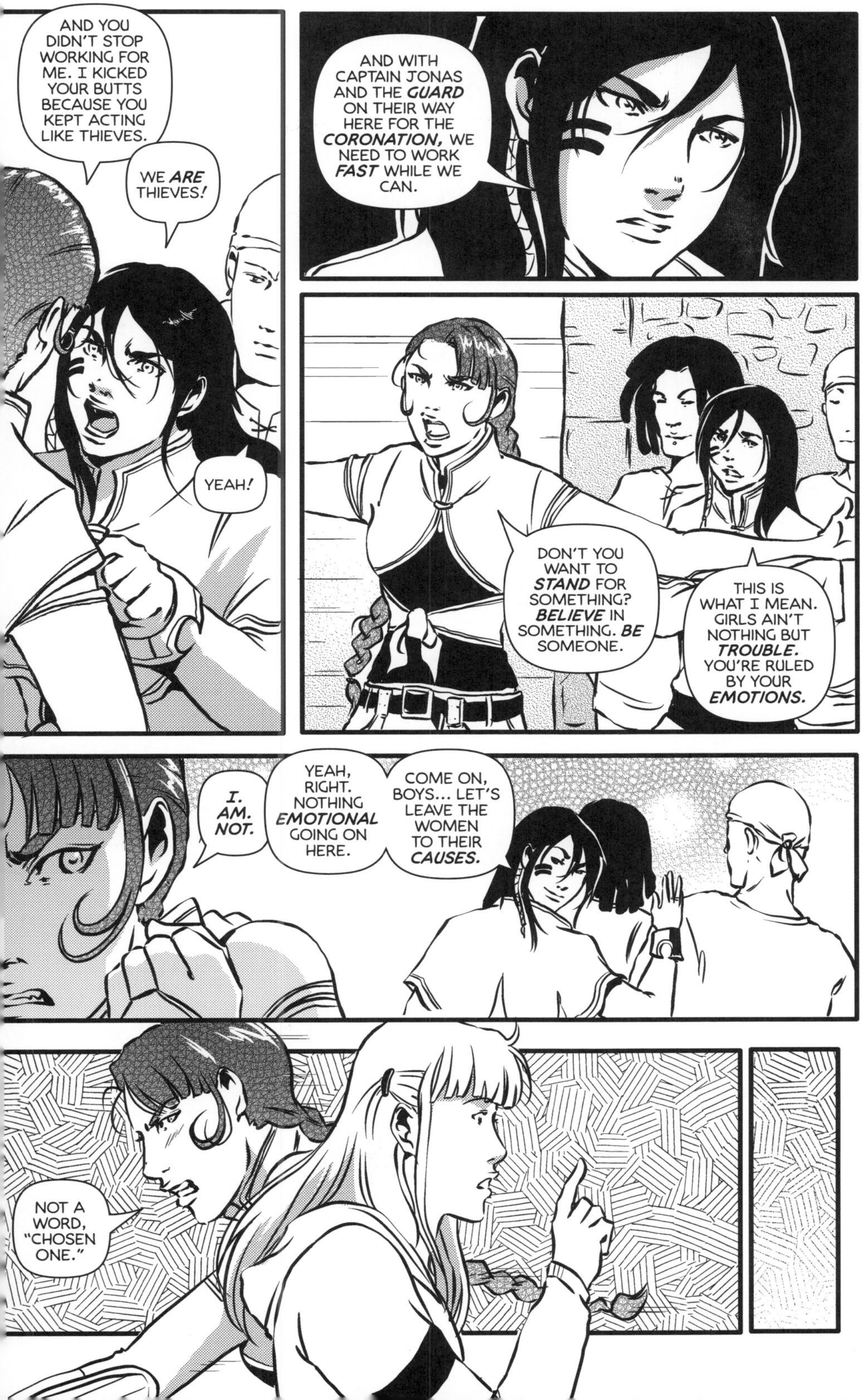
AND YOU DIDN'T STOP WORKING FOR ME. I KICKED YOUR BUTTS BECAUSE YOU KEPT ACTING LIKE THIEVES.
WE *ARE* THIEVES!
YEAH!
AND WITH CAPTAIN JONAS AND THE *GUARD* ON THEIR WAY HERE FOR THE *CORONATION,* WE NEED TO WORK *FAST* WHILE WE CAN.
DON'T YOU WANT TO *STAND* FOR SOMETHING? *BELIEVE* IN SOMETHING. *BE* SOMEONE.
THIS IS WHAT I MEAN. GIRLS AIN'T NOTHING BUT *TROUBLE.* YOU'RE RULED BY YOUR *EMOTIONS.*
I. AM. NOT.
YEAH, RIGHT. NOTHING *EMOTIONAL* GOING ON HERE.
COME ON, BOYS... LET'S LEAVE THE WOMEN TO THEIR *CAUSES.*
NOT A WORD, "CHOSEN ONE."

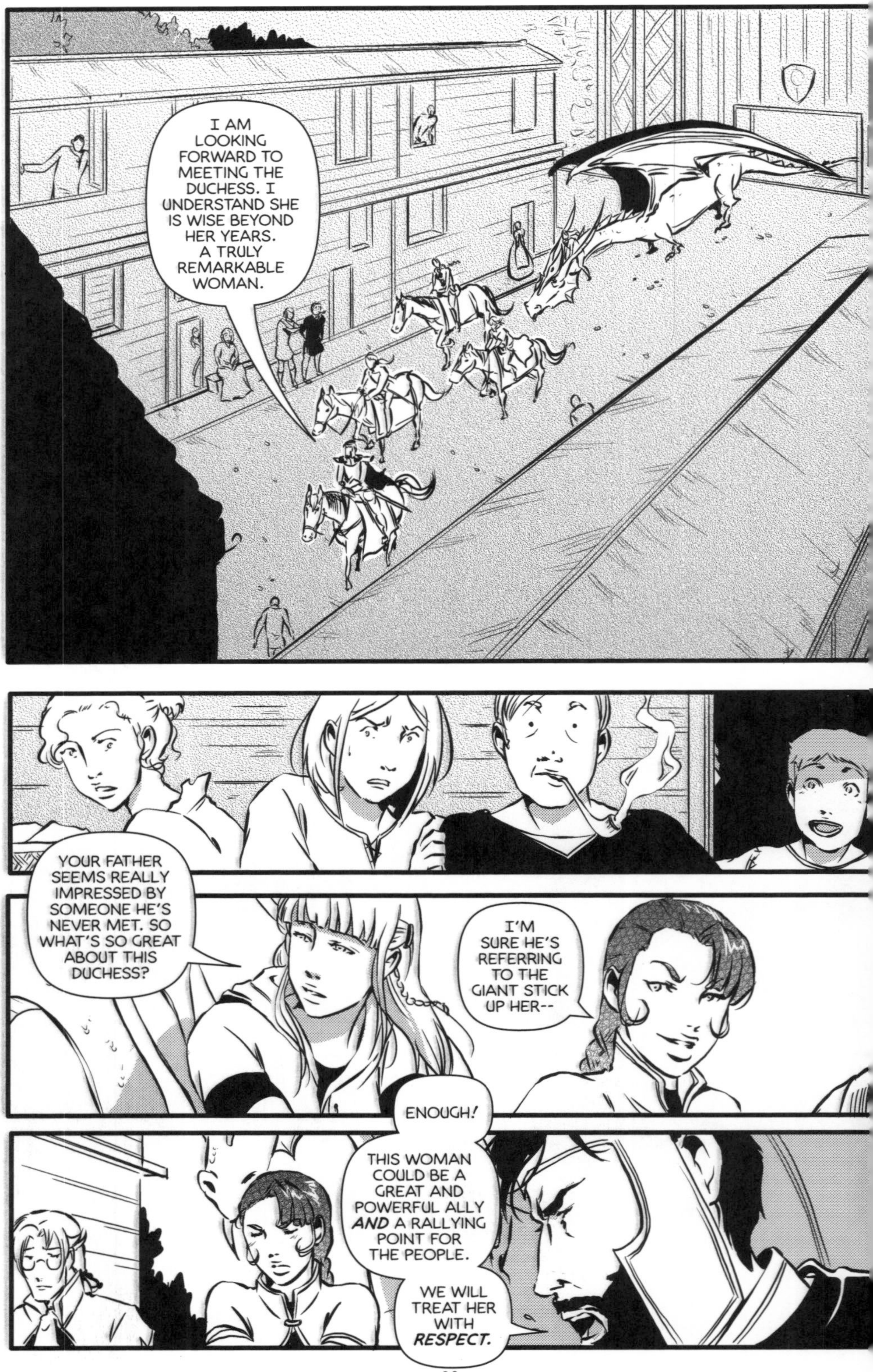
I AM LOOKING FORWARD TO MEETING THE DUCHESS. I UNDERSTAND SHE IS WISE BEYOND HER YEARS. A TRULY REMARKABLE WOMAN.
YOUR FATHER SEEMS REALLY IMPRESSED BY SOMEONE HE'S NEVER MET. SO WHAT'S SO GREAT ABOUT THIS DUCHESS?
I'M SURE HE'S REFERRING TO THE GIANT STICK UP HER--
ENOUGH!
THIS WOMAN COULD BE A GREAT AND POWERFUL ALLY *AND* A RALLYING POINT FOR THE PEOPLE.
WE WILL TREAT HER WITH ***RESPECT.***

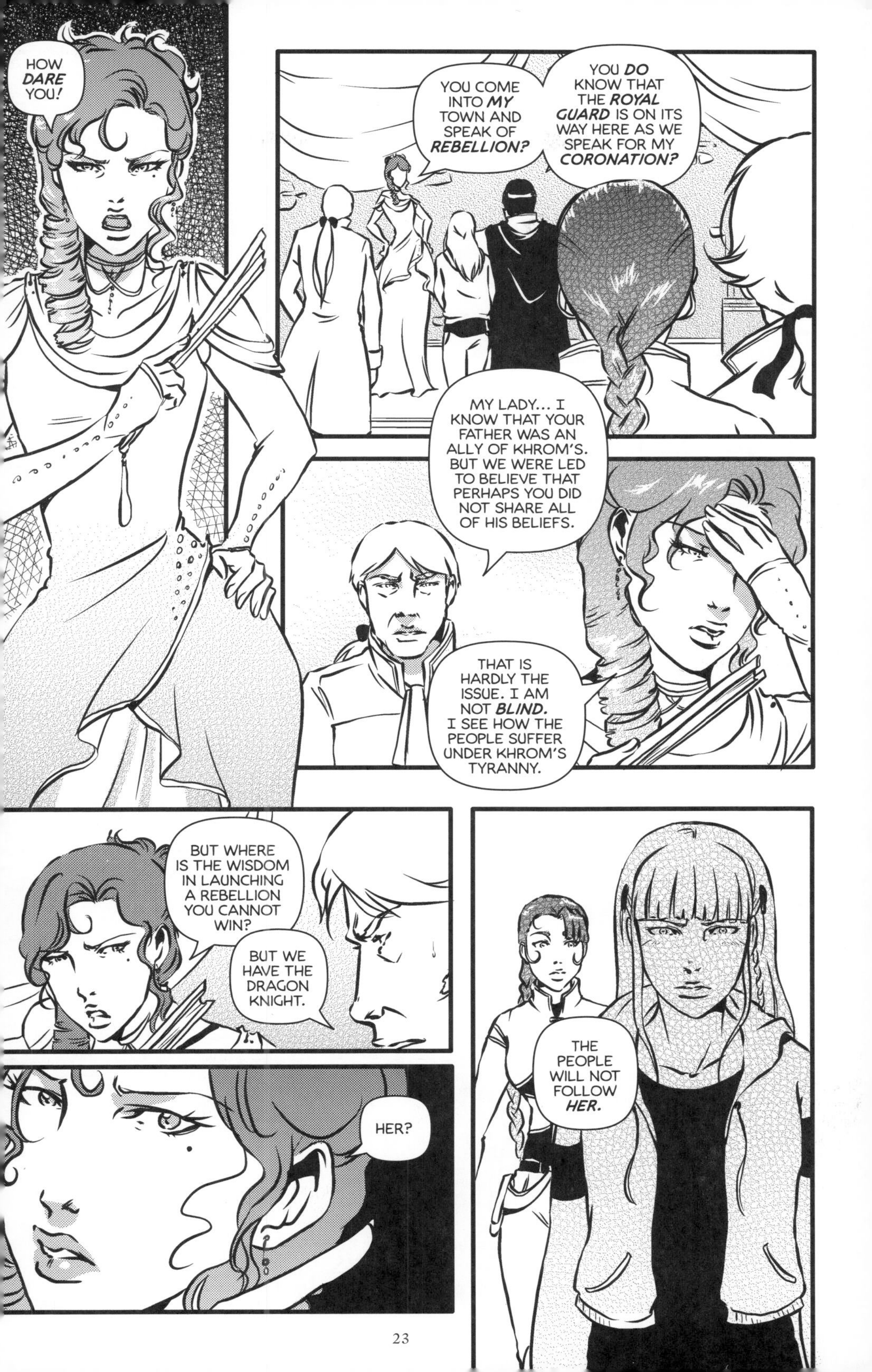
HOW DARE YOU!
YOU COME INTO MY TOWN AND SPEAK OF REBELLION?
YOU DO KNOW THAT THE ROYAL GUARD IS ON ITS WAY HERE AS WE SPEAK FOR MY CORONATION?
MY LADY... I KNOW THAT YOUR FATHER WAS AN ALLY OF KHROM'S. BUT WE WERE LED TO BELIEVE THAT PERHAPS YOU DID NOT SHARE ALL OF HIS BELIEFS.
THAT IS HARDLY THE ISSUE. I AM NOT BLIND. I SEE HOW THE PEOPLE SUFFER UNDER KHROM'S TYRANNY.
BUT WHERE IS THE WISDOM IN LAUNCHING A REBELLION YOU CANNOT WIN?
BUT WE HAVE THE DRAGON KNIGHT.
THE PEOPLE WILL NOT FOLLOW HER.
HER?

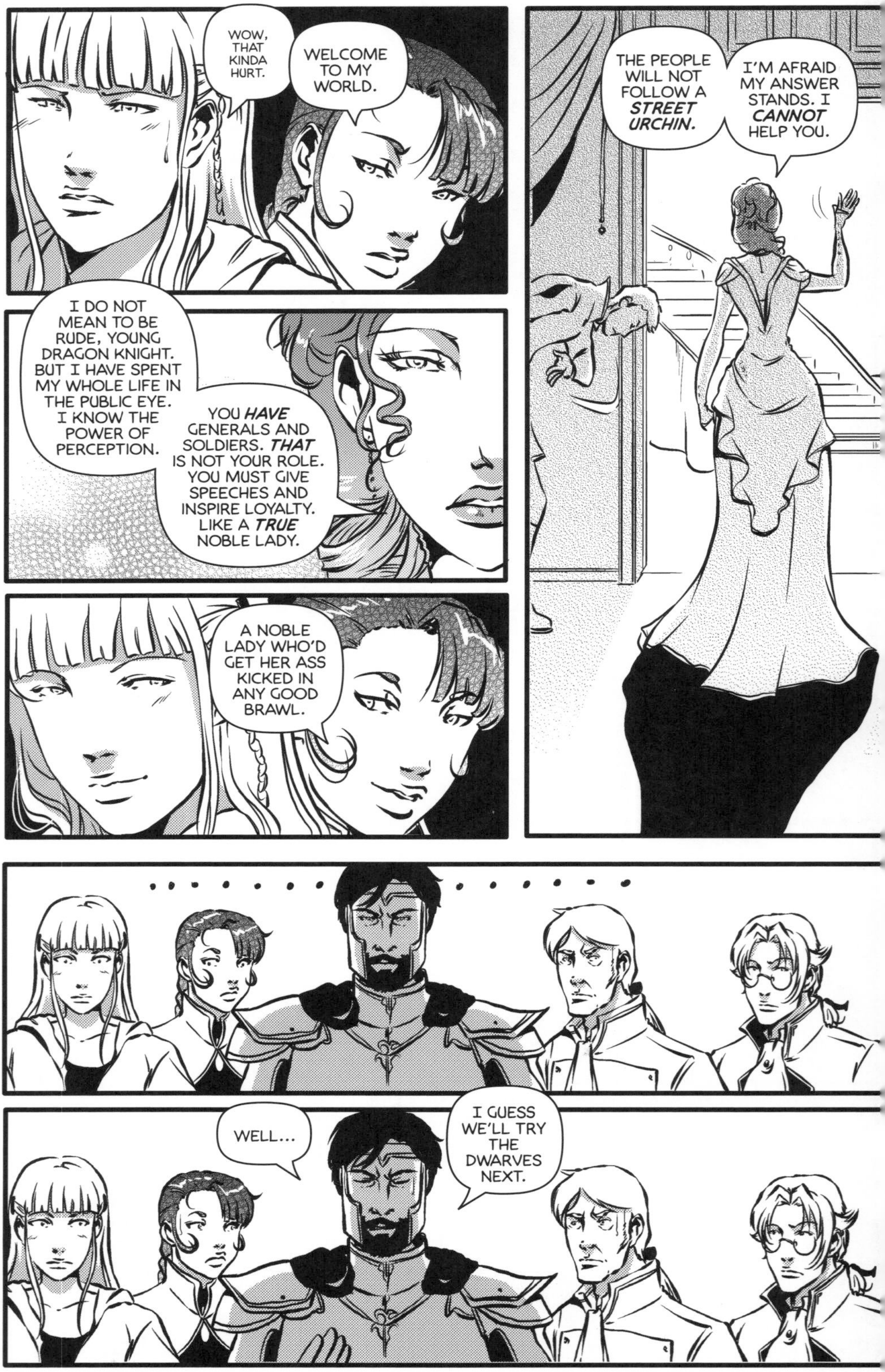
WOW, THAT KINDA HURT.
WELCOME TO MY WORLD.
I DO NOT MEAN TO BE RUDE, YOUNG DRAGON KNIGHT. BUT I HAVE SPENT MY WHOLE LIFE IN THE PUBLIC EYE. I KNOW THE POWER OF PERCEPTION.
YOU HAVE GENERALS AND SOLDIERS. THAT IS NOT YOUR ROLE. YOU MUST GIVE SPEECHES AND INSPIRE LOYALTY. LIKE A TRUE NOBLE LADY.
A NOBLE LADY WHO'D GET HER ASS KICKED IN ANY GOOD BRAWL.
THE PEOPLE WILL NOT FOLLOW A STREET URCHIN.
I'M AFRAID MY ANSWER STANDS. I CANNOT HELP YOU.
WELL...
I GUESS WE'LL TRY THE DWARVES NEXT.

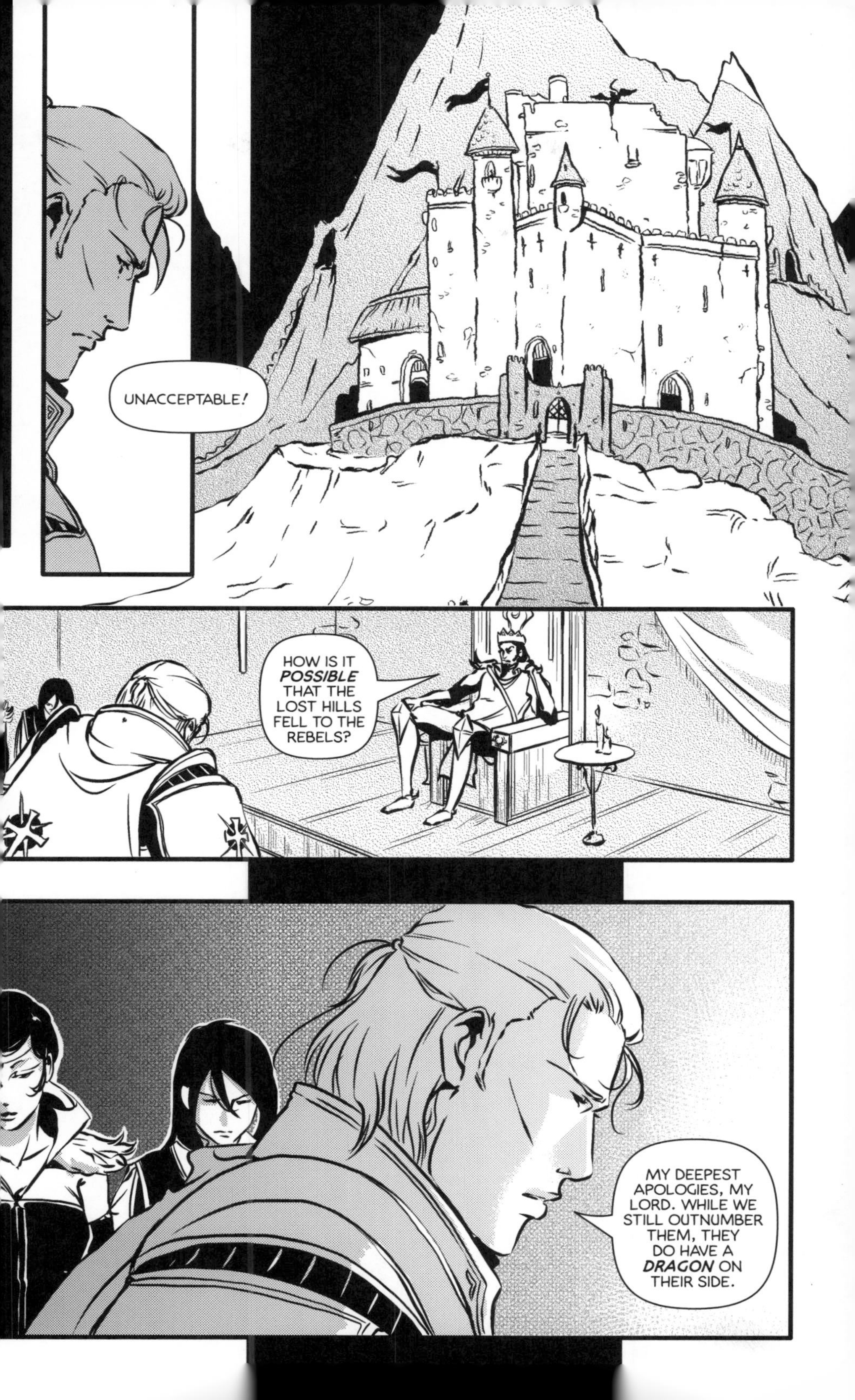
UNACCEPTABLE!
HOW IS IT *POSSIBLE* THAT THE LOST HILLS FELL TO THE REBELS?
MY DEEPEST APOLOGIES, MY LORD. WHILE WE STILL OUTNUMBER THEM, THEY DO HAVE A *DRAGON* ON THEIR SIDE.

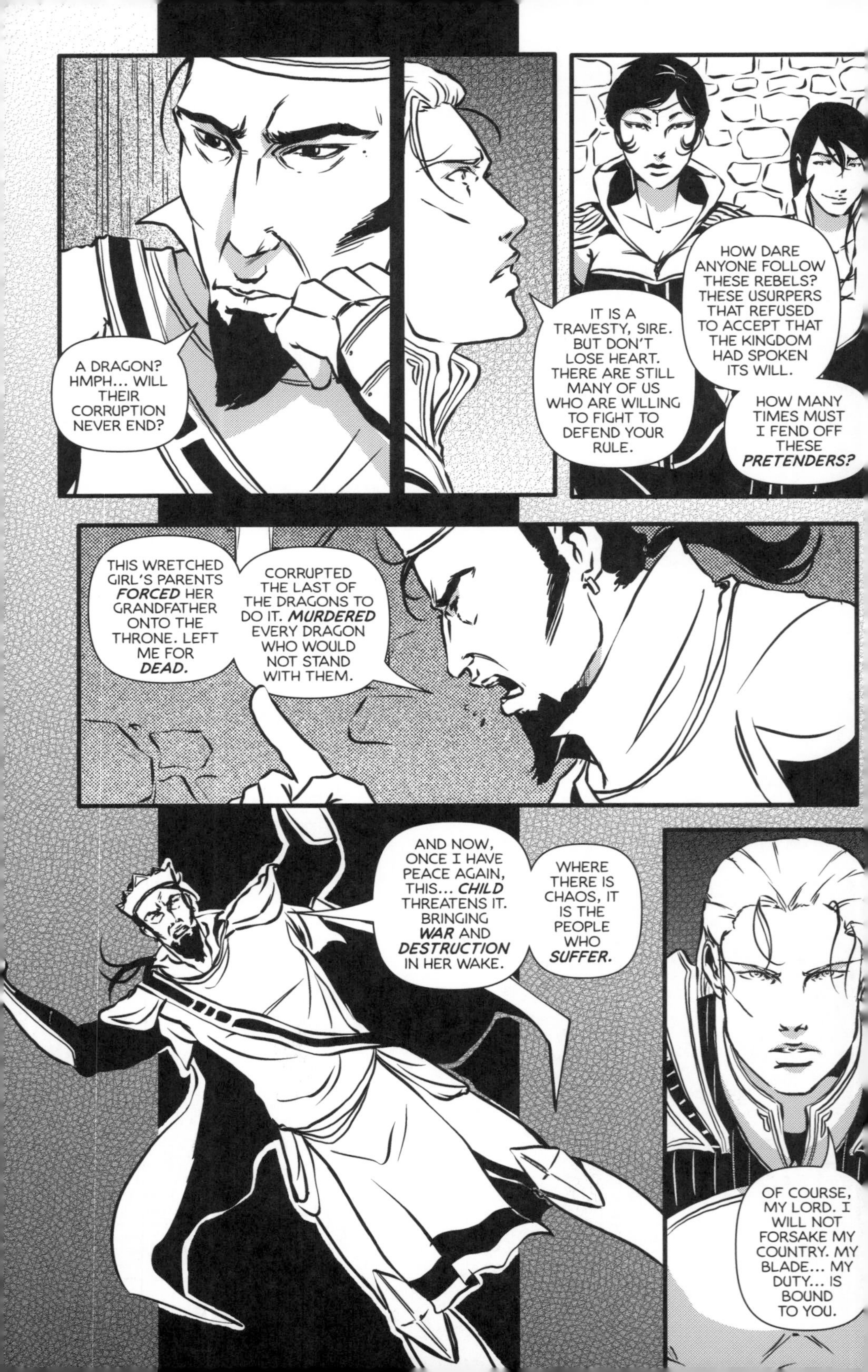
A DRAGON? HMPH... WILL THEIR CORRUPTION NEVER END?
IT IS A TRAVESTY, SIRE. BUT DON'T LOSE HEART. THERE ARE STILL MANY OF US WHO ARE WILLING TO FIGHT TO DEFEND YOUR RULE.
HOW DARE ANYONE FOLLOW THESE REBELS? THESE USURPERS THAT REFUSED TO ACCEPT THAT THE KINGDOM HAD SPOKEN ITS WILL.
HOW MANY TIMES MUST I FEND OFF THESE ***PRETENDERS?***
THIS WRETCHED GIRL'S PARENTS ***FORCED*** HER GRANDFATHER ONTO THE THRONE. LEFT ME FOR ***DEAD.***
CORRUPTED THE LAST OF THE DRAGONS TO DO IT. ***MURDERED*** EVERY DRAGON WHO WOULD NOT STAND WITH THEM.
AND NOW, ONCE I HAVE PEACE AGAIN, THIS... ***CHILD*** THREATENS IT. BRINGING ***WAR*** AND ***DESTRUCTION*** IN HER WAKE.
WHERE THERE IS CHAOS, IT IS THE PEOPLE WHO ***SUFFER.***
OF COURSE, MY LORD. I WILL NOT FORSAKE MY COUNTRY. MY BLADE... MY DUTY... IS BOUND TO YOU.

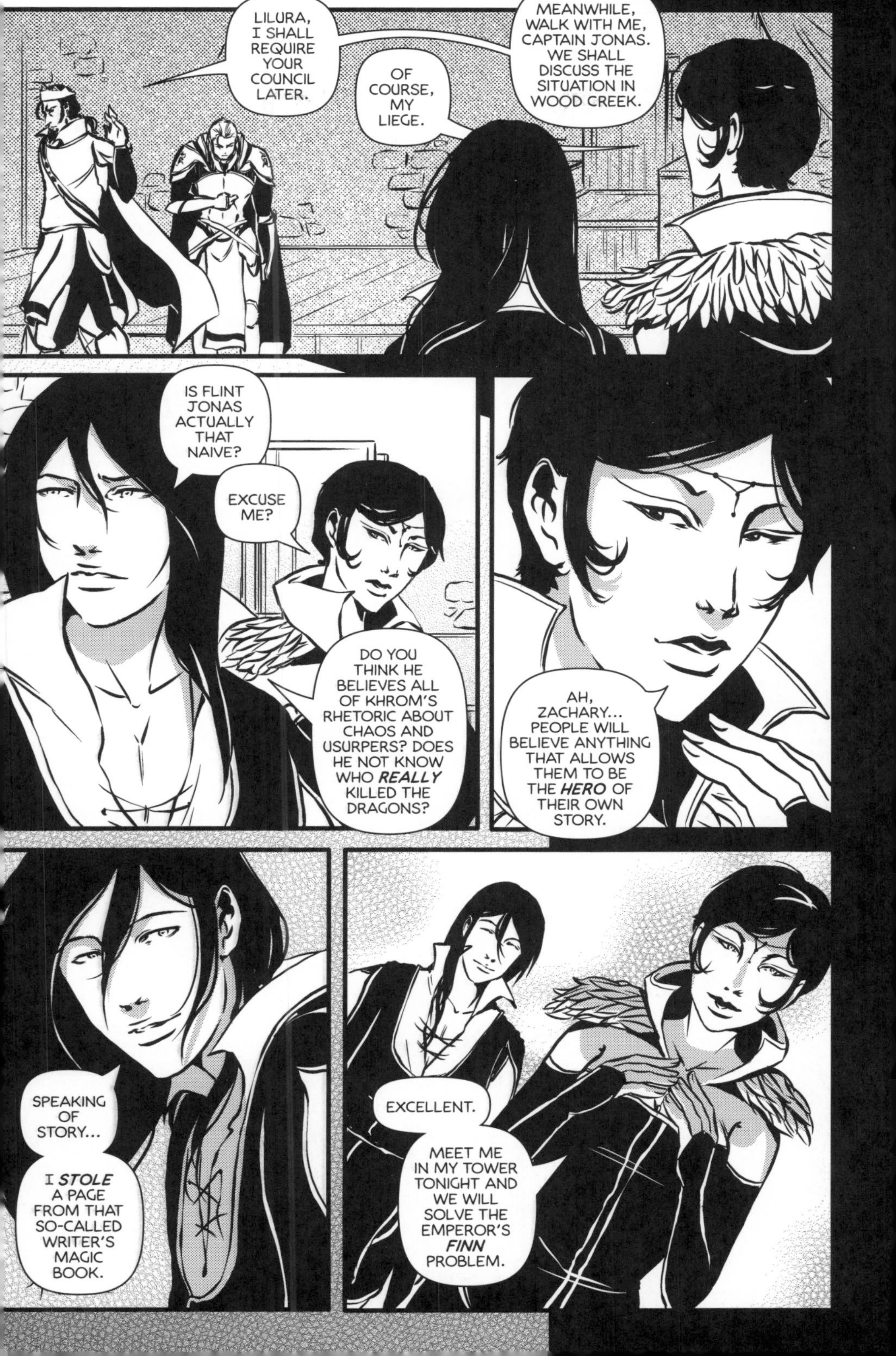
LILURA, I SHALL REQUIRE YOUR COUNCIL LATER.
OF COURSE, MY LIEGE.
MEANWHILE, WALK WITH ME, CAPTAIN JONAS. WE SHALL DISCUSS THE SITUATION IN WOOD CREEK.
IS FLINT JONAS ACTUALLY THAT NAIVE?
EXCUSE ME?
DO YOU THINK HE BELIEVES ALL OF KHROM'S RHETORIC ABOUT CHAOS AND USURPERS? DOES HE NOT KNOW WHO *REALLY* KILLED THE DRAGONS?
AH, ZACHARY... PEOPLE WILL BELIEVE ANYTHING THAT ALLOWS THEM TO BE THE *HERO* OF THEIR OWN STORY.
SPEAKING OF STORY...
I *STOLE* A PAGE FROM THAT SO-CALLED WRITER'S MAGIC BOOK.
EXCELLENT.
MEET ME IN MY TOWER TONIGHT AND WE WILL SOLVE THE EMPEROR'S *FINN* PROBLEM.

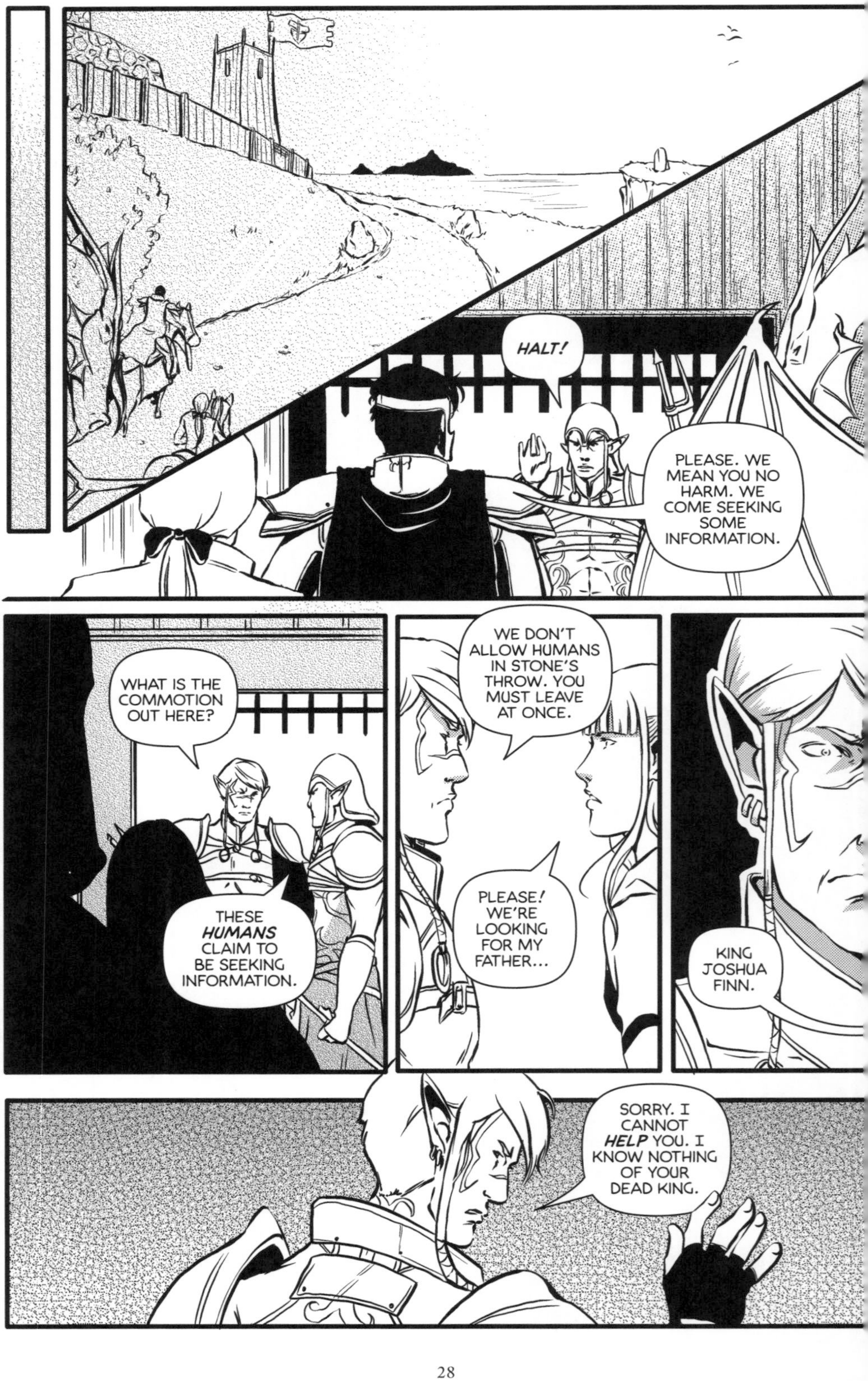
HALT!
PLEASE. WE MEAN YOU NO HARM. WE COME SEEKING SOME INFORMATION.
WHAT IS THE COMMOTION OUT HERE?
THESE *HUMANS* CLAIM TO BE SEEKING INFORMATION.
WE DON'T ALLOW HUMANS IN STONE'S THROW. YOU MUST LEAVE AT ONCE.
PLEASE! WE'RE LOOKING FOR MY FATHER...
KING JOSHUA FINN.
SORRY. I CANNOT *HELP* YOU. I KNOW NOTHING OF YOUR DEAD KING.

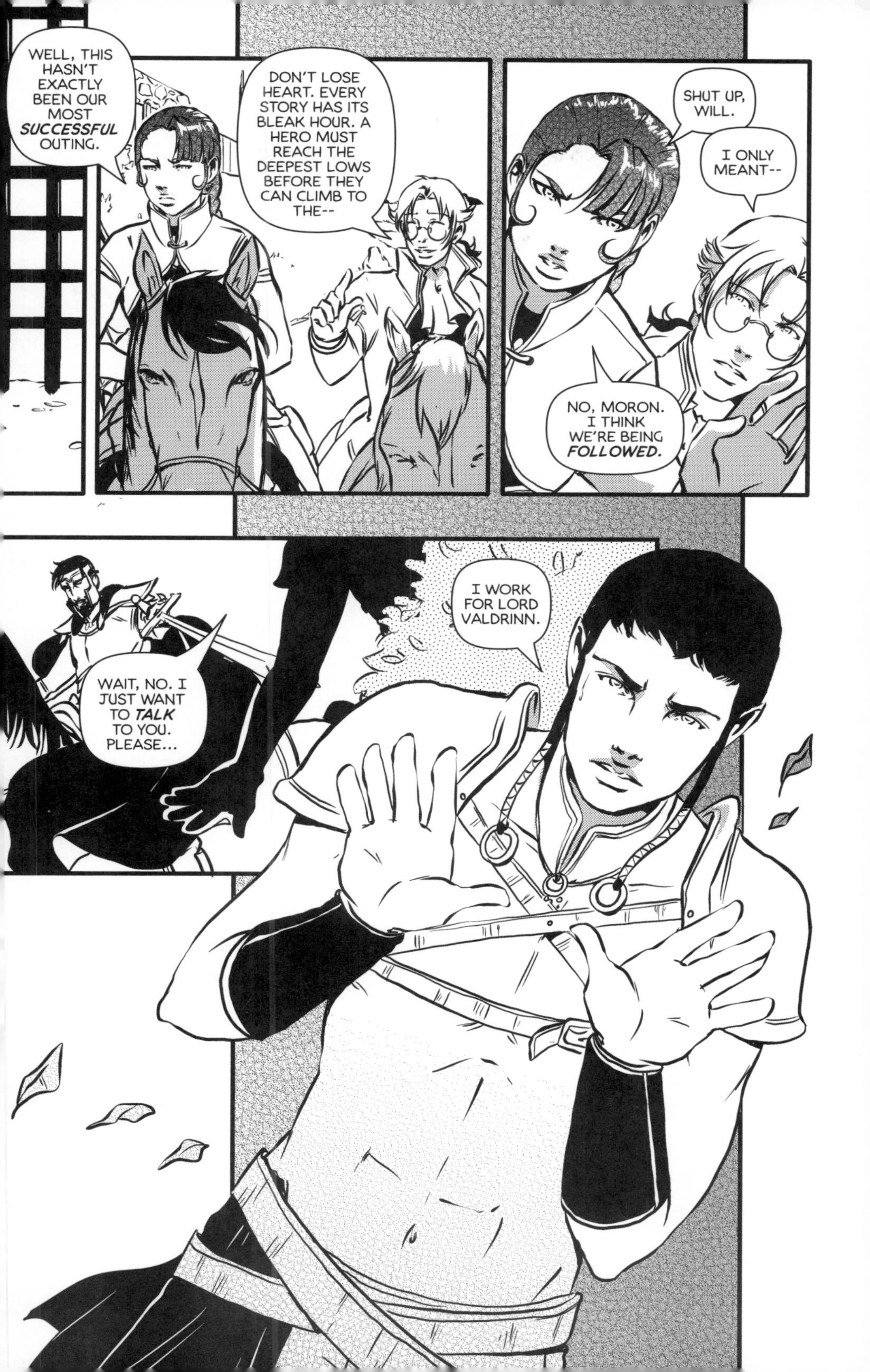
WELL, THIS HASN'T EXACTLY BEEN OUR MOST **SUCCESSFUL** OUTING.
DON'T LOSE HEART. EVERY STORY HAS ITS BLEAK HOUR. A HERO MUST REACH THE DEEPEST LOWS BEFORE THEY CAN CLIMB TO THE--
SHUT UP, WILL.
I ONLY MEANT--
NO, MORON. I THINK WE'RE BEING **FOLLOWED.**
I WORK FOR LORD VALDRINN.
WAIT, NO. I JUST WANT TO **TALK** TO YOU. PLEASE...

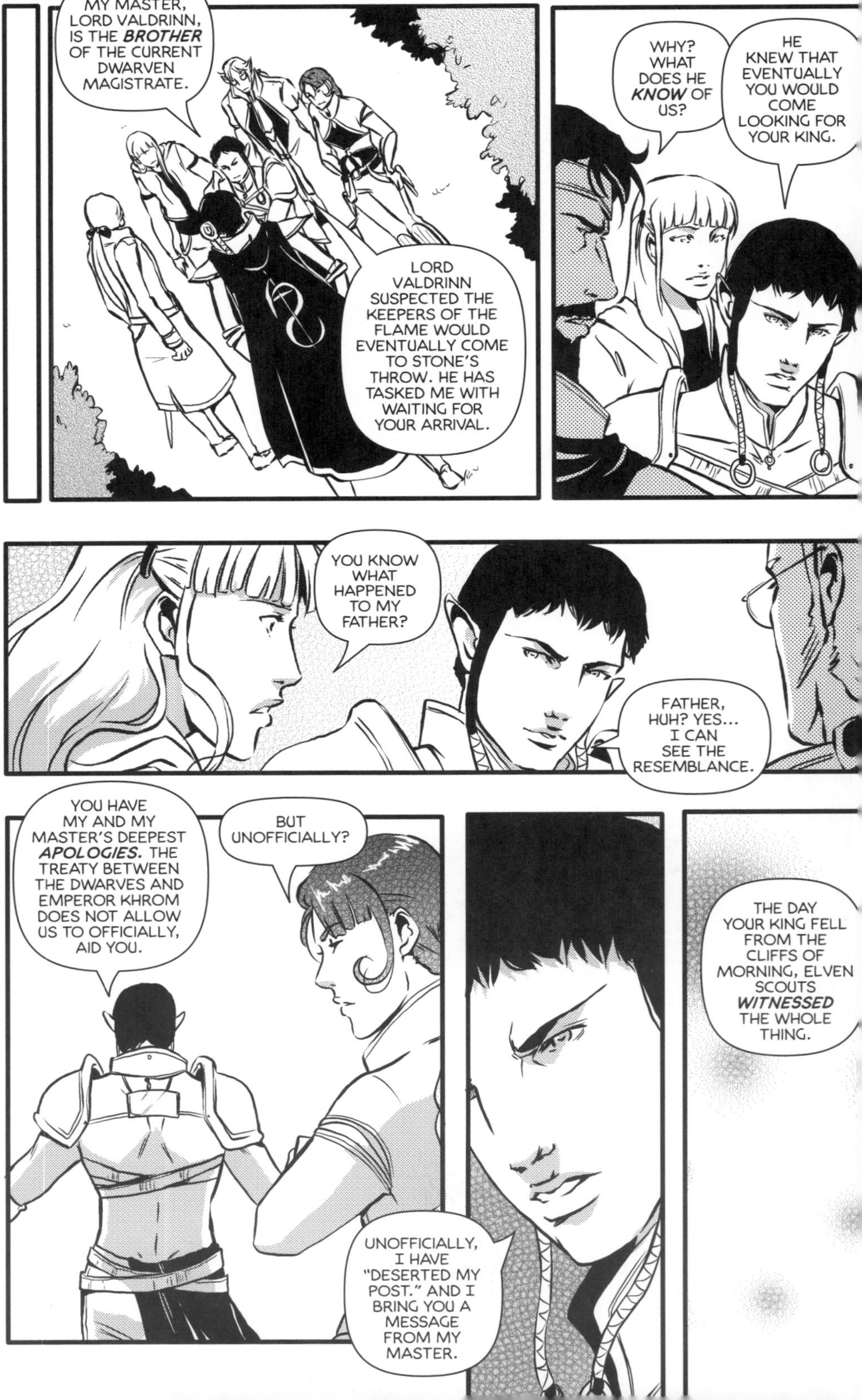

MY MASTER, LORD VALDRINN, IS THE ***BROTHER*** OF THE CURRENT DWARVEN MAGISTRATE.
LORD VALDRINN SUSPECTED THE KEEPERS OF THE FLAME WOULD EVENTUALLY COME TO STONE'S THROW. HE HAS TASKED ME WITH WAITING FOR YOUR ARRIVAL.
WHY? WHAT DOES HE ***KNOW*** OF US?
HE KNEW THAT EVENTUALLY YOU WOULD COME LOOKING FOR YOUR KING.
YOU KNOW WHAT HAPPENED TO MY FATHER?
FATHER, HUH? YES... I CAN SEE THE RESEMBLANCE.
YOU HAVE MY AND MY MASTER'S DEEPEST ***APOLOGIES.*** THE TREATY BETWEEN THE DWARVES AND EMPEROR KHROM DOES NOT ALLOW US TO OFFICIALLY, AID YOU.
BUT UNOFFICIALLY?
UNOFFICIALLY, I HAVE "DESERTED MY POST." AND I BRING YOU A MESSAGE FROM MY MASTER.
THE DAY YOUR KING FELL FROM THE CLIFFS OF MORNING, ELVEN SCOUTS ***WITNESSED*** THE WHOLE THING.

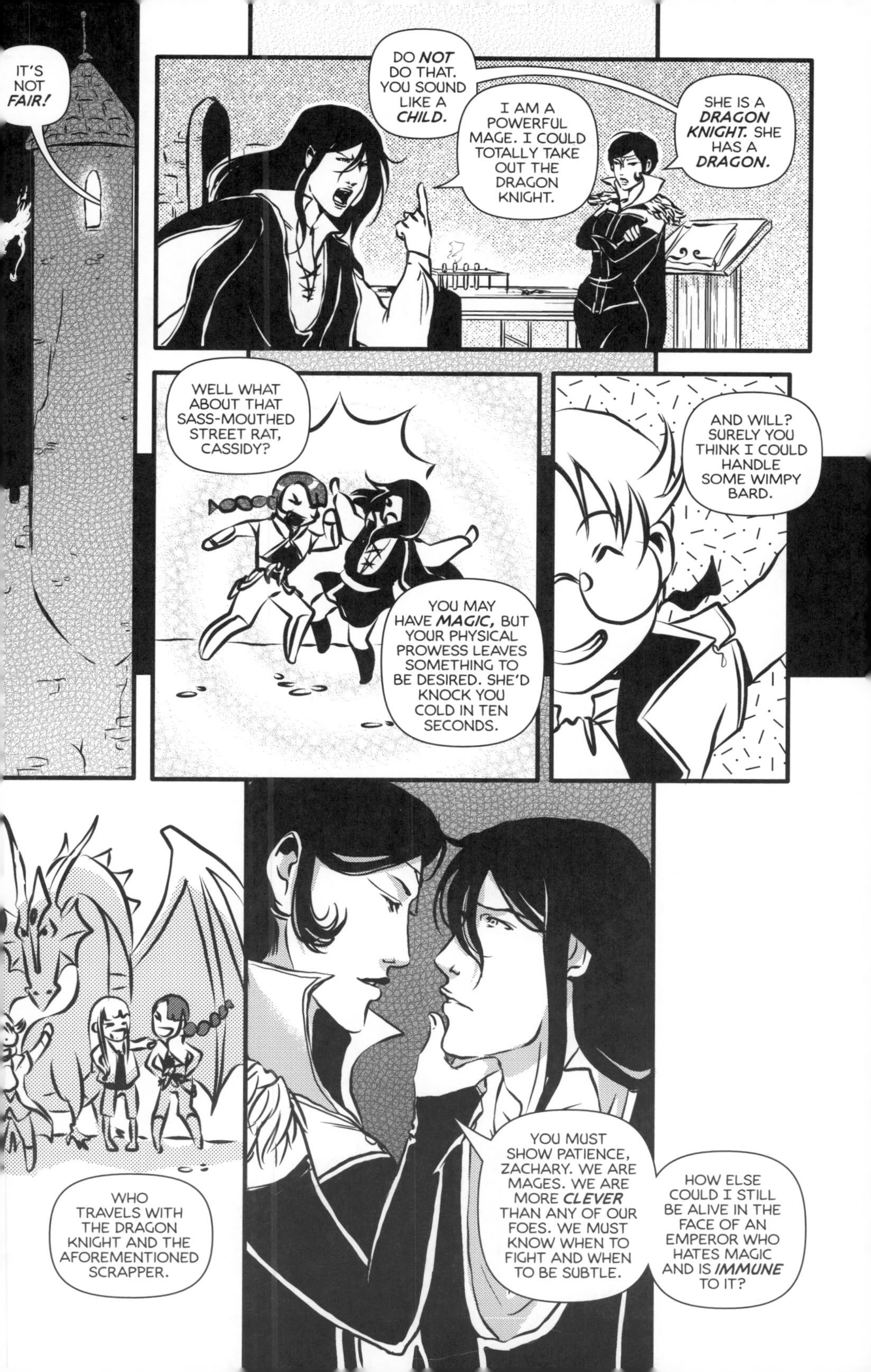
IT'S NOT *FAIR!*
DO *NOT* DO THAT. YOU SOUND LIKE A *CHILD.*
I AM A POWERFUL MAGE. I COULD TOTALLY TAKE OUT THE DRAGON KNIGHT.
SHE IS A *DRAGON KNIGHT.* SHE HAS A *DRAGON.*
WELL WHAT ABOUT THAT SASS-MOUTHED STREET RAT, CASSIDY?
YOU MAY HAVE *MAGIC,* BUT YOUR PHYSICAL PROWESS LEAVES SOMETHING TO BE DESIRED. SHE'D KNOCK YOU COLD IN TEN SECONDS.
AND WILL? SURELY YOU THINK I COULD HANDLE SOME WIMPY BARD.
WHO TRAVELS WITH THE DRAGON KNIGHT AND THE AFOREMENTIONED SCRAPPER.
YOU MUST SHOW PATIENCE, ZACHARY. WE ARE MAGES. WE ARE MORE *CLEVER* THAN ANY OF OUR FOES. WE MUST KNOW WHEN TO FIGHT AND WHEN TO BE SUBTLE.
HOW ELSE COULD I STILL BE ALIVE IN THE FACE OF AN EMPEROR WHO HATES MAGIC AND IS *IMMUNE* TO IT?

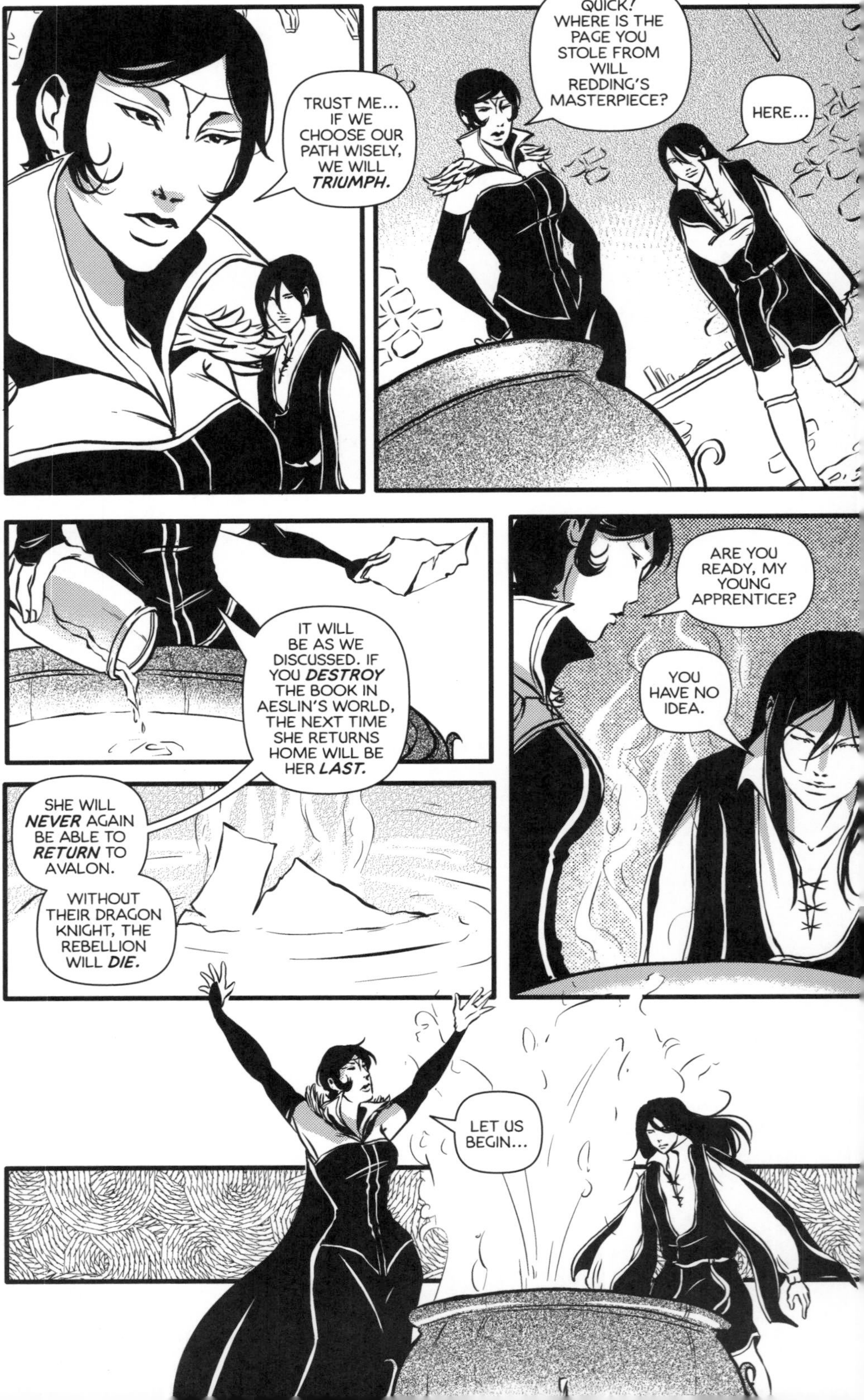
TRUST ME... IF WE CHOOSE OUR PATH WISELY, WE WILL TRIUMPH.
QUICK! WHERE IS THE PAGE YOU STOLE FROM WILL REDDING'S MASTERPIECE?
HERE...
IT WILL BE AS WE DISCUSSED. IF YOU DESTROY THE BOOK IN AESLIN'S WORLD, THE NEXT TIME SHE RETURNS HOME WILL BE HER LAST.
SHE WILL NEVER AGAIN BE ABLE TO RETURN TO AVALON.
WITHOUT THEIR DRAGON KNIGHT, THE REBELLION WILL DIE.
ARE YOU READY, MY YOUNG APPRENTICE?
YOU HAVE NO IDEA.
LET US BEGIN...

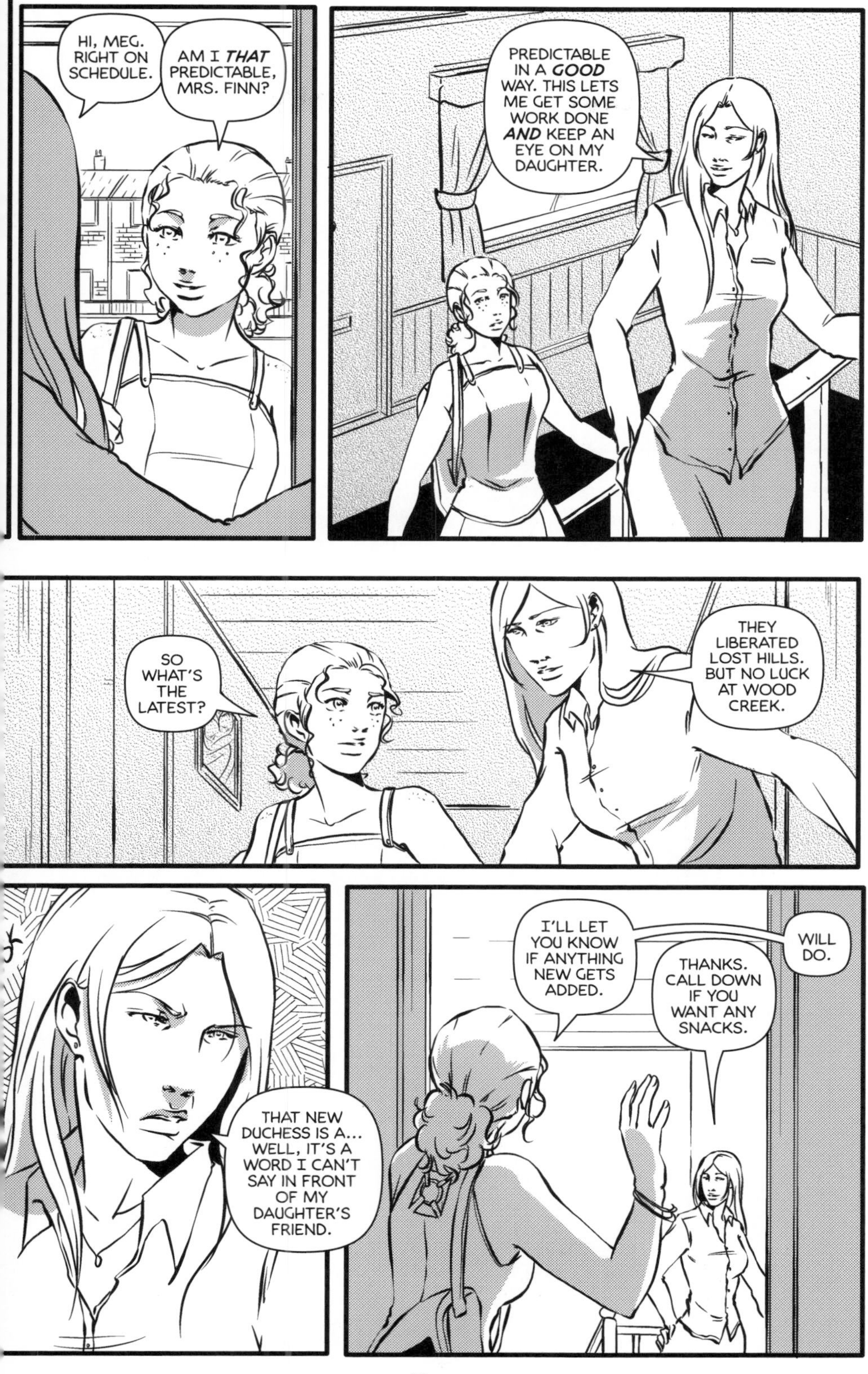
HI, MEG. RIGHT ON SCHEDULE.
AM I *THAT* PREDICTABLE, MRS. FINN?
PREDICTABLE IN A *GOOD* WAY. THIS LETS ME GET SOME WORK DONE *AND* KEEP AN EYE ON MY DAUGHTER.
SO WHAT'S THE LATEST?
THEY LIBERATED LOST HILLS. BUT NO LUCK AT WOOD CREEK.
THAT NEW DUCHESS IS A... WELL, IT'S A WORD I CAN'T SAY IN FRONT OF MY DAUGHTER'S FRIEND.
I'LL LET YOU KNOW IF ANYTHING NEW GETS ADDED.
WILL DO.
THANKS. CALL DOWN IF YOU WANT ANY SNACKS.

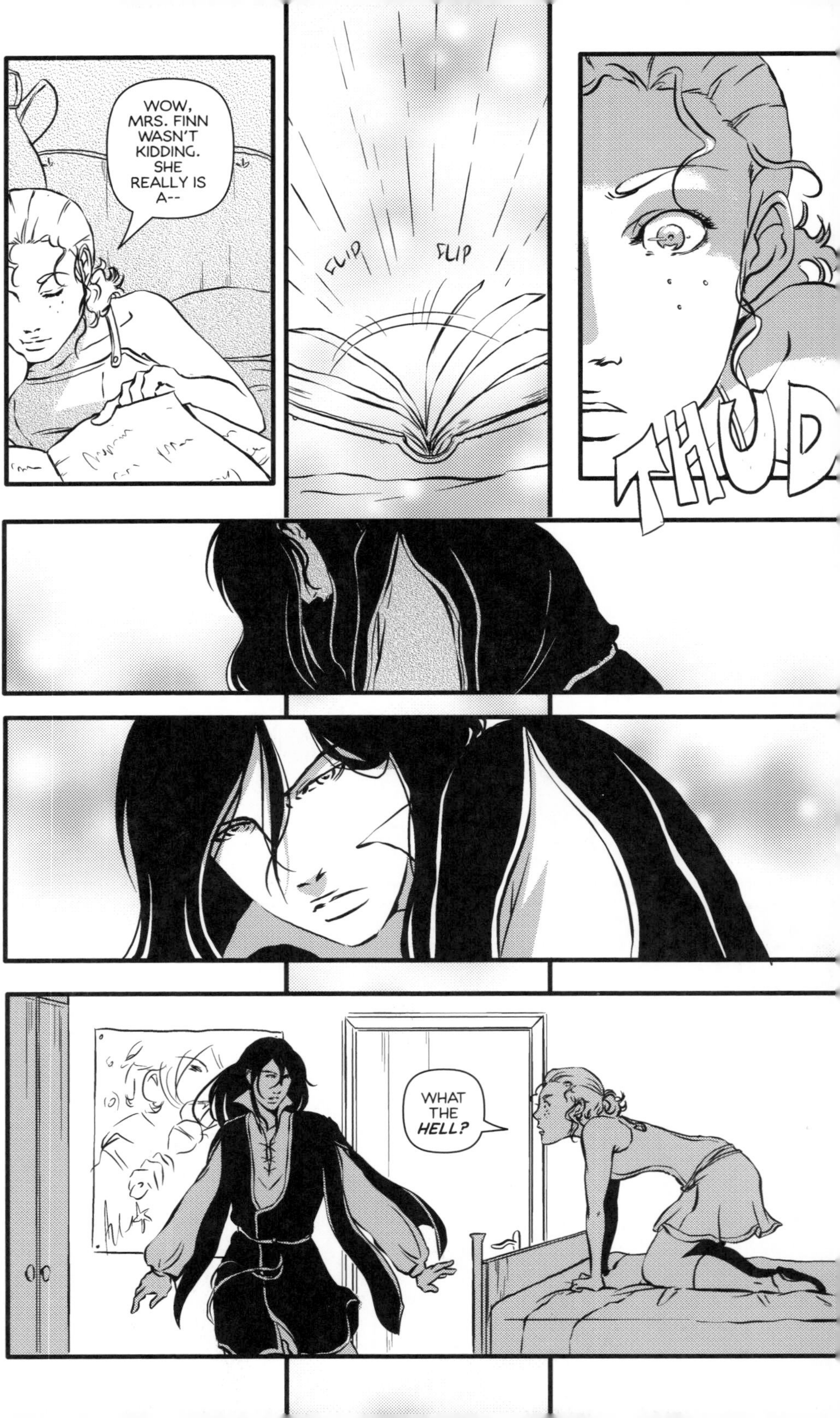
WOW, MRS. FINN WASN'T KIDDING. SHE REALLY IS A--
FLIP
FLIP
THUD
WHAT THE *HELL?*

Chapter 2

THE WAY OF THE ELVES

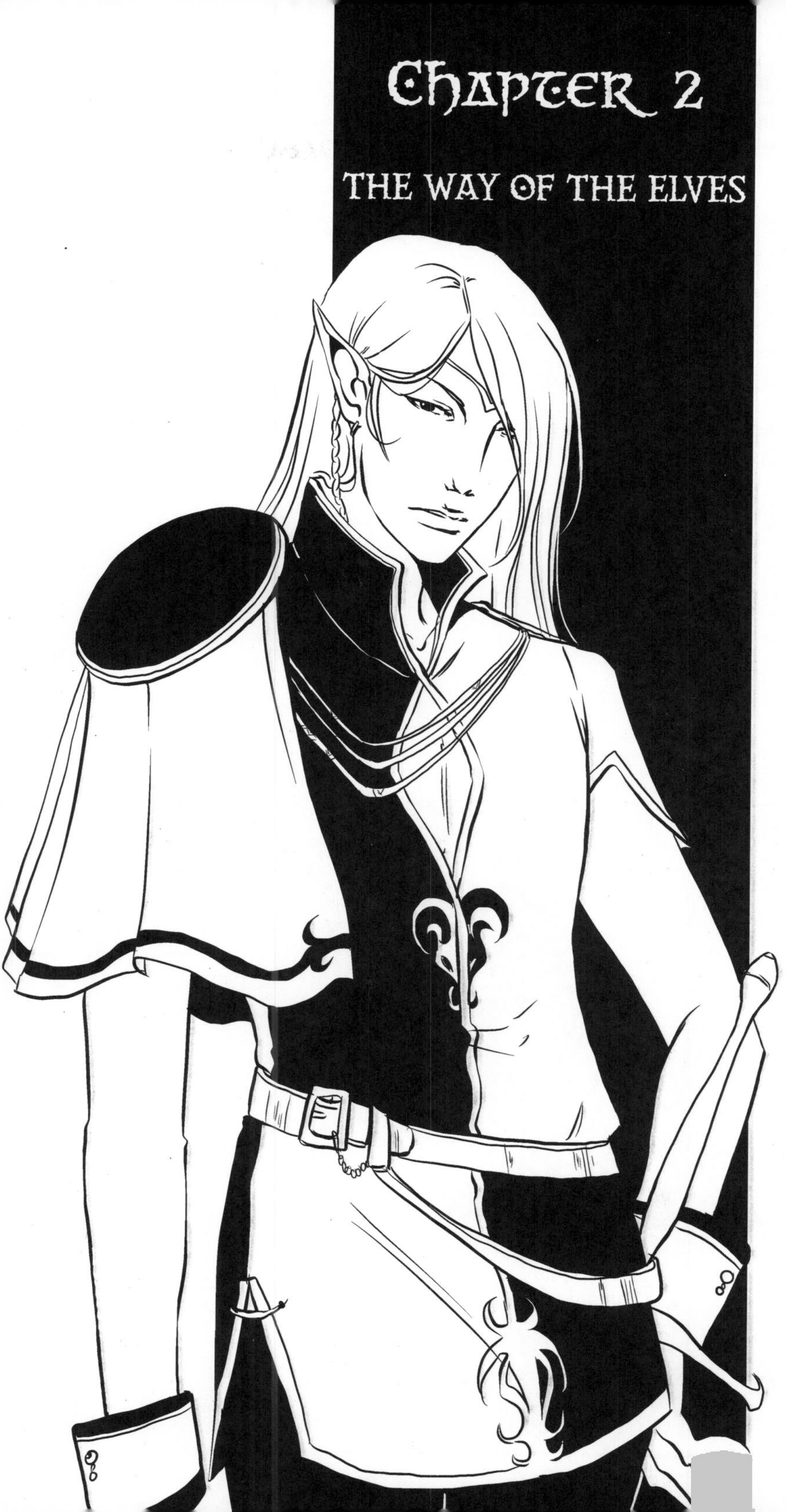

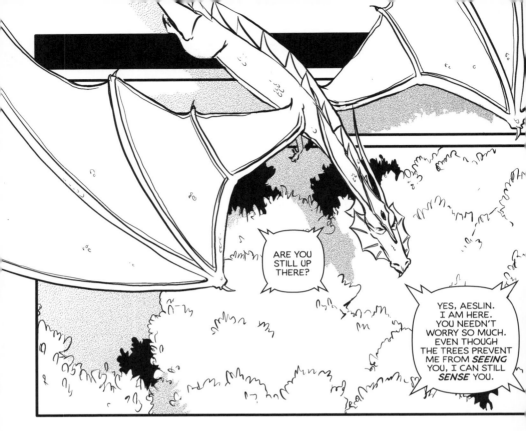

ARE YOU STILL UP THERE?

YES, AESLIN. I AM HERE. YOU NEEDN'T WORRY SO MUCH. EVEN THOUGH THE TREES PREVENT ME FROM *SEEING* YOU, I CAN STILL *SENSE* YOU.

I'M SORRY IT'S TOO *DENSE* FOR YOU DOWN HERE.

NO APOLOGIES, AESLIN. JUST FIND THE VILLAGE OF THE ELVES.

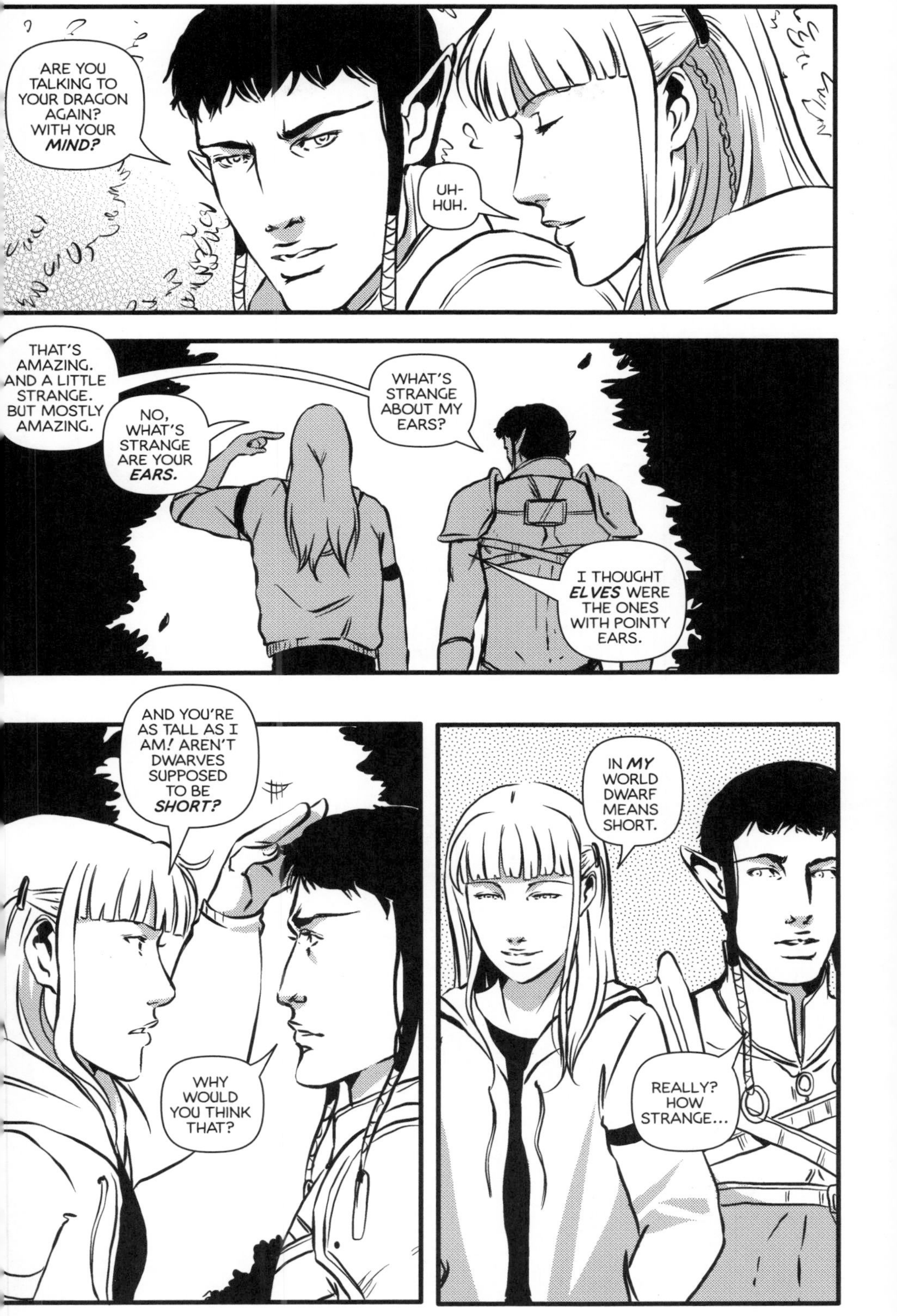
ARE YOU TALKING TO YOUR DRAGON AGAIN? WITH YOUR *MIND?*
UH-HUH.
THAT'S AMAZING. AND A LITTLE STRANGE. BUT MOSTLY AMAZING.
NO, WHAT'S STRANGE ARE YOUR *EARS.*
WHAT'S STRANGE ABOUT MY EARS?
I THOUGHT *ELVES* WERE THE ONES WITH POINTY EARS.
AND YOU'RE AS TALL AS I AM! AREN'T DWARVES SUPPOSED TO BE *SHORT?*
WHY WOULD YOU THINK THAT?
IN *MY* WORLD DWARF MEANS SHORT.
REALLY? HOW STRANGE...

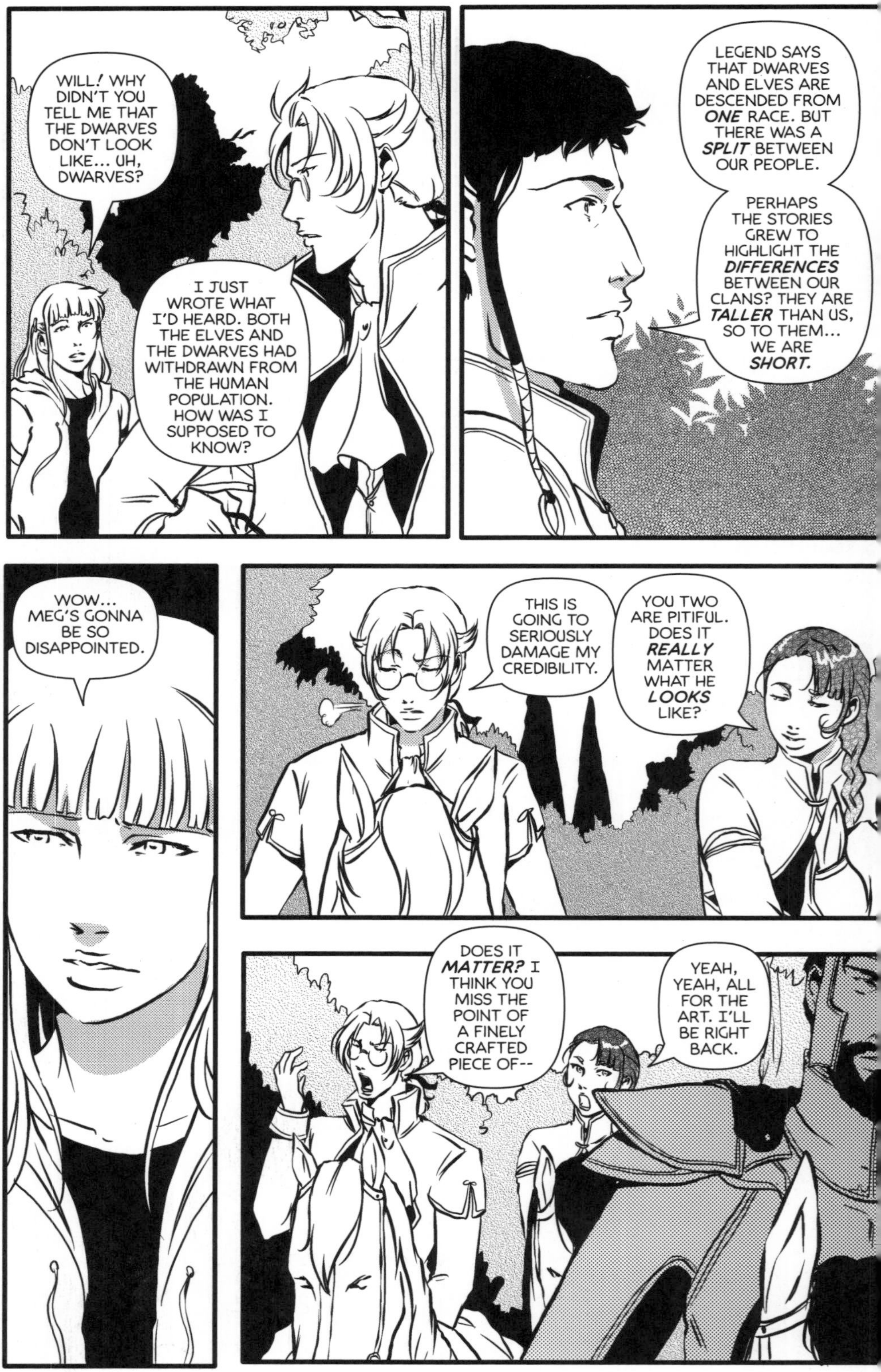
WILL! WHY DIDN'T YOU TELL ME THAT THE DWARVES DON'T LOOK LIKE... UH, DWARVES?
I JUST WROTE WHAT I'D HEARD. BOTH THE ELVES AND THE DWARVES HAD WITHDRAWN FROM THE HUMAN POPULATION. HOW WAS I SUPPOSED TO KNOW?
LEGEND SAYS THAT DWARVES AND ELVES ARE DESCENDED FROM ONE RACE. BUT THERE WAS A SPLIT BETWEEN OUR PEOPLE.
PERHAPS THE STORIES GREW TO HIGHLIGHT THE DIFFERENCES BETWEEN OUR CLANS? THEY ARE TALLER THAN US, SO TO THEM... WE ARE SHORT.
WOW... MEG'S GONNA BE SO DISAPPOINTED.
THIS IS GOING TO SERIOUSLY DAMAGE MY CREDIBILITY.
YOU TWO ARE PITIFUL. DOES IT REALLY MATTER WHAT HE LOOKS LIKE?
DOES IT MATTER? I THINK YOU MISS THE POINT OF A FINELY CRAFTED PIECE OF--
YEAH, YEAH, ALL FOR THE ART. I'LL BE RIGHT BACK.

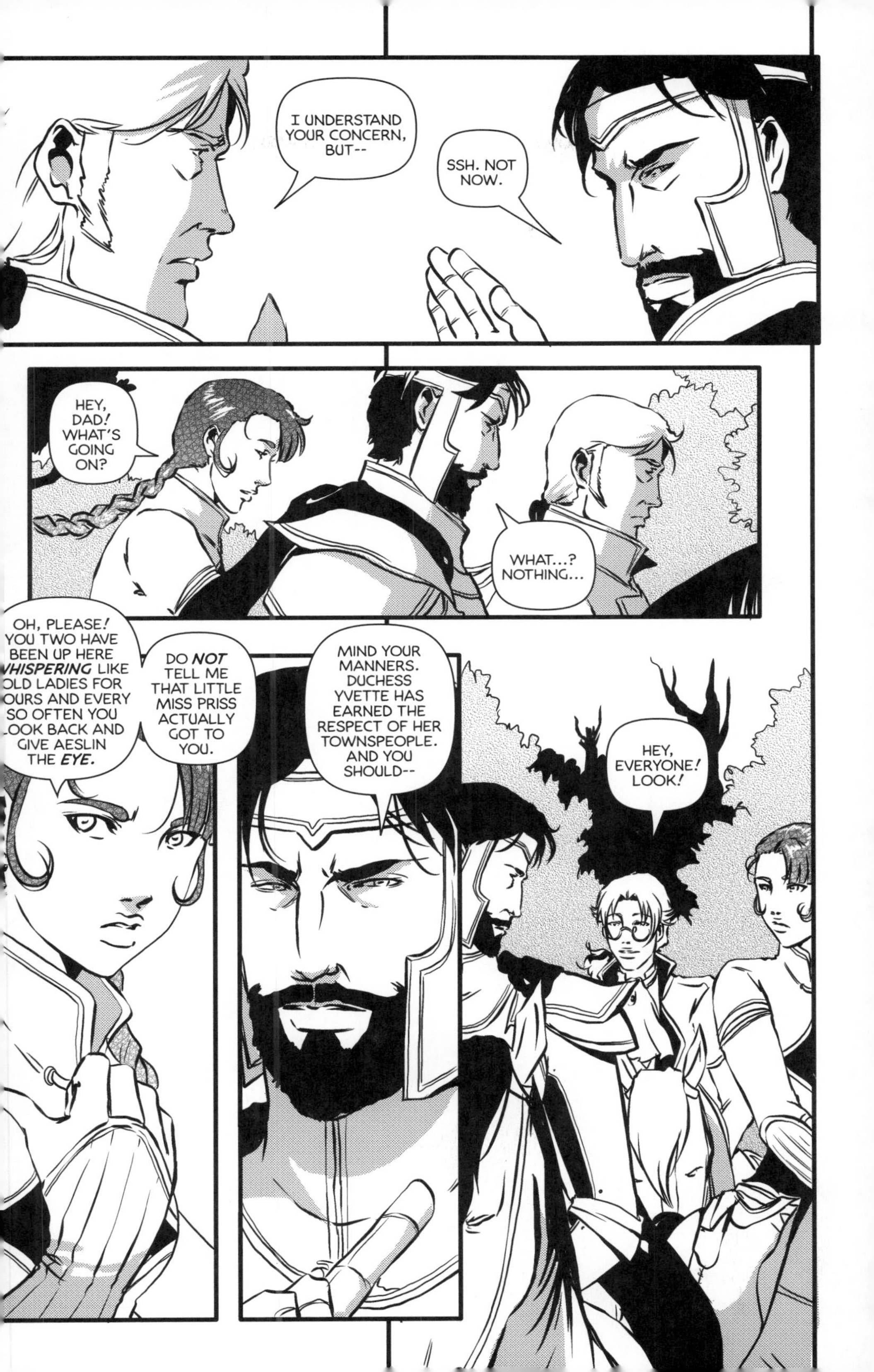
I UNDERSTAND YOUR CONCERN, BUT--
SSH. NOT NOW.
HEY, DAD! WHAT'S GOING ON?
WHAT...? NOTHING...
OH, PLEASE! YOU TWO HAVE BEEN UP HERE WHISPERING LIKE OLD LADIES FOR HOURS AND EVERY SO OFTEN YOU LOOK BACK AND GIVE AESLIN THE EYE.
DO NOT TELL ME THAT LITTLE MISS PRISS ACTUALLY GOT TO YOU.
MIND YOUR MANNERS. DUCHESS YVETTE HAS EARNED THE RESPECT OF HER TOWNSPEOPLE. AND YOU SHOULD--
HEY, EVERYONE! LOOK!

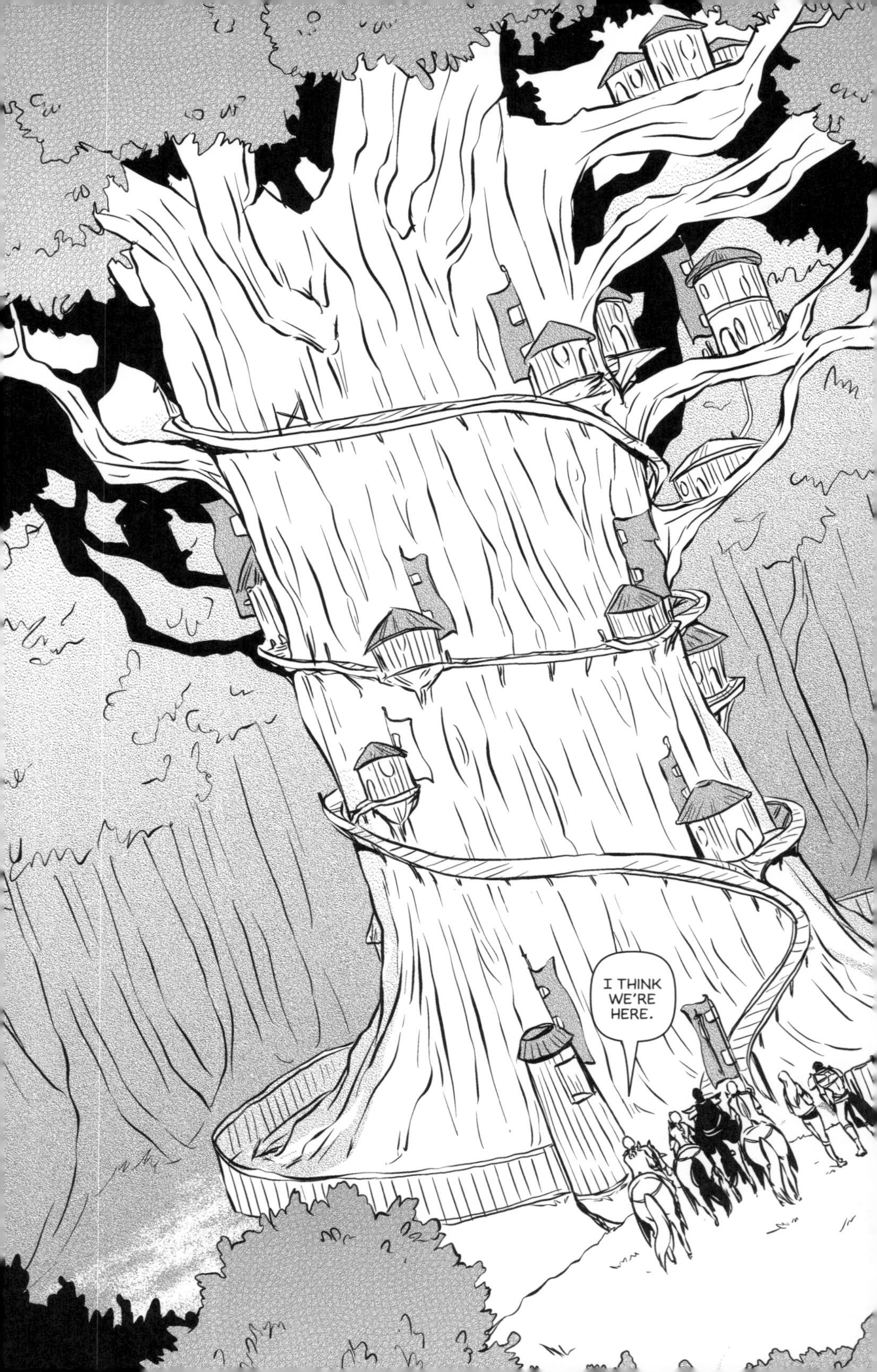
I THINK WE'RE HERE.

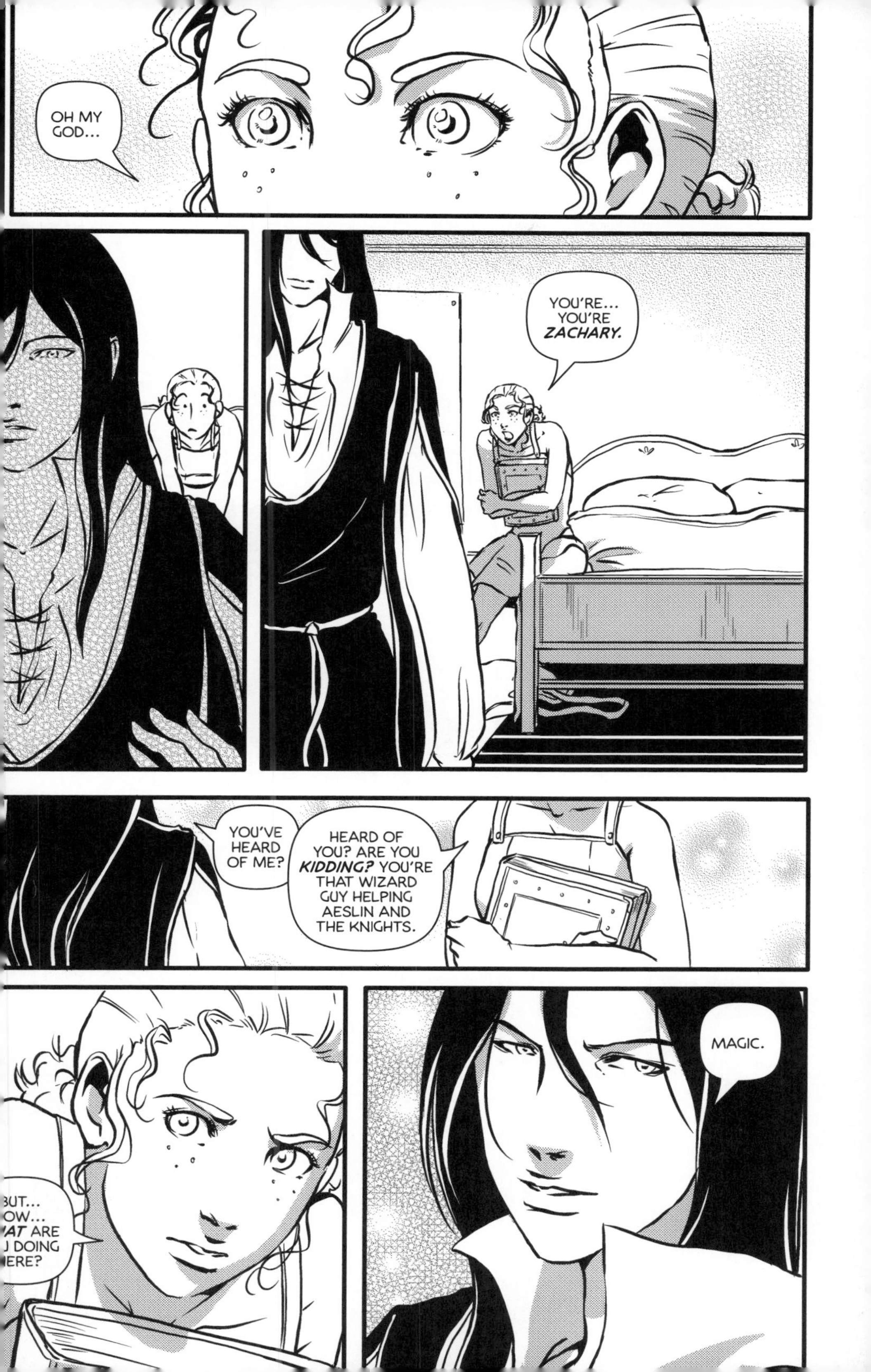
OH MY GOD…
YOU'RE… YOU'RE *ZACHARY.*
YOU'VE HEARD OF ME?
HEARD OF YOU? ARE YOU *KIDDING?* YOU'RE THAT WIZARD GUY HELPING AESLIN AND THE KNIGHTS.
BUT… OW… *AT* ARE U DOING ERE?
MAGIC.

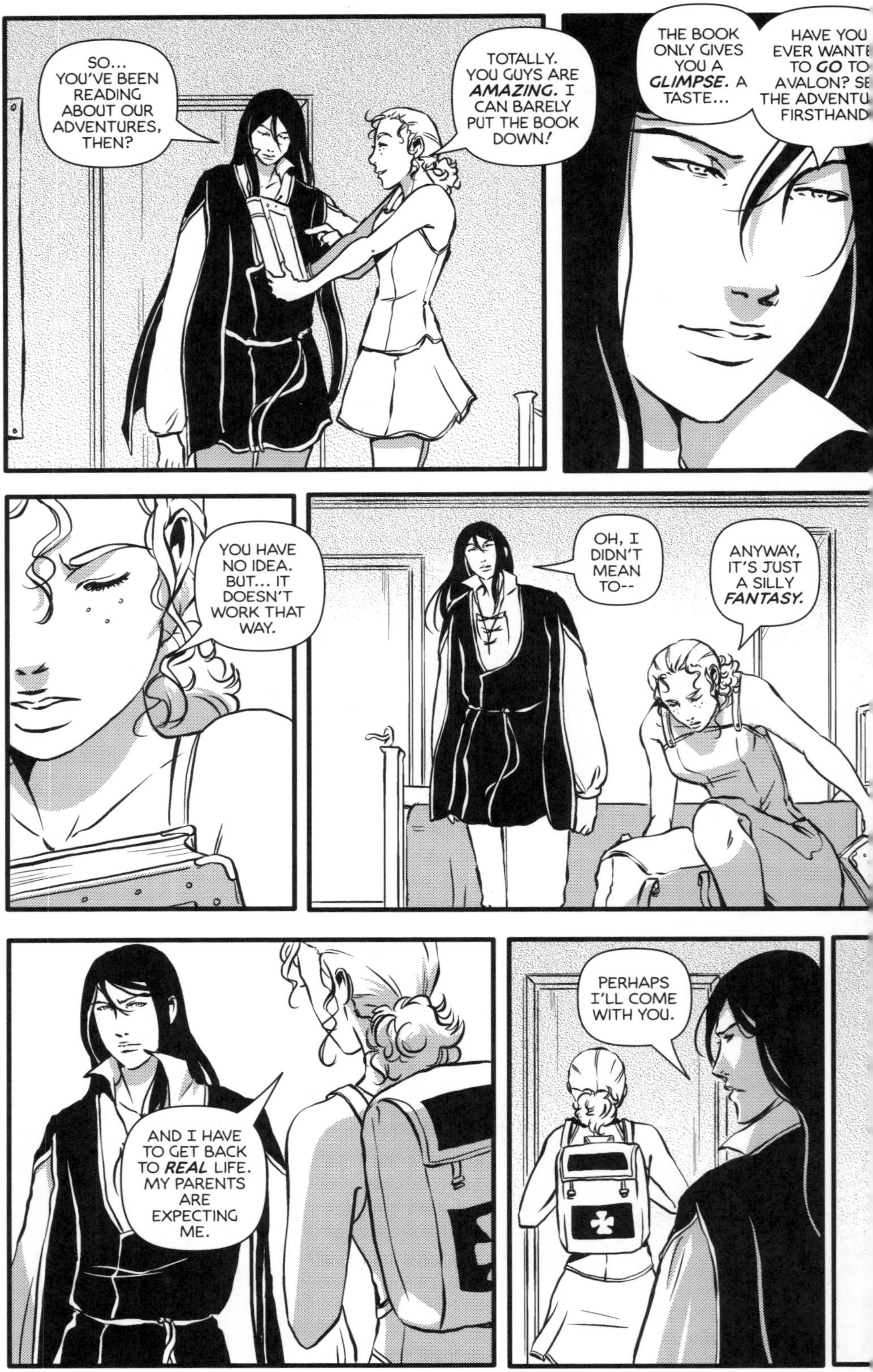
SO... YOU'VE BEEN READING ABOUT OUR ADVENTURES, THEN?
TOTALLY. YOU GUYS ARE AMAZING. I CAN BARELY PUT THE BOOK DOWN!
THE BOOK ONLY GIVES YOU A GLIMPSE. A TASTE...
HAVE YOU EVER WANTE TO GO TO AVALON? SE THE ADVENTU FIRSTHAND
YOU HAVE NO IDEA. BUT... IT DOESN'T WORK THAT WAY.
OH, I DIDN'T MEAN TO--
ANYWAY, IT'S JUST A SILLY FANTASY.
AND I HAVE TO GET BACK TO REAL LIFE. MY PARENTS ARE EXPECTING ME.
PERHAPS I'LL COME WITH YOU.

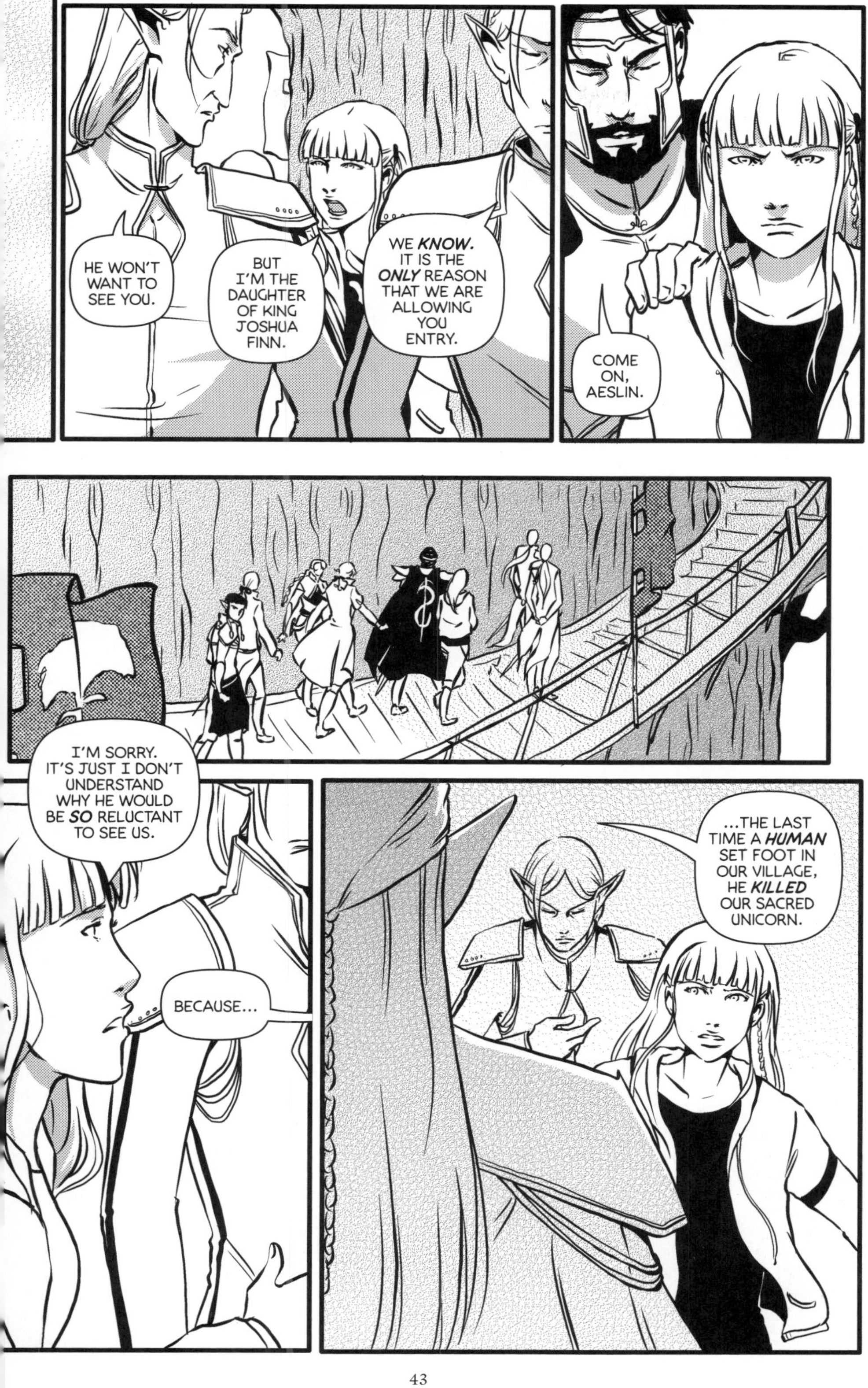
HE WON'T WANT TO SEE YOU.
BUT I'M THE DAUGHTER OF KING JOSHUA FINN.
WE *KNOW.* IT IS THE *ONLY* REASON THAT WE ARE ALLOWING YOU ENTRY.
COME ON, AESLIN.
I'M SORRY. IT'S JUST I DON'T UNDERSTAND WHY HE WOULD BE *SO* RELUCTANT TO SEE US.
BECAUSE...
...THE LAST TIME A *HUMAN* SET FOOT IN OUR VILLAGE, HE *KILLED* OUR SACRED UNICORN.

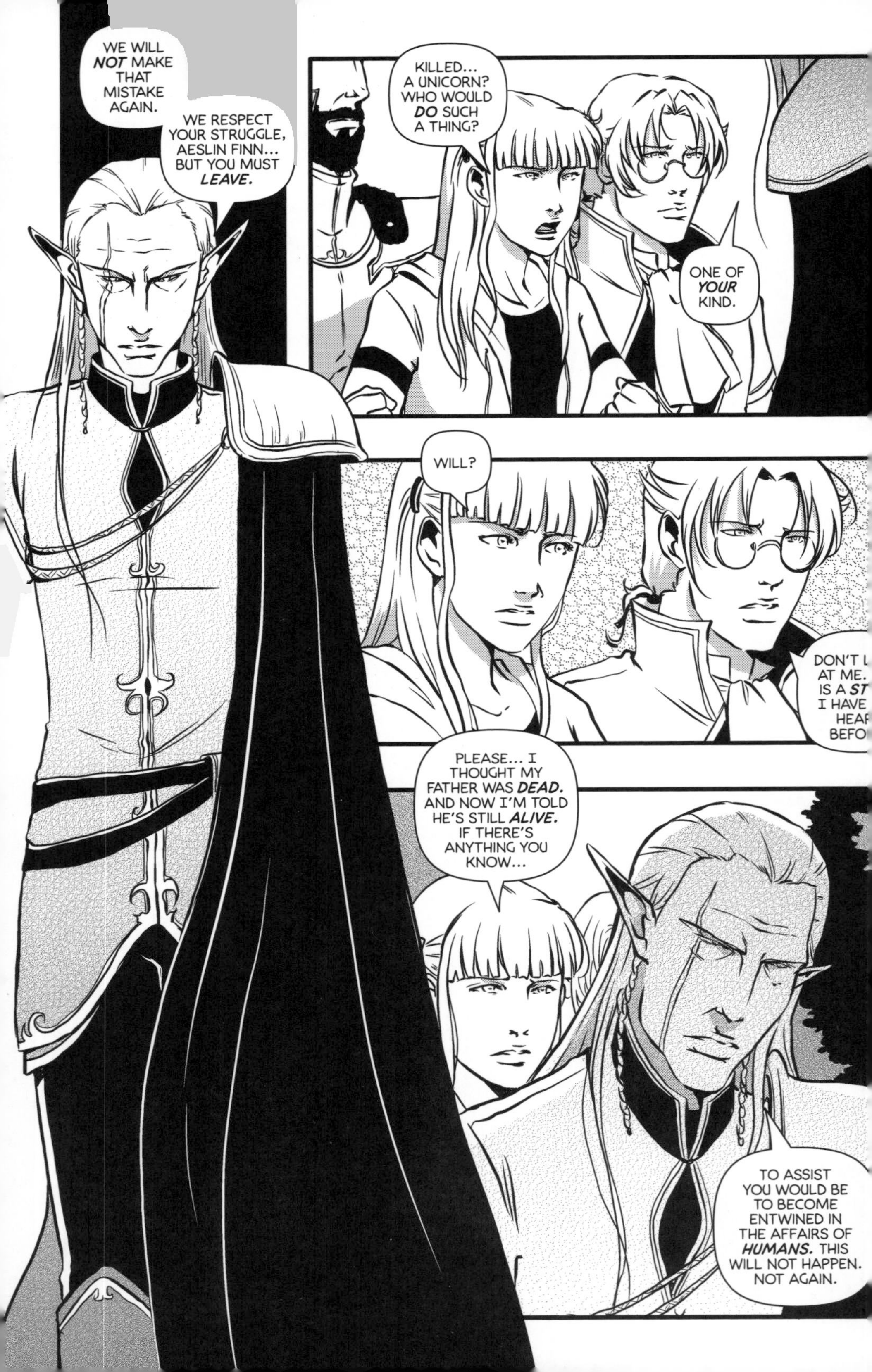

WE WILL NOT MAKE THAT MISTAKE AGAIN.
WE RESPECT YOUR STRUGGLE, AESLIN FINN... BUT YOU MUST LEAVE.
KILLED... A UNICORN? WHO WOULD DO SUCH A THING?
ONE OF YOUR KIND.
WILL?
PLEASE... I THOUGHT MY FATHER WAS DEAD. AND NOW I'M TOLD HE'S STILL ALIVE. IF THERE'S ANYTHING YOU KNOW...
TO ASSIST YOU WOULD BE TO BECOME ENTWINED IN THE AFFAIRS OF HUMANS. THIS WILL NOT HAPPEN. NOT AGAIN.

"YOU DO NOT KNOW YOUR RACE'S OWN CRIMES, SO THIS IS *ALL* THAT I WILL TELL YOU..."

"THE ELVES HAVE LONG SHARED A SACRED RELATIONSHIP WITH THE UNICORNS."

"THERE ARE ONLY EVER *TWO* UNICORNS. FATHER. AND SON.

"THE SON MATES WITH A MARE, A NORMAL HORSE, IN ORDER TO PRODUCE AN *HEIR.* AND ON THE NIGHT THAT NEW UNICORN IS BORN, THE FATHER *DIES* AND THE SON BECOMES THE FATHER.

"OUR PART OCCURS WHEN THE SON COMES OF AGE. THE SCION OF THE ELVES, THE SON'S COUNTERPART, PRESENTS THE SON WITH A HANDFUL OF ELVEN ATTENDANTS.

"THE SON THEN CHOOSES ONE ELVEN WOMAN TO HELP HIM IN HIS SEARCH FOR THE PERFECT MATE."

BUT ONE OF YOUR KIND CAME AND SHATTERED OUR SACRED TRUST.

"THE MAN WHO HAS CLAIMED YOUR THRONE.

RRENTLY, RE IS ONLY UNICORN. *SON.* HIS HER WAS LED ON NIGHT HE S BORN.

WHO...?

"KHROM."

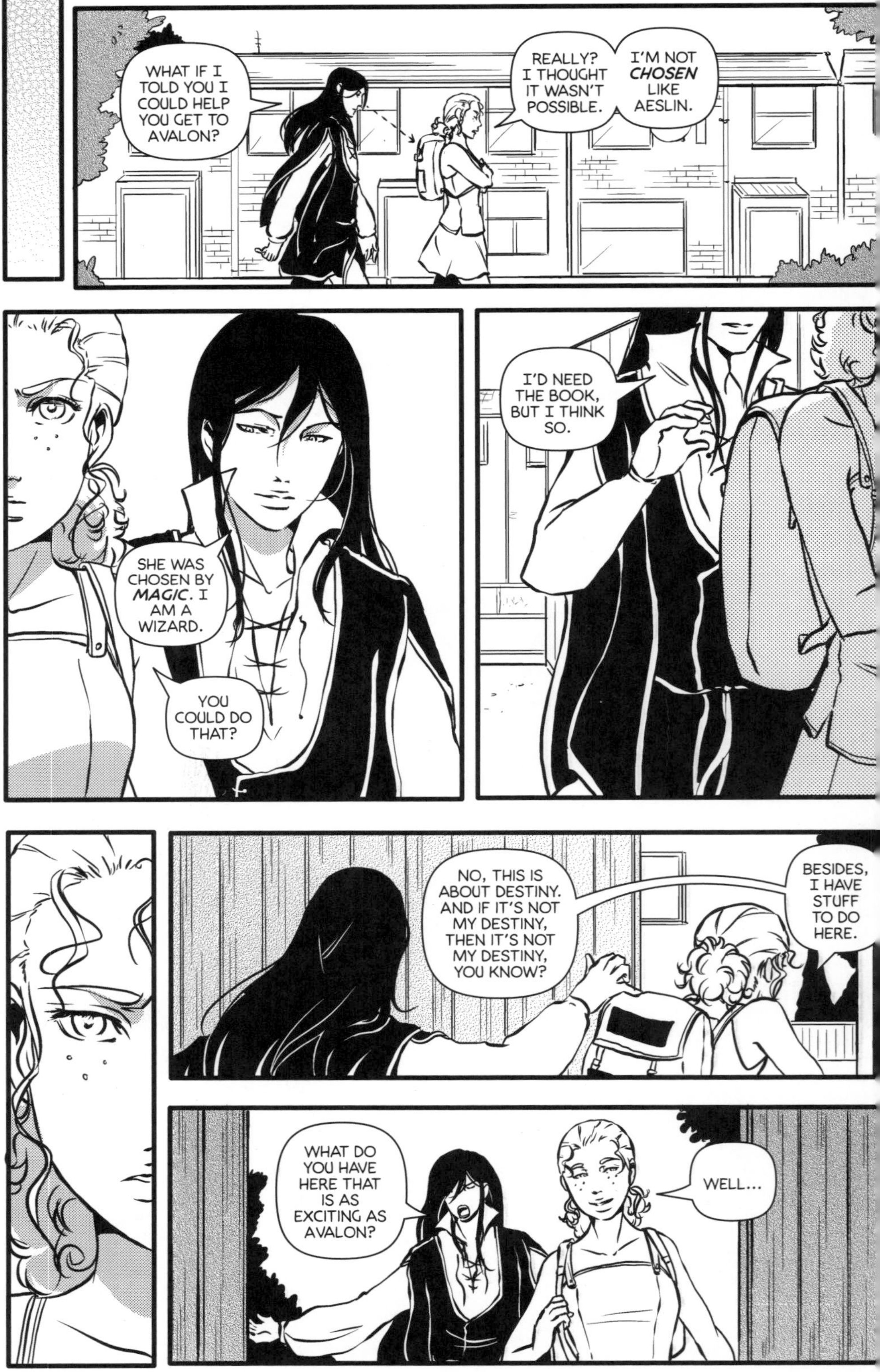
WHAT IF I TOLD YOU I COULD HELP YOU GET TO AVALON?
REALLY? I THOUGHT IT WASN'T POSSIBLE.
I'M NOT CHOSEN LIKE AESLIN.
SHE WAS CHOSEN BY MAGIC. I AM A WIZARD.
YOU COULD DO THAT?
I'D NEED THE BOOK, BUT I THINK SO.
NO, THIS IS ABOUT DESTINY. AND IF IT'S NOT MY DESTINY, THEN IT'S NOT MY DESTINY, YOU KNOW?
BESIDES, I HAVE STUFF TO DO HERE.
WHAT DO YOU HAVE HERE THAT IS AS EXCITING AS AVALON?
WELL...

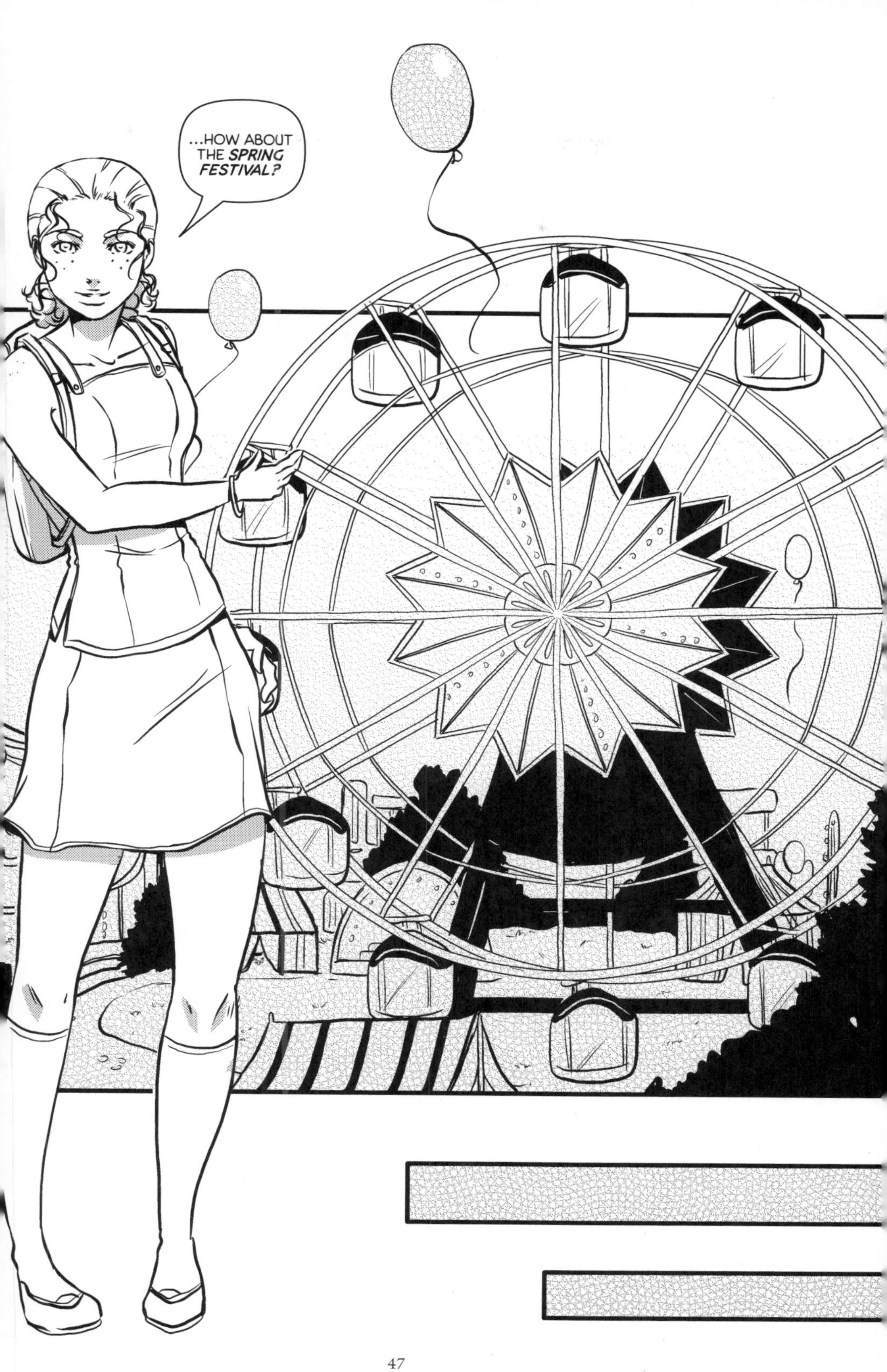
...HOW ABOUT THE *SPRING FESTIVAL?*

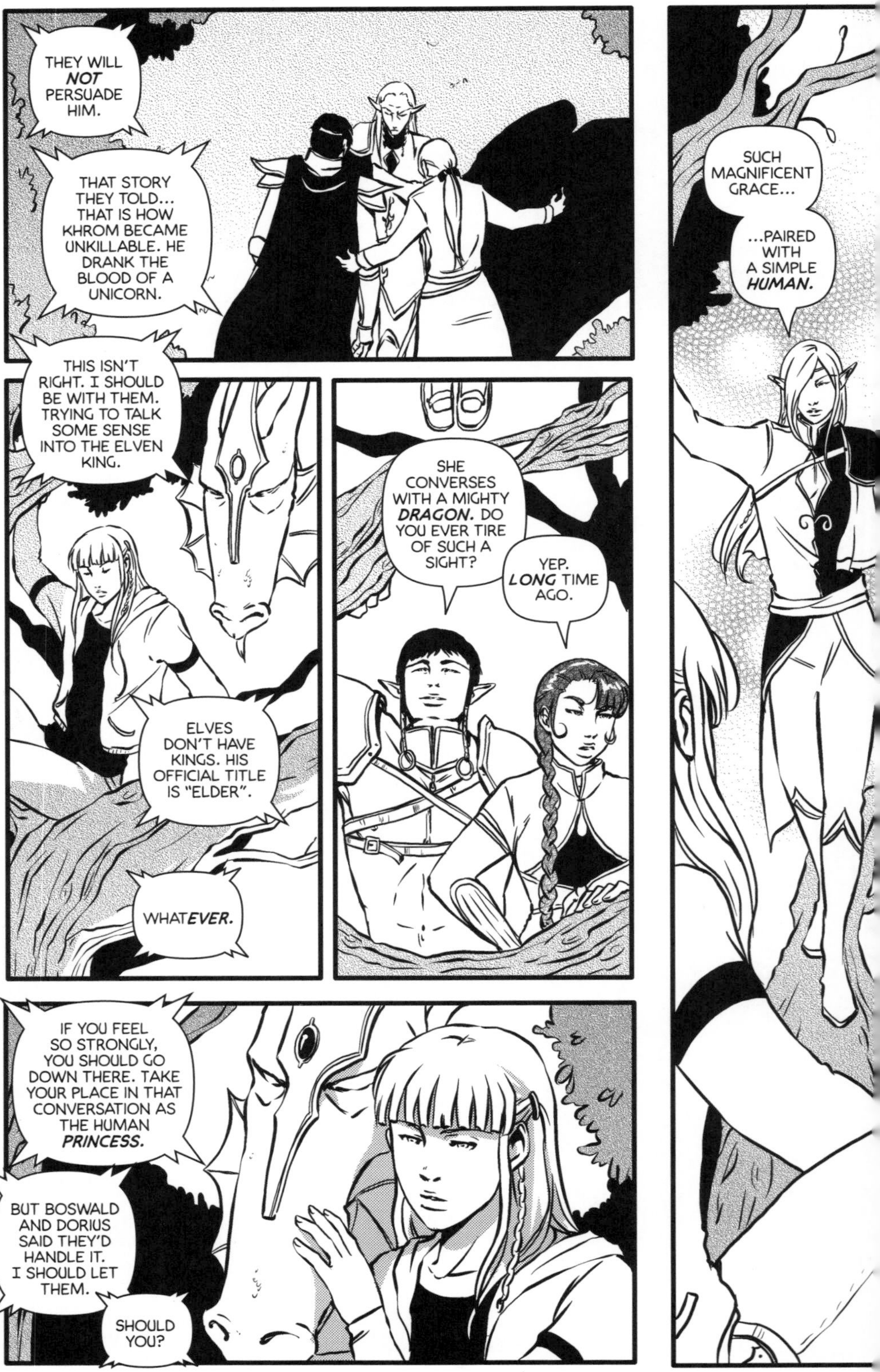
THEY WILL NOT PERSUADE HIM.
THAT STORY THEY TOLD... THAT IS HOW KHROM BECAME UNKILLABLE. HE DRANK THE BLOOD OF A UNICORN.
SUCH MAGNIFICENT GRACE...
...PAIRED WITH A SIMPLE HUMAN.
THIS ISN'T RIGHT. I SHOULD BE WITH THEM. TRYING TO TALK SOME SENSE INTO THE ELVEN KING.
ELVES DON'T HAVE KINGS. HIS OFFICIAL TITLE IS "ELDER".
WHATEVER.
SHE CONVERSES WITH A MIGHTY DRAGON. DO YOU EVER TIRE OF SUCH A SIGHT?
YEP. LONG TIME AGO.
IF YOU FEEL SO STRONGLY, YOU SHOULD GO DOWN THERE. TAKE YOUR PLACE IN THAT CONVERSATION AS THE HUMAN PRINCESS.
BUT BOSWALD AND DORIUS SAID THEY'D HANDLE IT. I SHOULD LET THEM.
SHOULD YOU?

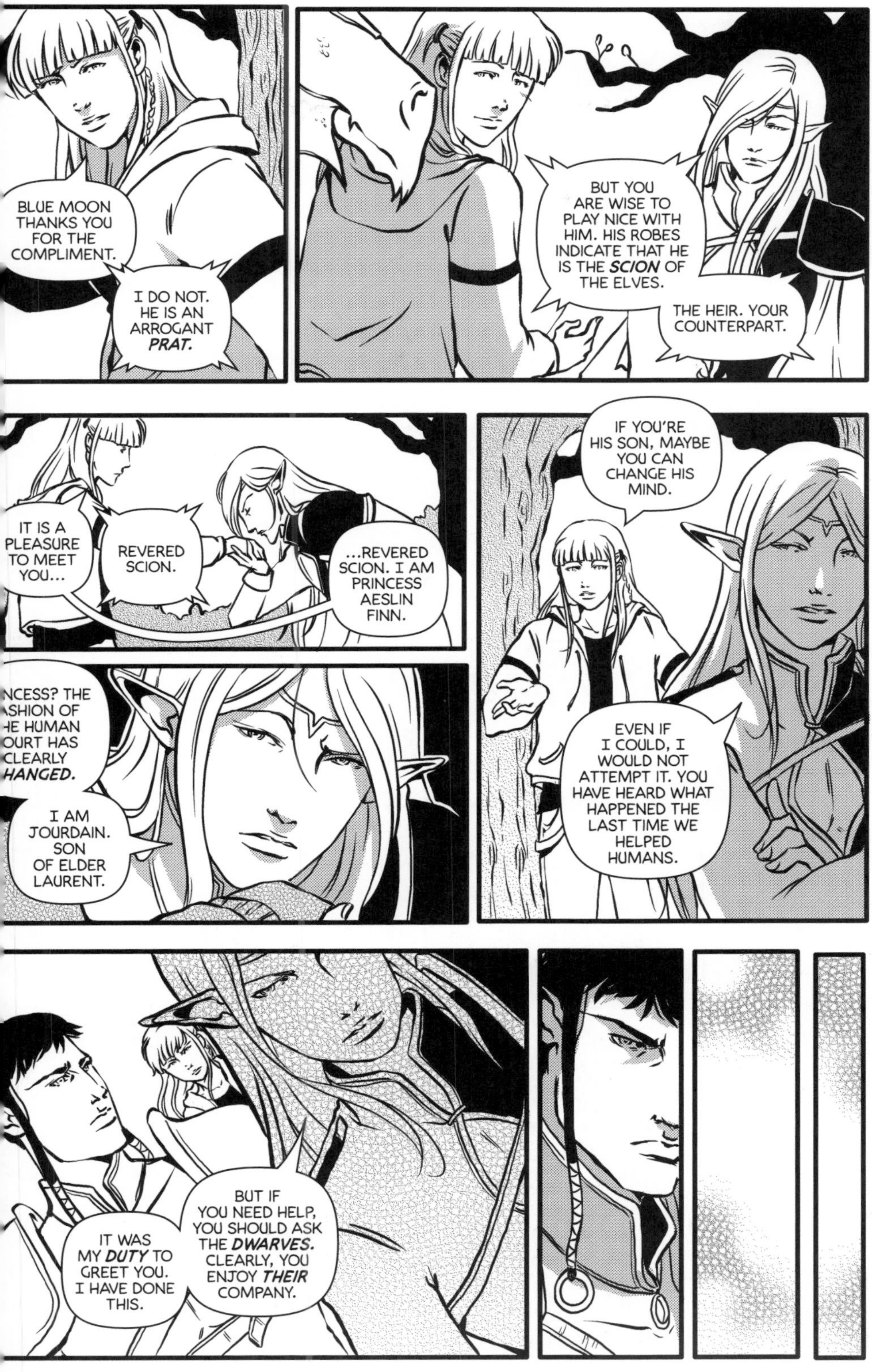
BLUE MOON THANKS YOU FOR THE COMPLIMENT.
I DO NOT. HE IS AN ARROGANT ***PRAT.***
BUT YOU ARE WISE TO PLAY NICE WITH HIM. HIS ROBES INDICATE THAT HE IS THE ***SCION*** OF THE ELVES.
THE HEIR. YOUR COUNTERPART.
IT IS A PLEASURE TO MEET YOU...
REVERED SCION.
...REVERED SCION. I AM PRINCESS AESLIN FINN.
NCESS? THE ASHION OF HE HUMAN OURT HAS CLEARLY ***HANGED.***
I AM JOURDAIN. SON OF ELDER LAURENT.
IF YOU'RE HIS SON, MAYBE YOU CAN CHANGE HIS MIND.
EVEN IF I COULD, I WOULD NOT ATTEMPT IT. YOU HAVE HEARD WHAT HAPPENED THE LAST TIME WE HELPED HUMANS.
IT WAS MY ***DUTY*** TO GREET YOU. I HAVE DONE THIS.
BUT IF YOU NEED HELP, YOU SHOULD ASK THE ***DWARVES.*** CLEARLY, YOU ENJOY ***THEIR*** COMPANY.

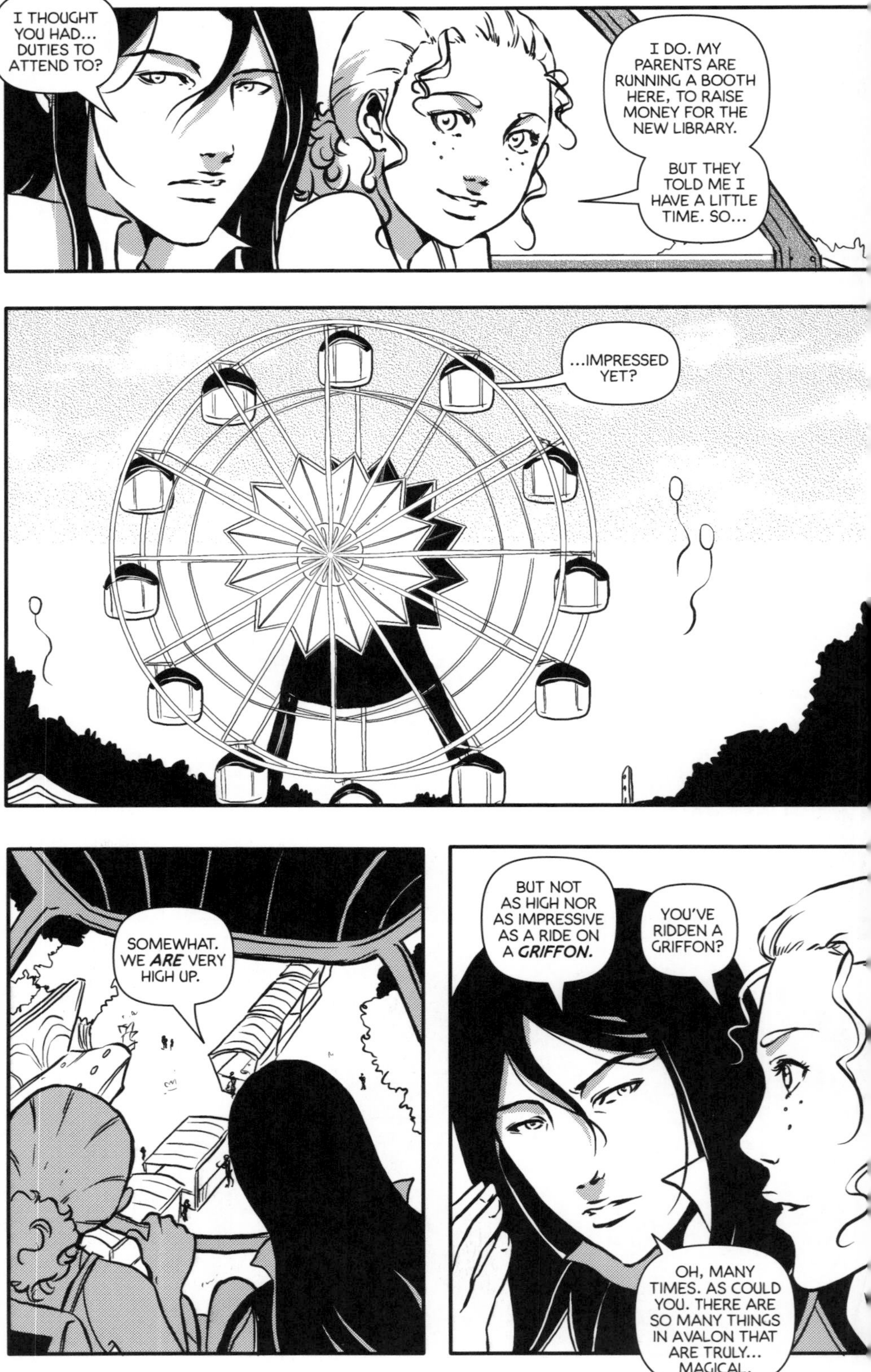
I THOUGHT YOU HAD... DUTIES TO ATTEND TO?
I DO. MY PARENTS ARE RUNNING A BOOTH HERE, TO RAISE MONEY FOR THE NEW LIBRARY.
BUT THEY TOLD ME I HAVE A LITTLE TIME. SO...
...IMPRESSED YET?
SOMEWHAT. WE ARE VERY HIGH UP.
BUT NOT AS HIGH NOR AS IMPRESSIVE AS A RIDE ON A GRIFFON.
YOU'VE RIDDEN A GRIFFON?
OH, MANY TIMES. AS COULD YOU. THERE ARE SO MANY THINGS IN AVALON THAT ARE TRULY... MAGICAL.

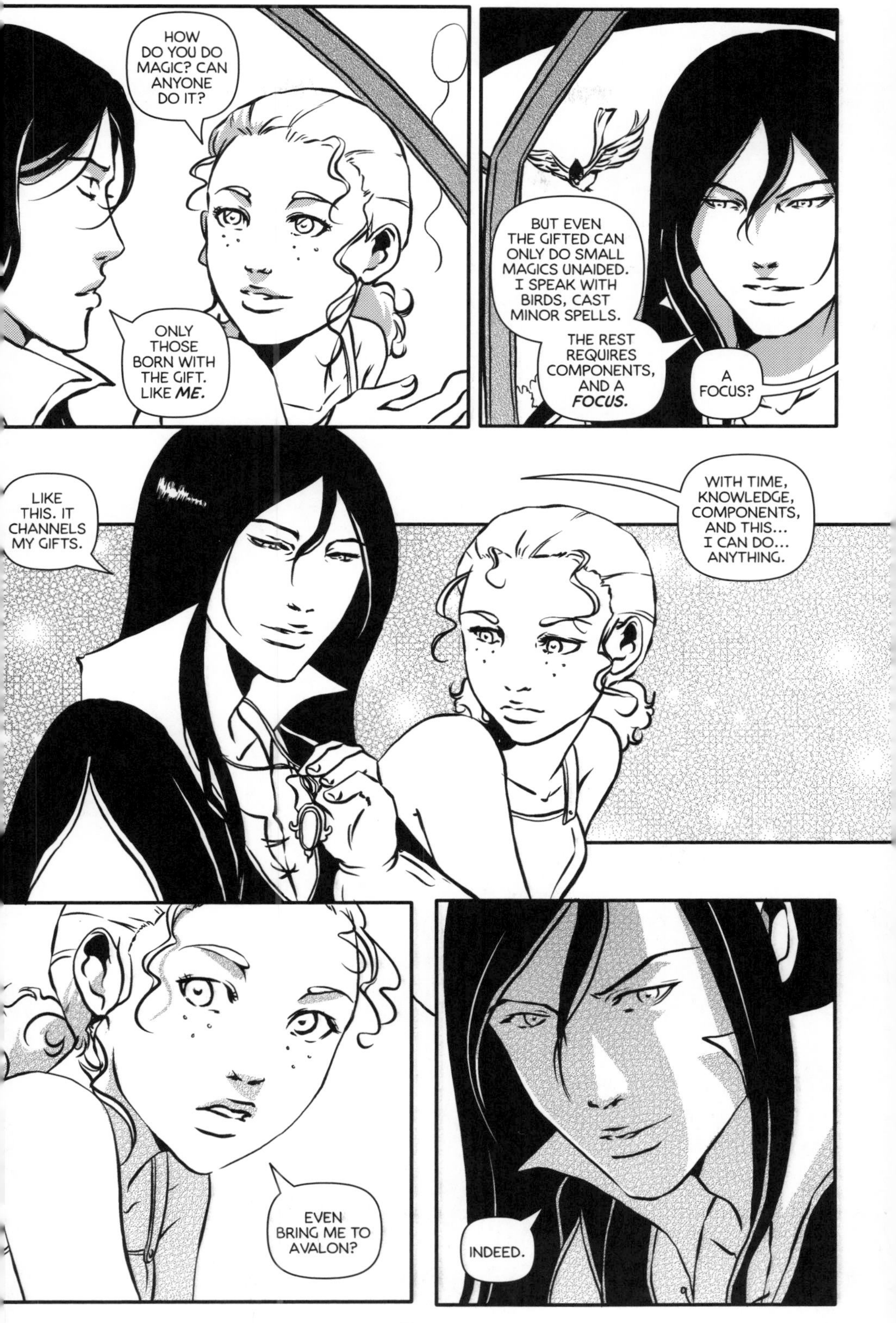
HOW DO YOU DO MAGIC? CAN ANYONE DO IT?
ONLY THOSE BORN WITH THE GIFT. LIKE *ME.*
BUT EVEN THE GIFTED CAN ONLY DO SMALL MAGICS UNAIDED. I SPEAK WITH BIRDS, CAST MINOR SPELLS.
THE REST REQUIRES COMPONENTS, AND A *FOCUS.*
A FOCUS?
LIKE THIS. IT CHANNELS MY GIFTS.
WITH TIME, KNOWLEDGE, COMPONENTS, AND THIS... I CAN DO... ANYTHING.
EVEN BRING ME TO AVALON?
INDEED.

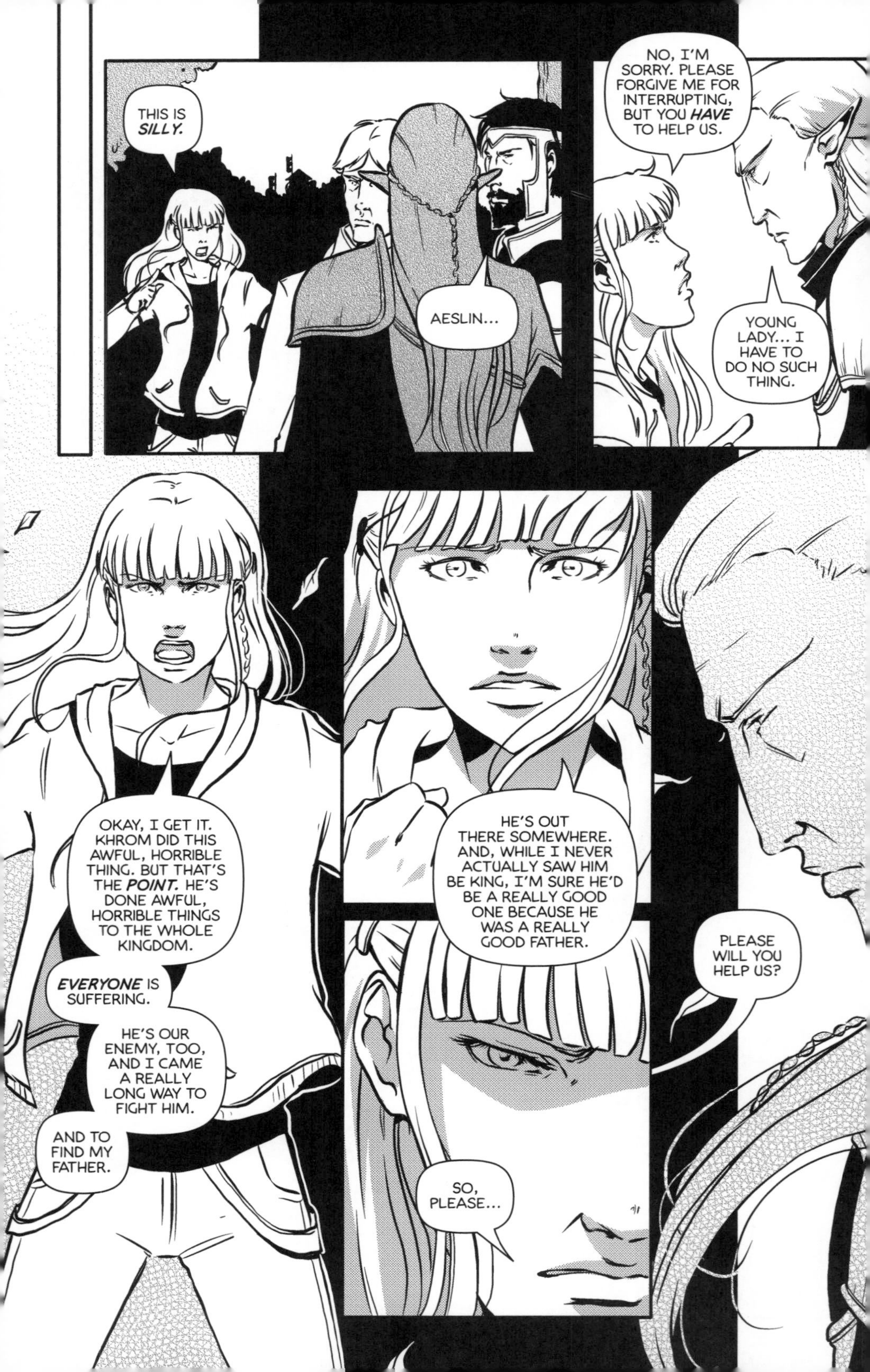
THIS IS SILLY.
AESLIN...
NO, I'M SORRY. PLEASE FORGIVE ME FOR INTERRUPTING, BUT YOU HAVE TO HELP US.
YOUNG LADY... I HAVE TO DO NO SUCH THING.
OKAY, I GET IT. KHROM DID THIS AWFUL, HORRIBLE THING. BUT THAT'S THE POINT. HE'S DONE AWFUL, HORRIBLE THINGS TO THE WHOLE KINGDOM.
EVERYONE IS SUFFERING.
HE'S OUR ENEMY, TOO, AND I CAME A REALLY LONG WAY TO FIGHT HIM.
AND TO FIND MY FATHER.
HE'S OUT THERE SOMEWHERE. AND, WHILE I NEVER ACTUALLY SAW HIM BE KING, I'M SURE HE'D BE A REALLY GOOD ONE BECAUSE HE WAS A REALLY GOOD FATHER.
SO, PLEASE...
PLEASE WILL YOU HELP US?

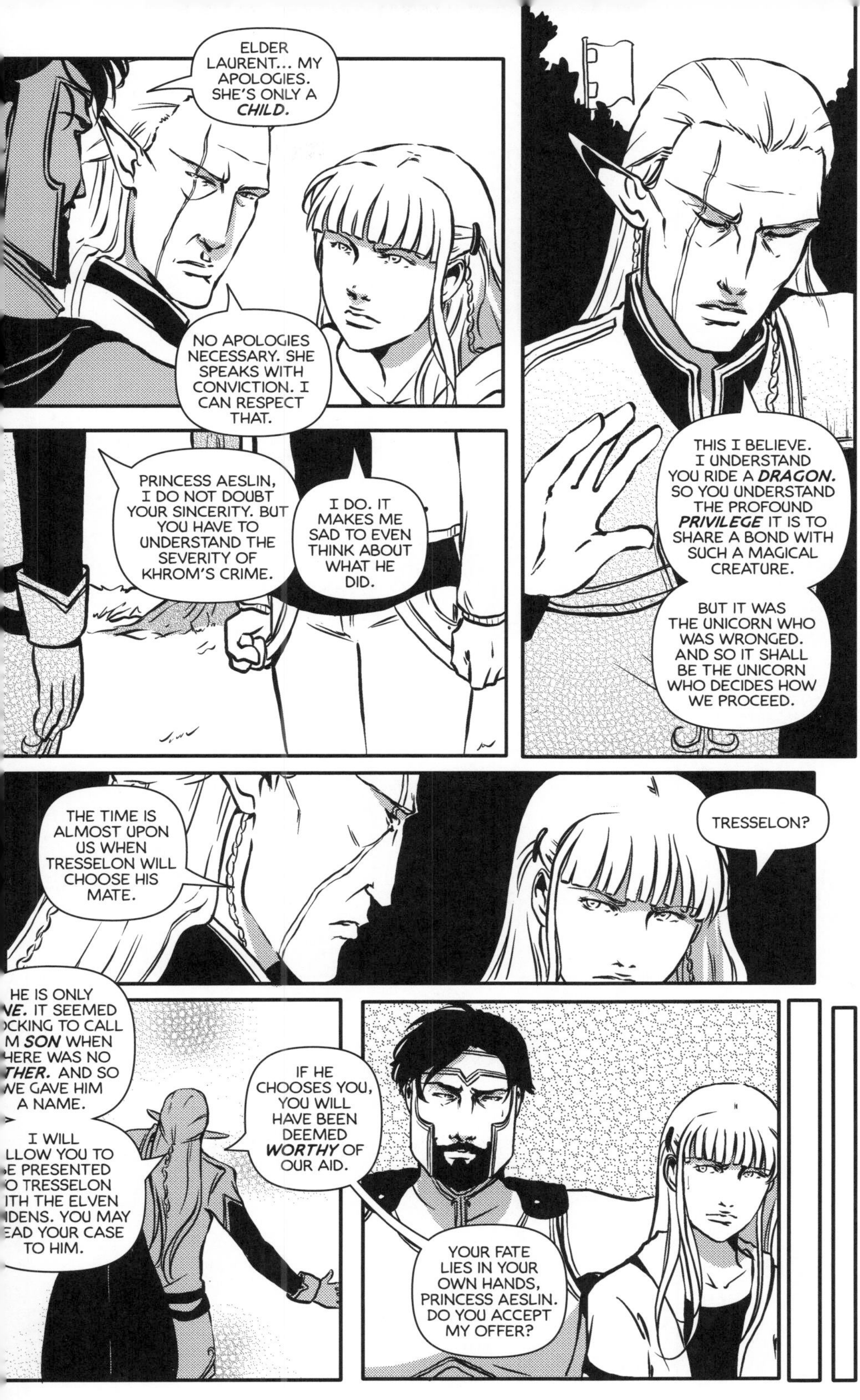
ELDER LAURENT... MY APOLOGIES. SHE'S ONLY A *CHILD.*
NO APOLOGIES NECESSARY. SHE SPEAKS WITH CONVICTION. I CAN RESPECT THAT.
THIS I BELIEVE. I UNDERSTAND YOU RIDE A *DRAGON.* SO YOU UNDERSTAND THE PROFOUND *PRIVILEGE* IT IS TO SHARE A BOND WITH SUCH A MAGICAL CREATURE.
BUT IT WAS THE UNICORN WHO WAS WRONGED. AND SO IT SHALL BE THE UNICORN WHO DECIDES HOW WE PROCEED.
PRINCESS AESLIN, I DO NOT DOUBT YOUR SINCERITY. BUT YOU HAVE TO UNDERSTAND THE SEVERITY OF KHROM'S CRIME.
I DO. IT MAKES ME SAD TO EVEN THINK ABOUT WHAT HE DID.
THE TIME IS ALMOST UPON US WHEN TRESSELON WILL CHOOSE HIS MATE.
TRESSELON?
HE IS ONLY NE. IT SEEMED CKING TO CALL M *SON* WHEN HERE WAS NO *THER.* AND SO WE GAVE HIM A NAME.
I WILL LLOW YOU TO E PRESENTED O TRESSELON ITH THE ELVEN IDENS. YOU MAY EAD YOUR CASE TO HIM.
IF HE CHOOSES YOU, YOU WILL HAVE BEEN DEEMED *WORTHY* OF OUR AID.
YOUR FATE LIES IN YOUR OWN HANDS, PRINCESS AESLIN. DO YOU ACCEPT MY OFFER?

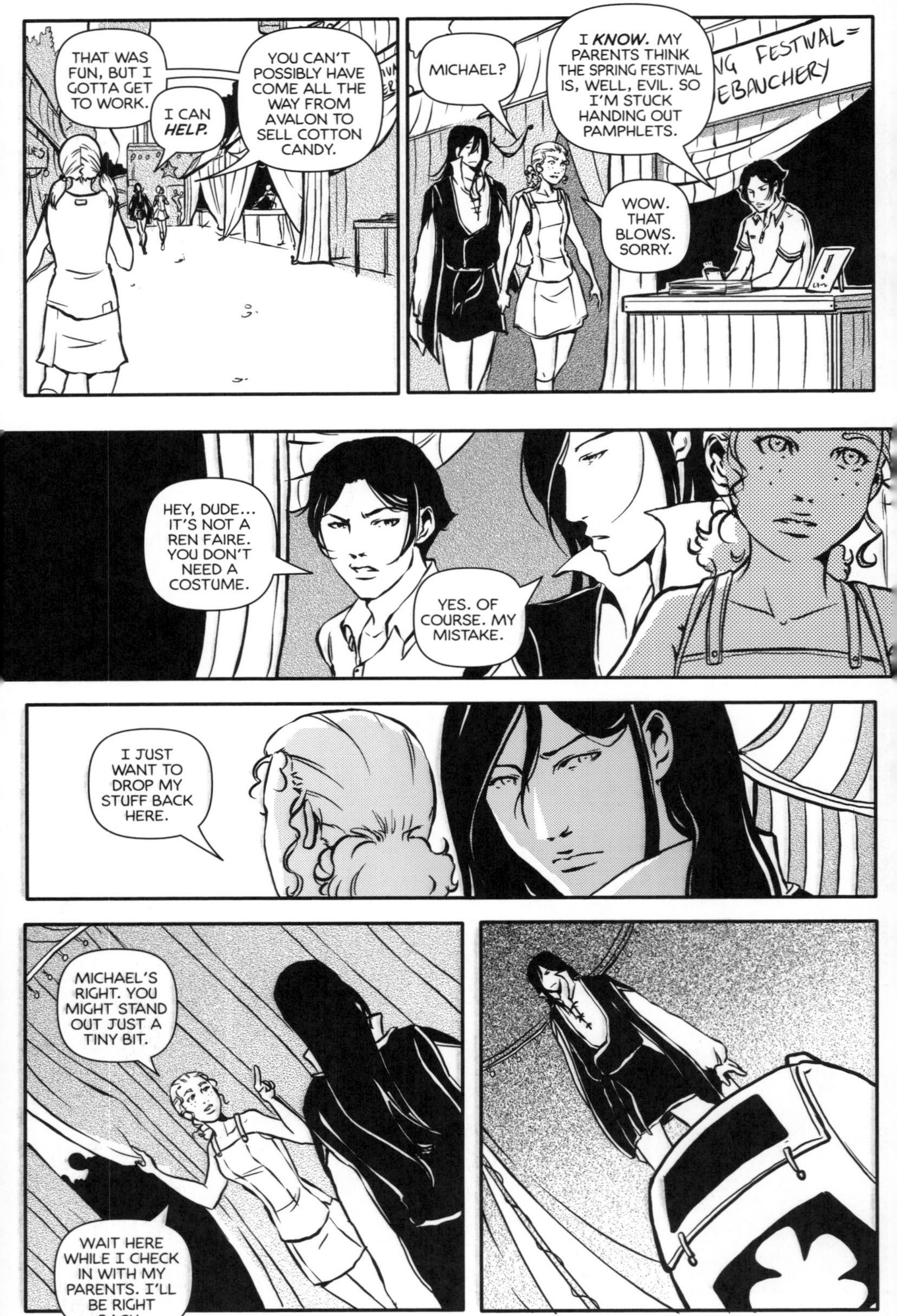
THAT WAS FUN, BUT I GOTTA GET TO WORK.
I CAN *HELP.*
YOU CAN'T POSSIBLY HAVE COME ALL THE WAY FROM AVALON TO SELL COTTON CANDY.
MICHAEL?
I *KNOW.* MY PARENTS THINK THE SPRING FESTIVAL IS, WELL, EVIL. SO I'M STUCK HANDING OUT PAMPHLETS.
NG FESTIVAL = EBAUCHERY
WOW. THAT BLOWS. SORRY.
HEY, DUDE... IT'S NOT A REN FAIRE. YOU DON'T NEED A COSTUME.
YES. OF COURSE. MY MISTAKE.
I JUST WANT TO DROP MY STUFF BACK HERE.
MICHAEL'S RIGHT. YOU MIGHT STAND OUT JUST A TINY BIT.
WAIT HERE WHILE I CHECK IN WITH MY PARENTS. I'LL BE RIGHT BACK.

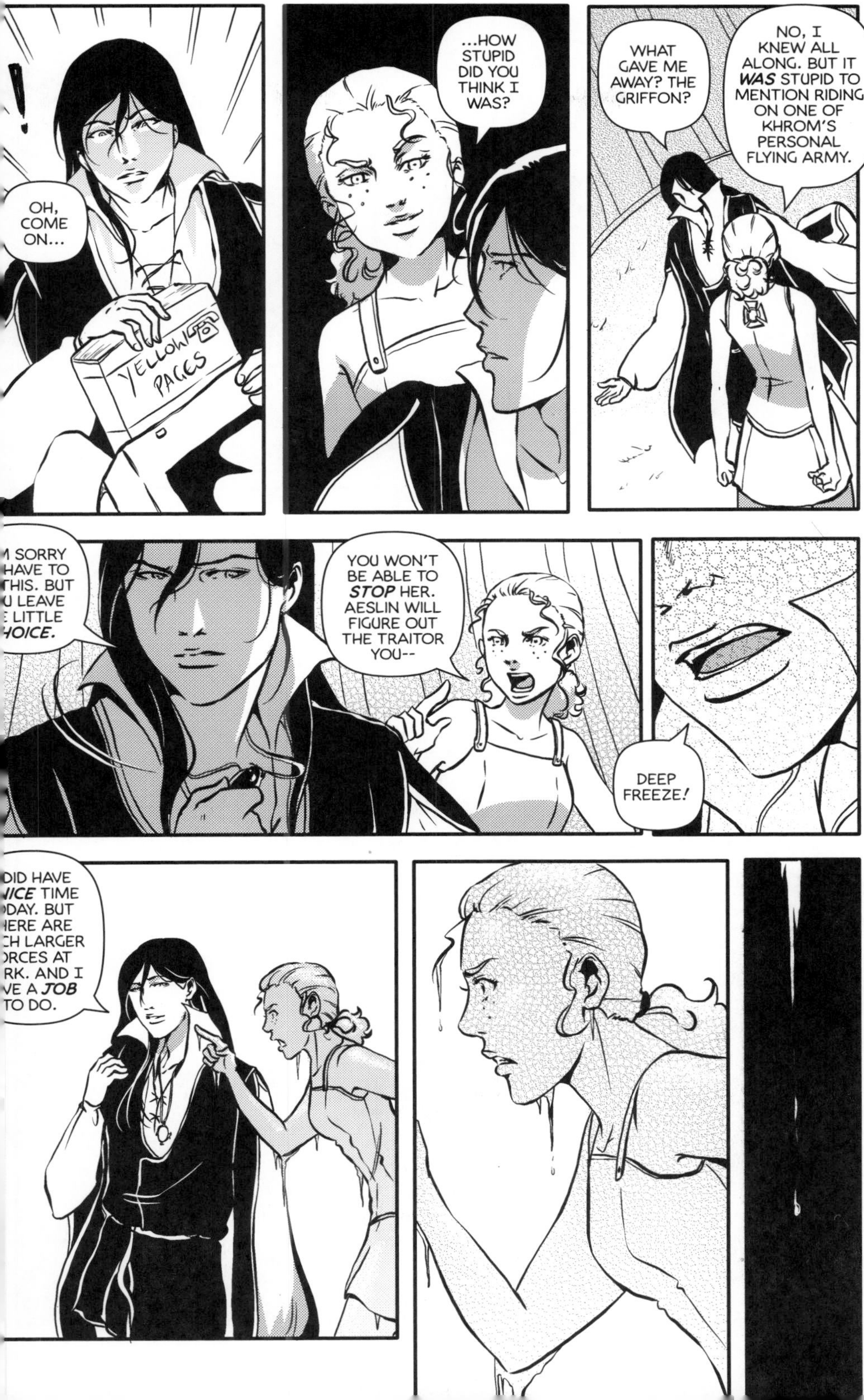
!
OH, COME ON...
YELLOW PAGES
...HOW STUPID DID YOU THINK I WAS?
WHAT GAVE ME AWAY? THE GRIFFON?
NO, I KNEW ALL ALONG. BUT IT WAS STUPID TO MENTION RIDING ON ONE OF KHROM'S PERSONAL FLYING ARMY.
M SORRY HAVE TO THIS. BUT U LEAVE E LITTLE HOICE.
YOU WON'T BE ABLE TO STOP HER. AESLIN WILL FIGURE OUT THE TRAITOR YOU--
DEEP FREEZE!
DID HAVE NICE TIME ODAY. BUT HERE ARE CH LARGER ORCES AT RK. AND I VE A JOB TO DO.

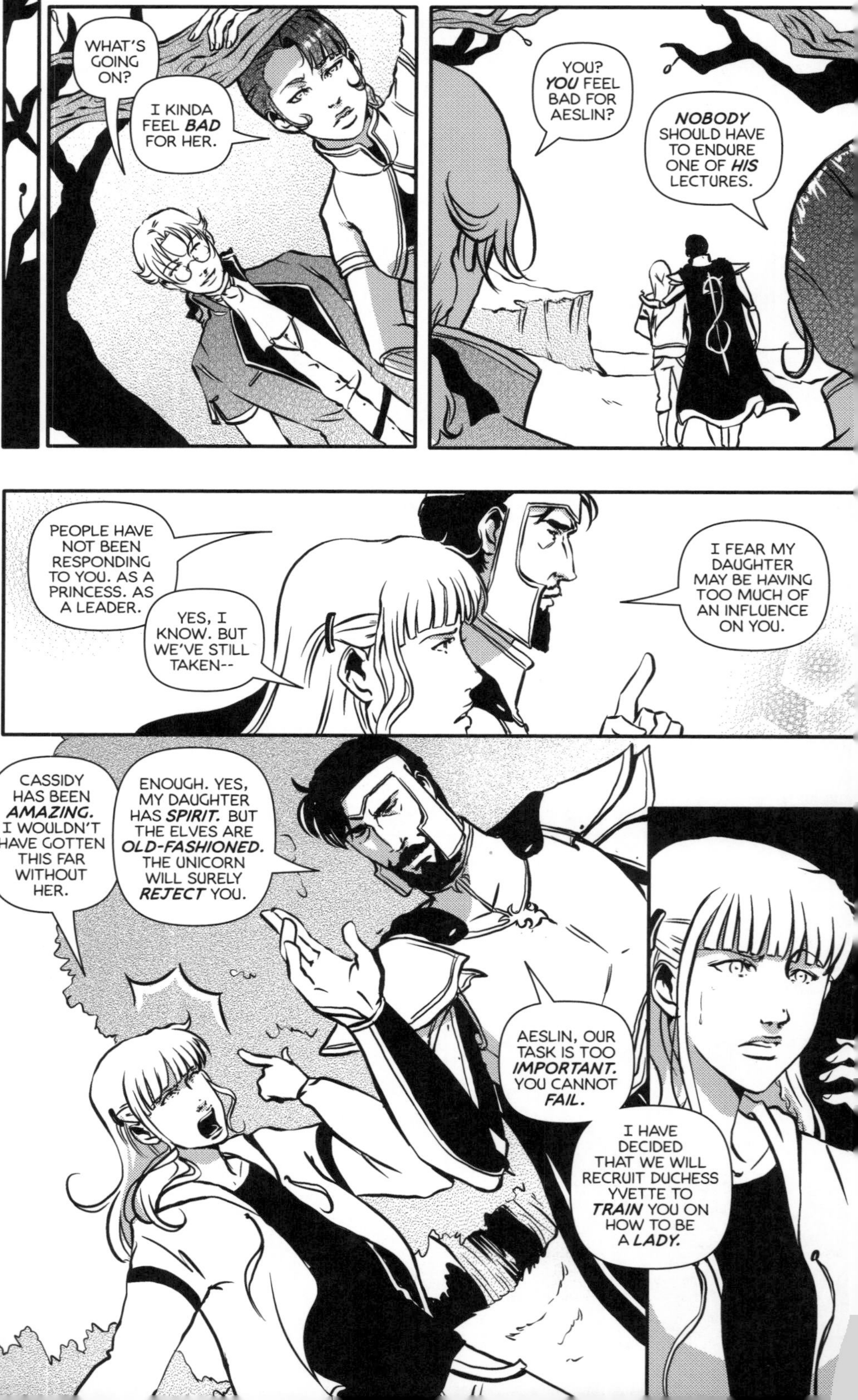
WHAT'S GOING ON?
I KINDA FEEL BAD FOR HER.
YOU? YOU FEEL BAD FOR AESLIN?
NOBODY SHOULD HAVE TO ENDURE ONE OF HIS LECTURES.
PEOPLE HAVE NOT BEEN RESPONDING TO YOU. AS A PRINCESS. AS A LEADER.
YES, I KNOW. BUT WE'VE STILL TAKEN--
I FEAR MY DAUGHTER MAY BE HAVING TOO MUCH OF AN INFLUENCE ON YOU.
CASSIDY HAS BEEN AMAZING. I WOULDN'T HAVE GOTTEN THIS FAR WITHOUT HER.
ENOUGH. YES, MY DAUGHTER HAS SPIRIT. BUT THE ELVES ARE OLD-FASHIONED. THE UNICORN WILL SURELY REJECT YOU.
AESLIN, OUR TASK IS TOO IMPORTANT. YOU CANNOT FAIL.
I HAVE DECIDED THAT WE WILL RECRUIT DUCHESS YVETTE TO TRAIN YOU ON HOW TO BE A LADY.

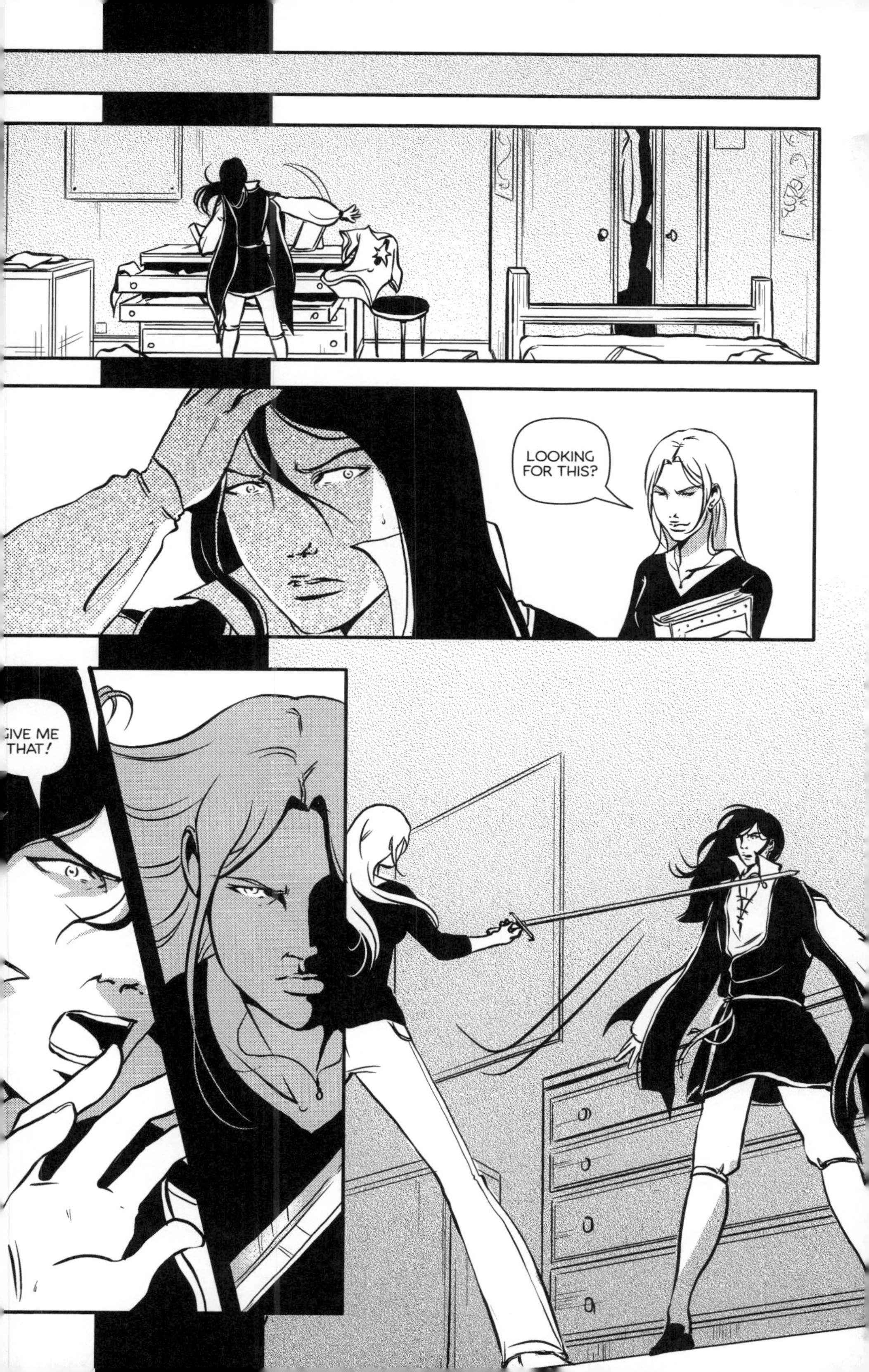
LOOKING FOR THIS?
GIVE ME THAT!

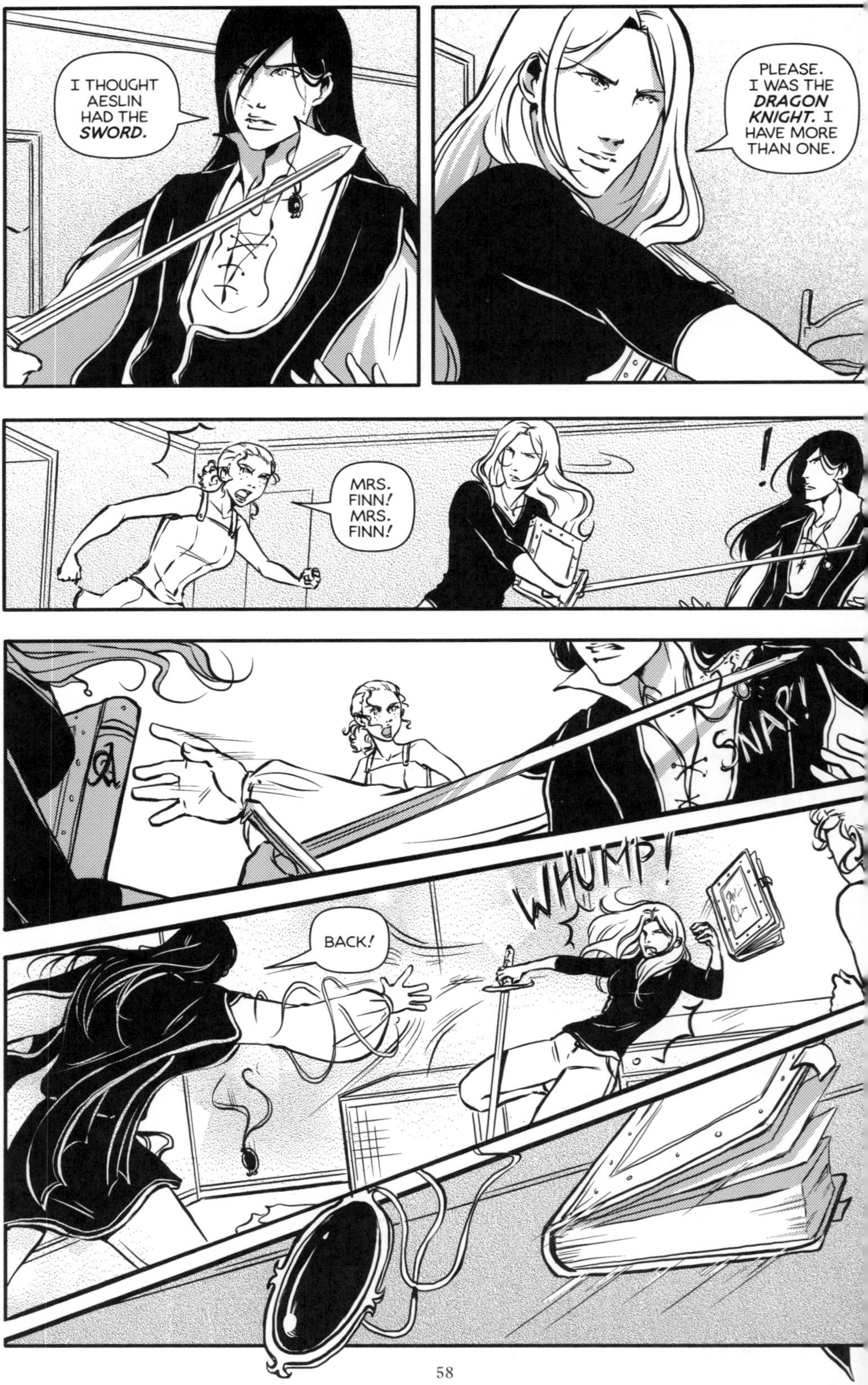
I THOUGHT AESLIN HAD THE *SWORD.*
PLEASE. I WAS THE *DRAGON KNIGHT.* I HAVE MORE THAN ONE.
!
MRS. FINN! MRS. FINN!
SNAP!
WHUMP!
BACK!

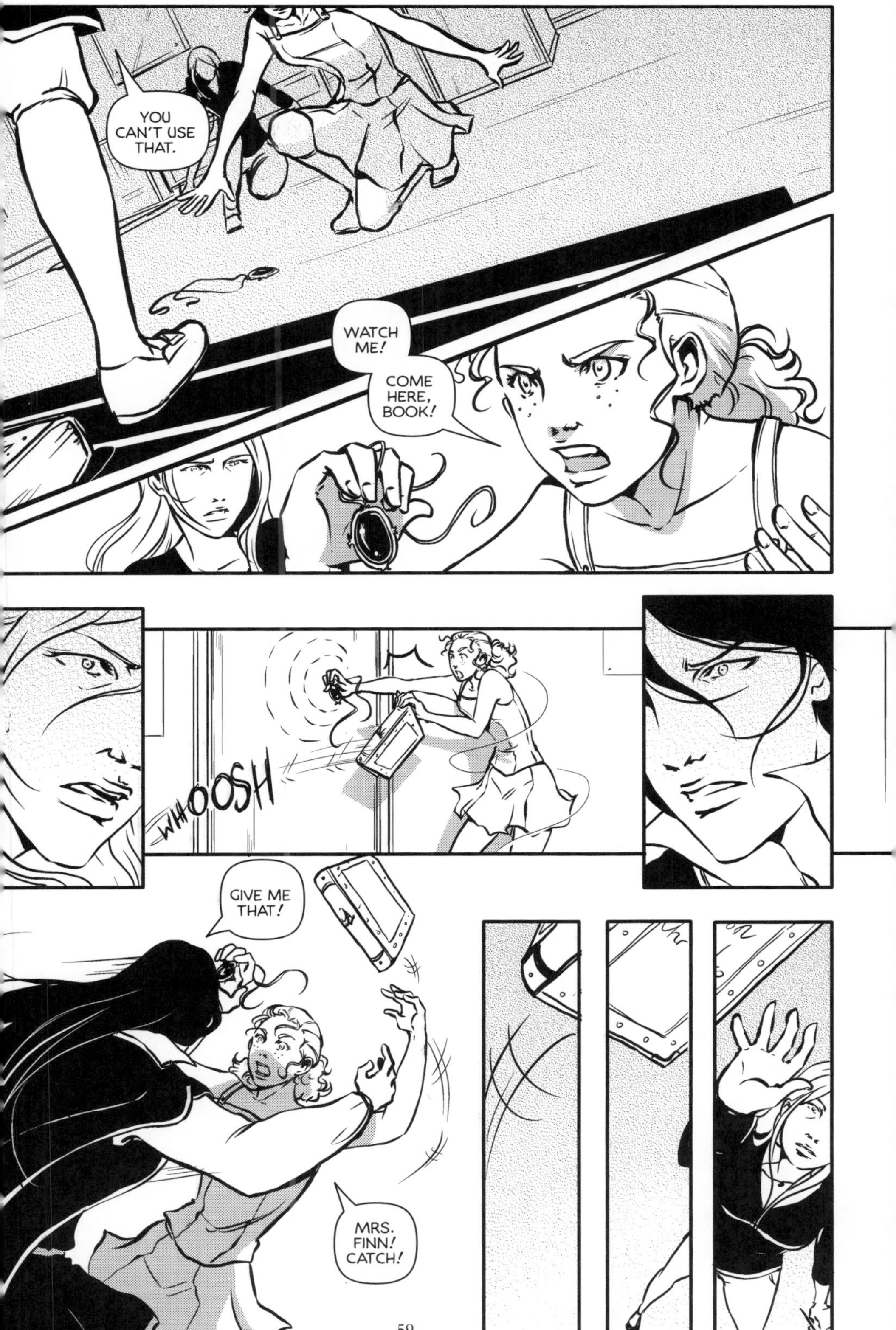

YOU CAN'T USE THAT.
WATCH ME!
COME HERE, BOOK!
WHOOSH
GIVE ME THAT!
MRS. FINN! CATCH!

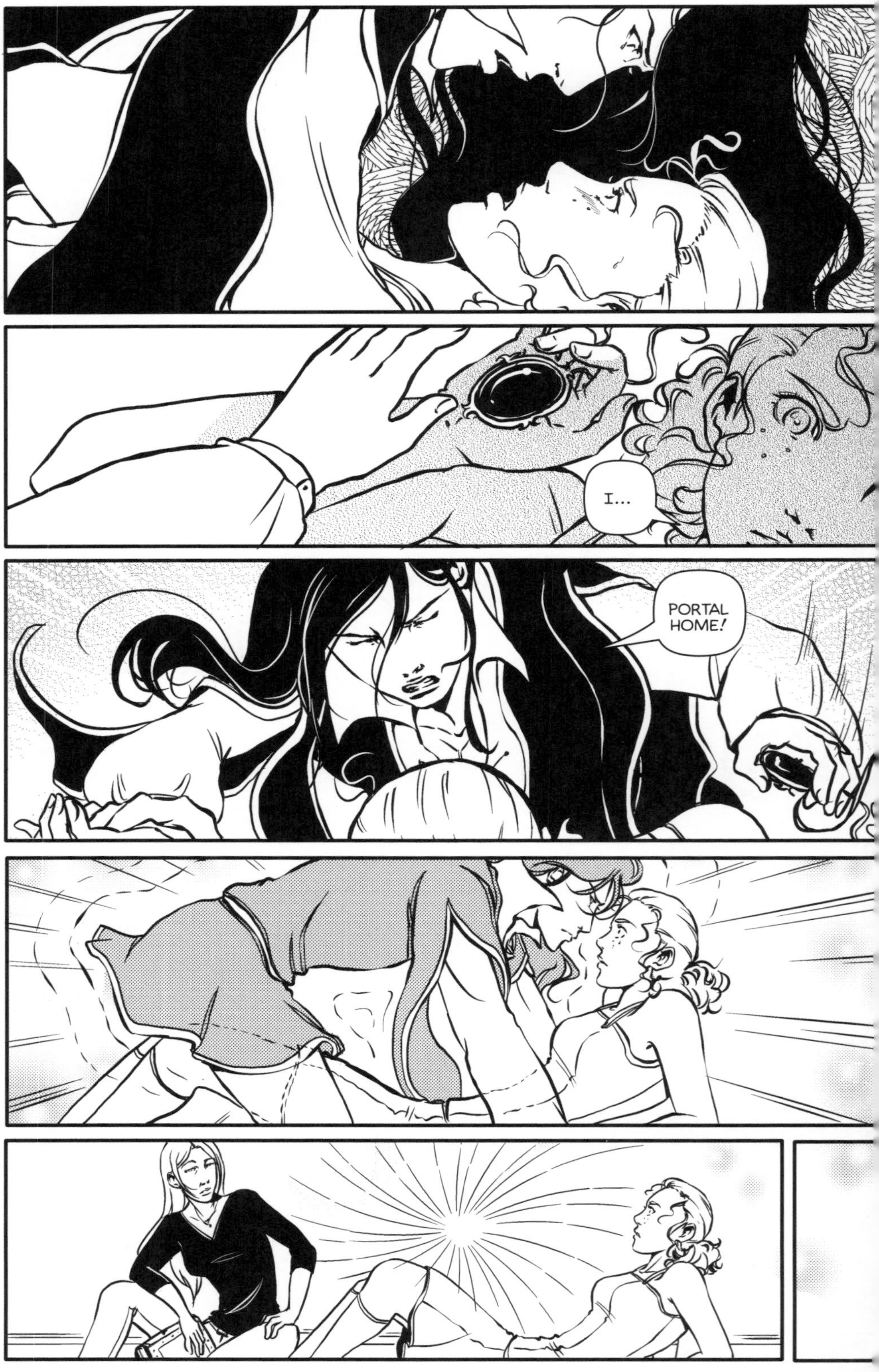
I...
PORTAL HOME!

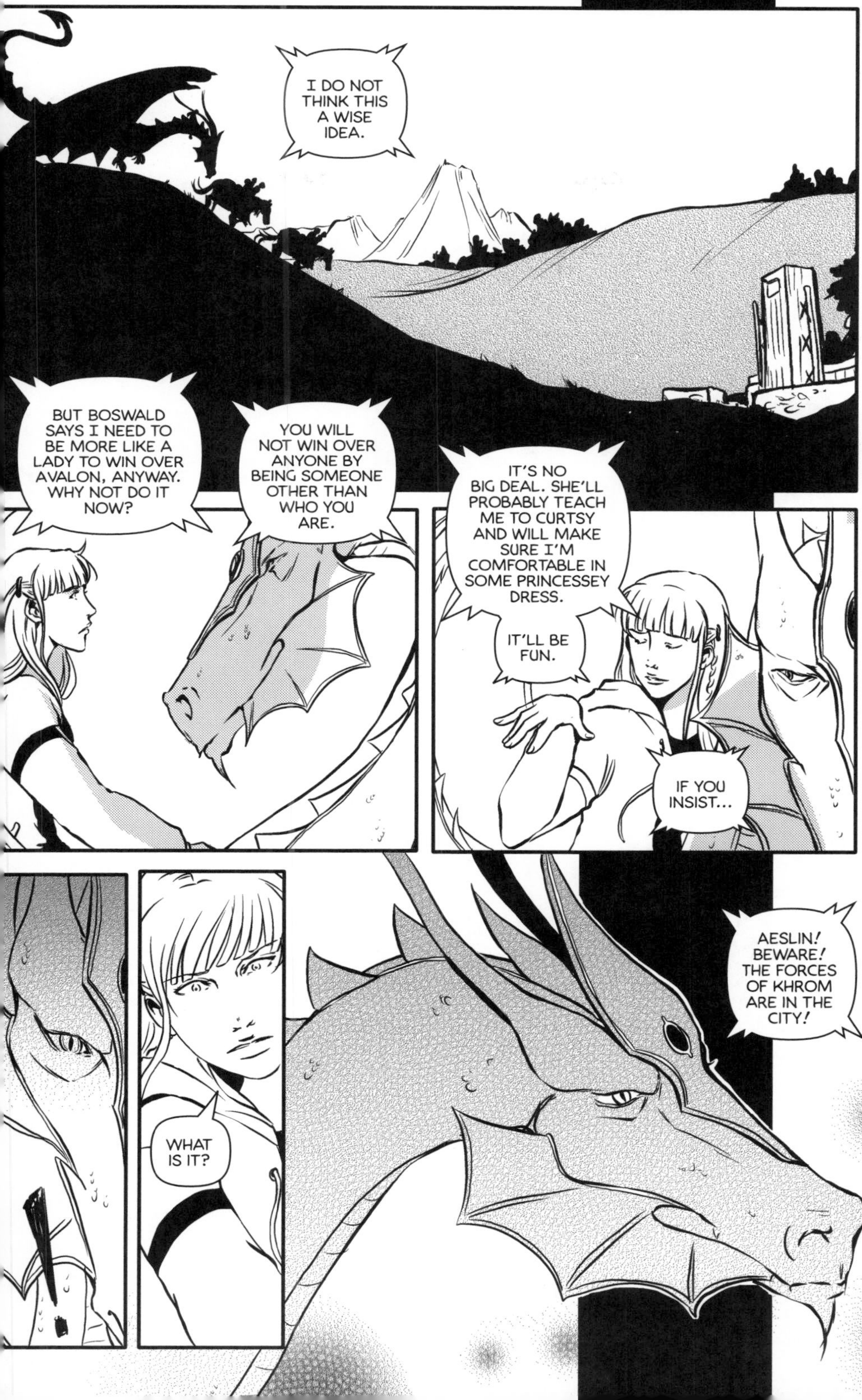

I DO NOT THINK THIS A WISE IDEA.
BUT BOSWALD SAYS I NEED TO BE MORE LIKE A LADY TO WIN OVER AVALON, ANYWAY. WHY NOT DO IT NOW?
YOU WILL NOT WIN OVER ANYONE BY BEING SOMEONE OTHER THAN WHO YOU ARE.
IT'S NO BIG DEAL. SHE'LL PROBABLY TEACH ME TO CURTSY AND WILL MAKE SURE I'M COMFORTABLE IN SOME PRINCESSEY DRESS.
IT'LL BE FUN.
IF YOU INSIST...
WHAT IS IT?
AESLIN! BEWARE! THE FORCES OF KHROM ARE IN THE CITY!

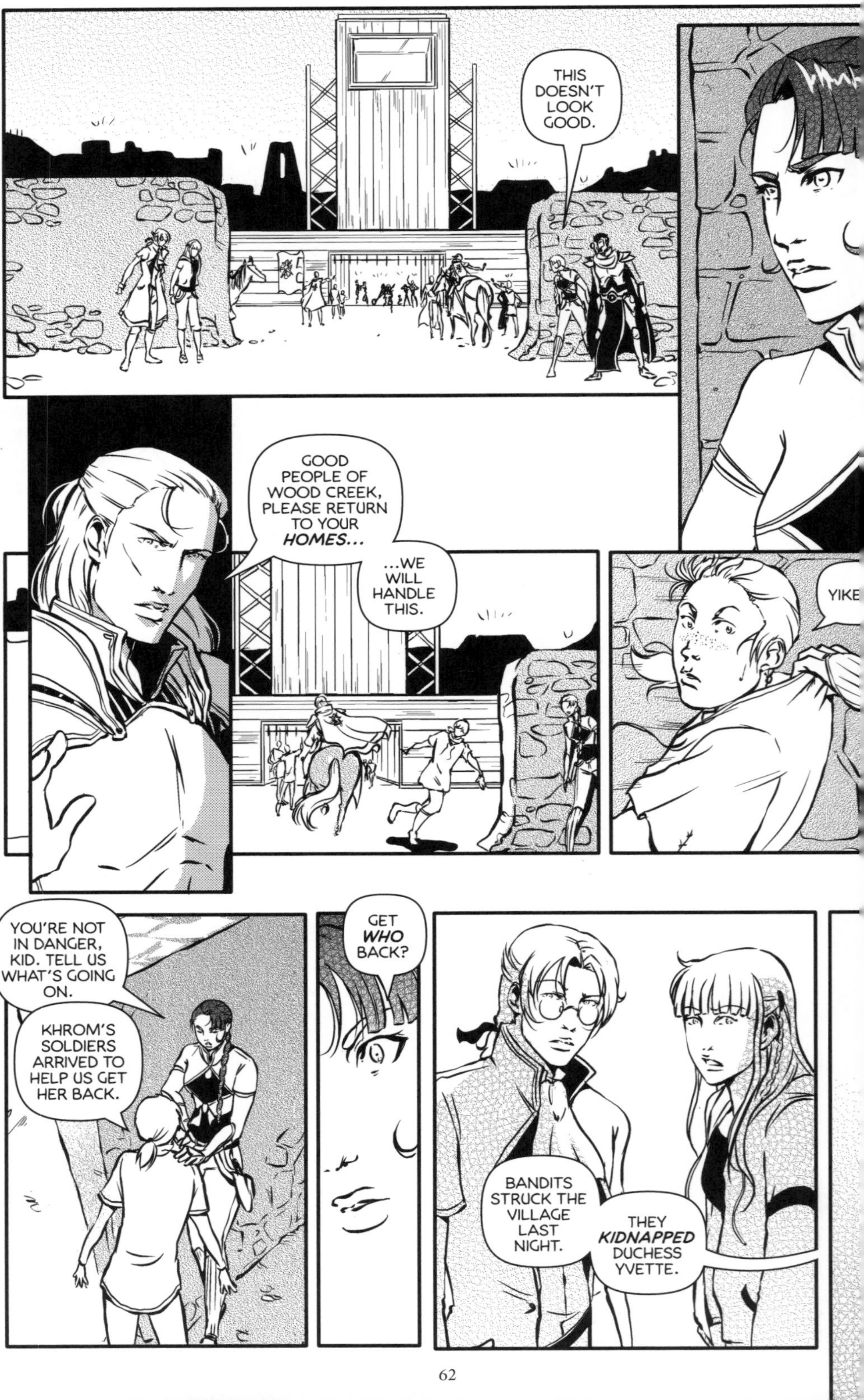
THIS DOESN'T LOOK GOOD.
GOOD PEOPLE OF WOOD CREEK, PLEASE RETURN TO YOUR *HOMES...*
...WE WILL HANDLE THIS.
YIKE
YOU'RE NOT IN DANGER, KID. TELL US WHAT'S GOING ON.
KHROM'S SOLDIERS ARRIVED TO HELP US GET HER BACK.
GET *WHO* BACK?
BANDITS STRUCK THE VILLAGE LAST NIGHT.
THEY *KIDNAPPED* DUCHESS YVETTE.

Chapter 3

GIRL, ABDUCTED

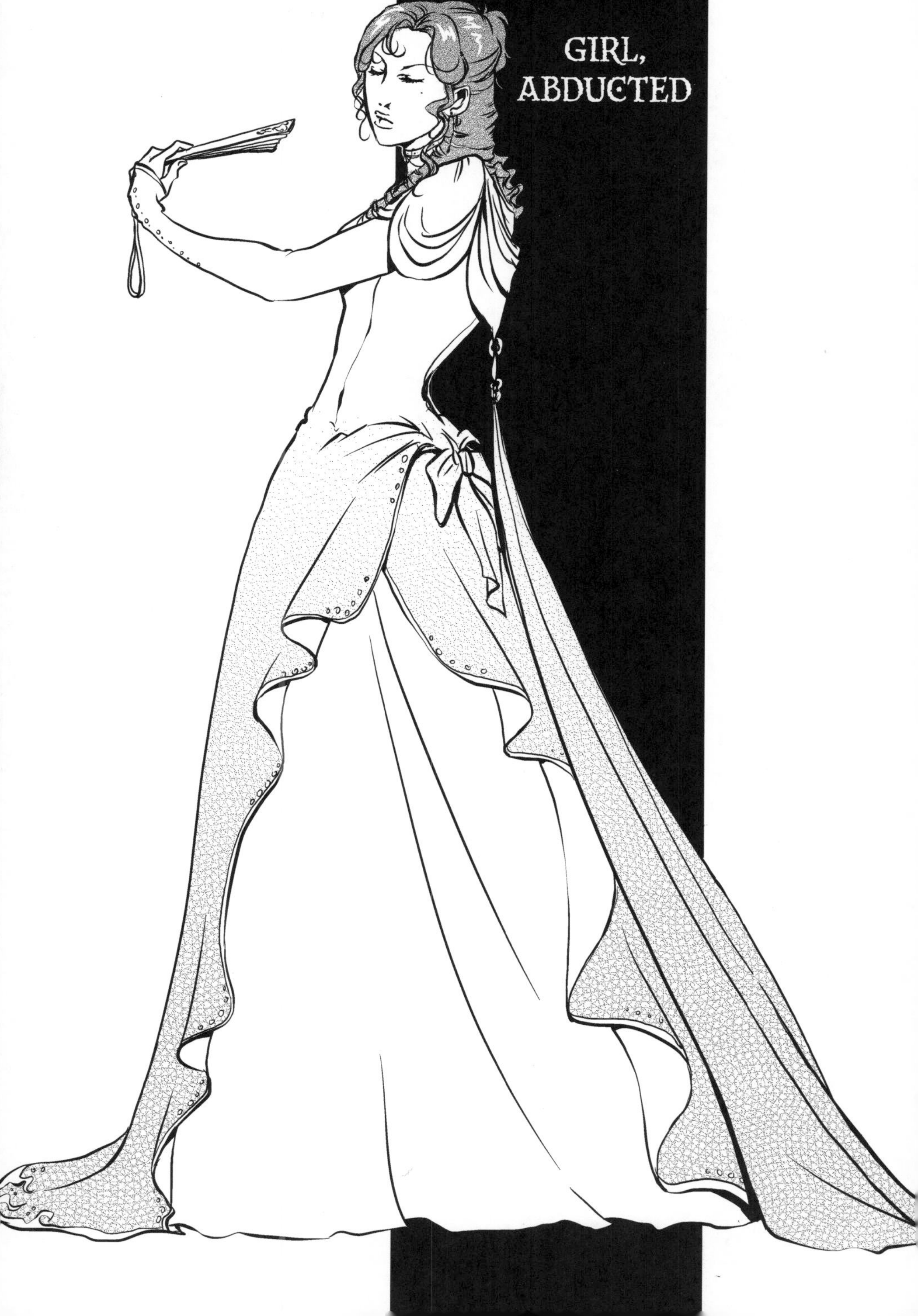

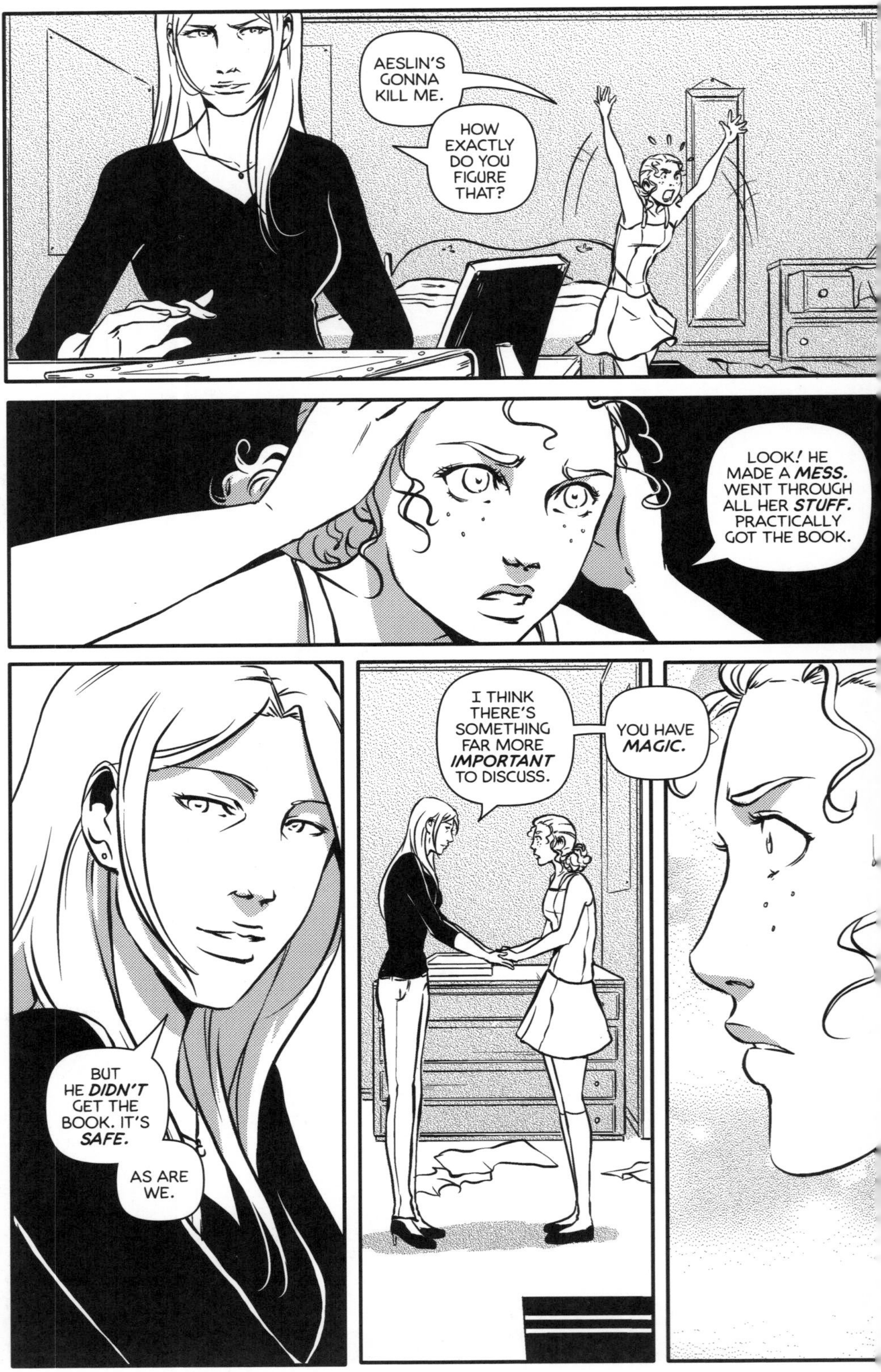
AESLIN'S GONNA KILL ME.
HOW EXACTLY DO YOU FIGURE THAT?
LOOK! HE MADE A MESS. WENT THROUGH ALL HER STUFF. PRACTICALLY GOT THE BOOK.
BUT HE DIDN'T GET THE BOOK. IT'S SAFE.
AS ARE WE.
I THINK THERE'S SOMETHING FAR MORE IMPORTANT TO DISCUSS.
YOU HAVE MAGIC.

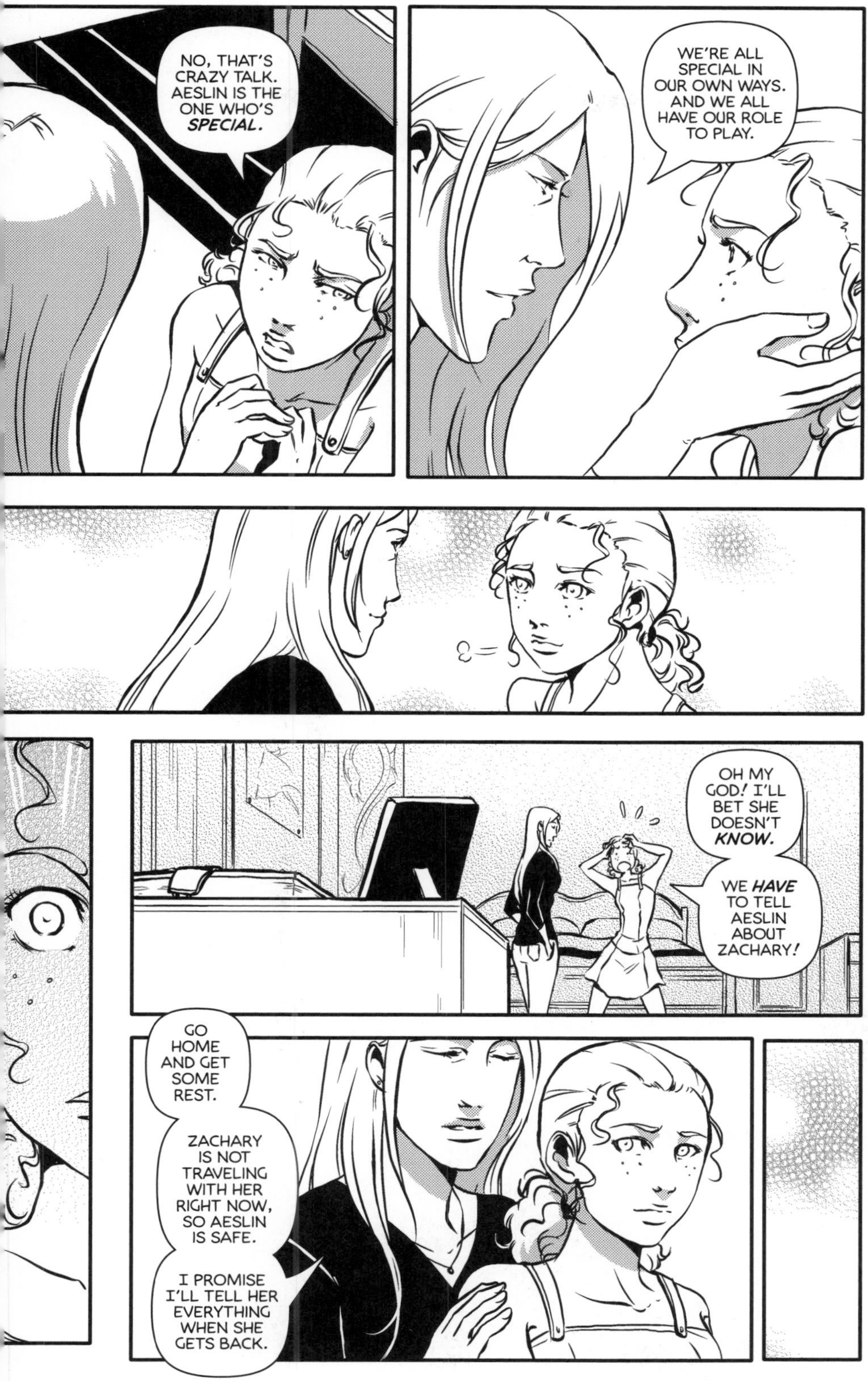
NO, THAT'S CRAZY TALK. AESLIN IS THE ONE WHO'S *SPECIAL.*
WE'RE ALL SPECIAL IN OUR OWN WAYS. AND WE ALL HAVE OUR ROLE TO PLAY.
OH MY GOD! I'LL BET SHE DOESN'T *KNOW.*
WE *HAVE* TO TELL AESLIN ABOUT ZACHARY!
GO HOME AND GET SOME REST.
ZACHARY IS NOT TRAVELING WITH HER RIGHT NOW, SO AESLIN IS SAFE.
I PROMISE I'LL TELL HER EVERYTHING WHEN SHE GETS BACK.

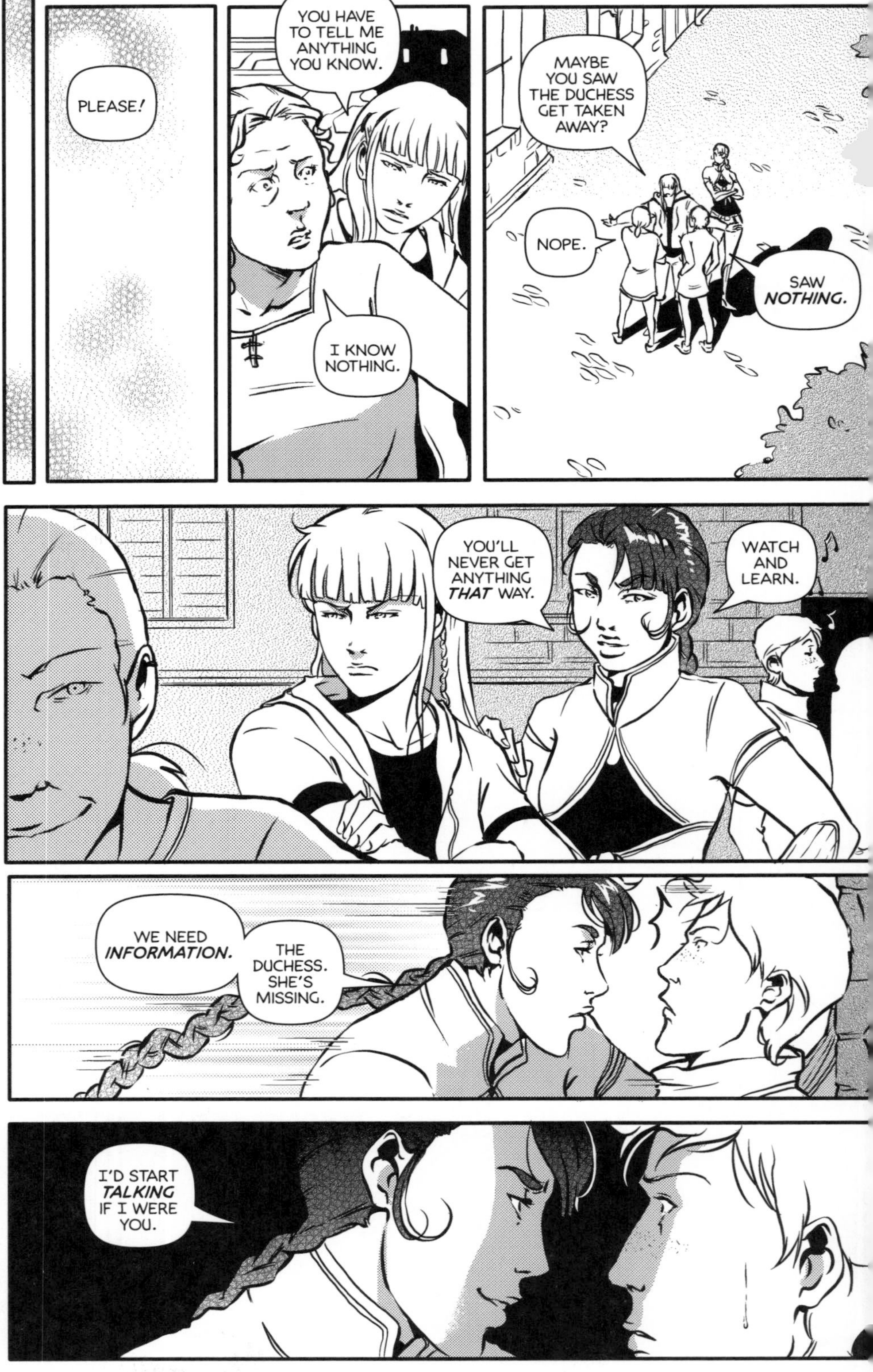
PLEASE!
YOU HAVE TO TELL ME ANYTHING YOU KNOW.
I KNOW NOTHING.
MAYBE YOU SAW THE DUCHESS GET TAKEN AWAY?
NOPE.
SAW NOTHING.
YOU'LL NEVER GET ANYTHING THAT WAY.
WATCH AND LEARN.
WE NEED INFORMATION.
THE DUCHESS. SHE'S MISSING.
I'D START TALKING IF I WERE YOU.

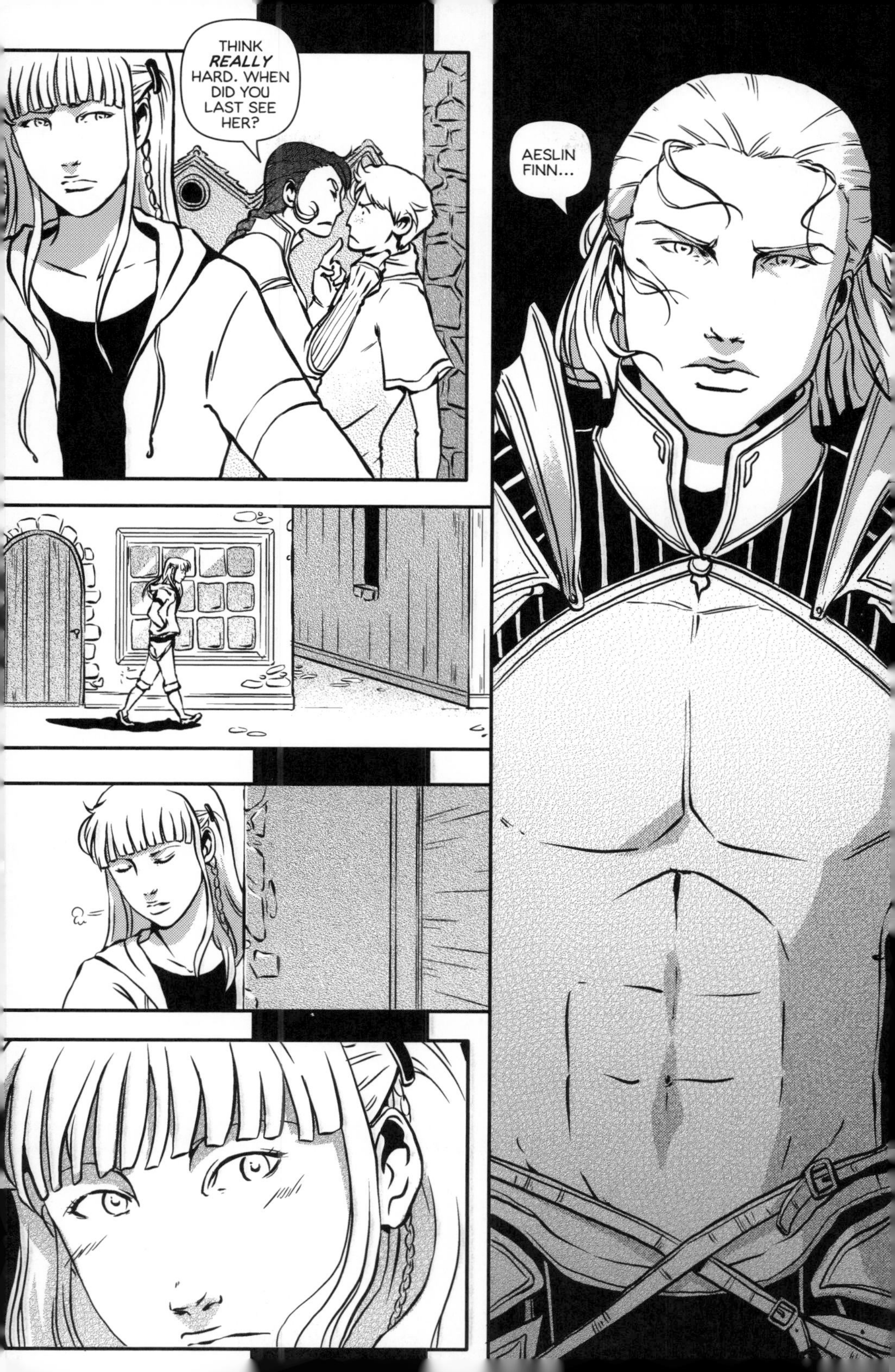
THINK *REALLY* HARD. WHEN DID YOU LAST SEE HER?
AESLIN FINN...

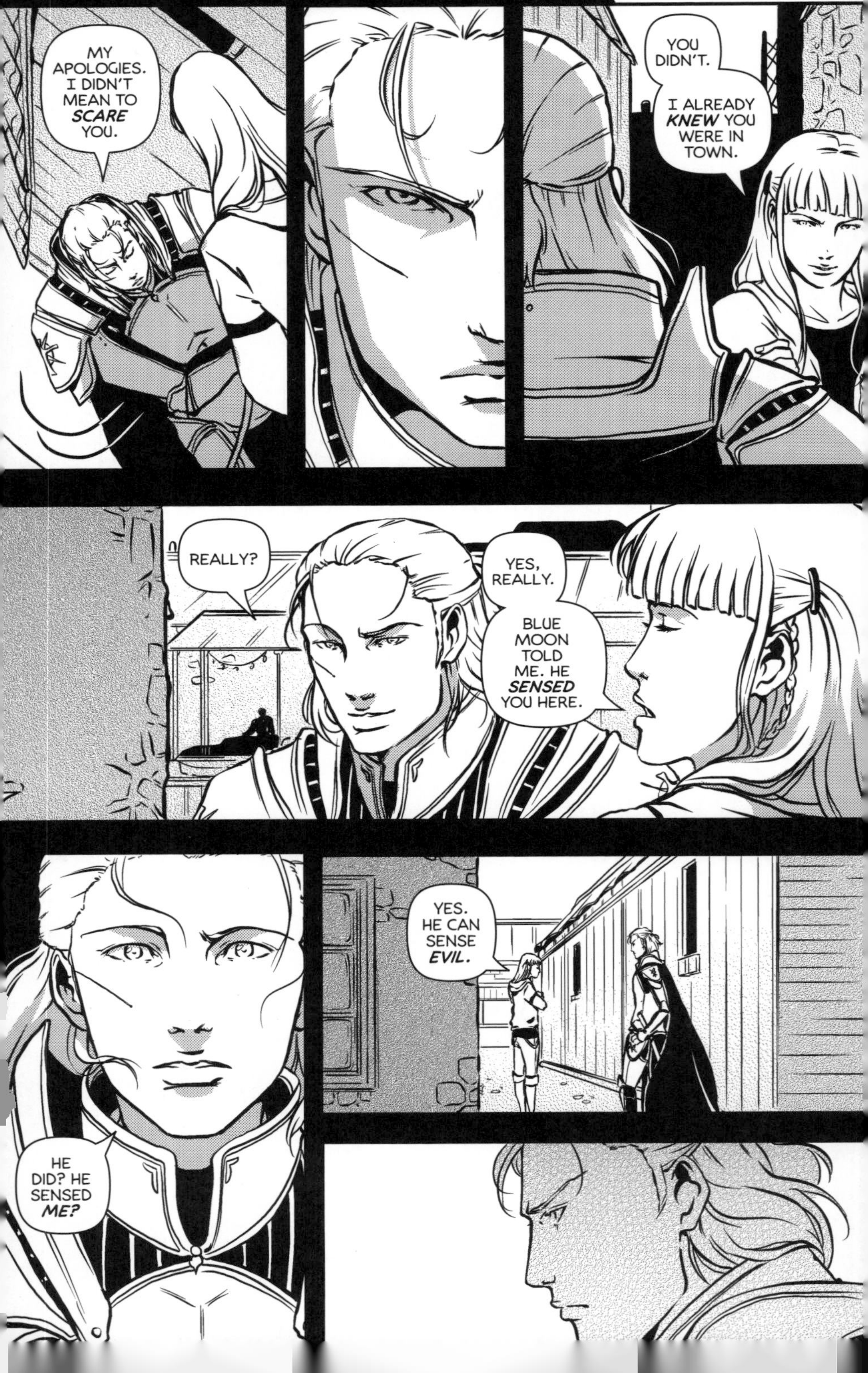
MY APOLOGIES. I DIDN'T MEAN TO SCARE YOU.
YOU DIDN'T.
I ALREADY KNEW YOU WERE IN TOWN.
REALLY?
YES, REALLY.
BLUE MOON TOLD ME. HE SENSED YOU HERE.
HE DID? HE SENSED ME?
YES. HE CAN SENSE EVIL.

I'M EVIL?

HELLO? ONLY ONE OF US WORKS FOR KHROM AND IT'S NOT *ME.*

YES, YOU ARE *SO* NOBLE. UNLESS, OF COURSE, YOU'RE BUSY *ABDUCTING* DUCHESSES.

ME? *ME?* I WOULD *NEVER* KIDNAP SOMEBODY. WHERE I COME FROM IT'S NOT A VERY *NICE* THING TO DO.

I'LL HAVE YOU KNOW WE'RE HERE TO *RESCUE* THE DUCHESS.

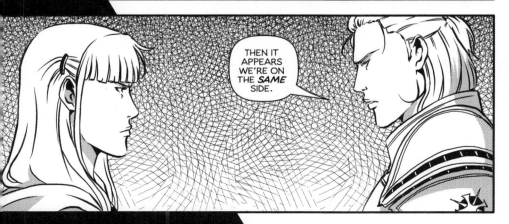

THEN IT APPEARS WE'RE ON THE *SAME* SIDE.

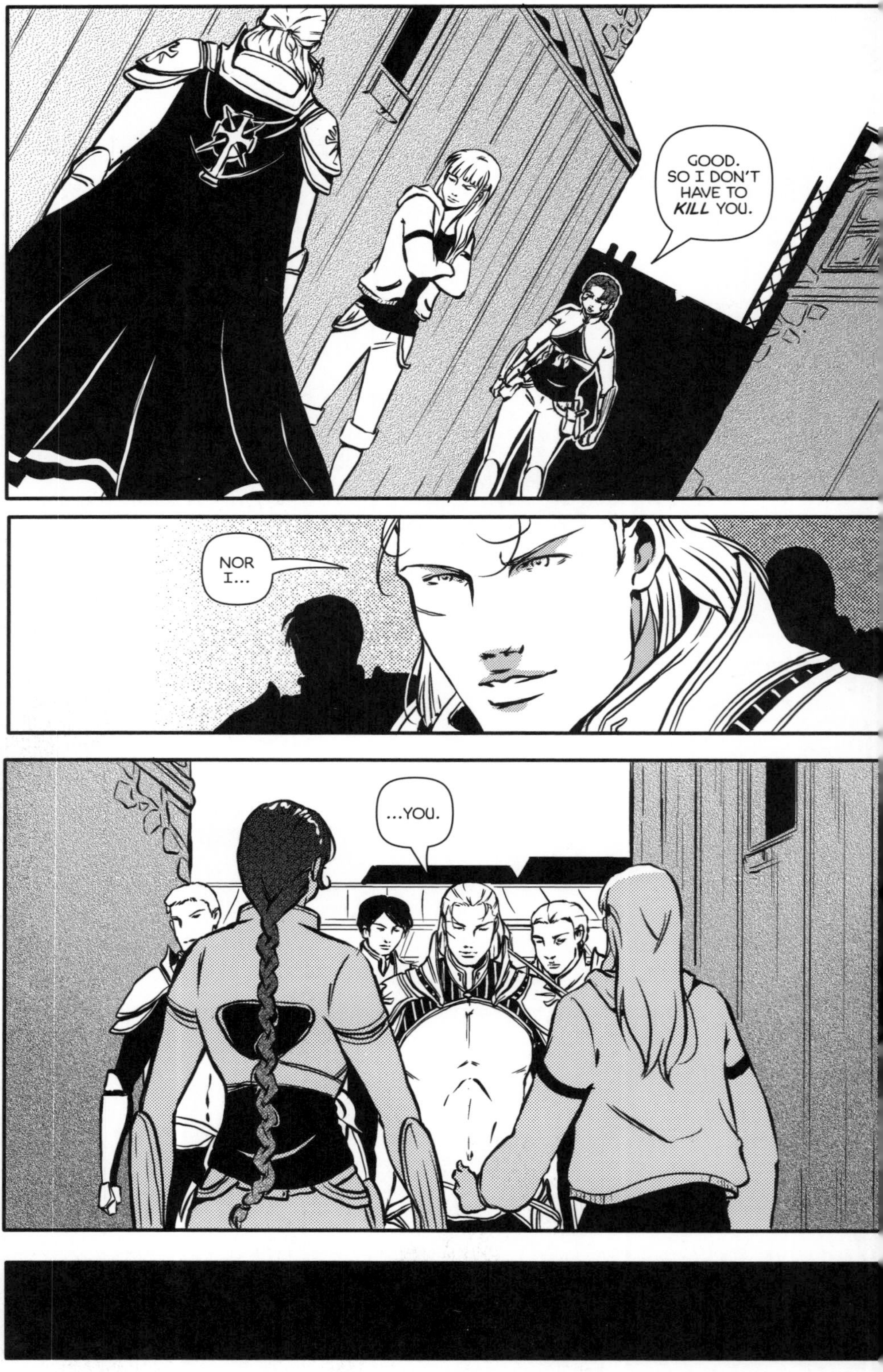
GOOD. SO I DON'T HAVE TO *KILL* YOU.
NOR I...
...YOU.

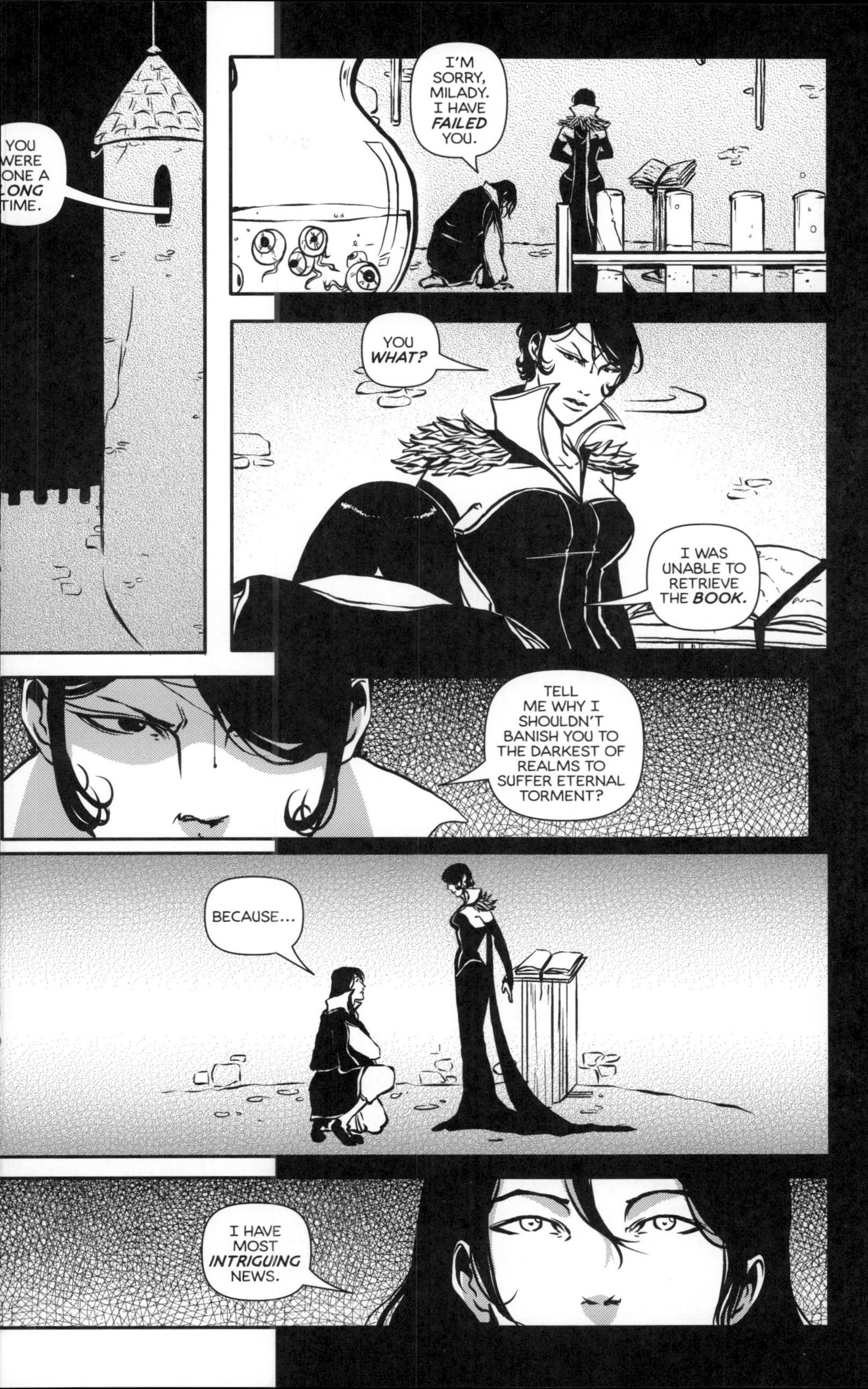
YOU WERE GONE A LONG TIME.
I'M SORRY, MILADY. I HAVE FAILED YOU.
YOU WHAT?
I WAS UNABLE TO RETRIEVE THE BOOK.
TELL ME WHY I SHOULDN'T BANISH YOU TO THE DARKEST OF REALMS TO SUFFER ETERNAL TORMENT?
BECAUSE...
I HAVE MOST INTRIGUING NEWS.

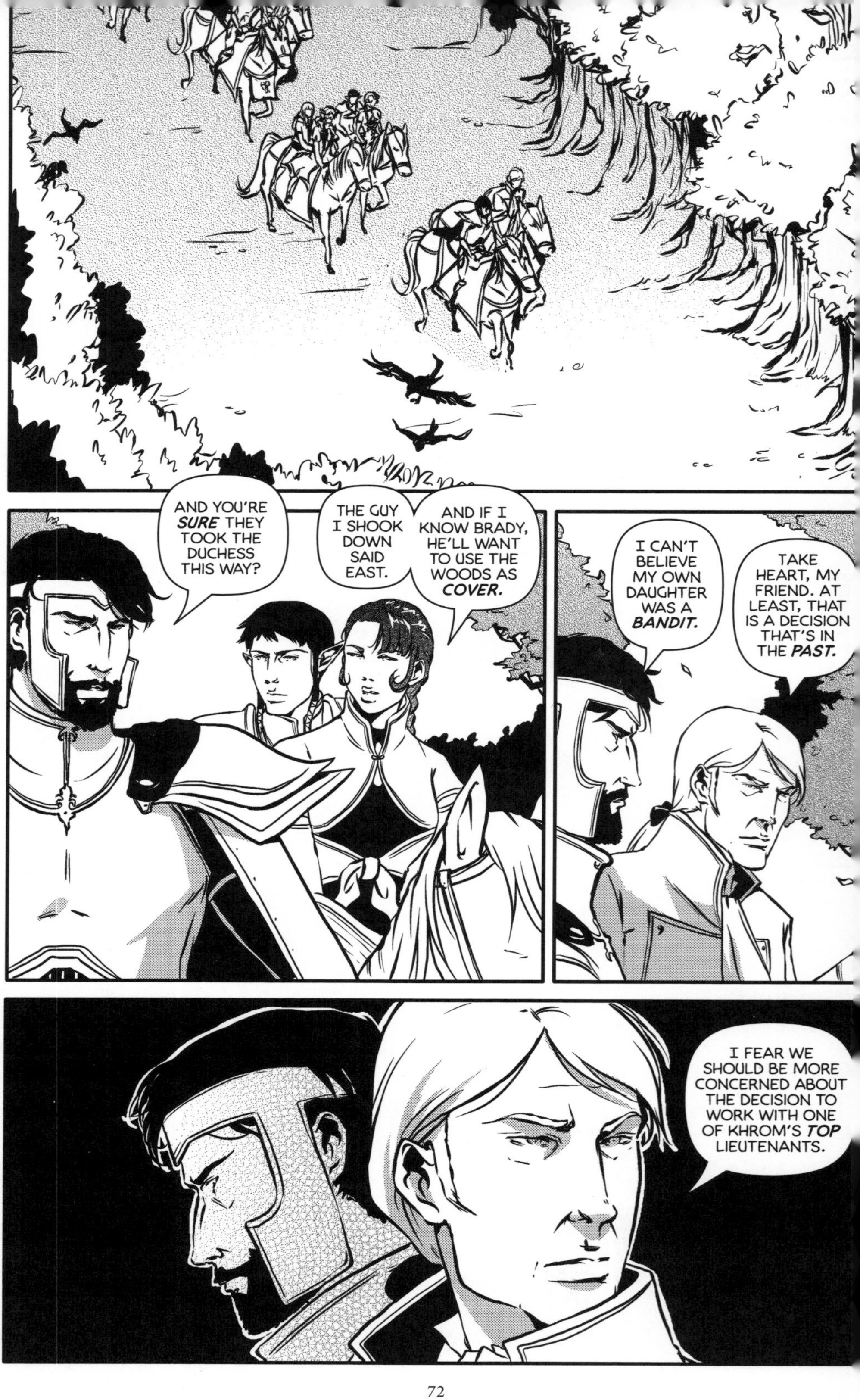
AND YOU'RE SURE THEY TOOK THE DUCHESS THIS WAY?
THE GUY I SHOOK DOWN SAID EAST.
AND IF I KNOW BRADY, HE'LL WANT TO USE THE WOODS AS COVER.
I CAN'T BELIEVE MY OWN DAUGHTER WAS A BANDIT.
TAKE HEART, MY FRIEND. AT LEAST, THAT IS A DECISION THAT'S IN THE PAST.
I FEAR WE SHOULD BE MORE CONCERNED ABOUT THE DECISION TO WORK WITH ONE OF KHROM'S TOP LIEUTENANTS.

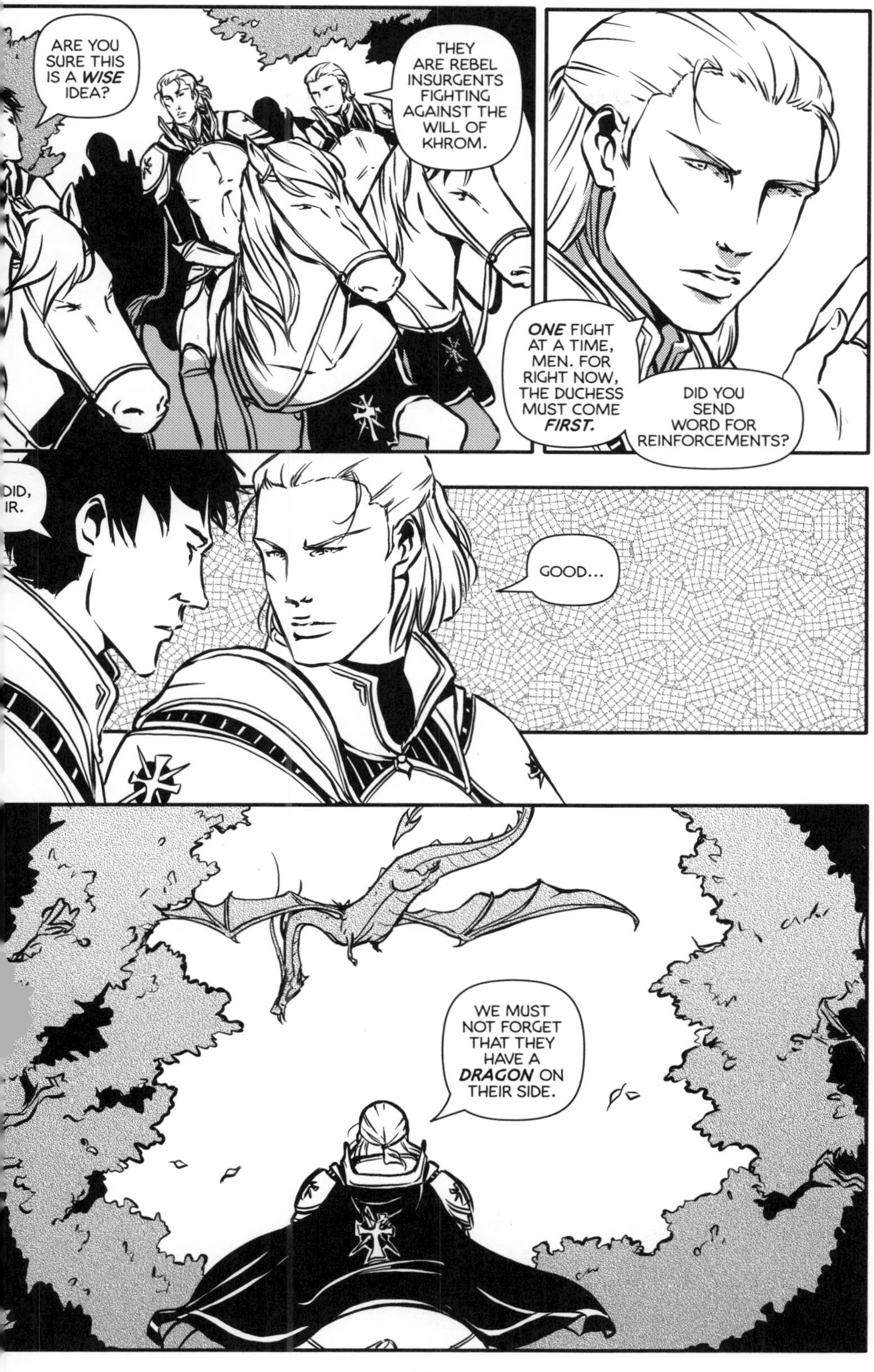
ARE YOU SURE THIS IS A *WISE* IDEA?
THEY ARE REBEL INSURGENTS FIGHTING AGAINST THE WILL OF KHROM.
ONE FIGHT AT A TIME, MEN. FOR RIGHT NOW, THE DUCHESS MUST COME *FIRST.*
DID YOU SEND WORD FOR REINFORCEMENTS?
DID, IR.
GOOD...
WE MUST NOT FORGET THAT THEY HAVE A *DRAGON* ON THEIR SIDE.

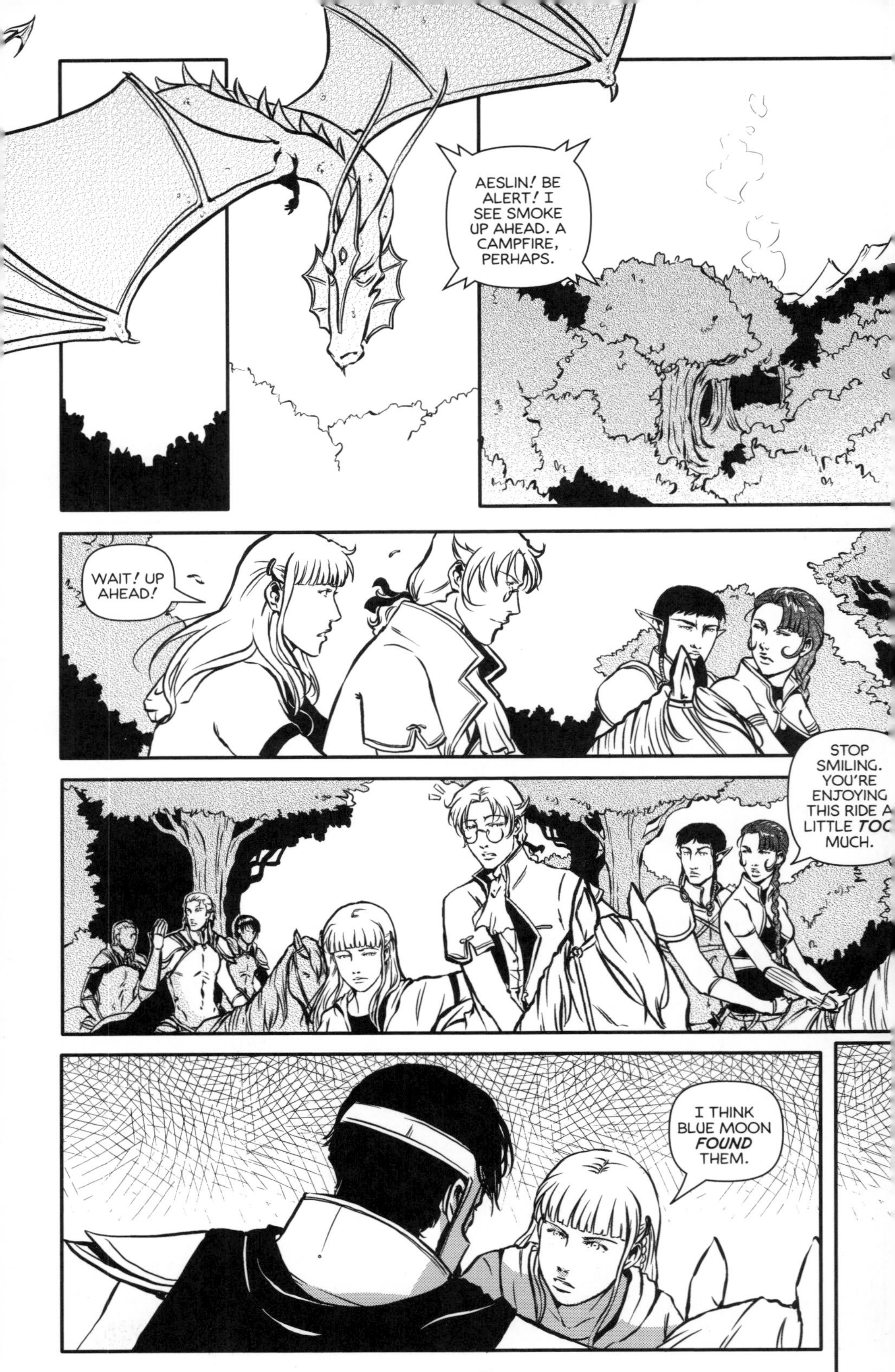
AESLIN! BE ALERT! I SEE SMOKE UP AHEAD. A CAMPFIRE, PERHAPS.
WAIT! UP AHEAD!
STOP SMILING. YOU'RE ENJOYING THIS RIDE A LITTLE *TOO* MUCH.
I THINK BLUE MOON *FOUND* THEM.

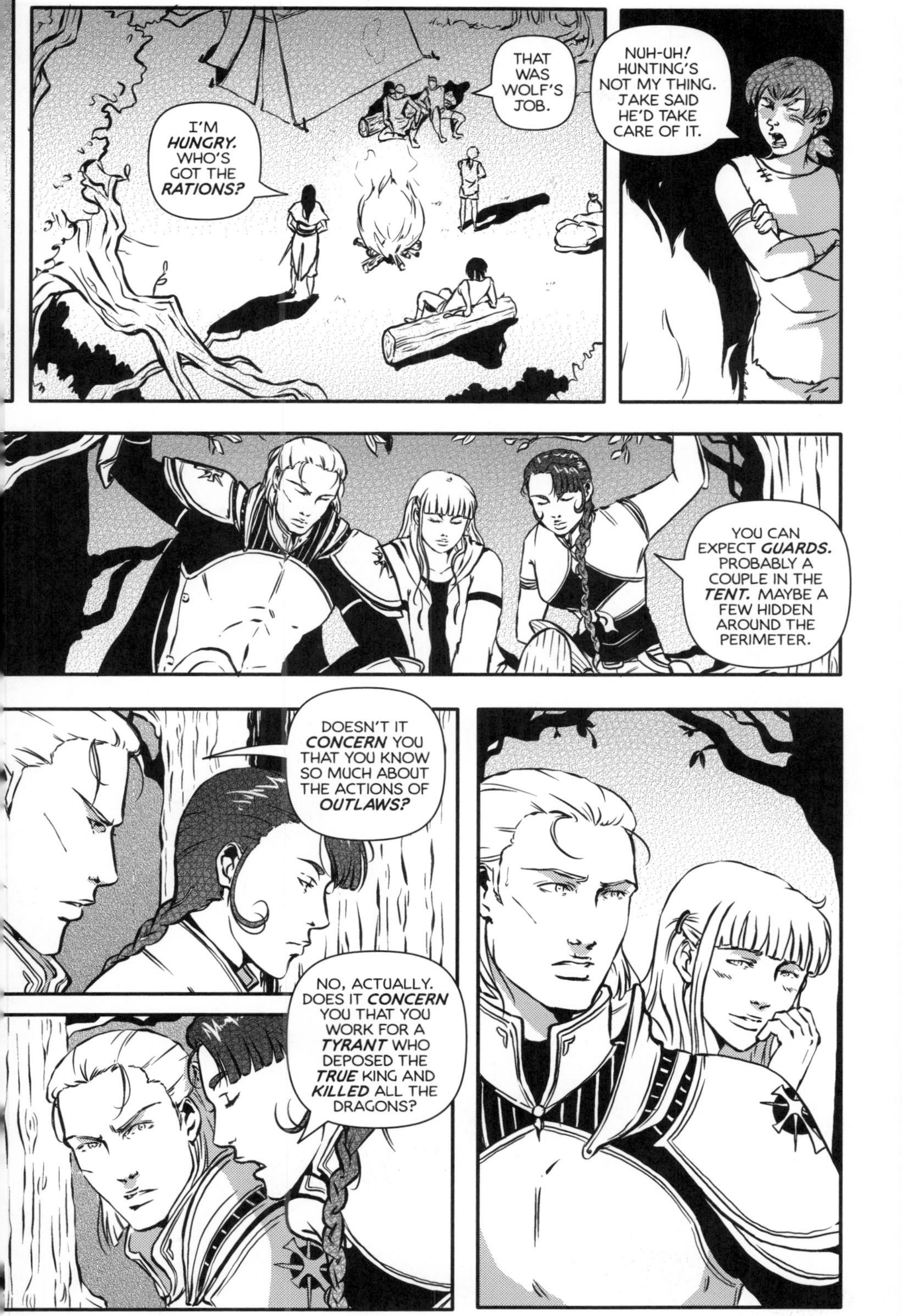
I'M HUNGRY. WHO'S GOT THE RATIONS?
THAT WAS WOLF'S JOB.
NUH-UH! HUNTING'S NOT MY THING. JAKE SAID HE'D TAKE CARE OF IT.
YOU CAN EXPECT GUARDS. PROBABLY A COUPLE IN THE TENT. MAYBE A FEW HIDDEN AROUND THE PERIMETER.
DOESN'T IT CONCERN YOU THAT YOU KNOW SO MUCH ABOUT THE ACTIONS OF OUTLAWS?
NO, ACTUALLY. DOES IT CONCERN YOU THAT YOU WORK FOR A TYRANT WHO DEPOSED THE TRUE KING AND KILLED ALL THE DRAGONS?

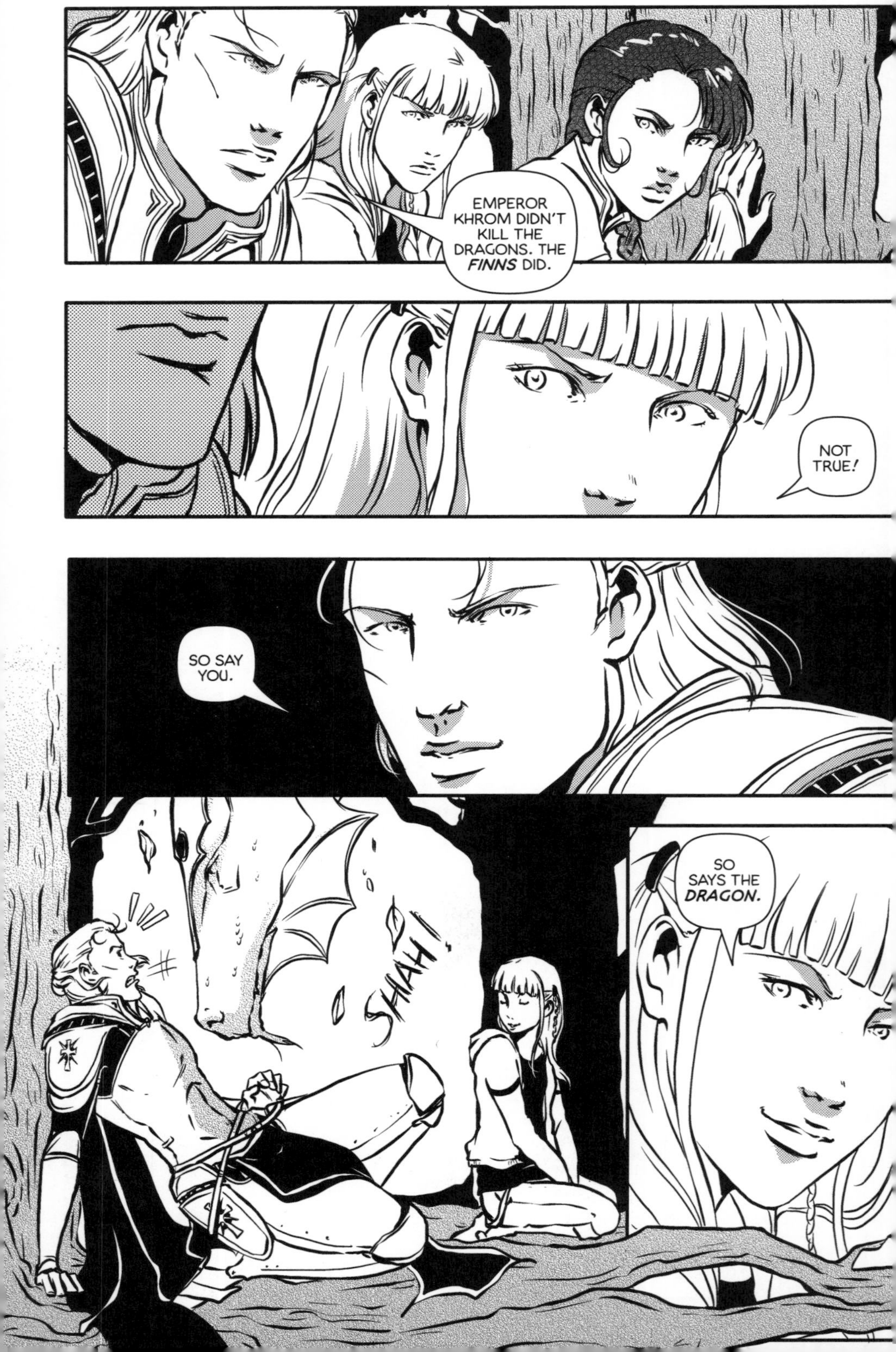

EMPEROR KHROM DIDN'T KILL THE DRAGONS. THE *FINNS* DID.
NOT TRUE!
SO SAY YOU.
SHAH!
SO SAYS THE *DRAGON*.

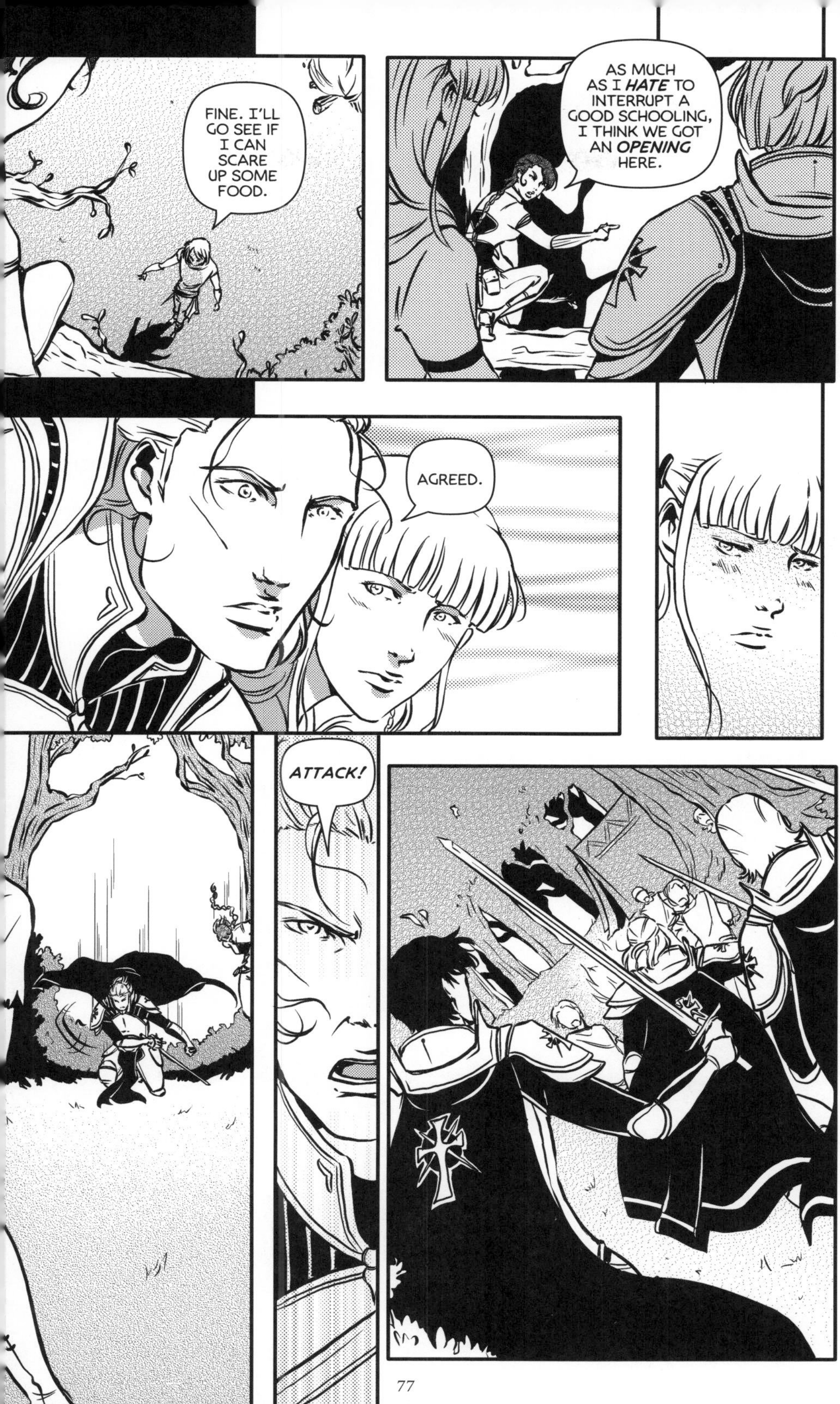
FINE. I'LL GO SEE IF I CAN SCARE UP SOME FOOD.
AS MUCH AS I HATE TO INTERRUPT A GOOD SCHOOLING, I THINK WE GOT AN OPENING HERE.
AGREED.
ATTACK!

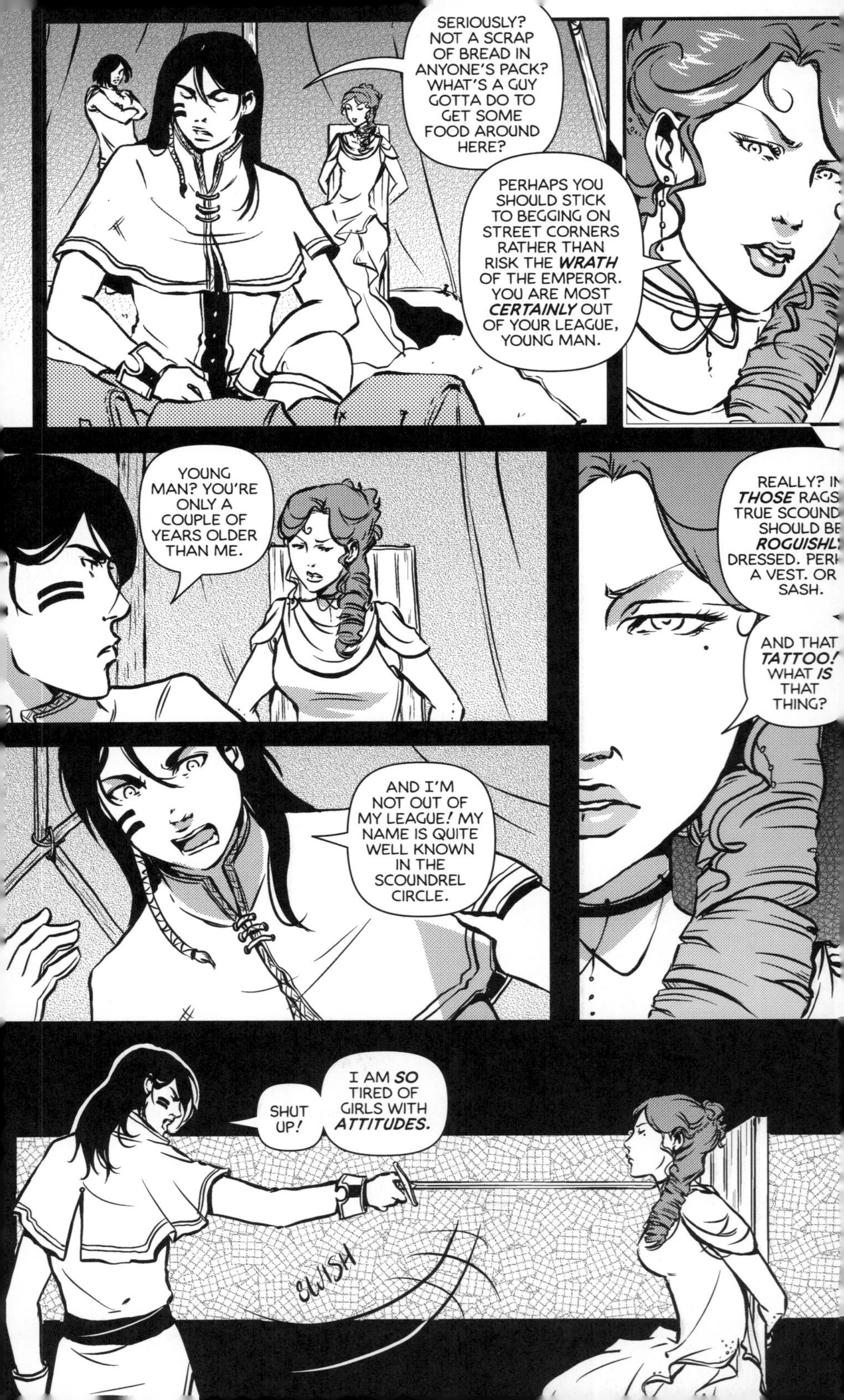

SERIOUSLY? NOT A SCRAP OF BREAD IN ANYONE'S PACK? WHAT'S A GUY GOTTA DO TO GET SOME FOOD AROUND HERE?
PERHAPS YOU SHOULD STICK TO BEGGING ON STREET CORNERS RATHER THAN RISK THE WRATH OF THE EMPEROR. YOU ARE MOST CERTAINLY OUT OF YOUR LEAGUE, YOUNG MAN.
YOUNG MAN? YOU'RE ONLY A COUPLE OF YEARS OLDER THAN ME.
AND I'M NOT OUT OF MY LEAGUE! MY NAME IS QUITE WELL KNOWN IN THE SCOUNDREL CIRCLE.
AND THAT TATTOO! WHAT IS THAT THING?
SHUT UP!
I AM SO TIRED OF GIRLS WITH ATTITUDES.
SWISH

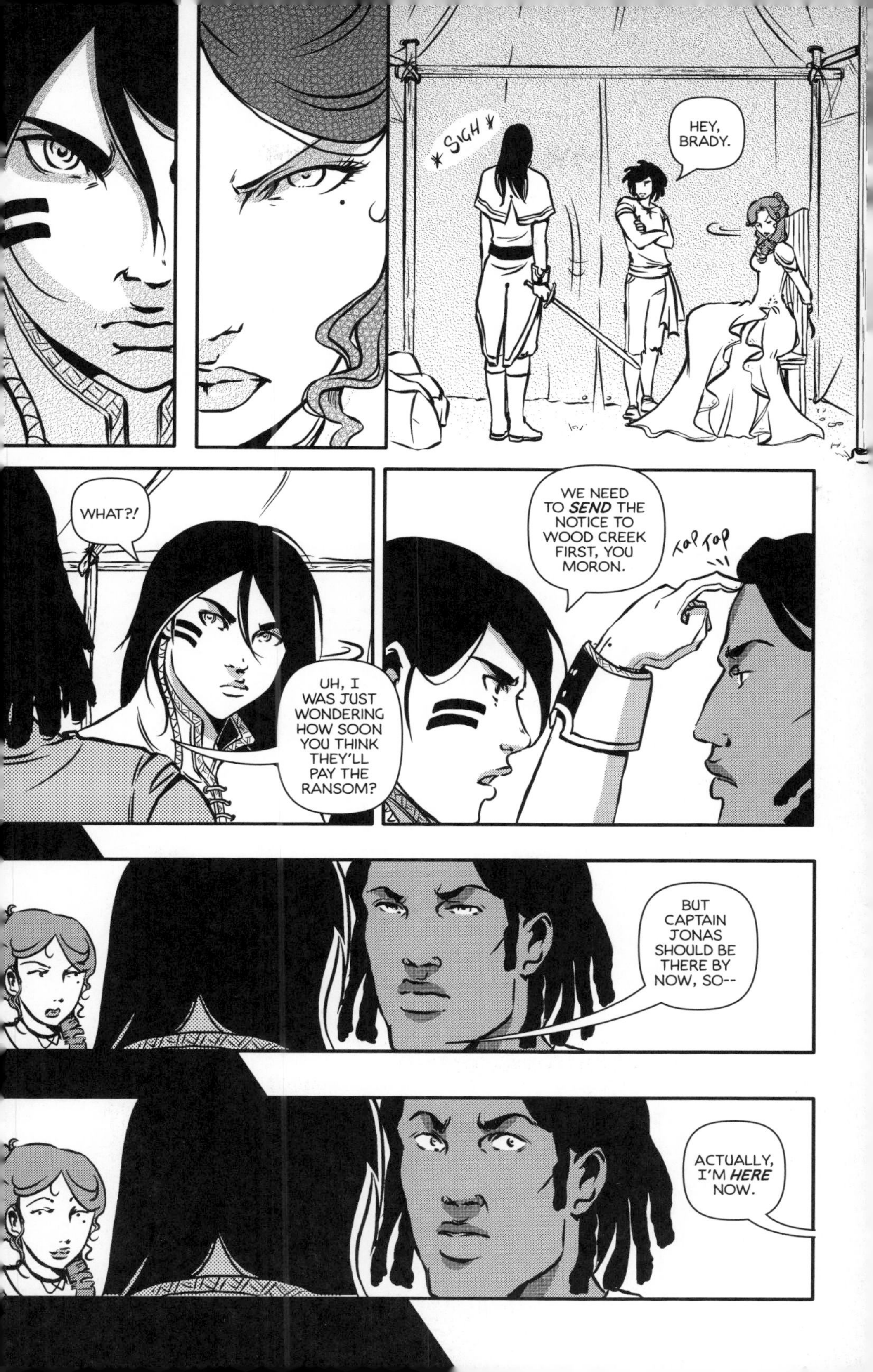

SIGH
HEY, BRADY.
WHAT?!
UH, I WAS JUST WONDERING HOW SOON YOU THINK THEY'LL PAY THE RANSOM?
WE NEED TO SEND THE NOTICE TO WOOD CREEK FIRST, YOU MORON.
TAP TAP
BUT CAPTAIN JONAS SHOULD BE THERE BY NOW, SO--
ACTUALLY, I'M HERE NOW.

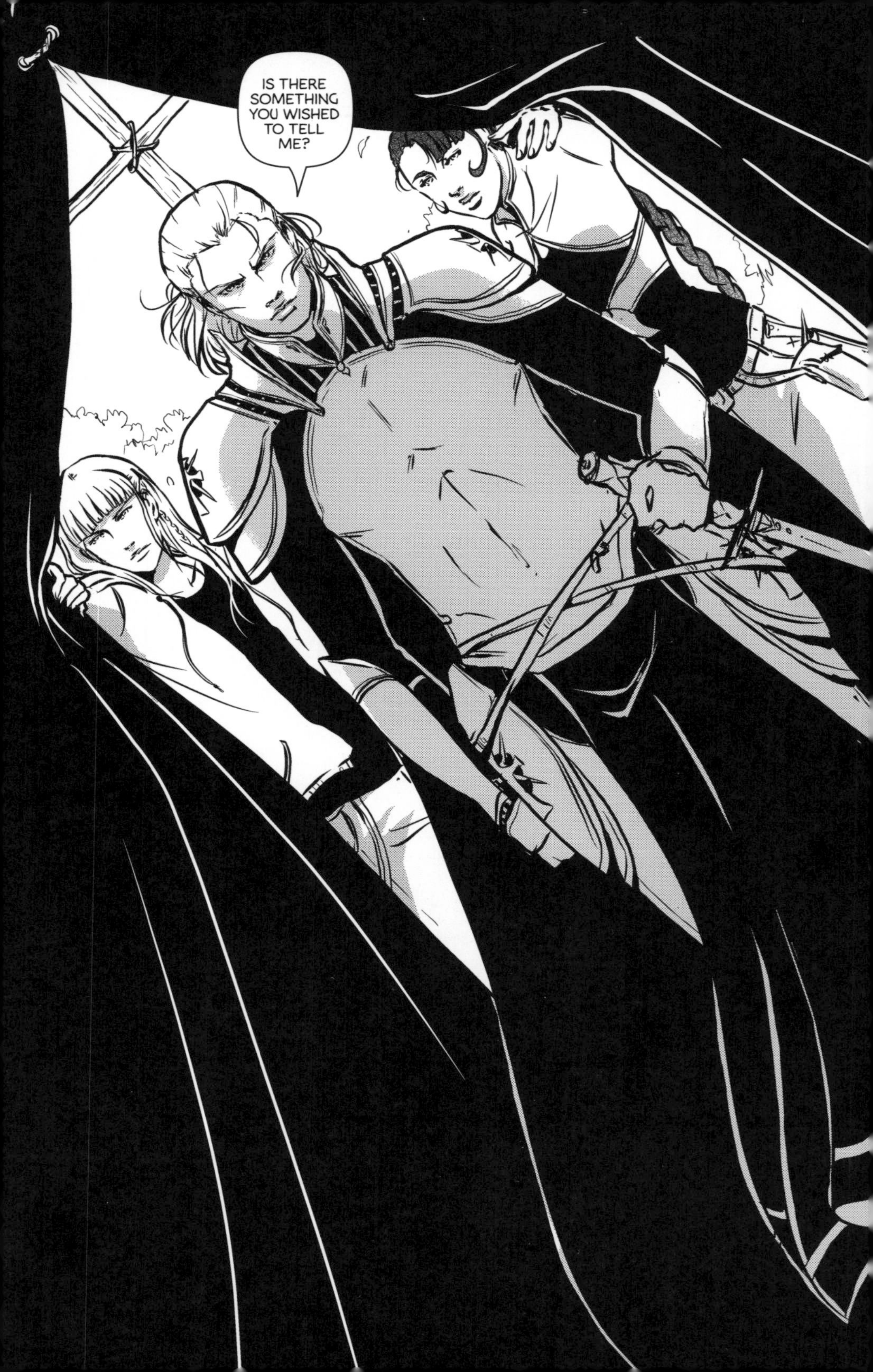
IS THERE SOMETHING YOU WISHED TO TELL ME?

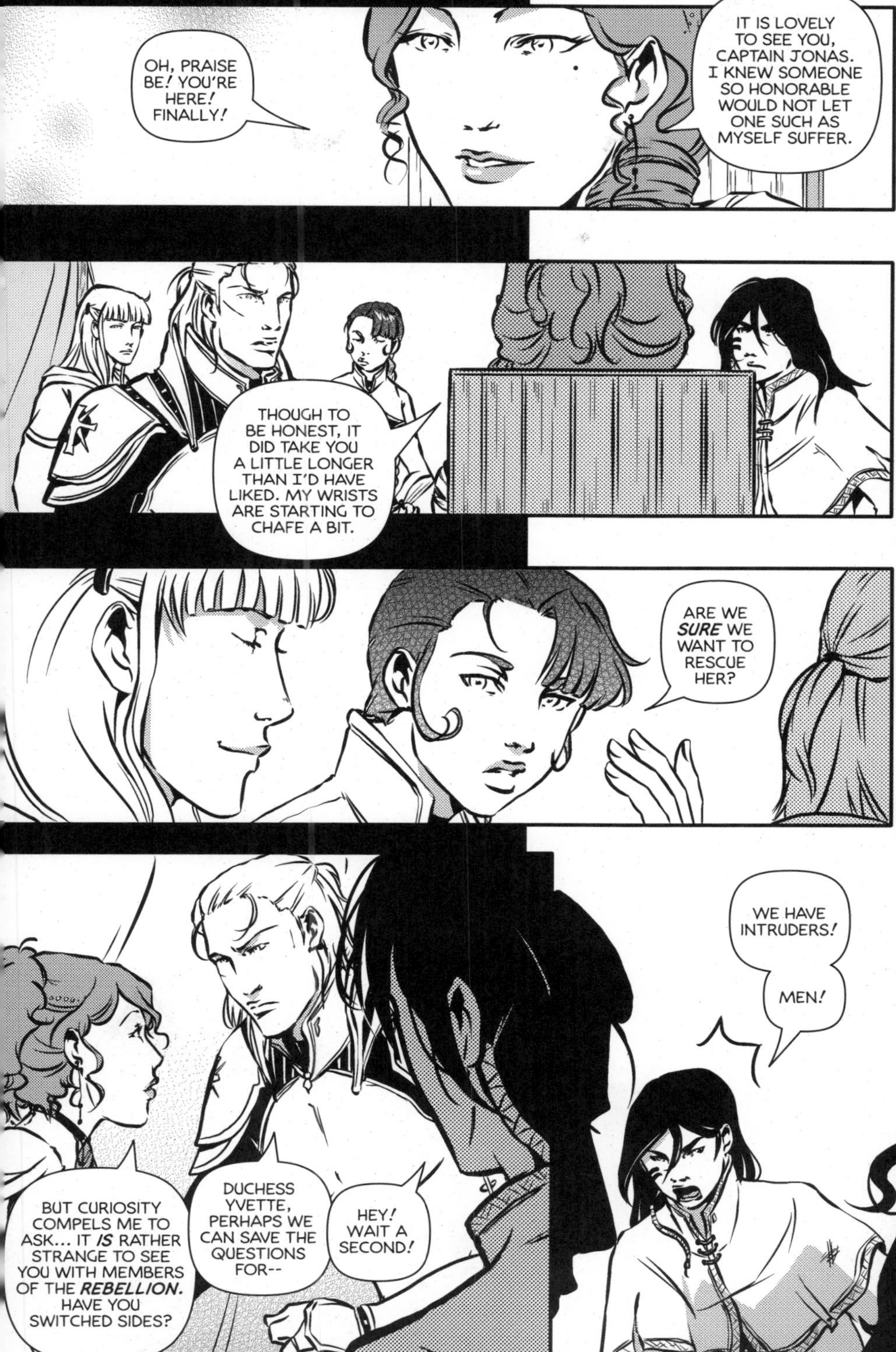
OH, PRAISE BE! YOU'RE HERE! FINALLY!
IT IS LOVELY TO SEE YOU, CAPTAIN JONAS. I KNEW SOMEONE SO HONORABLE WOULD NOT LET ONE SUCH AS MYSELF SUFFER.
THOUGH TO BE HONEST, IT DID TAKE YOU A LITTLE LONGER THAN I'D HAVE LIKED. MY WRISTS ARE STARTING TO CHAFE A BIT.
ARE WE SURE WE WANT TO RESCUE HER?
BUT CURIOSITY COMPELS ME TO ASK... IT IS RATHER STRANGE TO SEE YOU WITH MEMBERS OF THE REBELLION. HAVE YOU SWITCHED SIDES?
DUCHESS YVETTE, PERHAPS WE CAN SAVE THE QUESTIONS FOR--
HEY! WAIT A SECOND!
WE HAVE INTRUDERS!
MEN!

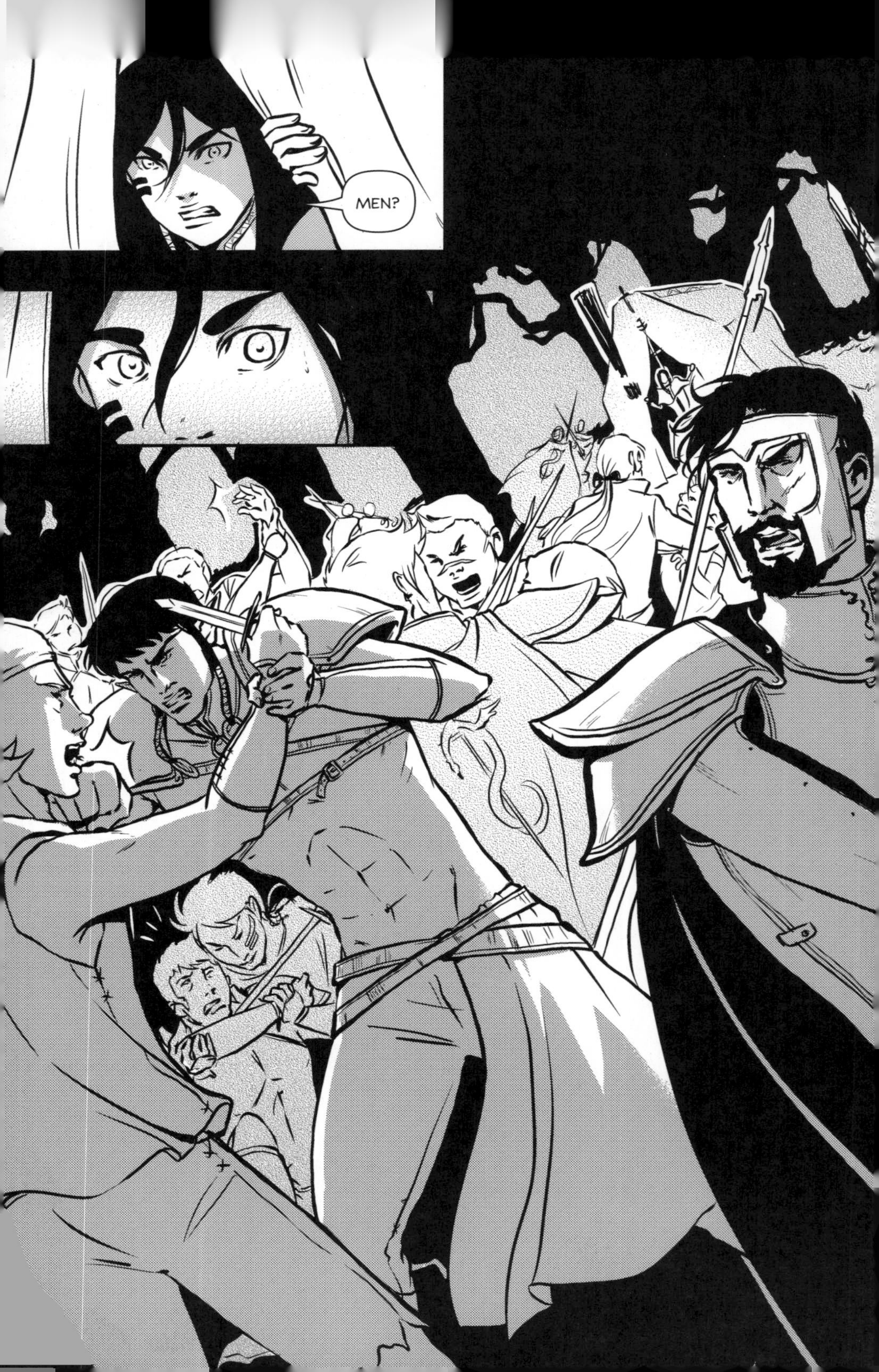
MEN?

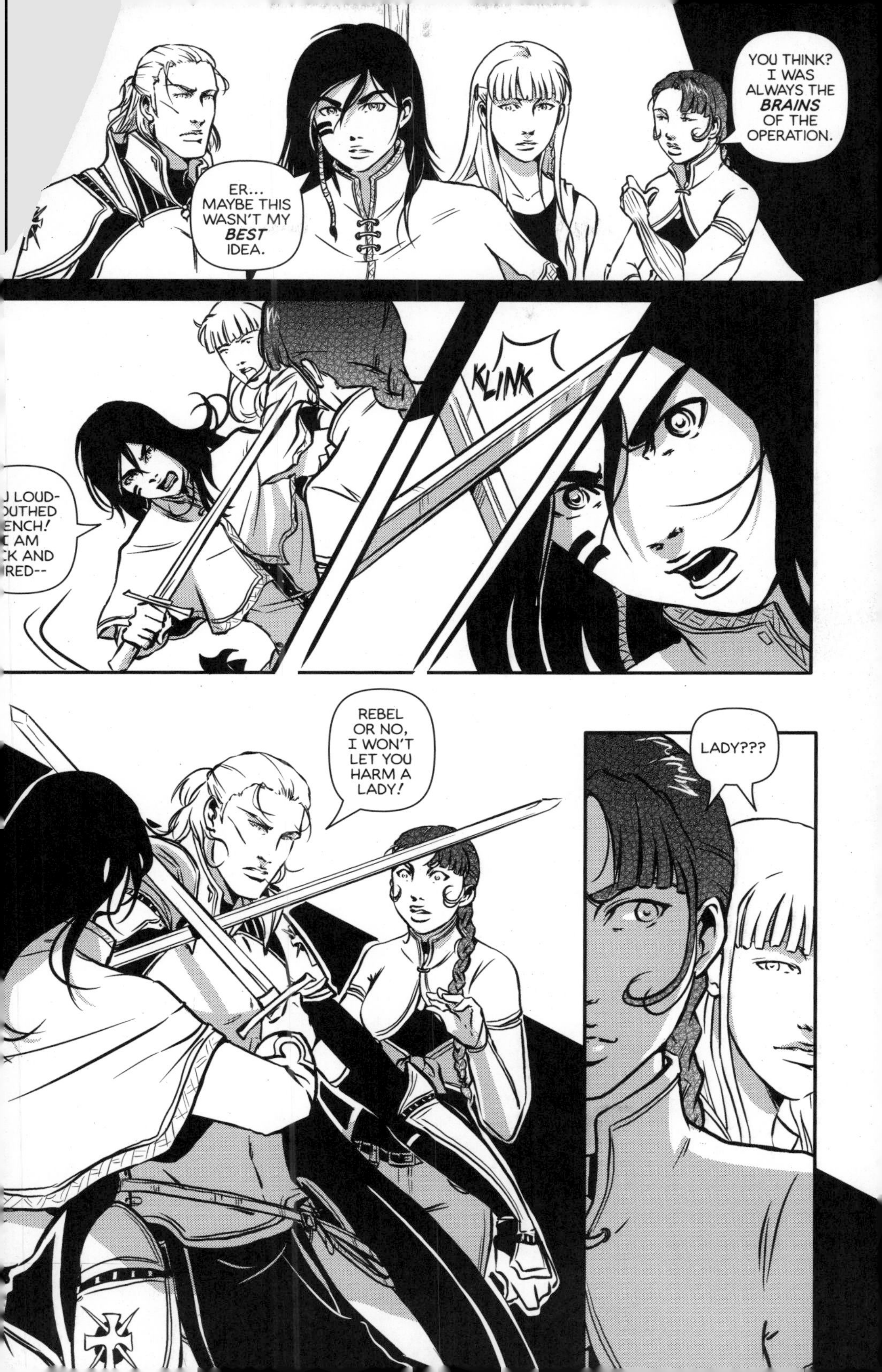
ER... MAYBE THIS WASN'T MY ***BEST*** IDEA.
YOU THINK? I WAS ALWAYS THE ***BRAINS*** OF THE OPERATION.
U LOUD- OUTHED ENCH! AM CK AND RED--
KLINK
REBEL OR NO, I WON'T LET YOU HARM A LADY!
LADY???

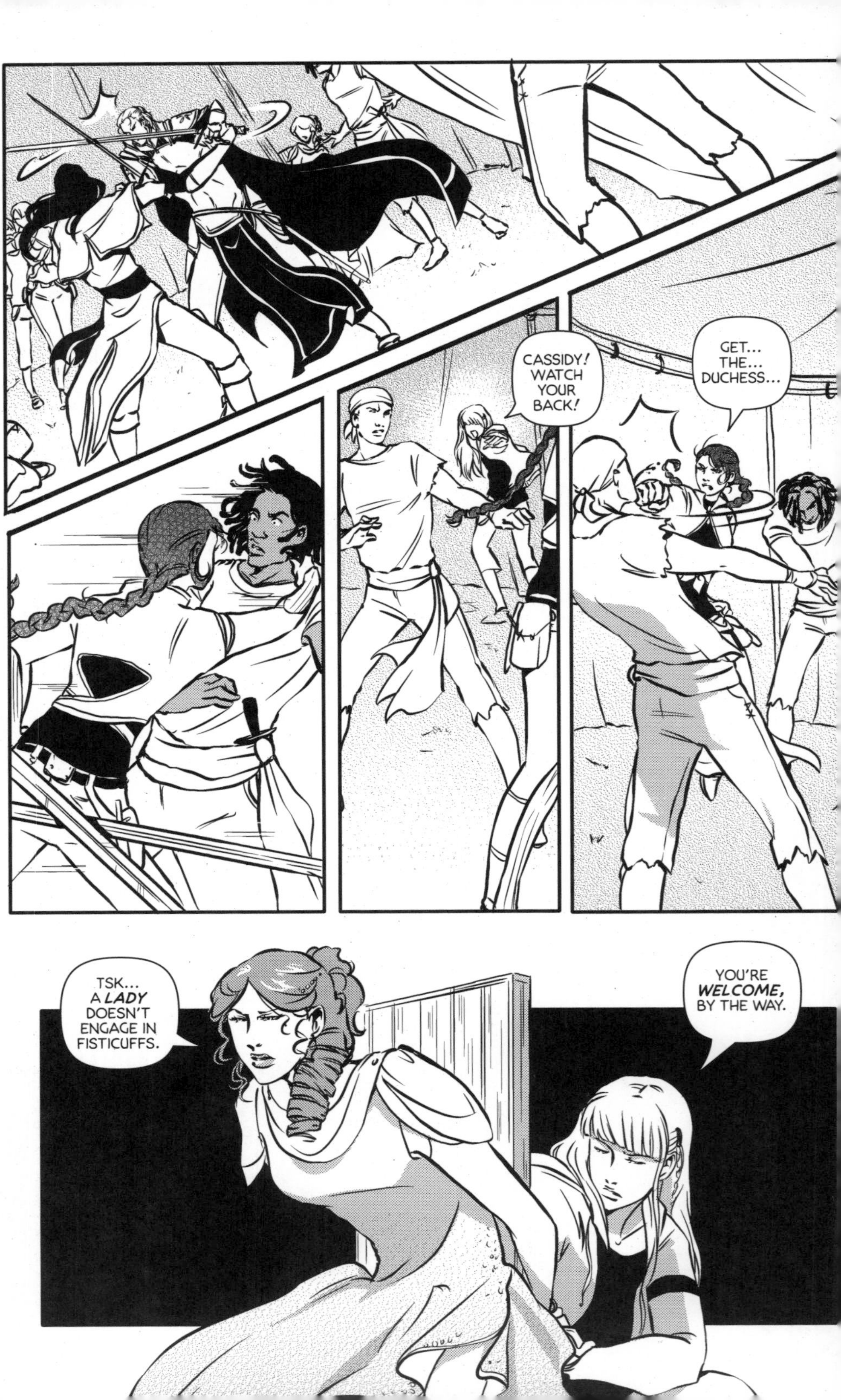
CASSIDY! WATCH YOUR BACK!
GET... THE... DUCHESS...
TSK... A *LADY* DOESN'T ENGAGE IN FISTICUFFS.
YOU'RE ***WELCOME,*** BY THE WAY.

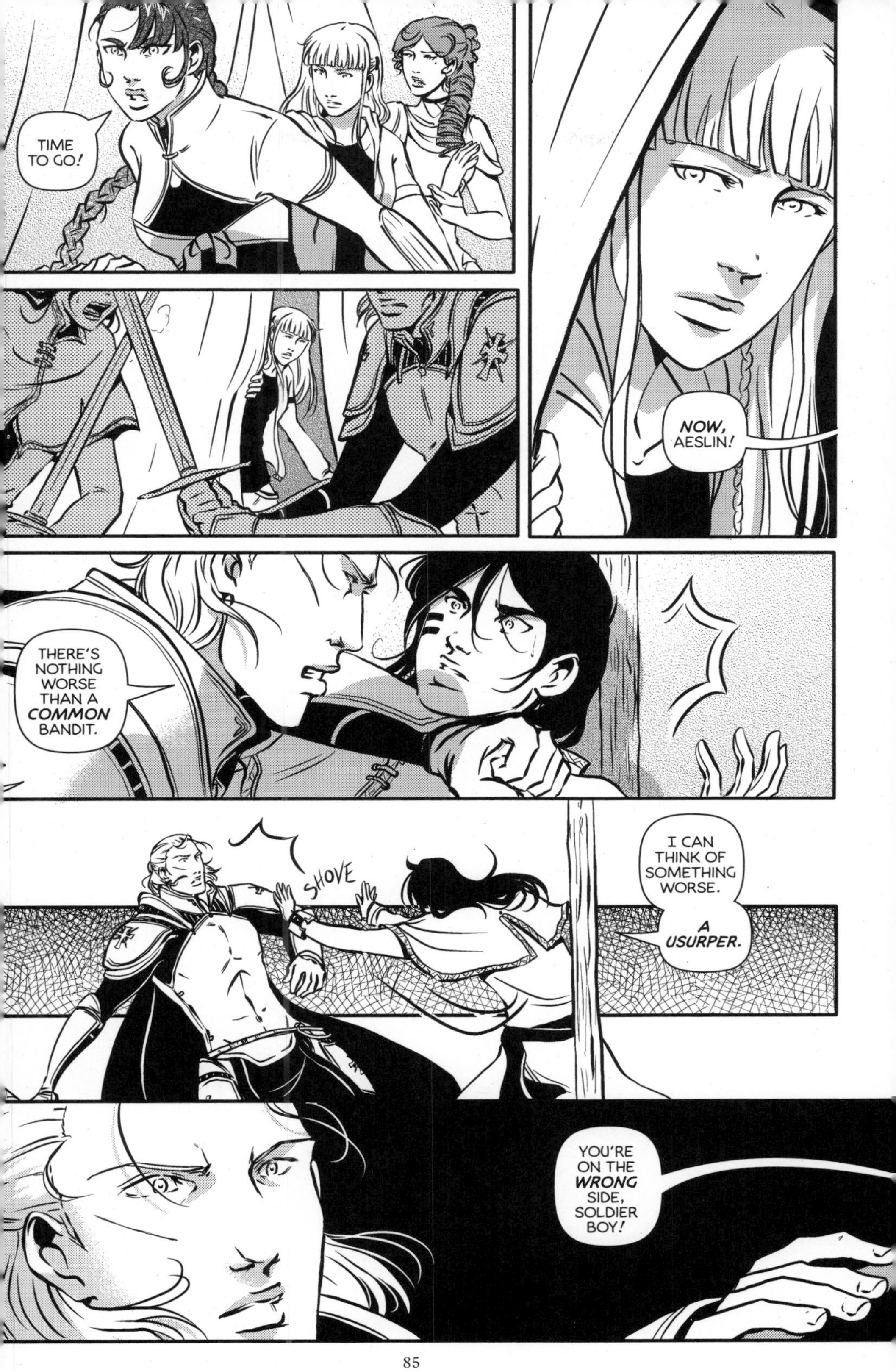
TIME TO GO!
NOW, AESLIN!
THERE'S NOTHING WORSE THAN A COMMON BANDIT.
SHOVE
I CAN THINK OF SOMETHING WORSE.
A USURPER.
YOU'RE ON THE WRONG SIDE, SOLDIER BOY!

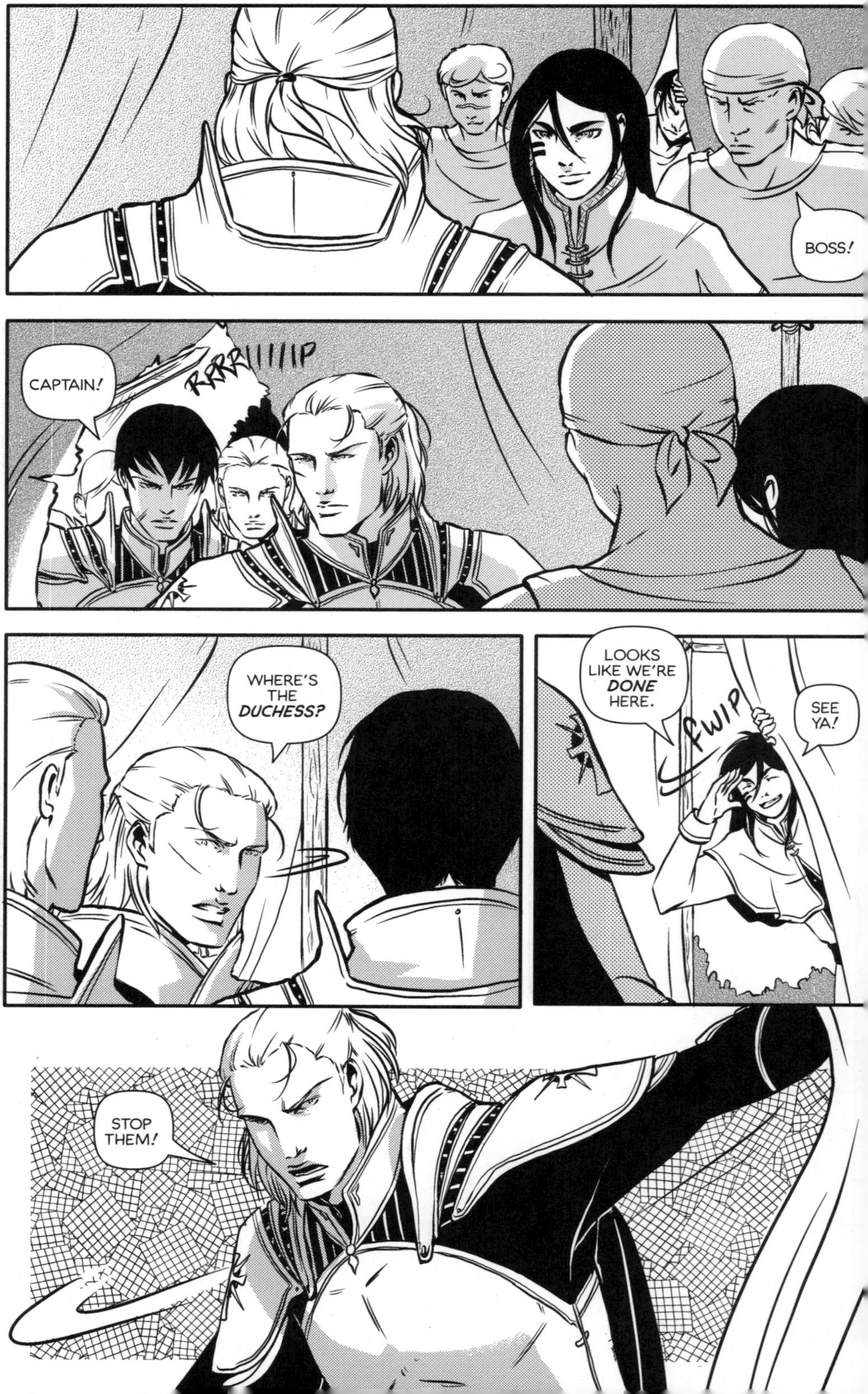
BOSS!
CAPTAIN!
RRRRIIIIIIP
WHERE'S THE DUCHESS?
LOOKS LIKE WE'RE DONE HERE.
FWIP
SEE YA!
STOP THEM!

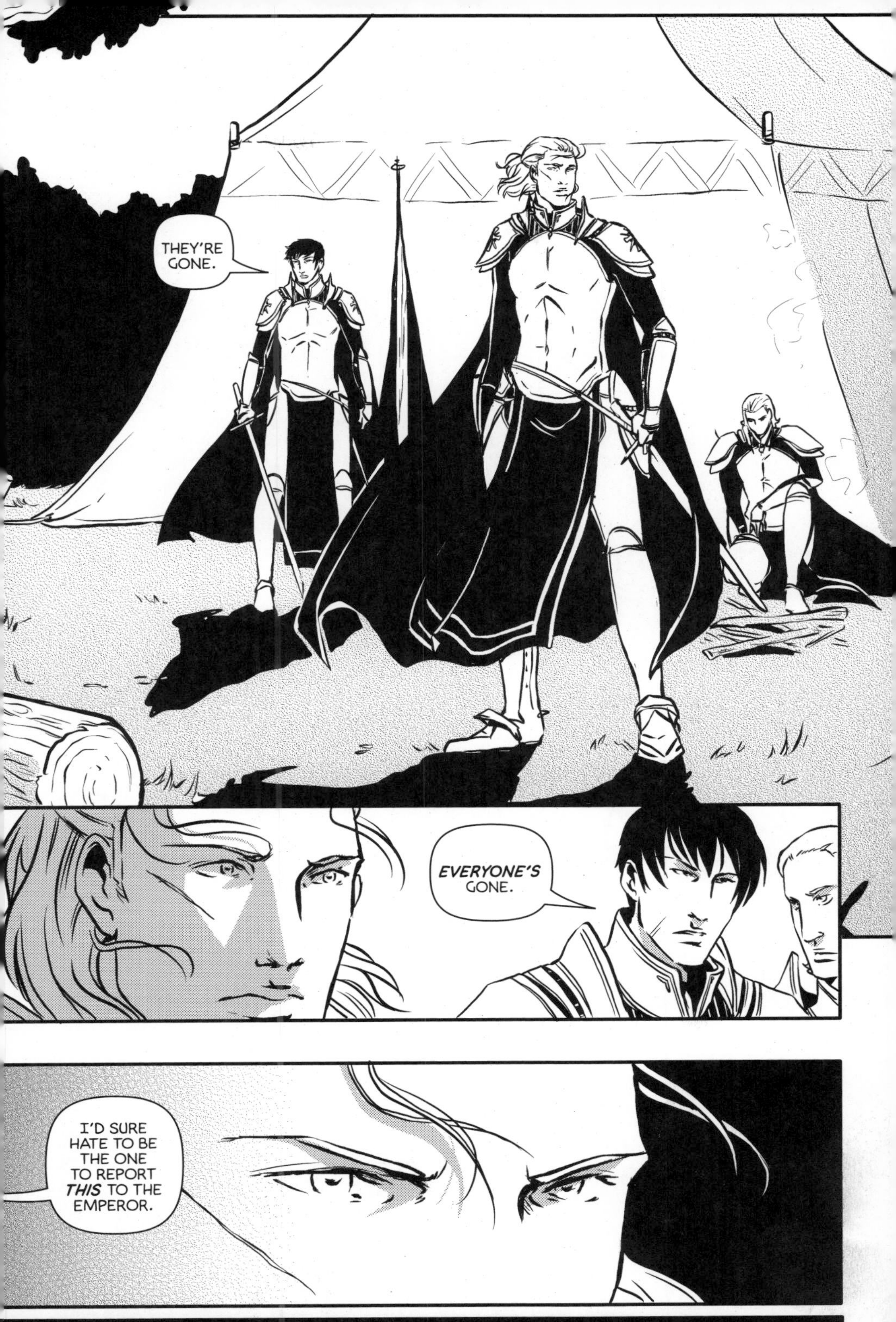
THEY'RE GONE.
EVERYONE'S GONE.
I'D SURE HATE TO BE THE ONE TO REPORT THIS TO THE EMPEROR.

Chapter 4

THE GIRL & THE UNICORN

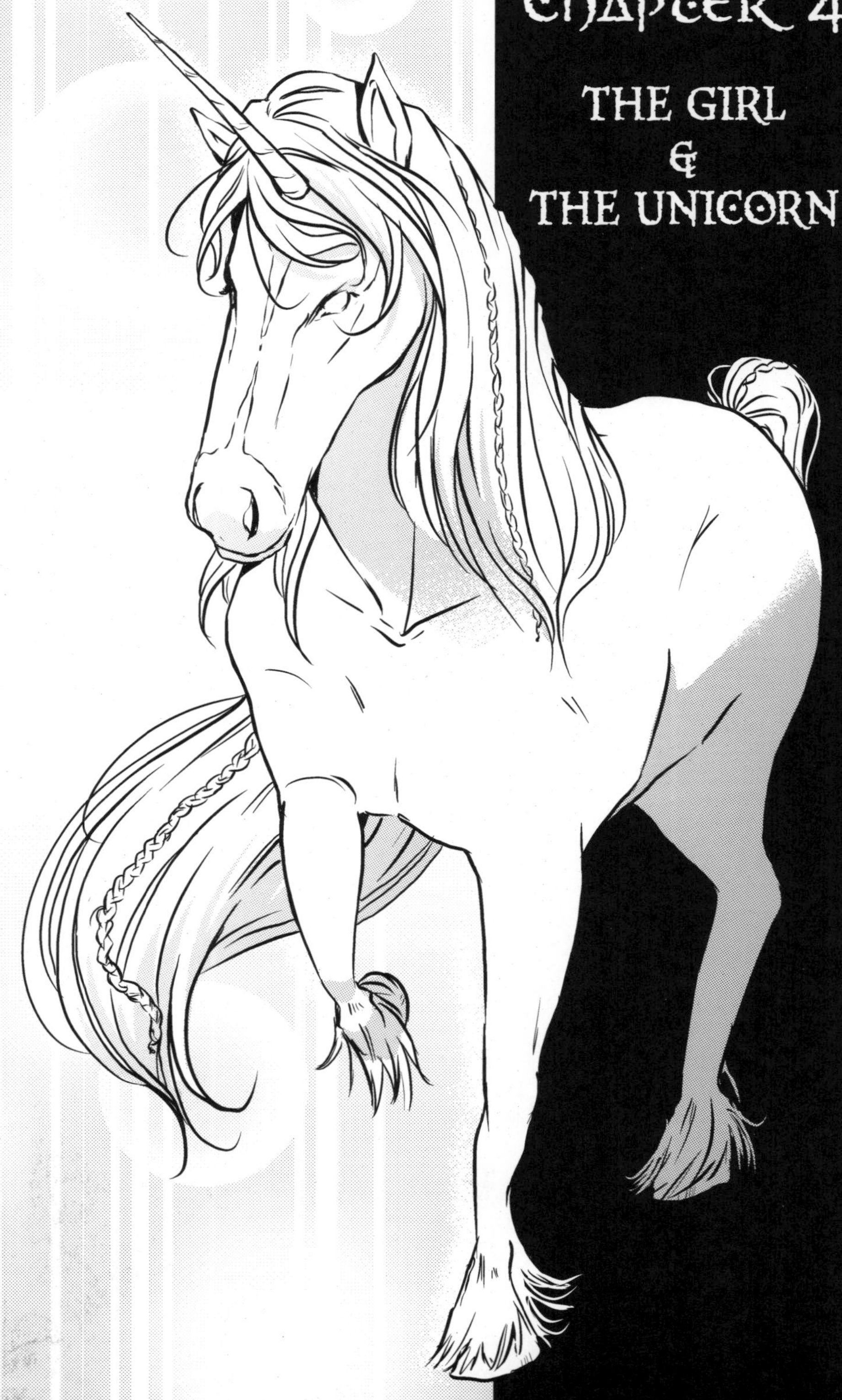

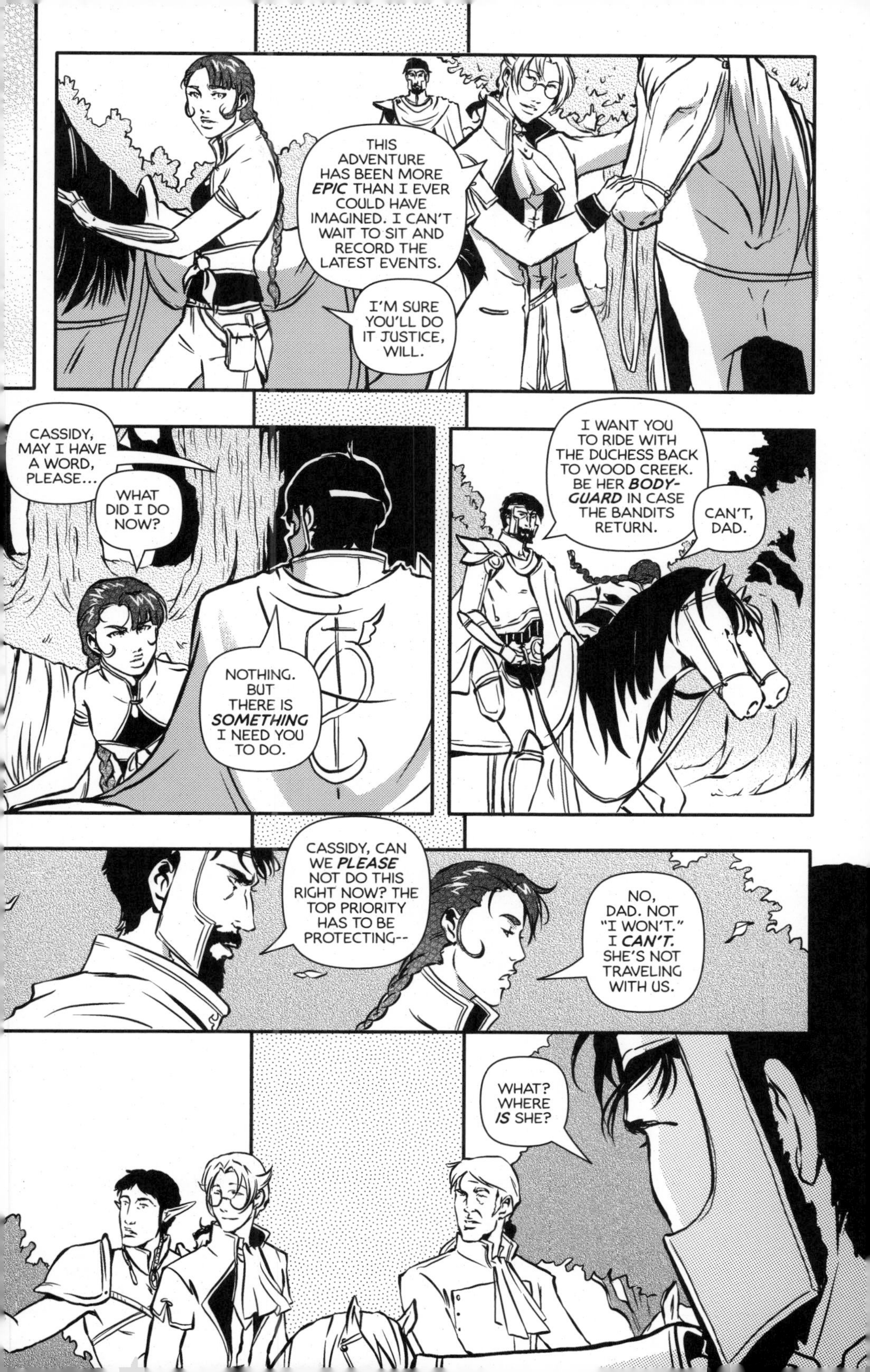
THIS ADVENTURE HAS BEEN MORE EPIC THAN I EVER COULD HAVE IMAGINED. I CAN'T WAIT TO SIT AND RECORD THE LATEST EVENTS.
I'M SURE YOU'LL DO IT JUSTICE, WILL.
CASSIDY, MAY I HAVE A WORD, PLEASE...
WHAT DID I DO NOW?
NOTHING. BUT THERE IS SOMETHING I NEED YOU TO DO.
I WANT YOU TO RIDE WITH THE DUCHESS BACK TO WOOD CREEK. BE HER BODY-GUARD IN CASE THE BANDITS RETURN.
CAN'T, DAD.
CASSIDY, CAN WE PLEASE NOT DO THIS RIGHT NOW? THE TOP PRIORITY HAS TO BE PROTECTING--
NO, DAD. NOT "I WON'T." I CAN'T. SHE'S NOT TRAVELING WITH US.
WHAT? WHERE IS SHE?

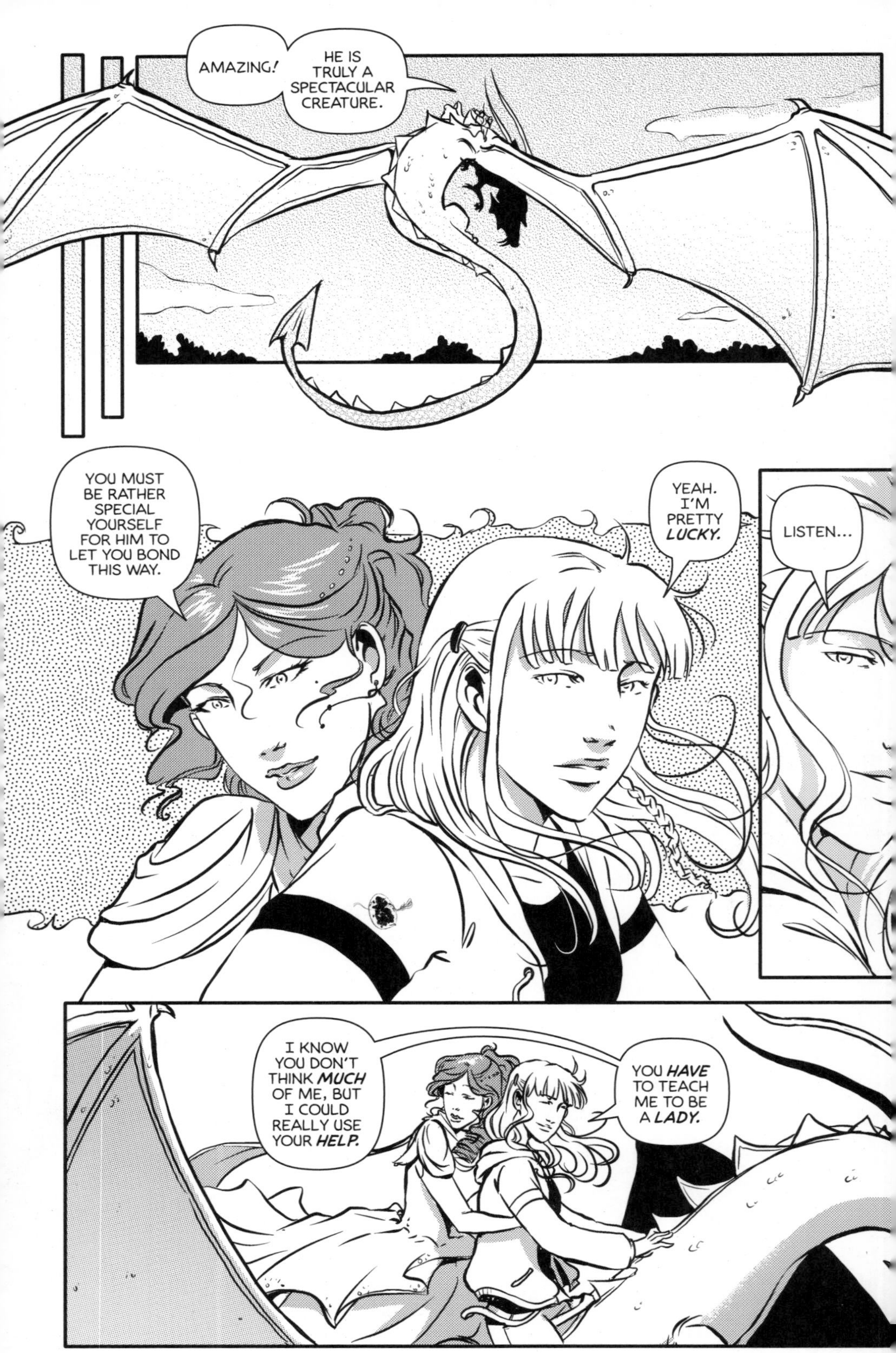
AMAZING!
HE IS TRULY A SPECTACULAR CREATURE.
YOU MUST BE RATHER SPECIAL YOURSELF FOR HIM TO LET YOU BOND THIS WAY.
YEAH. I'M PRETTY *LUCKY.*
LISTEN...
I KNOW YOU DON'T THINK *MUCH* OF ME, BUT I COULD REALLY USE YOUR *HELP.*
YOU *HAVE* TO TEACH ME TO BE A *LADY.*

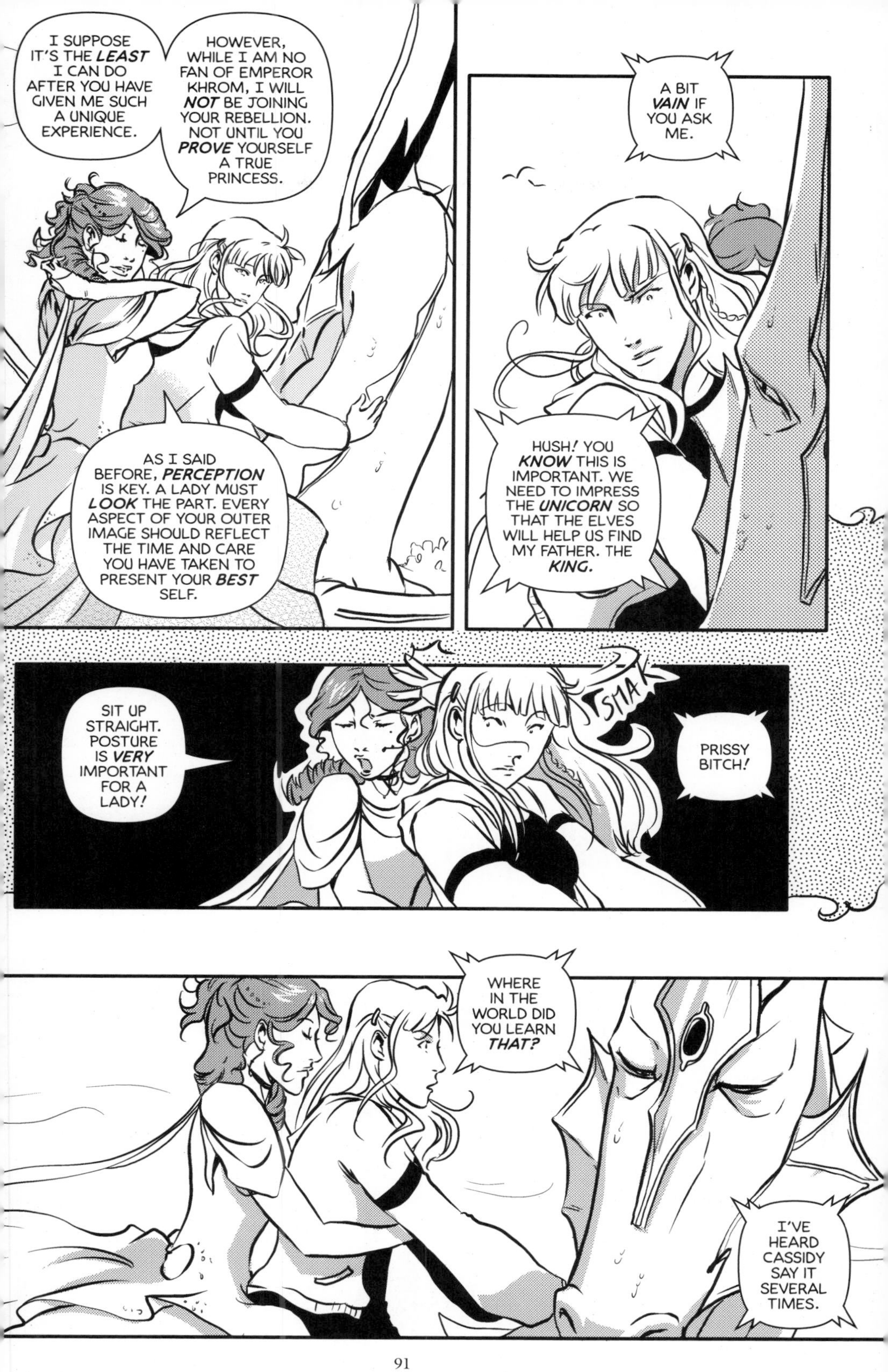
I SUPPOSE IT'S THE ***LEAST*** I CAN DO AFTER YOU HAVE GIVEN ME SUCH A UNIQUE EXPERIENCE.
HOWEVER, WHILE I AM NO FAN OF EMPEROR KHROM, I WILL ***NOT*** BE JOINING YOUR REBELLION. NOT UNTIL YOU ***PROVE*** YOURSELF A TRUE PRINCESS.
AS I SAID BEFORE, ***PERCEPTION*** IS KEY. A LADY MUST ***LOOK*** THE PART. EVERY ASPECT OF YOUR OUTER IMAGE SHOULD REFLECT THE TIME AND CARE YOU HAVE TAKEN TO PRESENT YOUR ***BEST*** SELF.
A BIT ***VAIN*** IF YOU ASK ME.
HUSH! YOU ***KNOW*** THIS IS IMPORTANT. WE NEED TO IMPRESS THE ***UNICORN*** SO THAT THE ELVES WILL HELP US FIND MY FATHER. THE ***KING.***
SIT UP STRAIGHT. POSTURE IS ***VERY*** IMPORTANT FOR A LADY!
SMAK
PRISSY BITCH!
WHERE IN THE WORLD DID YOU LEARN ***THAT?***
I'VE HEARD CASSIDY SAY IT SEVERAL TIMES.

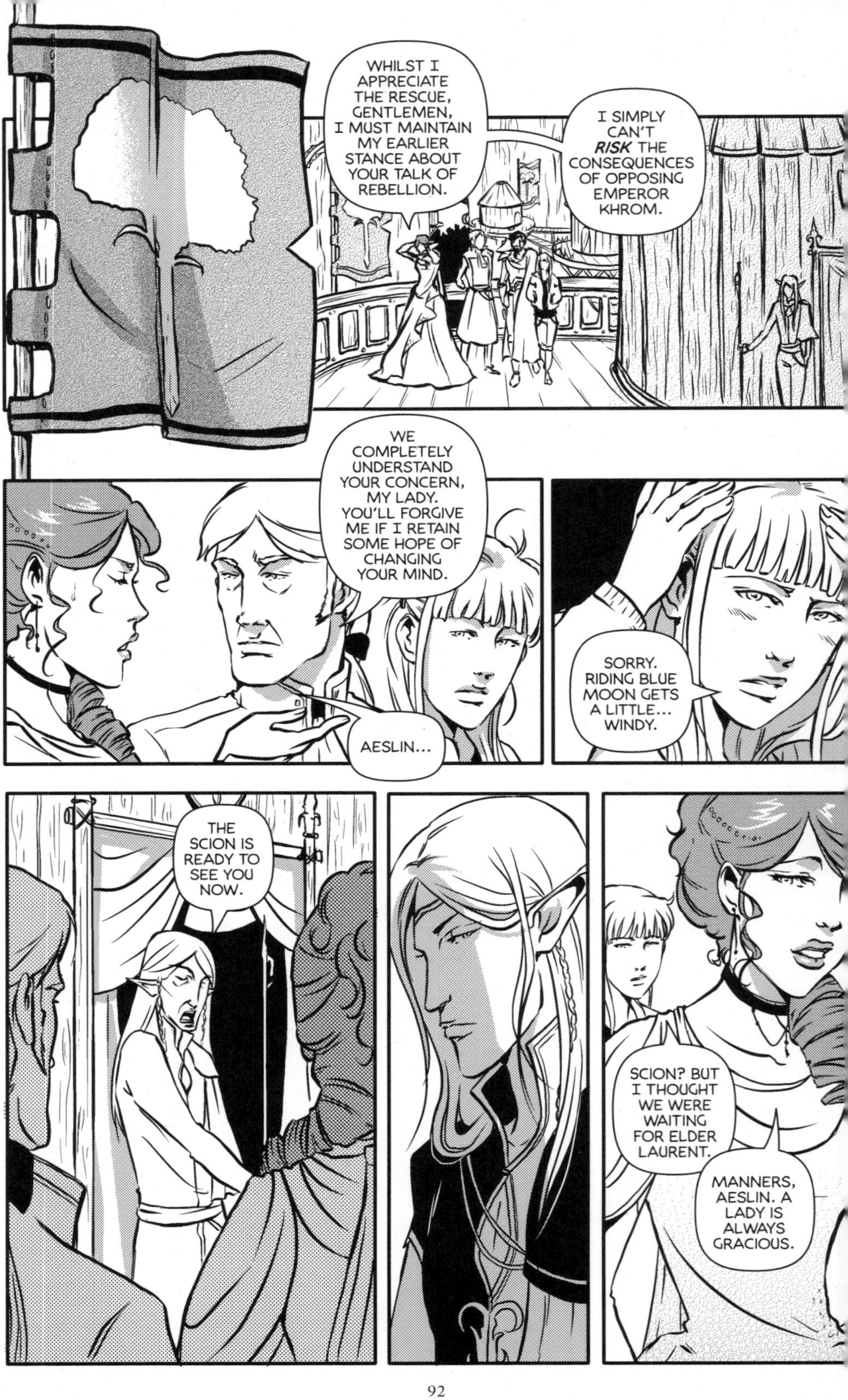
WHILST I APPRECIATE THE RESCUE, GENTLEMEN, I MUST MAINTAIN MY EARLIER STANCE ABOUT YOUR TALK OF REBELLION.
I SIMPLY CAN'T RISK THE CONSEQUENCES OF OPPOSING EMPEROR KHROM.
WE COMPLETELY UNDERSTAND YOUR CONCERN, MY LADY. YOU'LL FORGIVE ME IF I RETAIN SOME HOPE OF CHANGING YOUR MIND.
AESLIN...
SORRY. RIDING BLUE MOON GETS A LITTLE... WINDY.
THE SCION IS READY TO SEE YOU NOW.
SCION? BUT I THOUGHT WE WERE WAITING FOR ELDER LAURENT.
MANNERS, AESLIN. A LADY IS ALWAYS GRACIOUS.

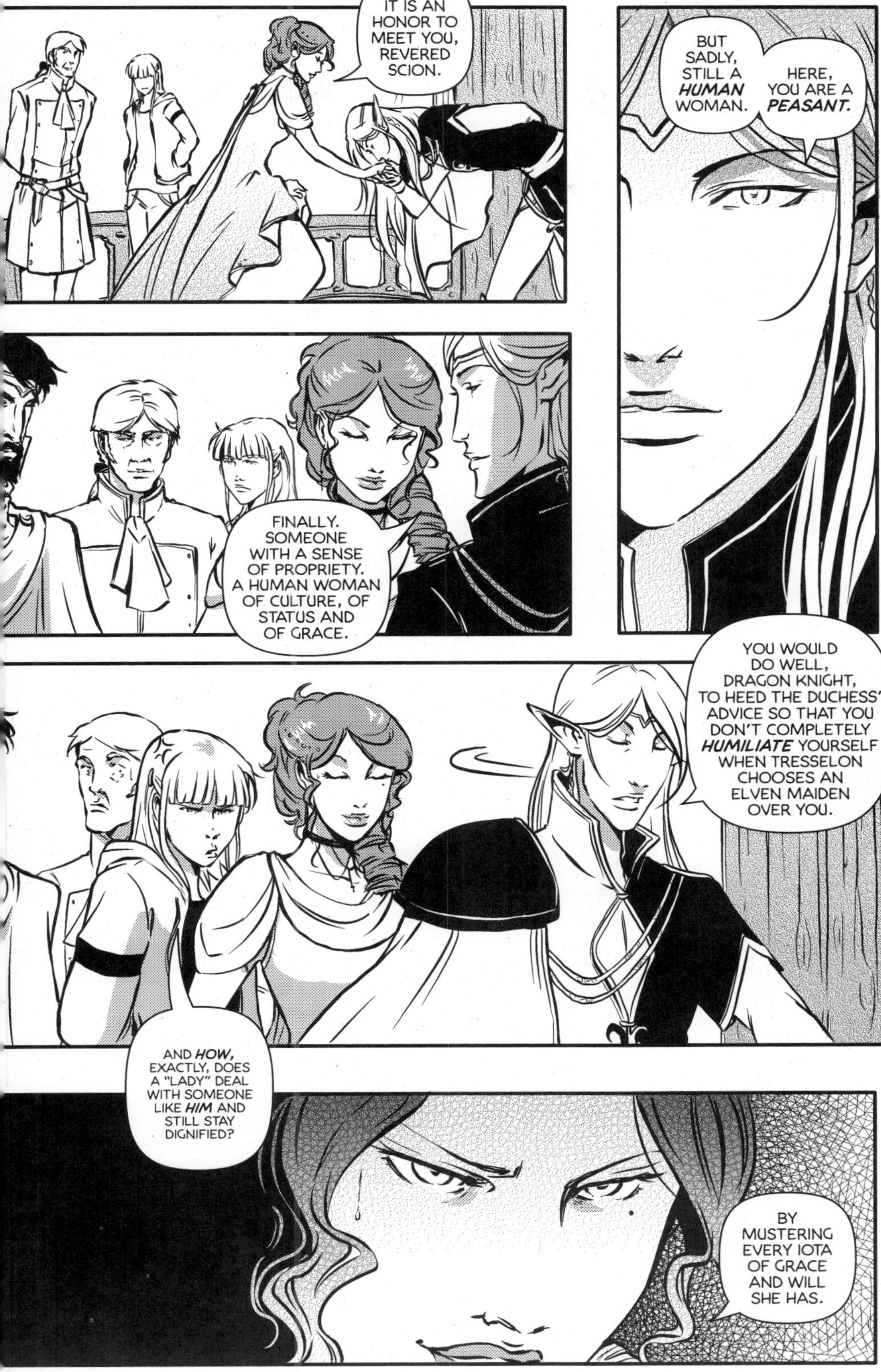

IT IS AN HONOR TO MEET YOU, REVERED SCION.
BUT SADLY, STILL A *HUMAN* WOMAN.
HERE, YOU ARE A *PEASANT.*
FINALLY. SOMEONE WITH A SENSE OF PROPRIETY. A HUMAN WOMAN OF CULTURE, OF STATUS AND OF GRACE.
YOU WOULD DO WELL, DRAGON KNIGHT, TO HEED THE DUCHESS' ADVICE SO THAT YOU DON'T COMPLETELY *HUMILIATE* YOURSELF WHEN TRESSELON CHOOSES AN ELVEN MAIDEN OVER YOU.
AND *HOW,* EXACTLY, DOES A "LADY" DEAL WITH SOMEONE LIKE *HIM* AND STILL STAY DIGNIFIED?
BY MUSTERING EVERY IOTA OF GRACE AND WILL SHE HAS.

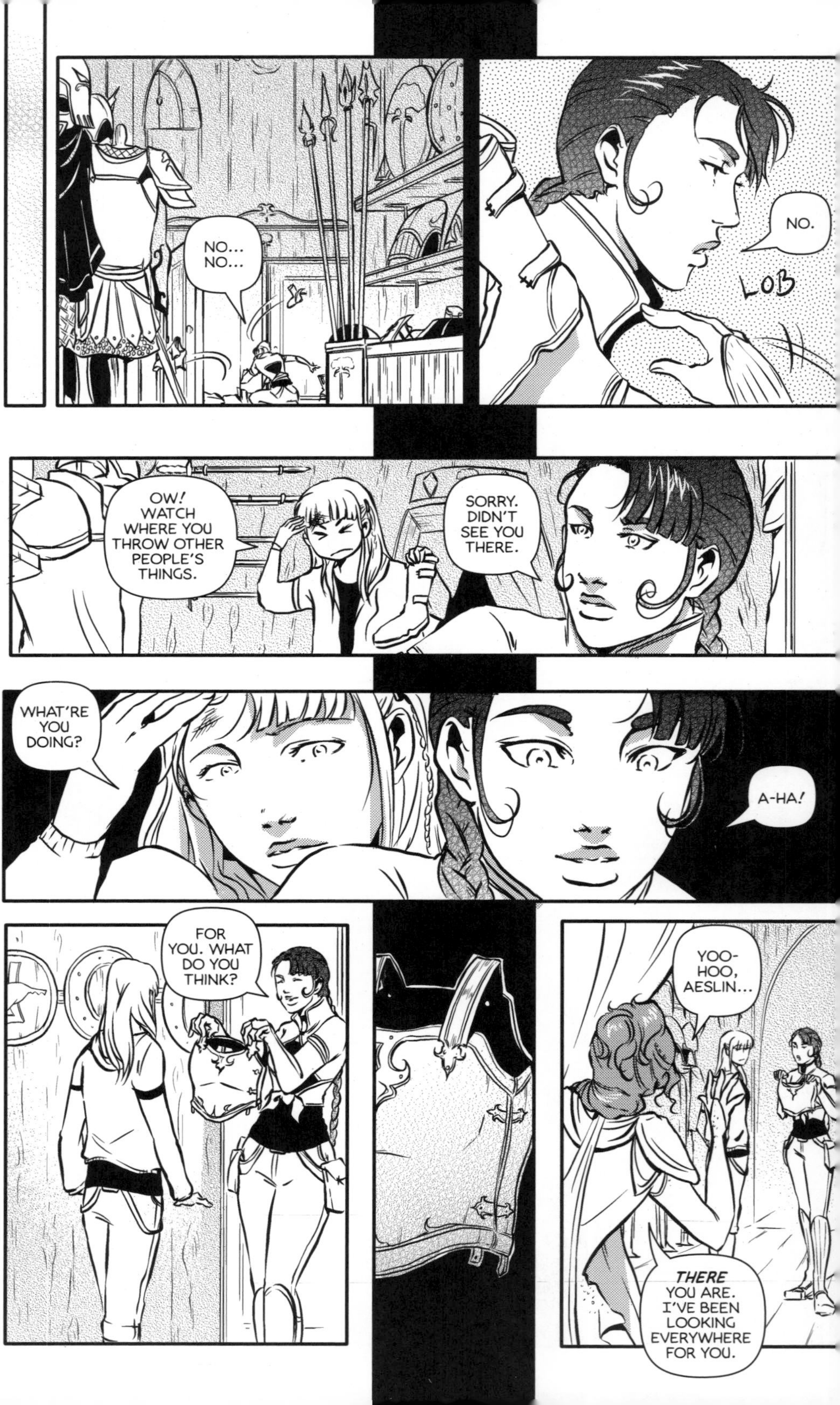
NO...
NO...
NO.
LOB
OW! WATCH WHERE YOU THROW OTHER PEOPLE'S THINGS.
SORRY. DIDN'T SEE YOU THERE.
WHAT'RE YOU DOING?
A-HA!
FOR YOU. WHAT DO YOU THINK?
YOO-HOO, AESLIN...
THERE YOU ARE. I'VE BEEN LOOKING EVERYWHERE FOR YOU.

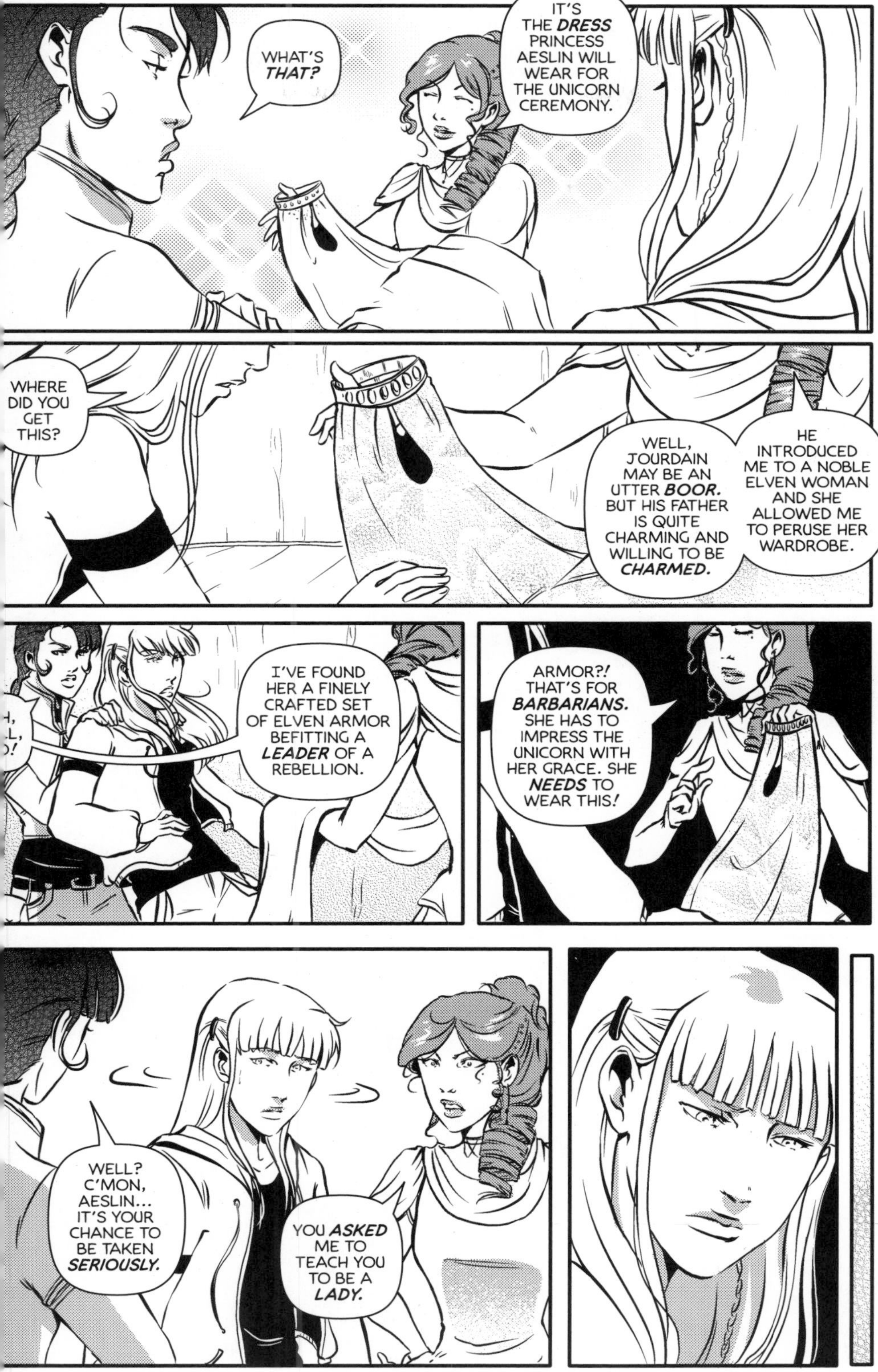
WHAT'S *THAT?*
IT'S THE ***DRESS*** PRINCESS AESLIN WILL WEAR FOR THE UNICORN CEREMONY.
WHERE DID YOU GET THIS?
WELL, JOURDAIN MAY BE AN UTTER ***BOOR.*** BUT HIS FATHER IS QUITE CHARMING AND WILLING TO BE ***CHARMED.***
HE INTRODUCED ME TO A NOBLE ELVEN WOMAN AND SHE ALLOWED ME TO PERUSE HER WARDROBE.
I'VE FOUND HER A FINELY CRAFTED SET OF ELVEN ARMOR BEFITTING A ***LEADER*** OF A REBELLION.
ARMOR?! THAT'S FOR ***BARBARIANS.*** SHE HAS TO IMPRESS THE UNICORN WITH HER GRACE. SHE ***NEEDS*** TO WEAR THIS!
WELL? C'MON, AESLIN... IT'S YOUR CHANCE TO BE TAKEN ***SERIOUSLY.***
YOU ***ASKED*** ME TO TEACH YOU TO BE A ***LADY.***

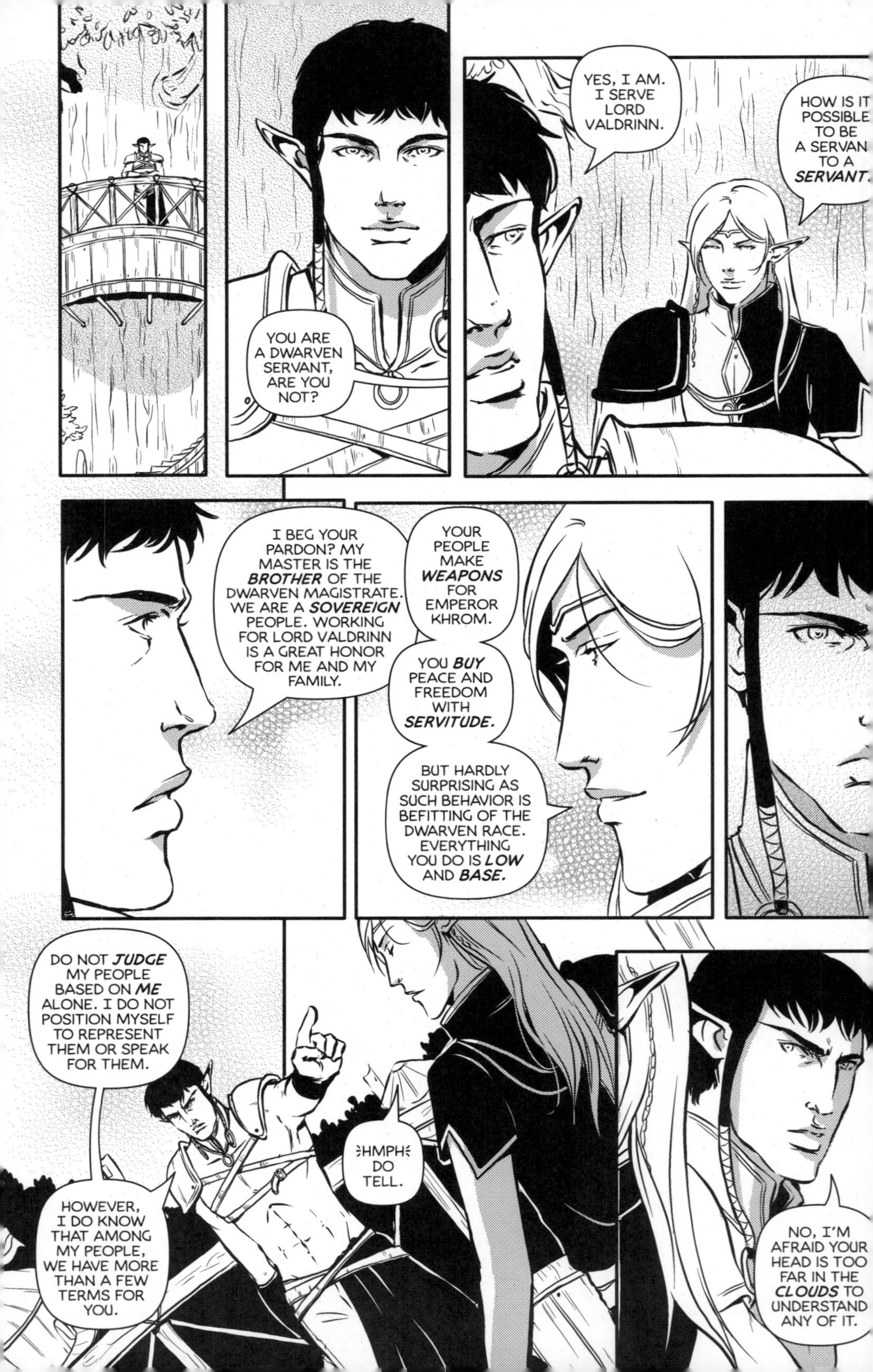
YOU ARE A DWARVEN SERVANT, ARE YOU NOT?
YES, I AM. I SERVE LORD VALDRINN.
HOW IS IT POSSIBLE TO BE A SERVAN TO A SERVANT.
I BEG YOUR PARDON? MY MASTER IS THE BROTHER OF THE DWARVEN MAGISTRATE. WE ARE A SOVEREIGN PEOPLE. WORKING FOR LORD VALDRINN IS A GREAT HONOR FOR ME AND MY FAMILY.
YOUR PEOPLE MAKE WEAPONS FOR EMPEROR KHROM.
YOU BUY PEACE AND FREEDOM WITH SERVITUDE.
BUT HARDLY SURPRISING AS SUCH BEHAVIOR IS BEFITTING OF THE DWARVEN RACE. EVERYTHING YOU DO IS LOW AND BASE.
DO NOT JUDGE MY PEOPLE BASED ON ME ALONE. I DO NOT POSITION MYSELF TO REPRESENT THEM OR SPEAK FOR THEM.
HOWEVER, I DO KNOW THAT AMONG MY PEOPLE, WE HAVE MORE THAN A FEW TERMS FOR YOU.
HMPH DO TELL.
NO, I'M AFRAID YOUR HEAD IS TOO FAR IN THE CLOUDS TO UNDERSTAND ANY OF IT.

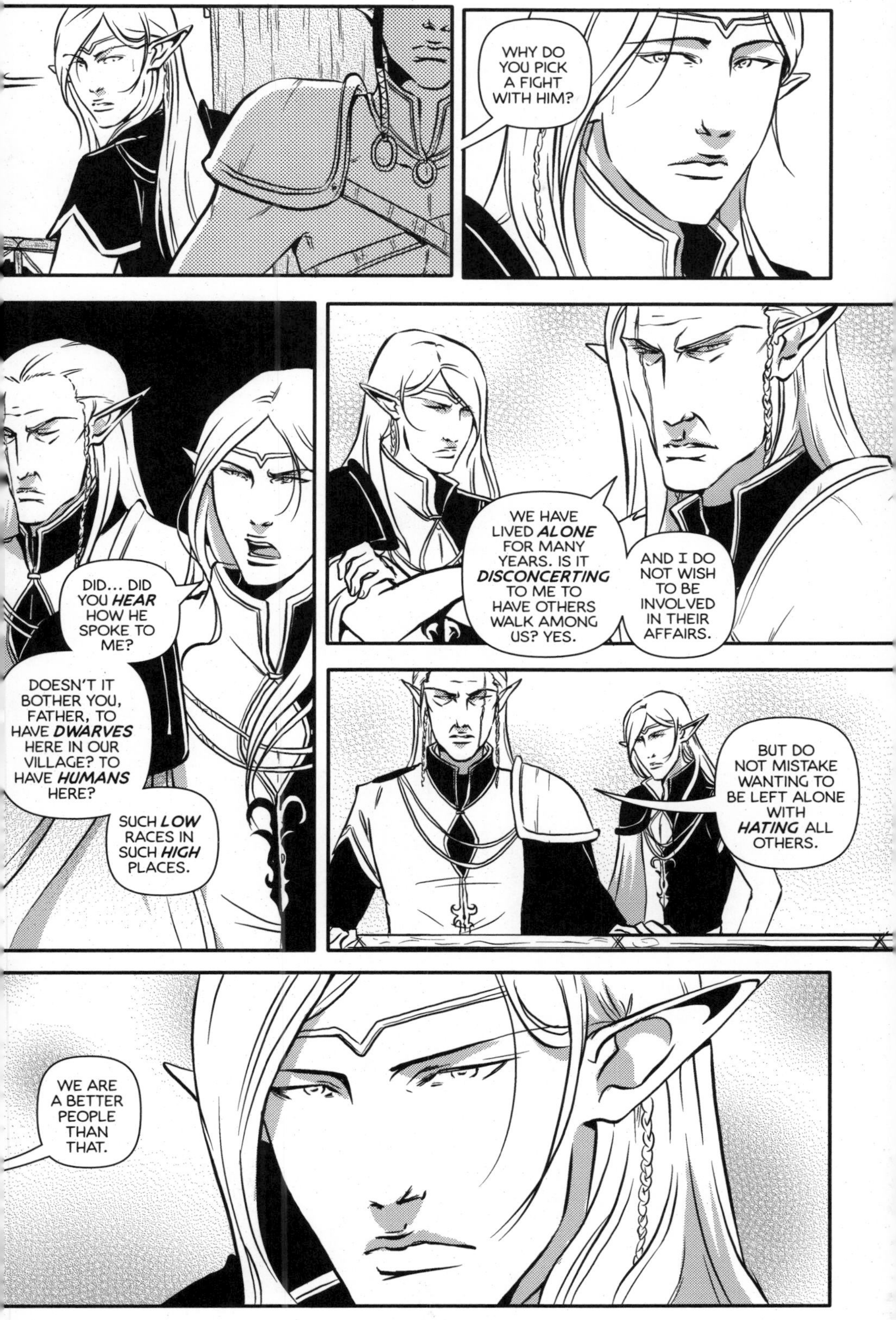
WHY DO YOU PICK A FIGHT WITH HIM?
DID... DID YOU HEAR HOW HE SPOKE TO ME?
DOESN'T IT BOTHER YOU, FATHER, TO HAVE DWARVES HERE IN OUR VILLAGE? TO HAVE HUMANS HERE?
SUCH LOW RACES IN SUCH HIGH PLACES.
WE HAVE LIVED ALONE FOR MANY YEARS. IS IT DISCONCERTING TO ME TO HAVE OTHERS WALK AMONG US? YES.
AND I DO NOT WISH TO BE INVOLVED IN THEIR AFFAIRS.
BUT DO NOT MISTAKE WANTING TO BE LEFT ALONE WITH HATING ALL OTHERS.
WE ARE A BETTER PEOPLE THAN THAT.

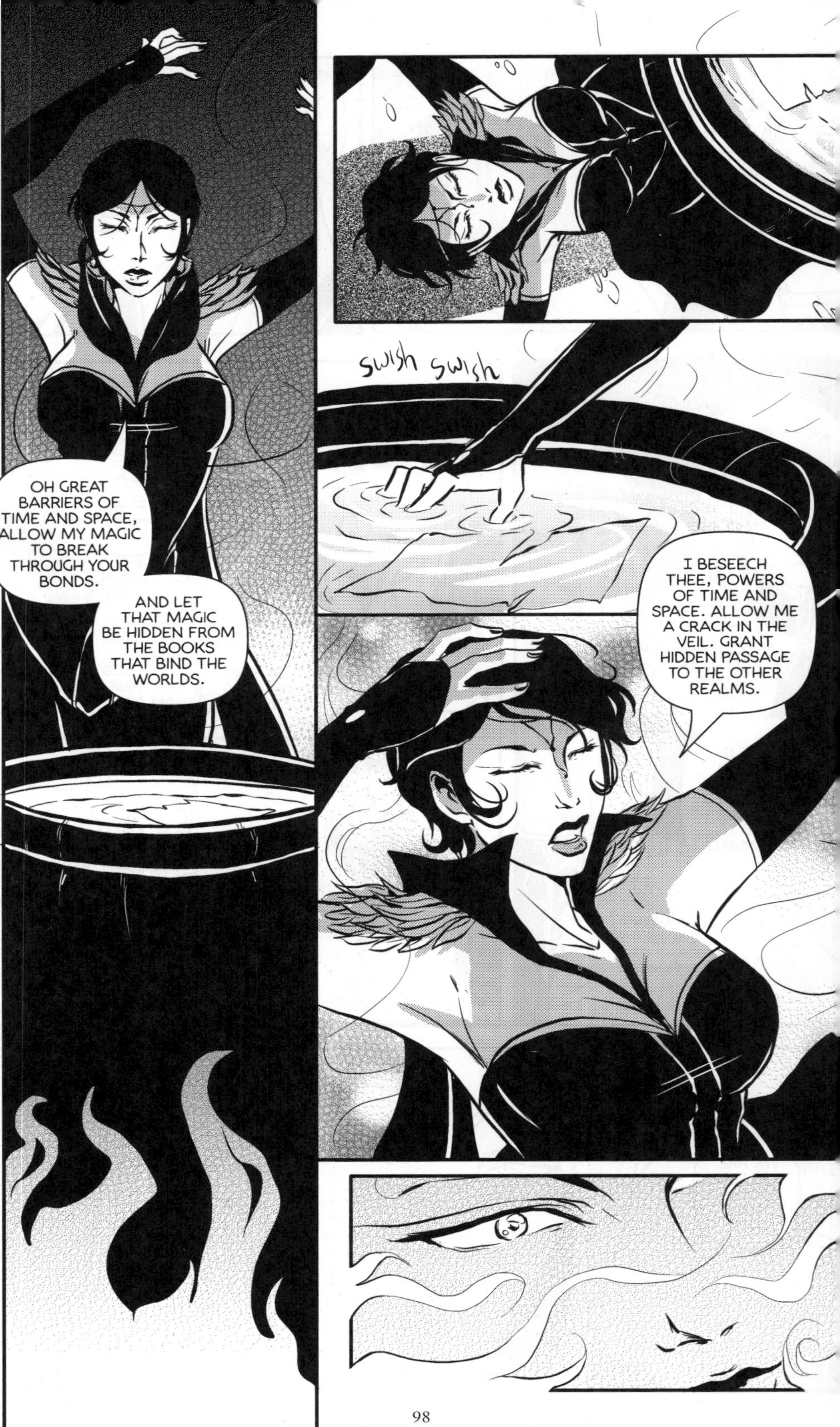
OH GREAT BARRIERS OF TIME AND SPACE, ALLOW MY MAGIC TO BREAK THROUGH YOUR BONDS.
AND LET THAT MAGIC BE HIDDEN FROM THE BOOKS THAT BIND THE WORLDS.
SWISH SWISH
I BESEECH THEE, POWERS OF TIME AND SPACE. ALLOW ME A CRACK IN THE VEIL. GRANT HIDDEN PASSAGE TO THE OTHER REALMS.

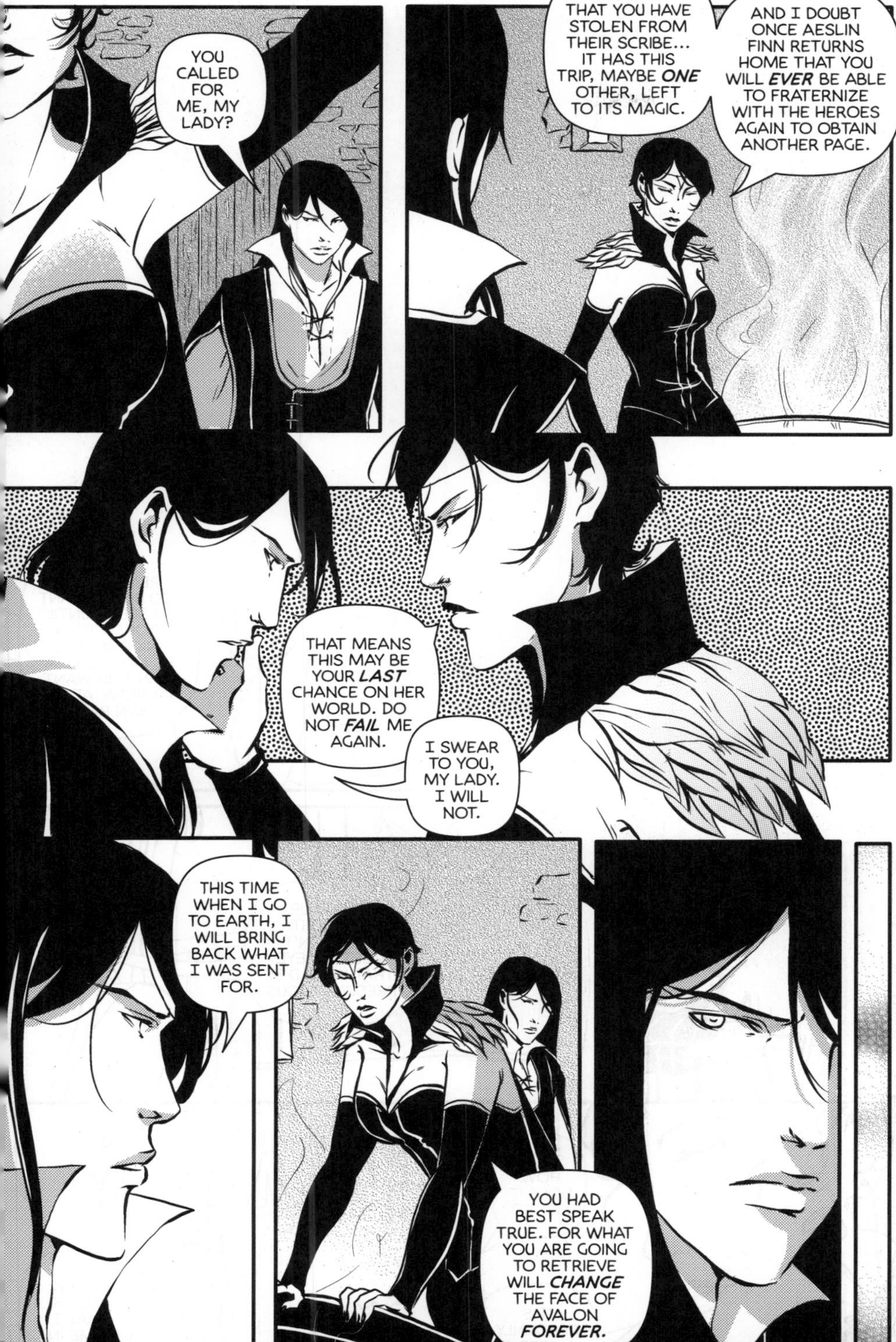
YOU CALLED FOR ME, MY LADY?
THIS PAGE THAT YOU HAVE STOLEN FROM THEIR SCRIBE... IT HAS THIS TRIP, MAYBE ***ONE*** OTHER, LEFT TO ITS MAGIC.
AND I DOUBT ONCE AESLIN FINN RETURNS HOME THAT YOU WILL ***EVER*** BE ABLE TO FRATERNIZE WITH THE HEROES AGAIN TO OBTAIN ANOTHER PAGE.
THAT MEANS THIS MAY BE YOUR ***LAST*** CHANCE ON HER WORLD. DO NOT ***FAIL*** ME AGAIN.
I SWEAR TO YOU, MY LADY. I WILL NOT.
THIS TIME WHEN I GO TO EARTH, I WILL BRING BACK WHAT I WAS SENT FOR.
YOU HAD BEST SPEAK TRUE. FOR WHAT YOU ARE GOING TO RETRIEVE WILL ***CHANGE*** THE FACE OF AVALON ***FOREVER.***

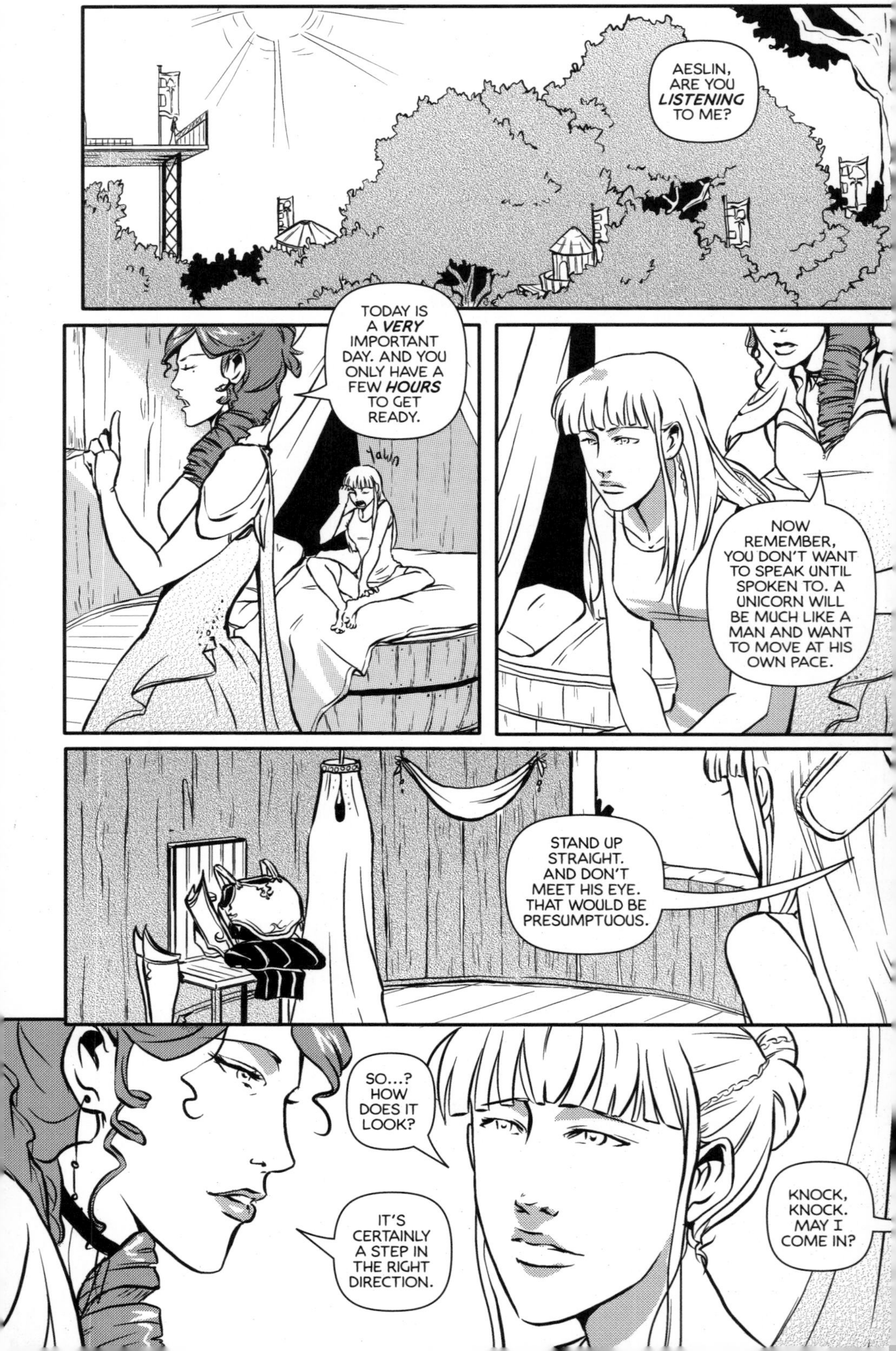
AESLIN, ARE YOU LISTENING TO ME?
TODAY IS A VERY IMPORTANT DAY. AND YOU ONLY HAVE A FEW HOURS TO GET READY.
YAWN
NOW REMEMBER, YOU DON'T WANT TO SPEAK UNTIL SPOKEN TO. A UNICORN WILL BE MUCH LIKE A MAN AND WANT TO MOVE AT HIS OWN PACE.
STAND UP STRAIGHT. AND DON'T MEET HIS EYE. THAT WOULD BE PRESUMPTUOUS.
SO...? HOW DOES IT LOOK?
IT'S CERTAINLY A STEP IN THE RIGHT DIRECTION.
KNOCK, KNOCK. MAY I COME IN?

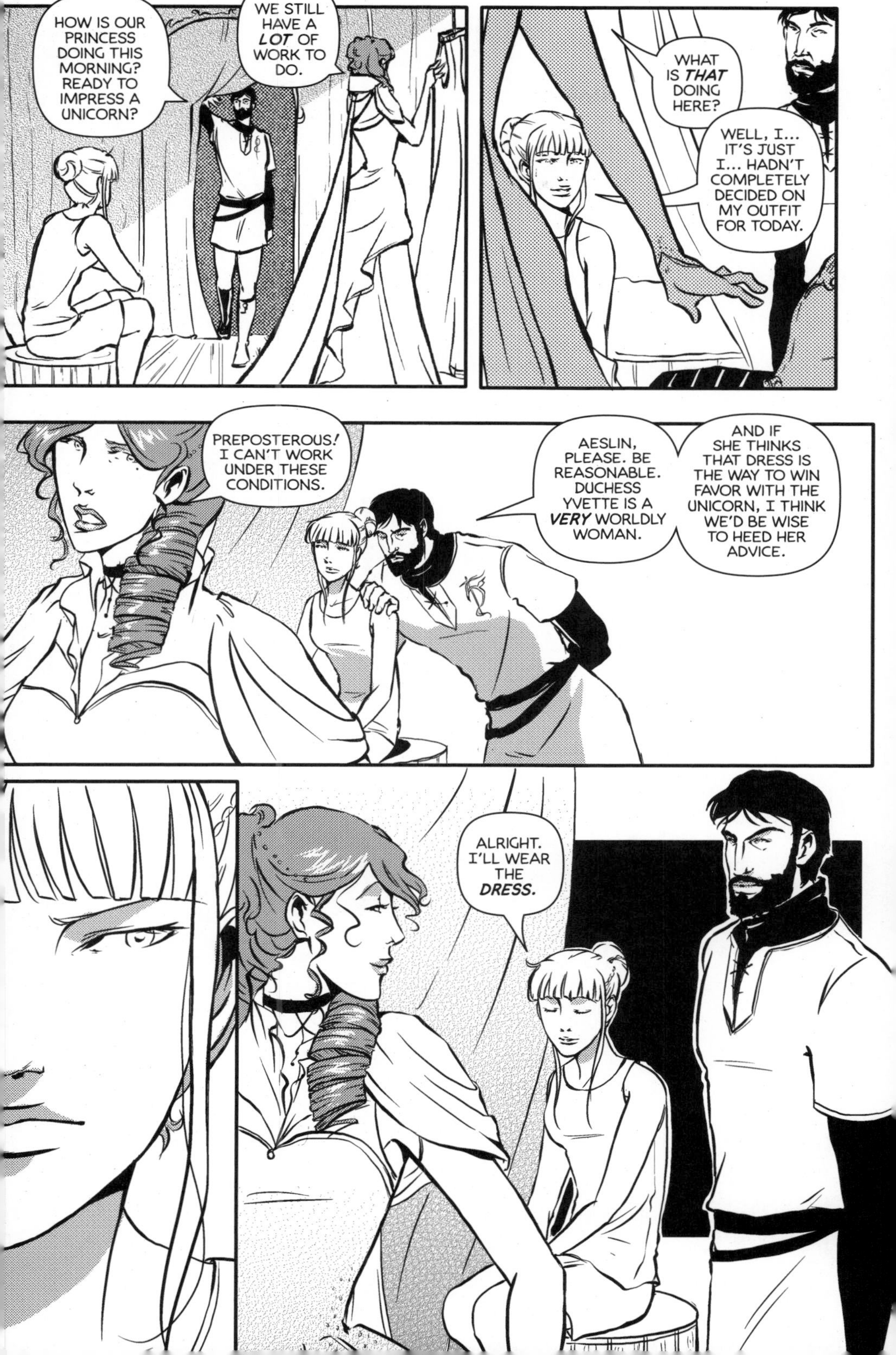
HOW IS OUR PRINCESS DOING THIS MORNING? READY TO IMPRESS A UNICORN?
WE STILL HAVE A LOT OF WORK TO DO.
WHAT IS THAT DOING HERE?
WELL, I... IT'S JUST I... HADN'T COMPLETELY DECIDED ON MY OUTFIT FOR TODAY.
PREPOSTEROUS! I CAN'T WORK UNDER THESE CONDITIONS.
AESLIN, PLEASE. BE REASONABLE. DUCHESS YVETTE IS A VERY WORLDLY WOMAN.
AND IF SHE THINKS THAT DRESS IS THE WAY TO WIN FAVOR WITH THE UNICORN, I THINK WE'D BE WISE TO HEED HER ADVICE.
ALRIGHT. I'LL WEAR THE DRESS.

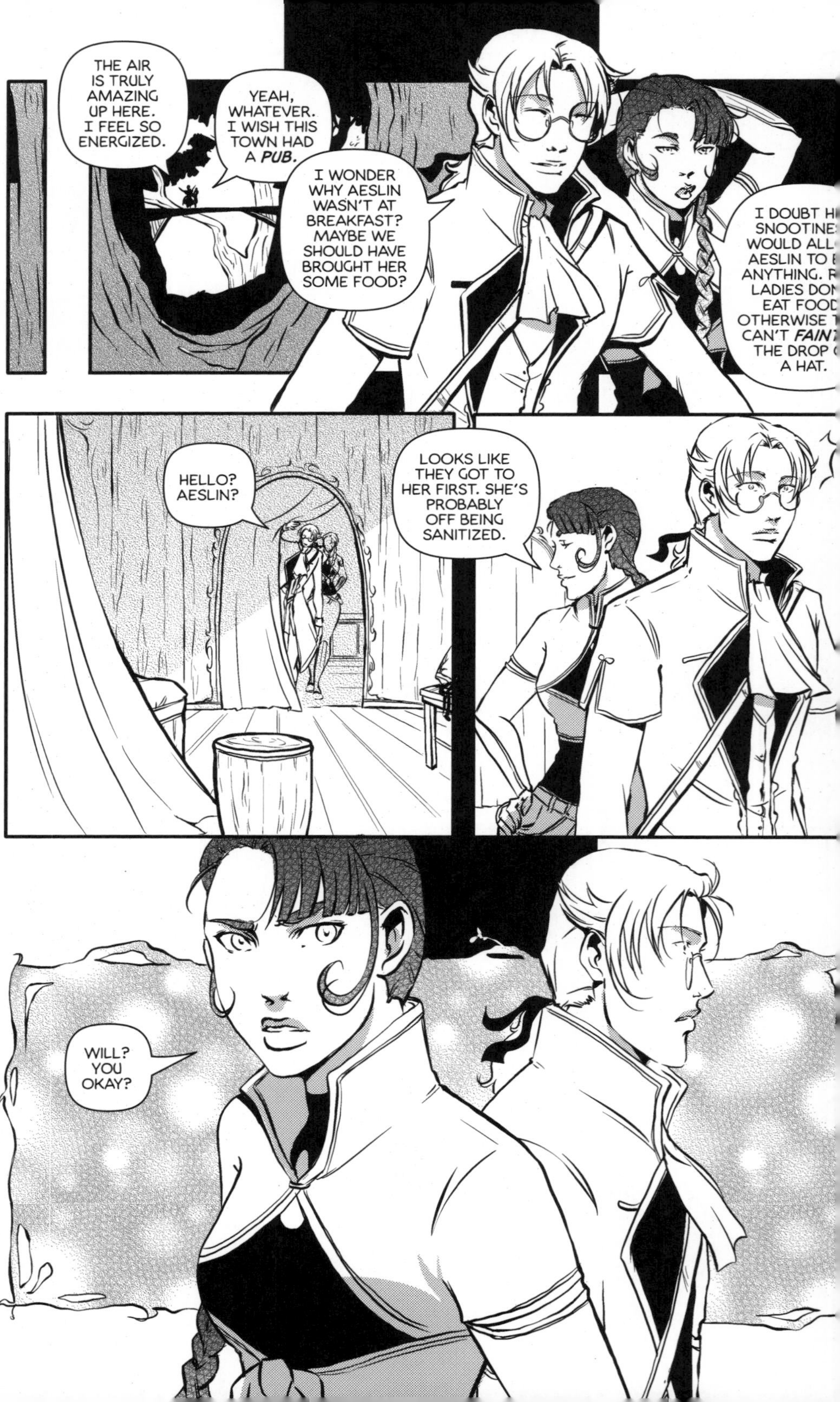
THE AIR IS TRULY AMAZING UP HERE. I FEEL SO ENERGIZED.
YEAH, WHATEVER. I WISH THIS TOWN HAD A ***PUB.***
I WONDER WHY AESLIN WASN'T AT BREAKFAST? MAYBE WE SHOULD HAVE BROUGHT HER SOME FOOD?
I DOUBT H SNOOTINES WOULD ALL AESLIN TO ANYTHING. R LADIES DON EAT FOOD OTHERWISE CAN'T ***FAIN*** THE DROP A HAT.
HELLO? AESLIN?
LOOKS LIKE THEY GOT TO HER FIRST. SHE'S PROBABLY OFF BEING SANITIZED.
WILL? YOU OKAY?

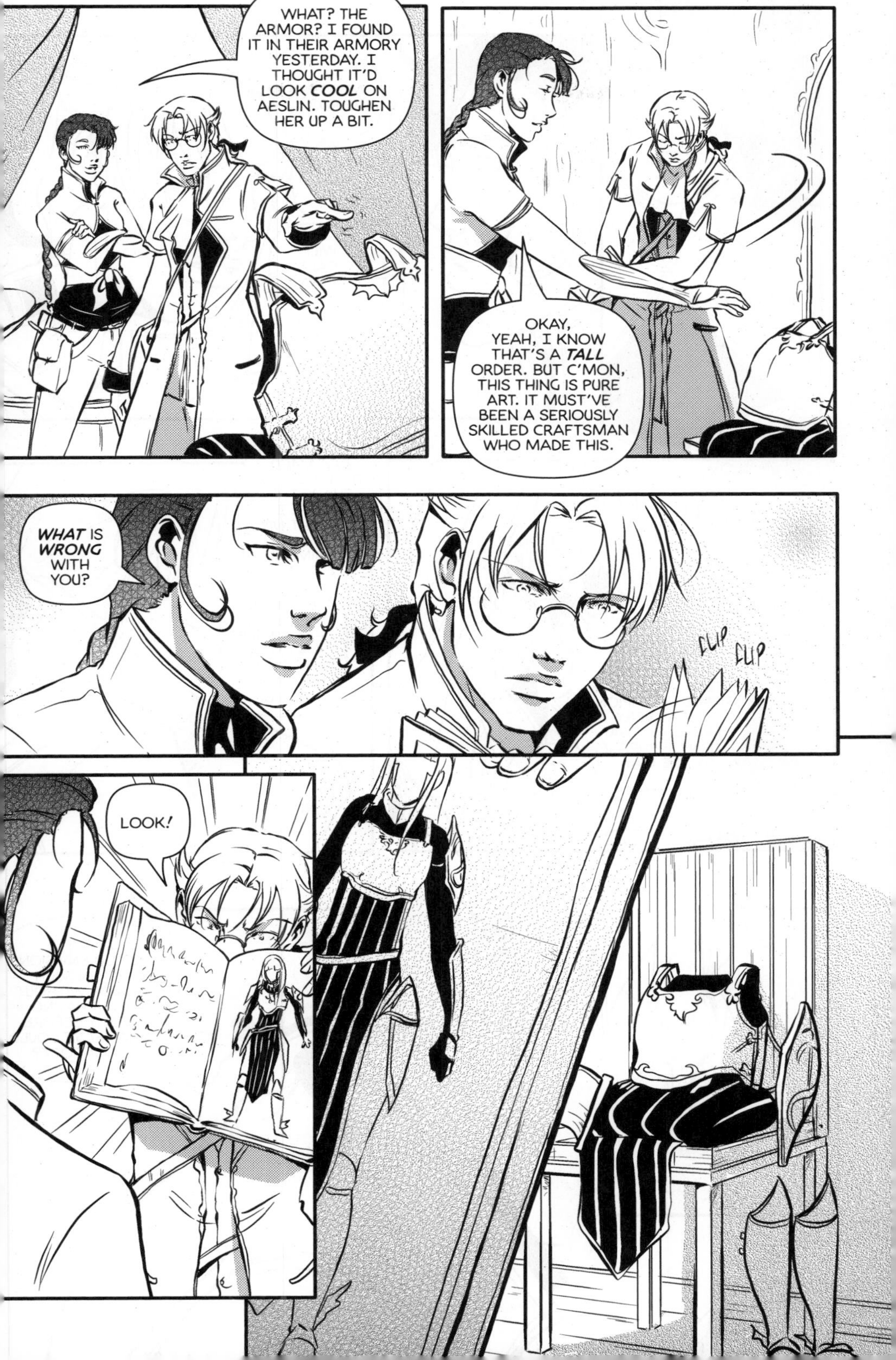
WHAT? THE ARMOR? I FOUND IT IN THEIR ARMORY YESTERDAY. I THOUGHT IT'D LOOK COOL ON AESLIN. TOUGHEN HER UP A BIT.
OKAY, YEAH, I KNOW THAT'S A TALL ORDER. BUT C'MON, THIS THING IS PURE ART. IT MUST'VE BEEN A SERIOUSLY SKILLED CRAFTSMAN WHO MADE THIS.
WHAT IS WRONG WITH YOU?
FLIP FLIP
LOOK!

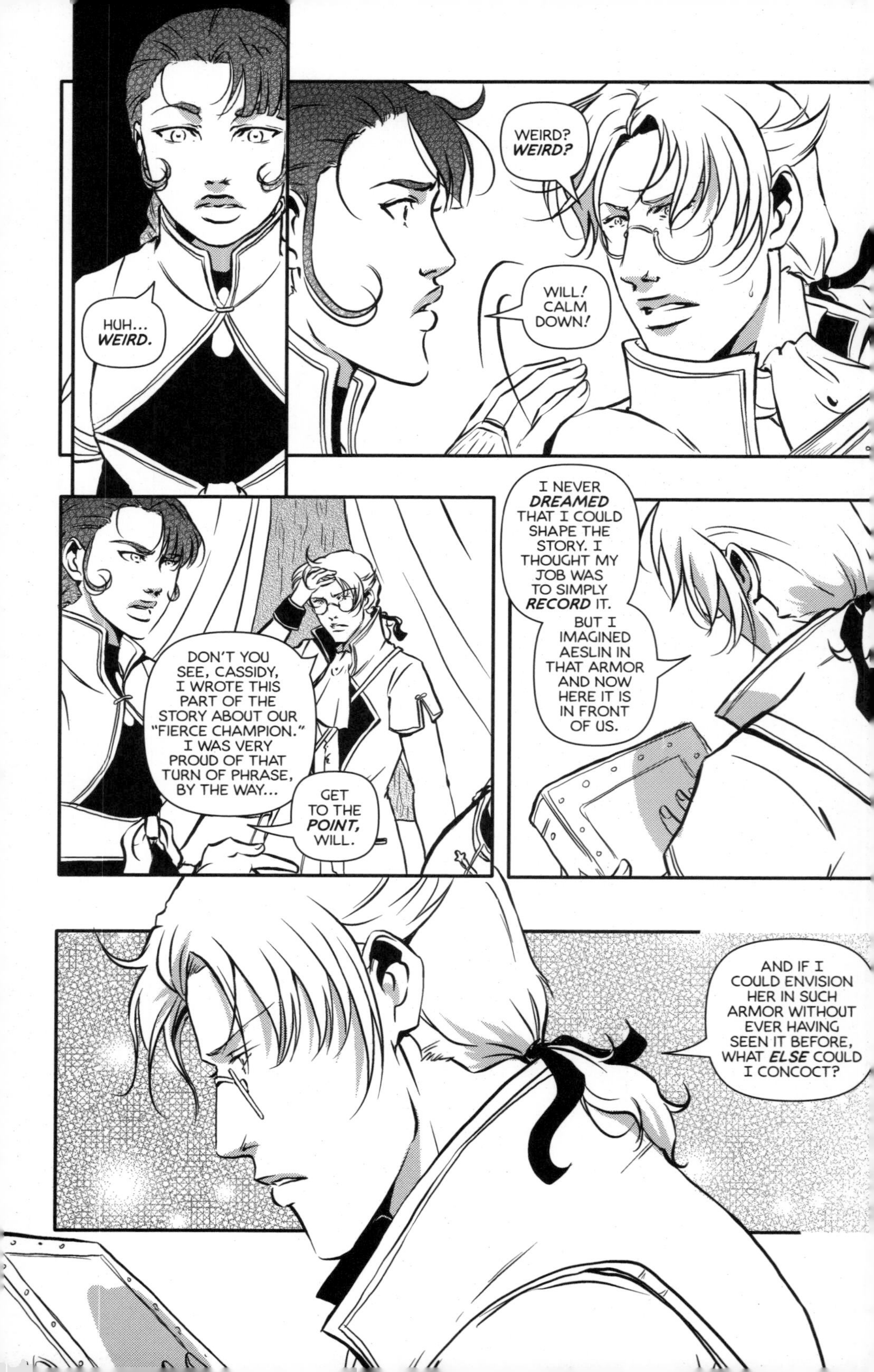
HUH... WEIRD.
WEIRD? WEIRD?
WILL! CALM DOWN!
DON'T YOU SEE, CASSIDY, I WROTE THIS PART OF THE STORY ABOUT OUR "FIERCE CHAMPION." I WAS VERY PROUD OF THAT TURN OF PHRASE, BY THE WAY...
GET TO THE POINT, WILL.
I NEVER DREAMED THAT I COULD SHAPE THE STORY. I THOUGHT MY JOB WAS TO SIMPLY RECORD IT.
BUT I IMAGINED AESLIN IN THAT ARMOR AND NOW HERE IT IS IN FRONT OF US.
AND IF I COULD ENVISION HER IN SUCH ARMOR WITHOUT EVER HAVING SEEN IT BEFORE, WHAT ELSE COULD I CONCOCT?

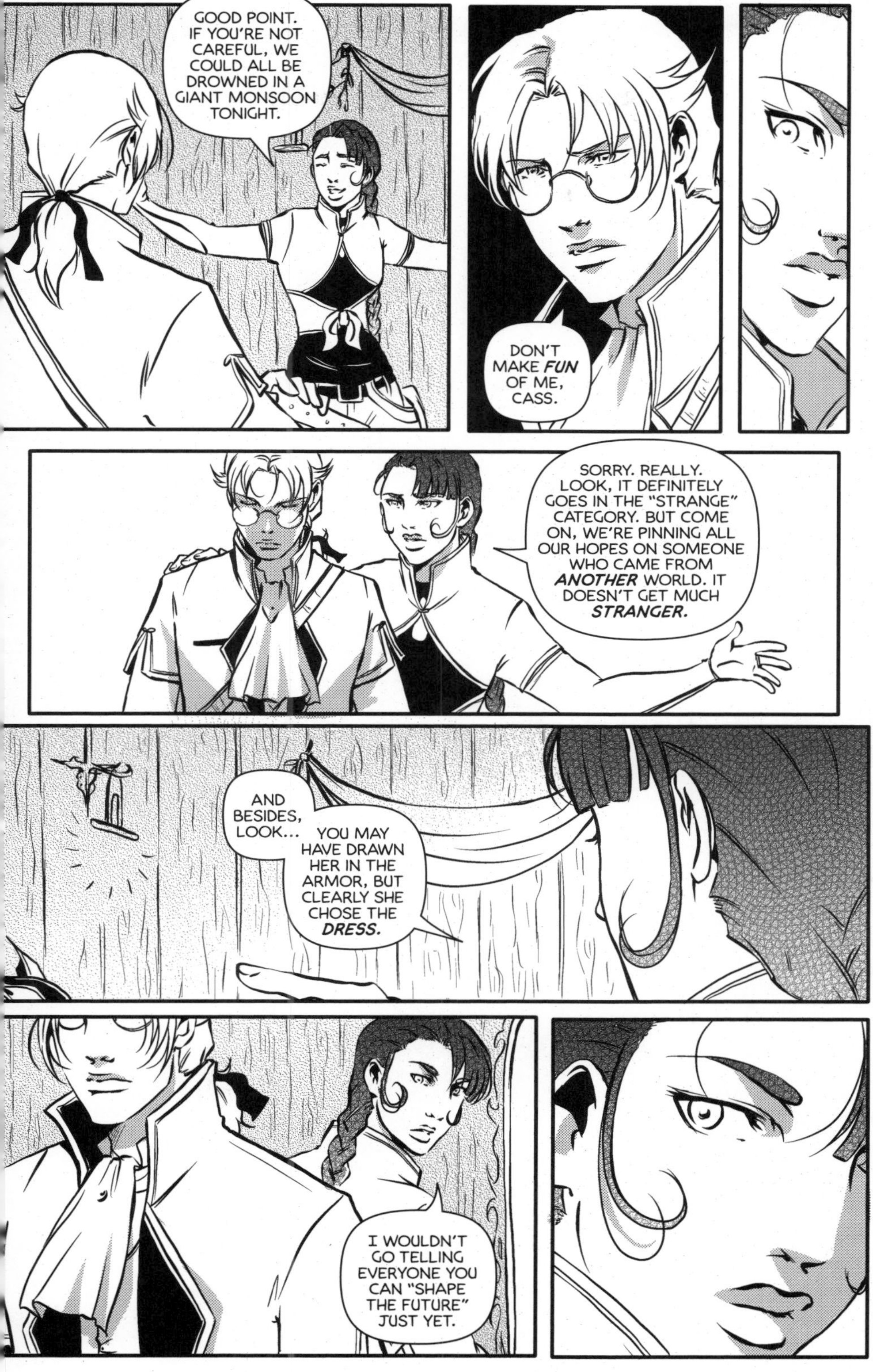
GOOD POINT. IF YOU'RE NOT CAREFUL, WE COULD ALL BE DROWNED IN A GIANT MONSOON TONIGHT.
DON'T MAKE *FUN* OF ME, CASS.
SORRY. REALLY. LOOK, IT DEFINITELY GOES IN THE "STRANGE" CATEGORY. BUT COME ON, WE'RE PINNING ALL OUR HOPES ON SOMEONE WHO CAME FROM *ANOTHER* WORLD. IT DOESN'T GET MUCH *STRANGER.*
AND BESIDES, LOOK...
YOU MAY HAVE DRAWN HER IN THE ARMOR, BUT CLEARLY SHE CHOSE THE *DRESS.*
I WOULDN'T GO TELLING EVERYONE YOU CAN "SHAPE THE FUTURE" JUST YET.

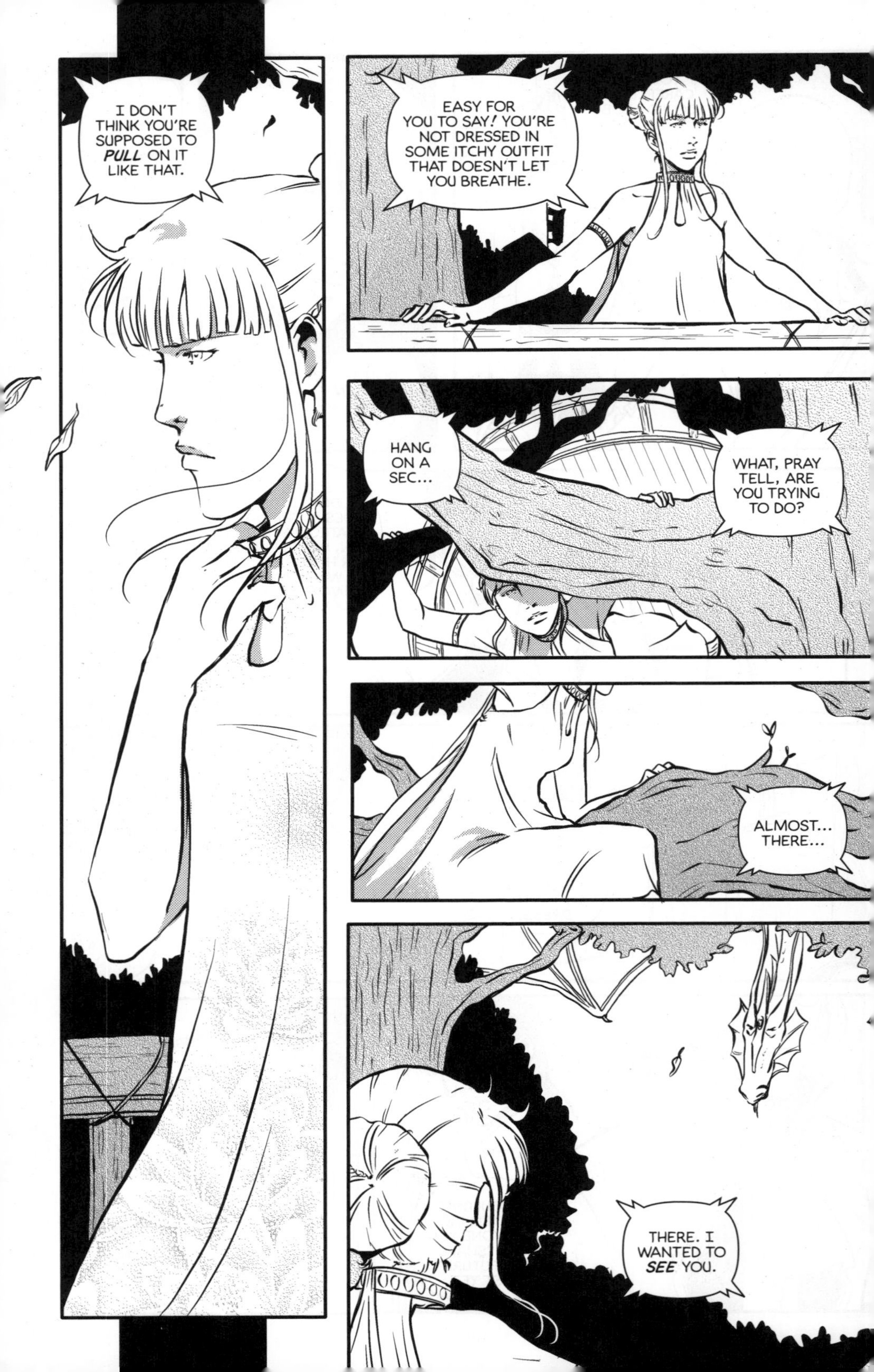
I DON'T THINK YOU'RE SUPPOSED TO *PULL* ON IT LIKE THAT.
EASY FOR YOU TO SAY*!* YOU'RE NOT DRESSED IN SOME ITCHY OUTFIT THAT DOESN'T LET YOU BREATHE.
HANG ON A SEC...
WHAT, PRAY TELL, ARE YOU TRYING TO DO?
ALMOST... THERE...
THERE. I WANTED TO *SEE* YOU.

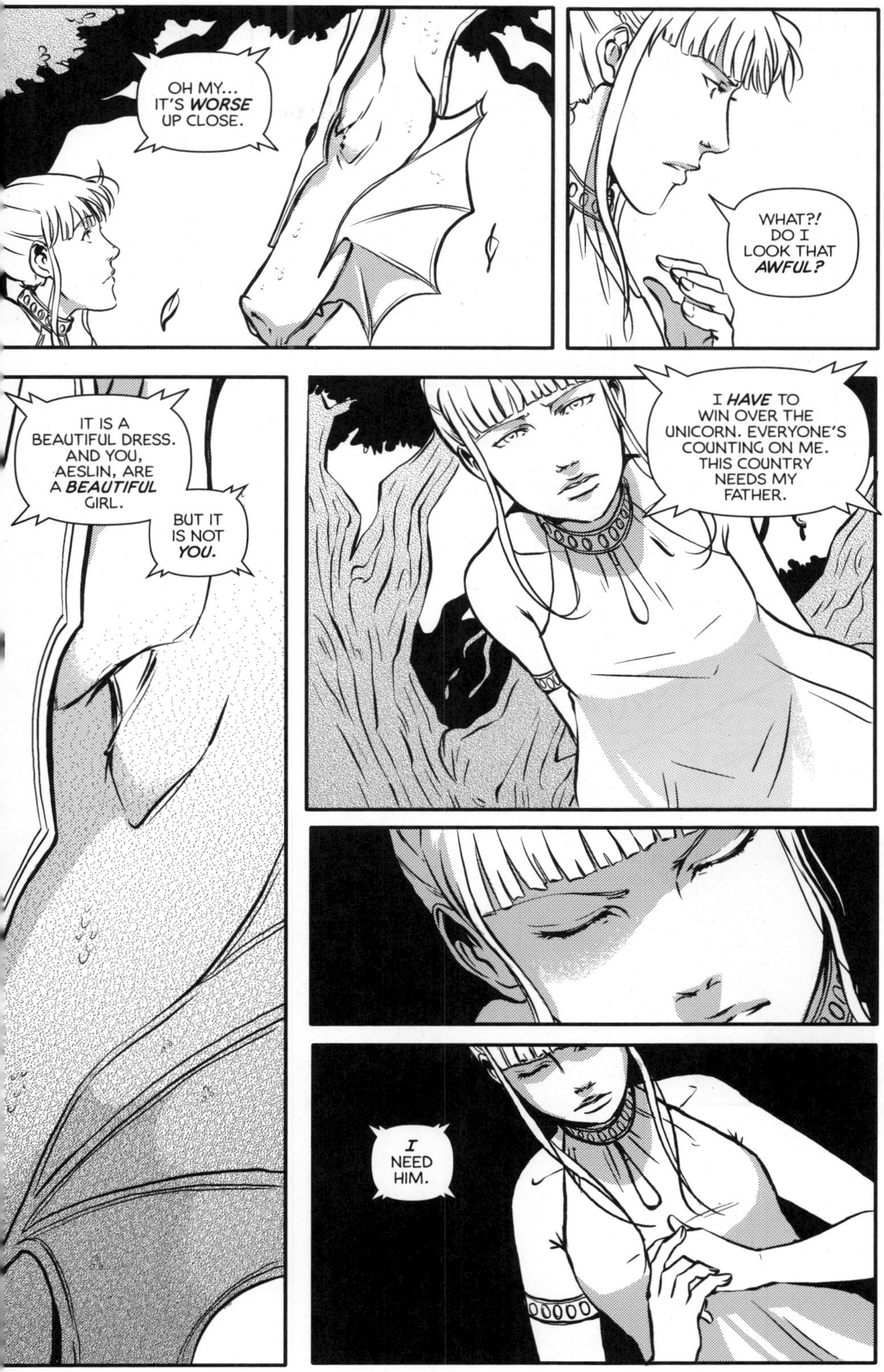
OH MY... IT'S WORSE UP CLOSE.
WHAT?! DO I LOOK THAT AWFUL?
IT IS A BEAUTIFUL DRESS. AND YOU, AESLIN, ARE A BEAUTIFUL GIRL.
BUT IT IS NOT YOU.
I HAVE TO WIN OVER THE UNICORN. EVERYONE'S COUNTING ON ME. THIS COUNTRY NEEDS MY FATHER.
I NEED HIM.

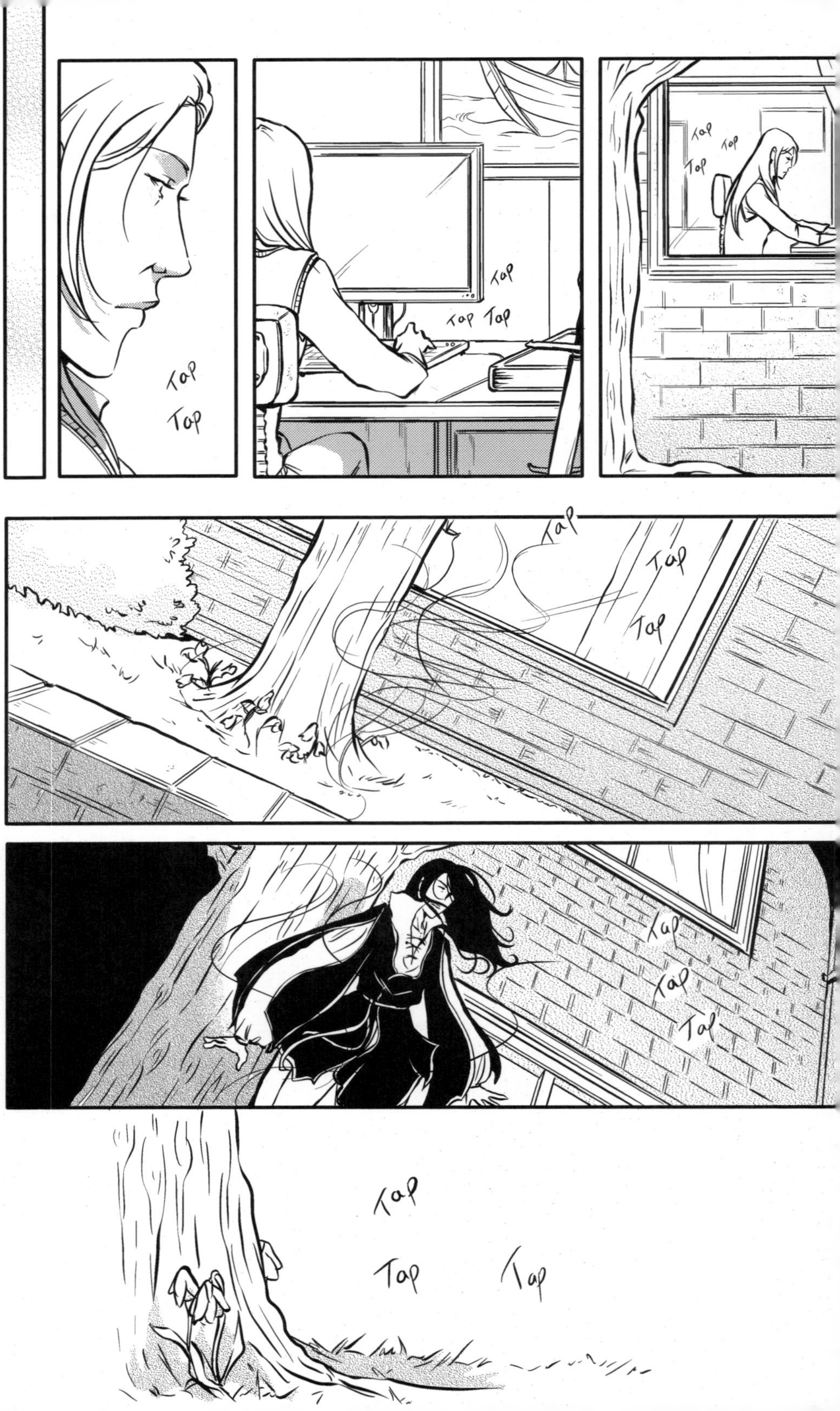
Tap
Tap
Tap
Tap
Tap
Tap
Tap
Tap
Tap
Tap
Tap
Tap
Tap
Tap
Tap
Tap
Tap

YOU LOOK MAGNIFICENT.
I LOOK LIKE AN IDIOT.
NO ARGUMENT FROM ME.
PRINCESS AESLIN...
...IT'S TIME.

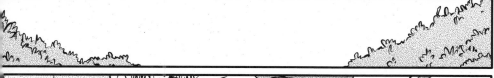

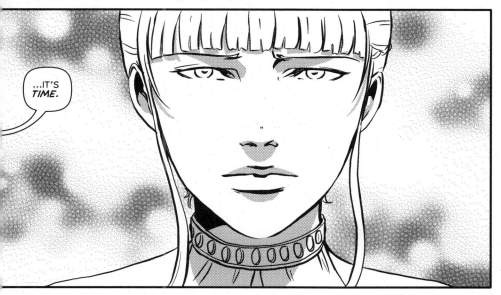

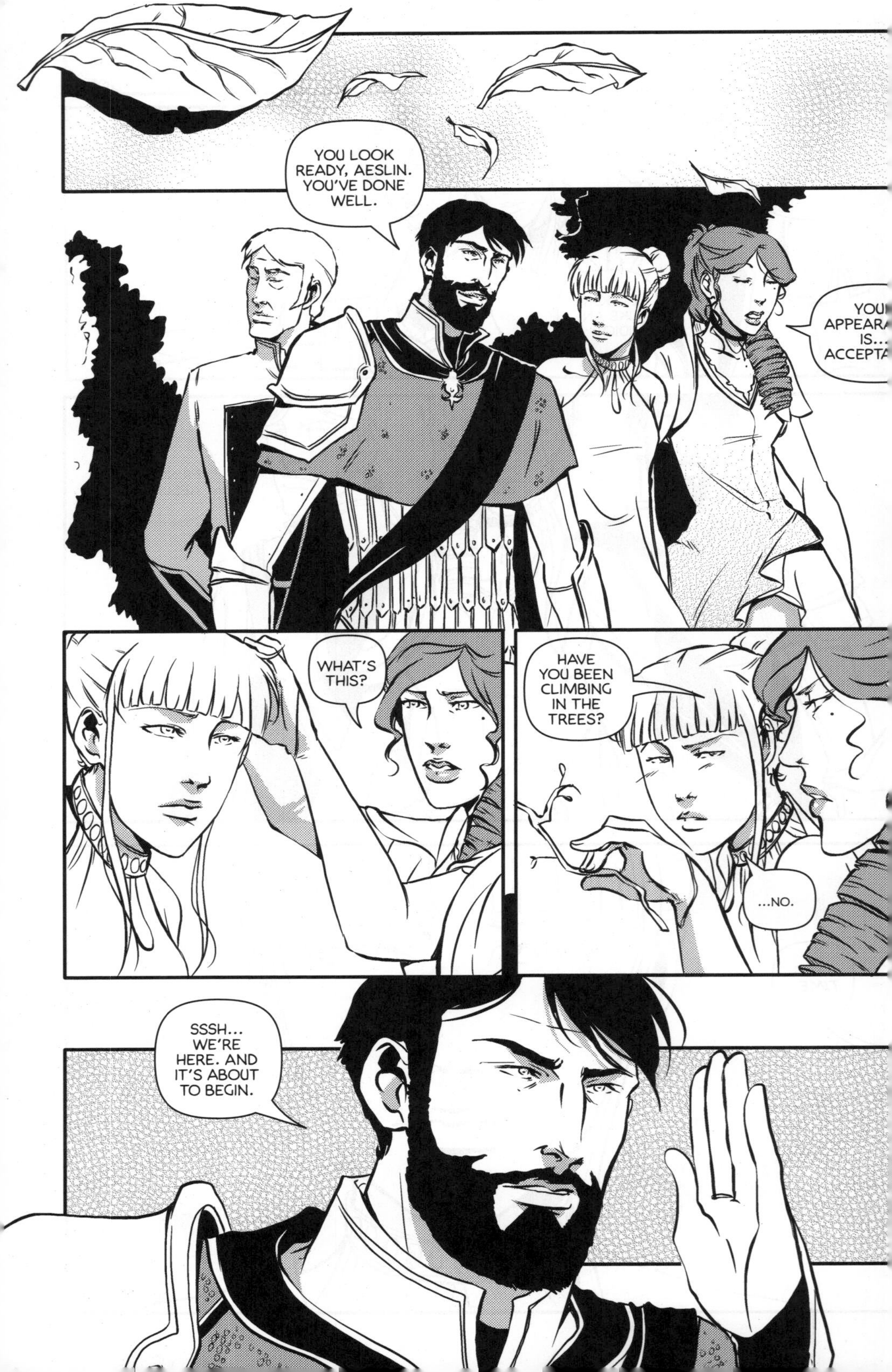
YOU LOOK READY, AESLIN. YOU'VE DONE WELL.
YOUR APPEARA IS... ACCEPTA
WHAT'S THIS?
HAVE YOU BEEN CLIMBING IN THE TREES?
...NO.
SSSH... WE'RE HERE. AND IT'S ABOUT TO BEGIN.

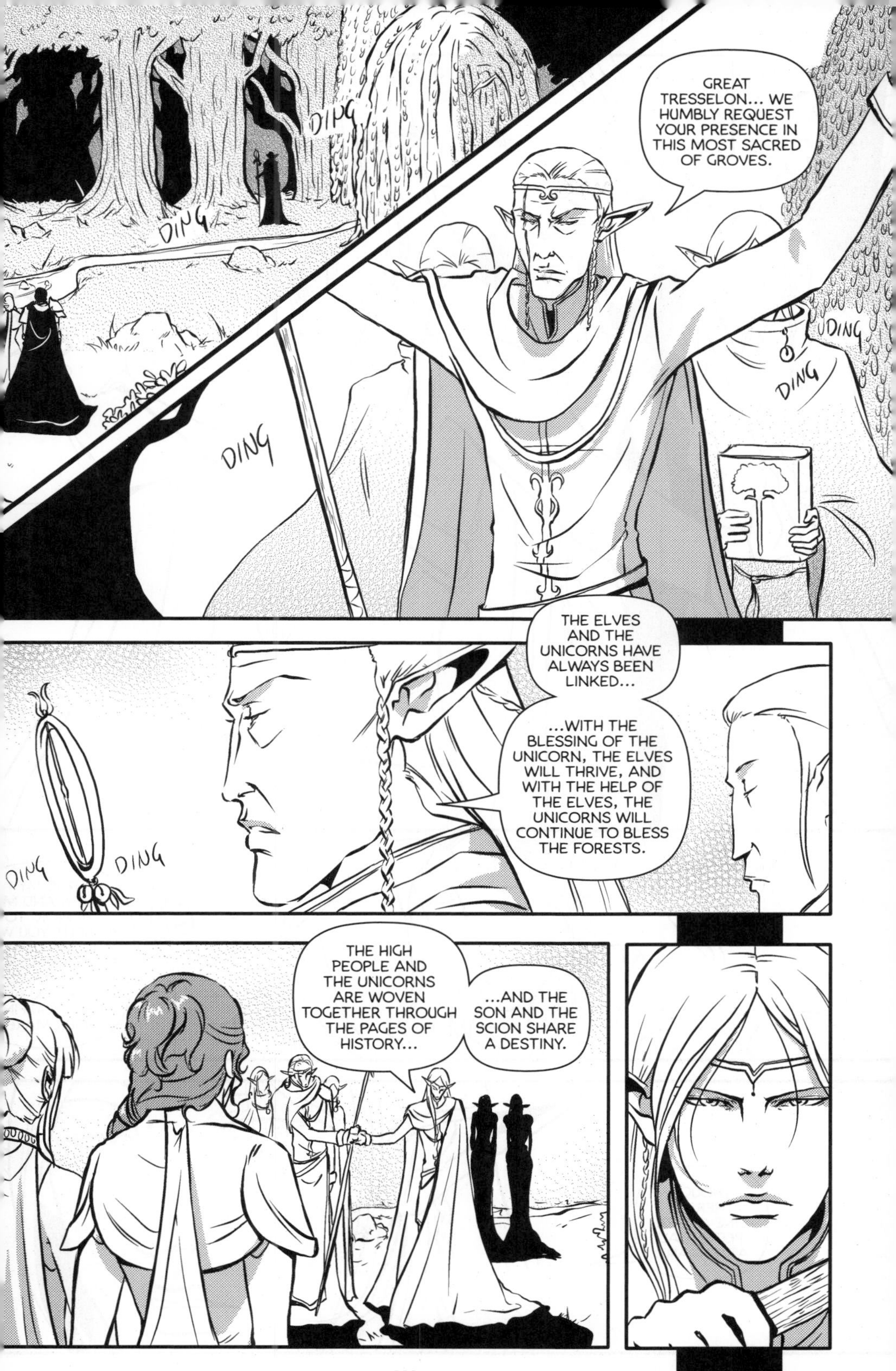
DING
DING
GREAT TRESSELON... WE HUMBLY REQUEST YOUR PRESENCE IN THIS MOST SACRED OF GROVES.
DING
DING
DING
THE ELVES AND THE UNICORNS HAVE ALWAYS BEEN LINKED...
...WITH THE BLESSING OF THE UNICORN, THE ELVES WILL THRIVE, AND WITH THE HELP OF THE ELVES, THE UNICORNS WILL CONTINUE TO BLESS THE FORESTS.
DING
DING
THE HIGH PEOPLE AND THE UNICORNS ARE WOVEN TOGETHER THROUGH THE PAGES OF HISTORY...
...AND THE SON AND THE SCION SHARE A DESTINY.

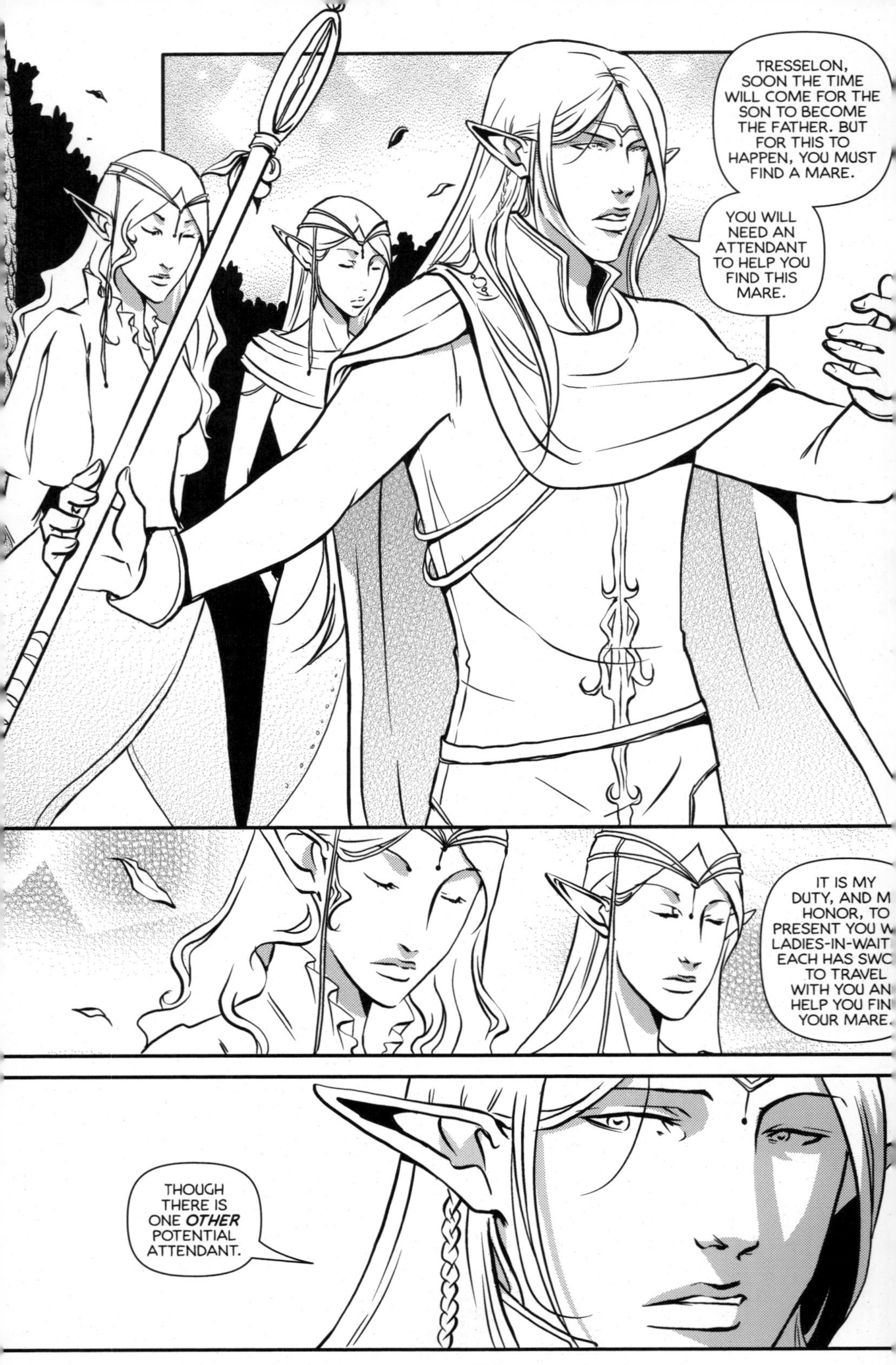
TRESSELON, SOON THE TIME WILL COME FOR THE SON TO BECOME THE FATHER. BUT FOR THIS TO HAPPEN, YOU MUST FIND A MARE.
YOU WILL NEED AN ATTENDANT TO HELP YOU FIND THIS MARE.
IT IS MY DUTY, AND M HONOR, TO PRESENT YOU W LADIES-IN-WAIT EACH HAS SWO TO TRAVEL WITH YOU AN HELP YOU FIN YOUR MARE.
THOUGH THERE IS ONE *OTHER* POTENTIAL ATTENDANT.

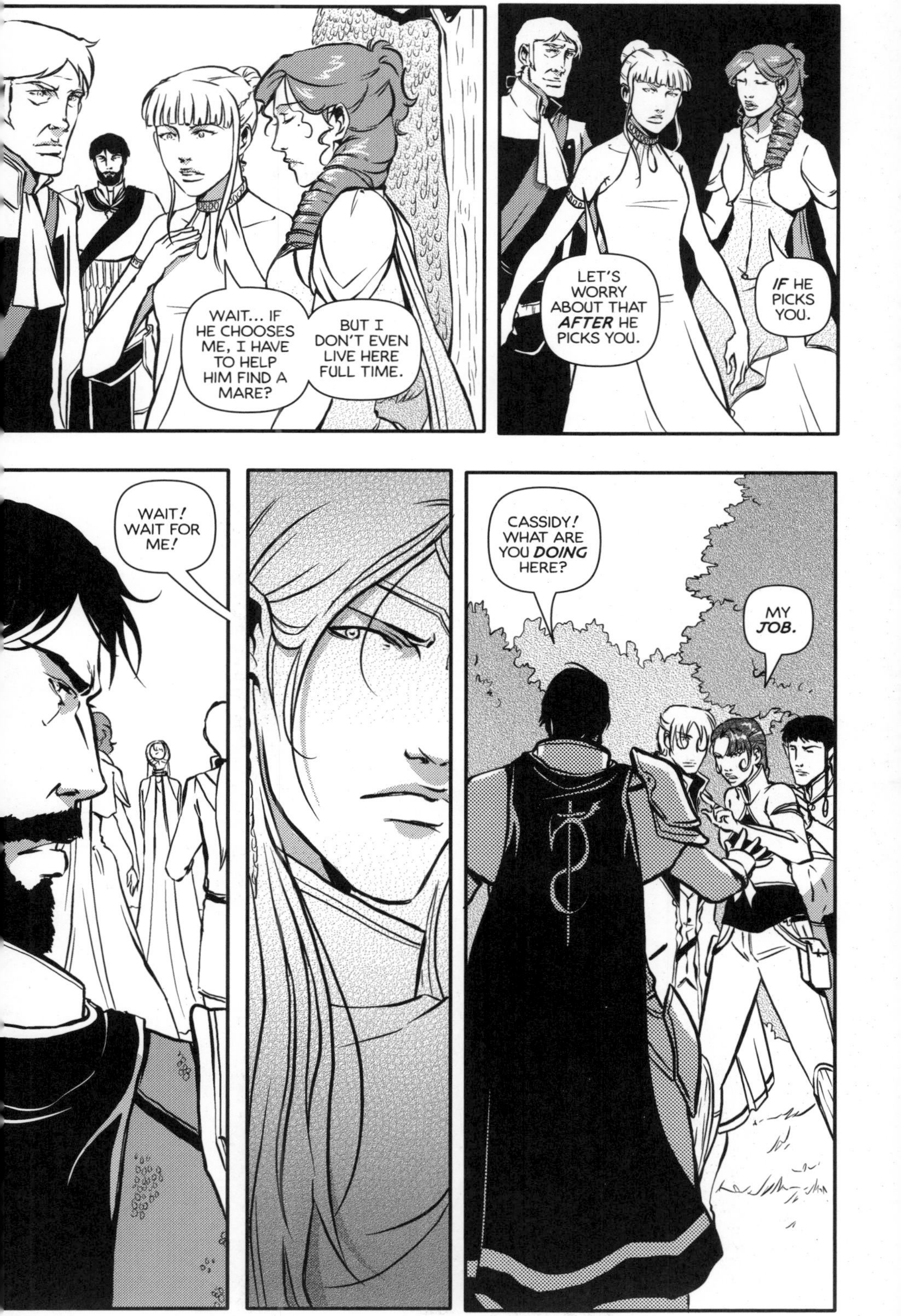
WAIT... IF HE CHOOSES ME, I HAVE TO HELP HIM FIND A MARE?
BUT I DON'T EVEN LIVE HERE FULL TIME.
LET'S WORRY ABOUT THAT AFTER HE PICKS YOU.
IF HE PICKS YOU.
WAIT! WAIT FOR ME!
CASSIDY! WHAT ARE YOU DOING HERE?
MY JOB.

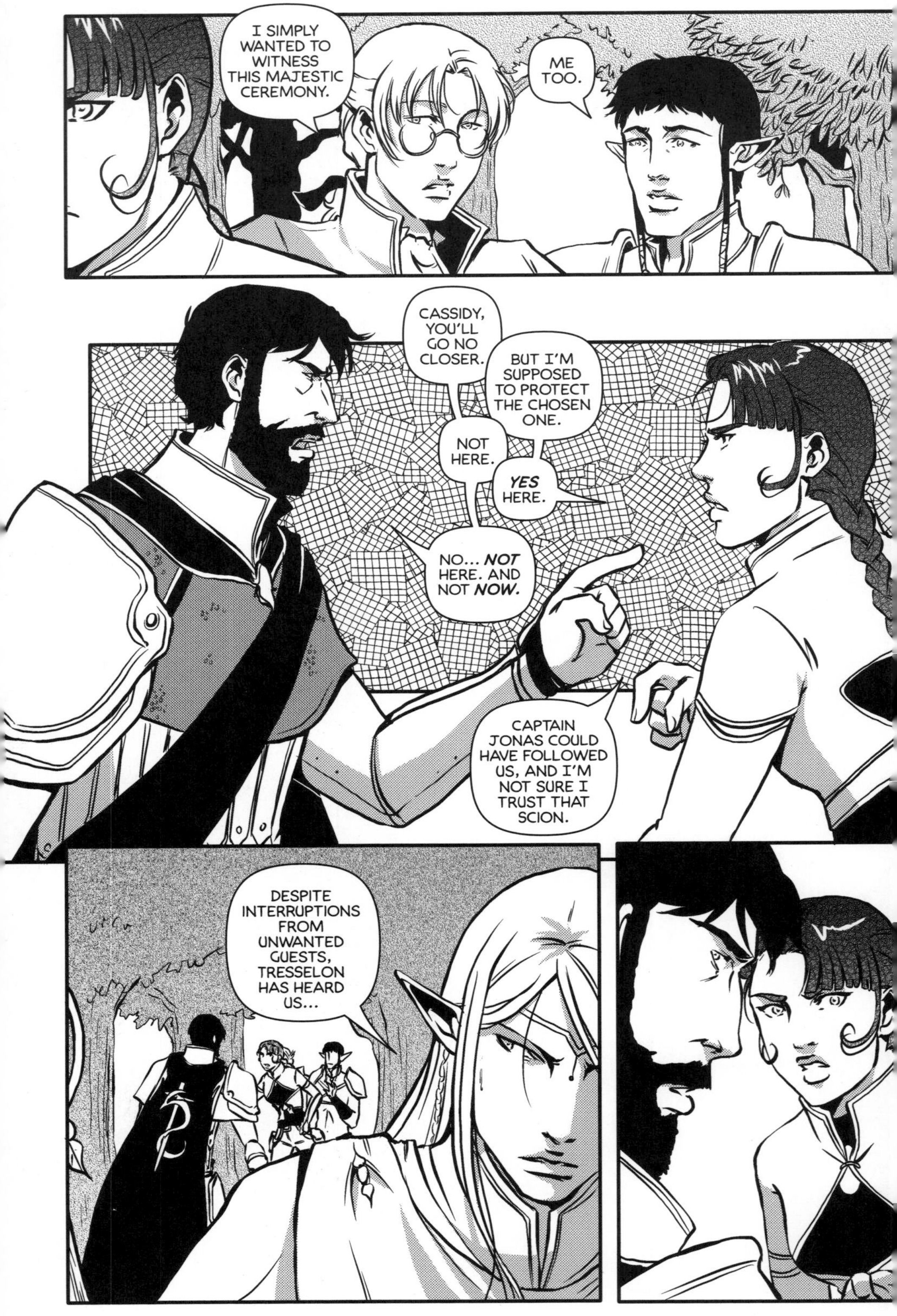
I SIMPLY WANTED TO WITNESS THIS MAJESTIC CEREMONY.
ME TOO.
CASSIDY, YOU'LL GO NO CLOSER.
BUT I'M SUPPOSED TO PROTECT THE CHOSEN ONE.
NOT HERE.
YES HERE.
NO... *NOT* HERE. AND NOT *NOW.*
CAPTAIN JONAS COULD HAVE FOLLOWED US, AND I'M NOT SURE I TRUST THAT SCION.
DESPITE INTERRUPTIONS FROM UNWANTED GUESTS, TRESSELON HAS HEARD US...

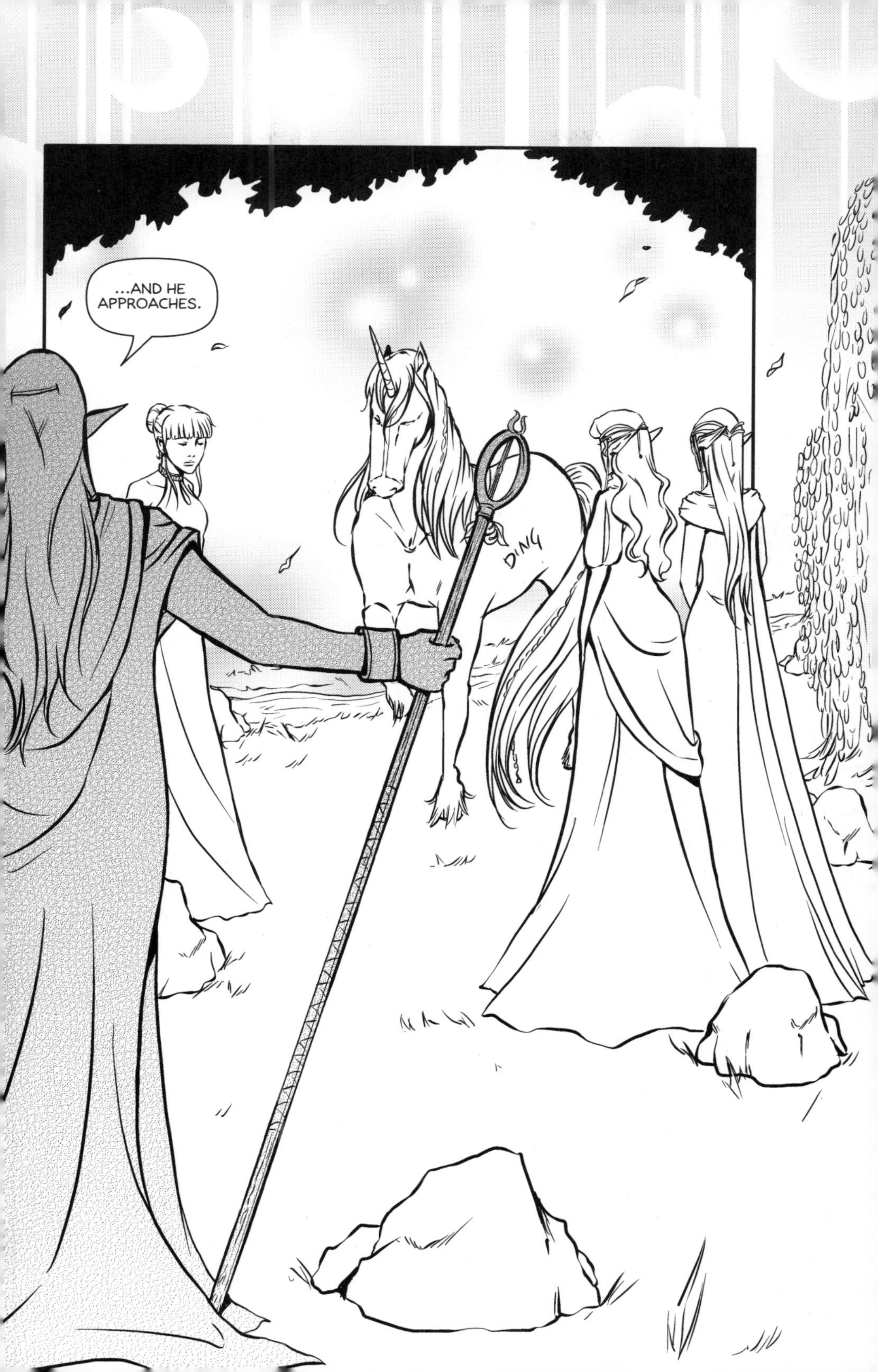
...AND HE APPROACHES.
DING

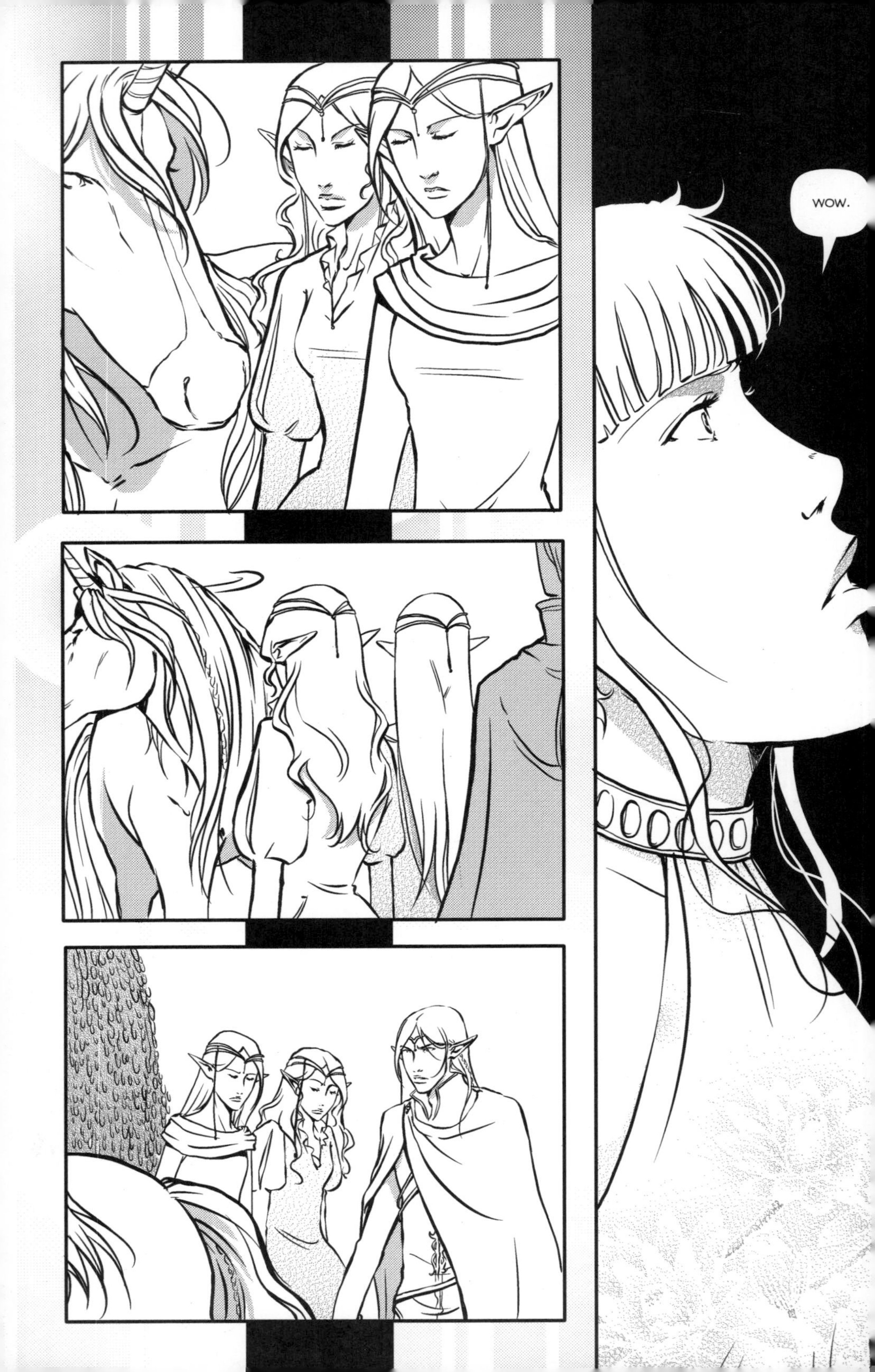
WOW.

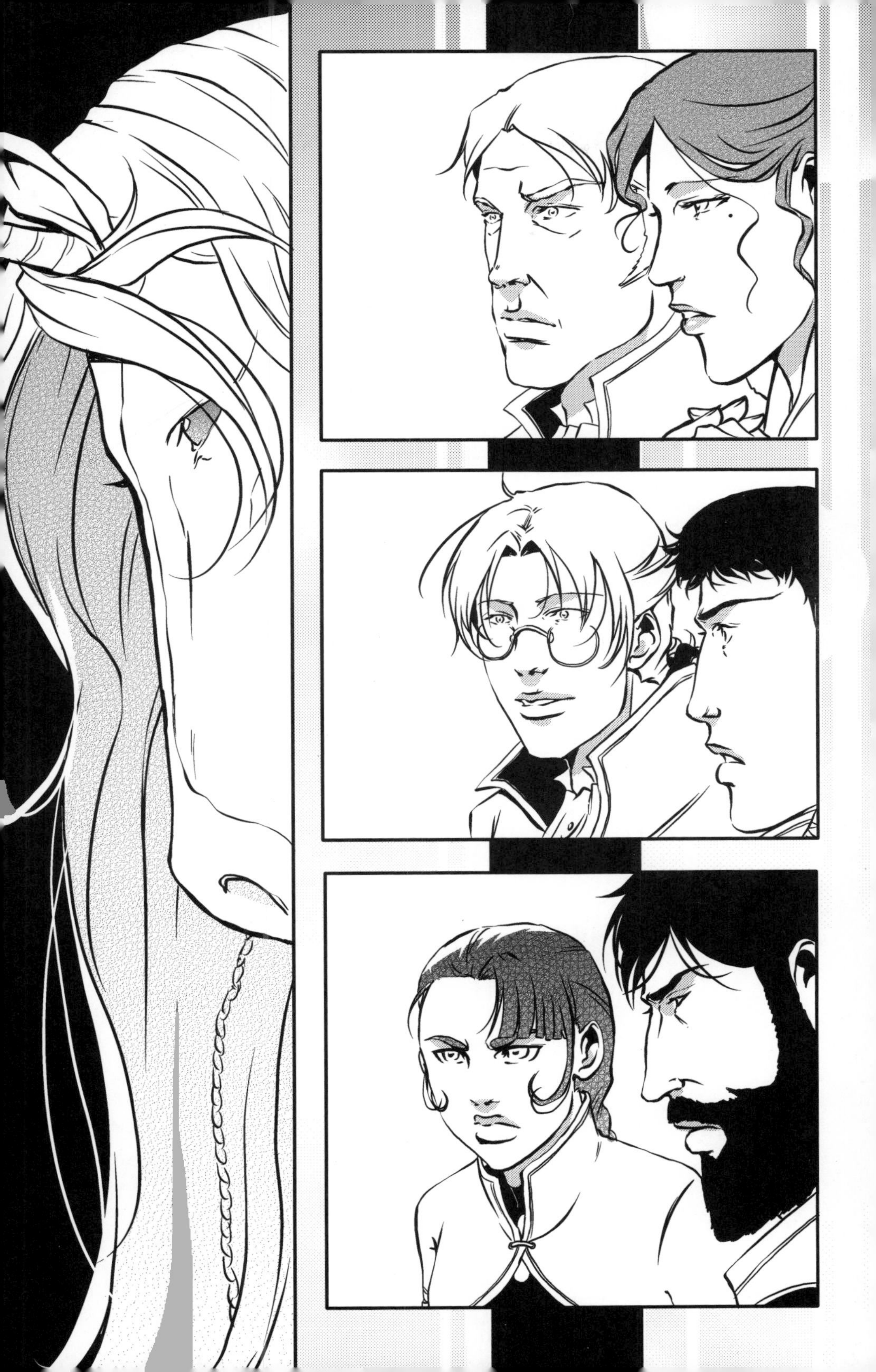

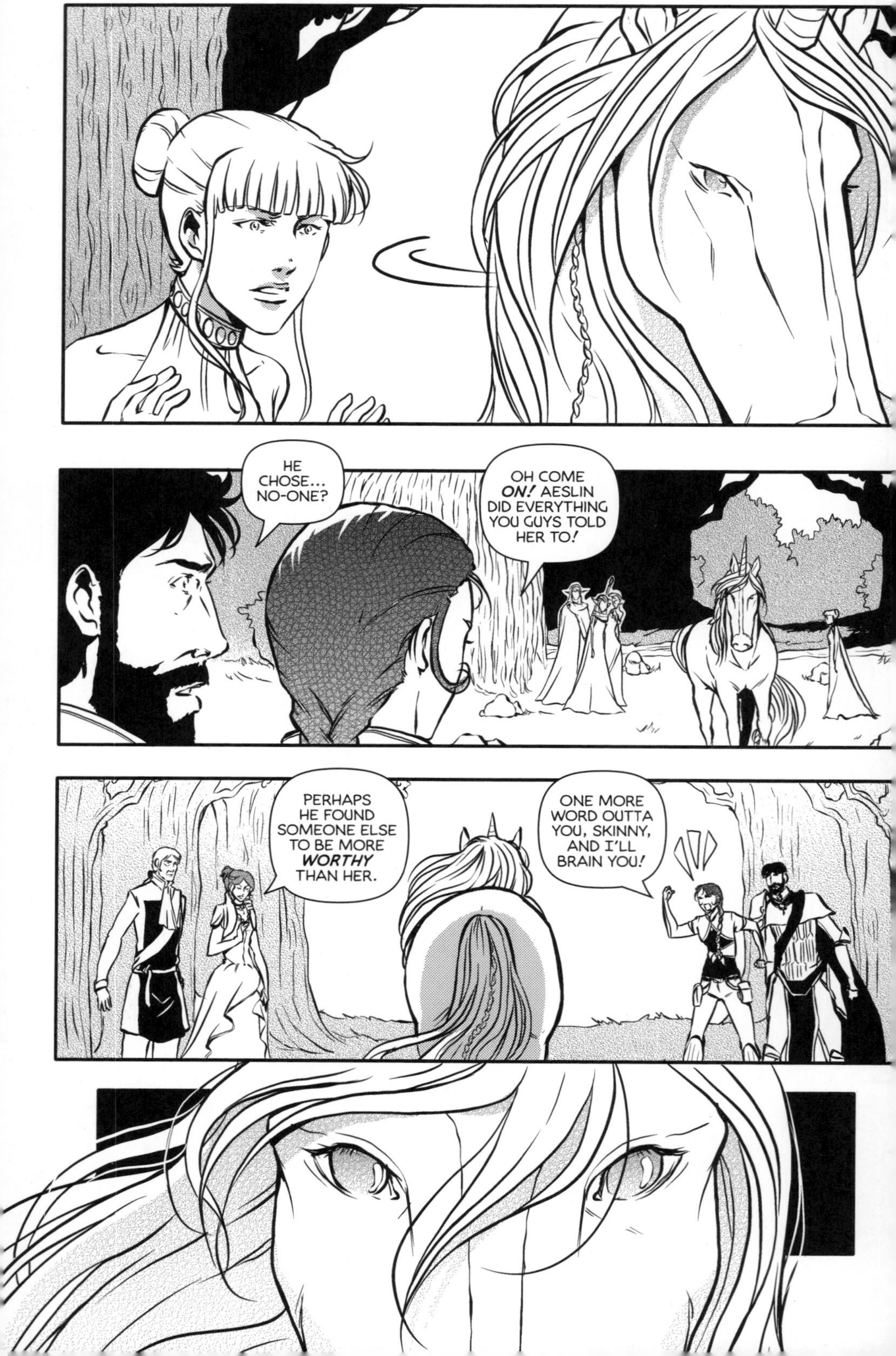
HE CHOSE... NO-ONE?
OH COME *ON!* AESLIN DID EVERYTHING YOU GUYS TOLD HER TO!
PERHAPS HE FOUND SOMEONE ELSE TO BE MORE *WORTHY* THAN HER.
ONE MORE WORD OUTTA YOU, SKINNY, AND I'LL BRAIN YOU!

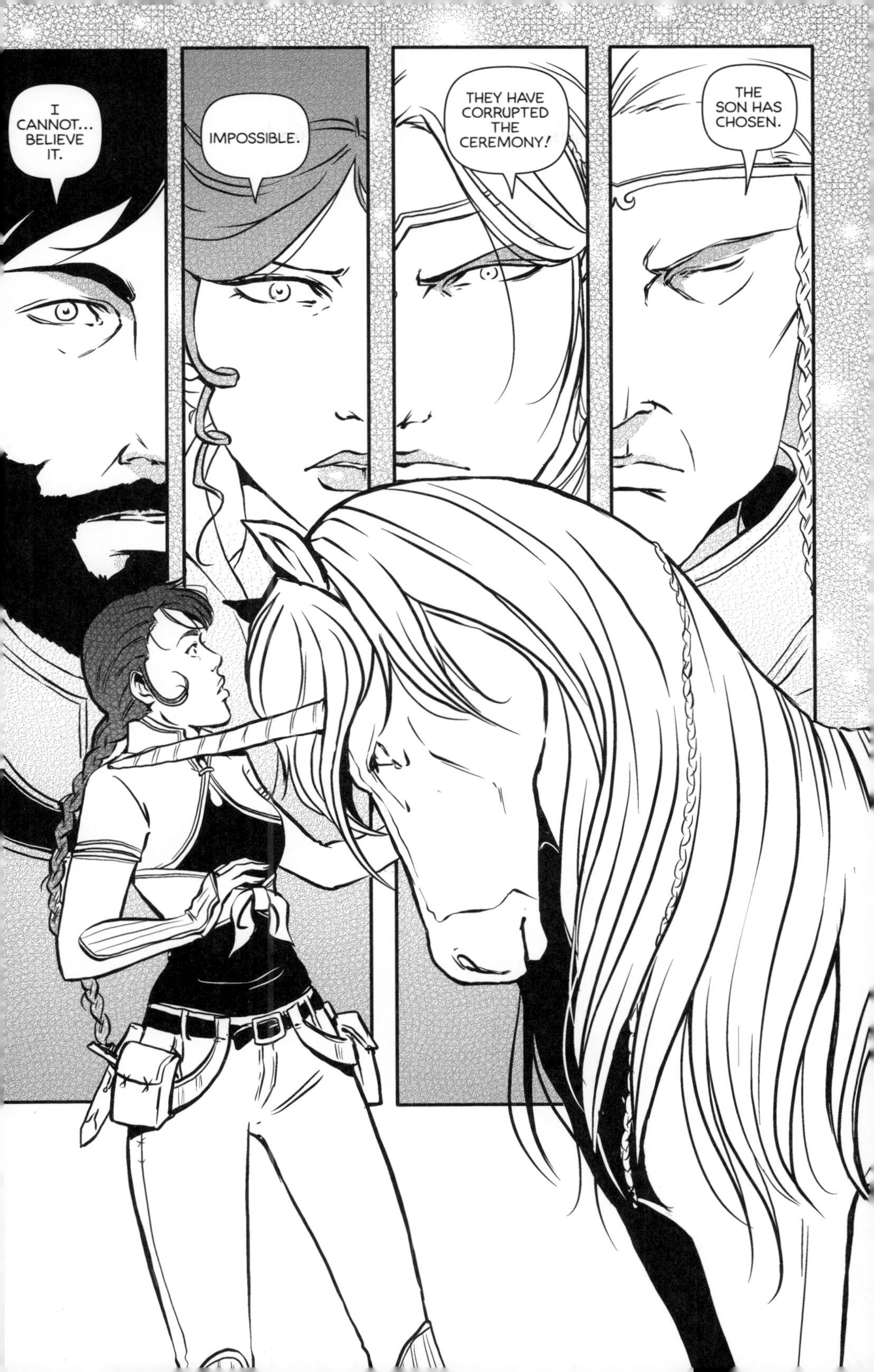
I CANNOT... BELIEVE IT.
IMPOSSIBLE.
THEY HAVE CORRUPTED THE CEREMONY!
THE SON HAS CHOSEN.

Chapter 5

THE BATTLE OF WOOD CREEK

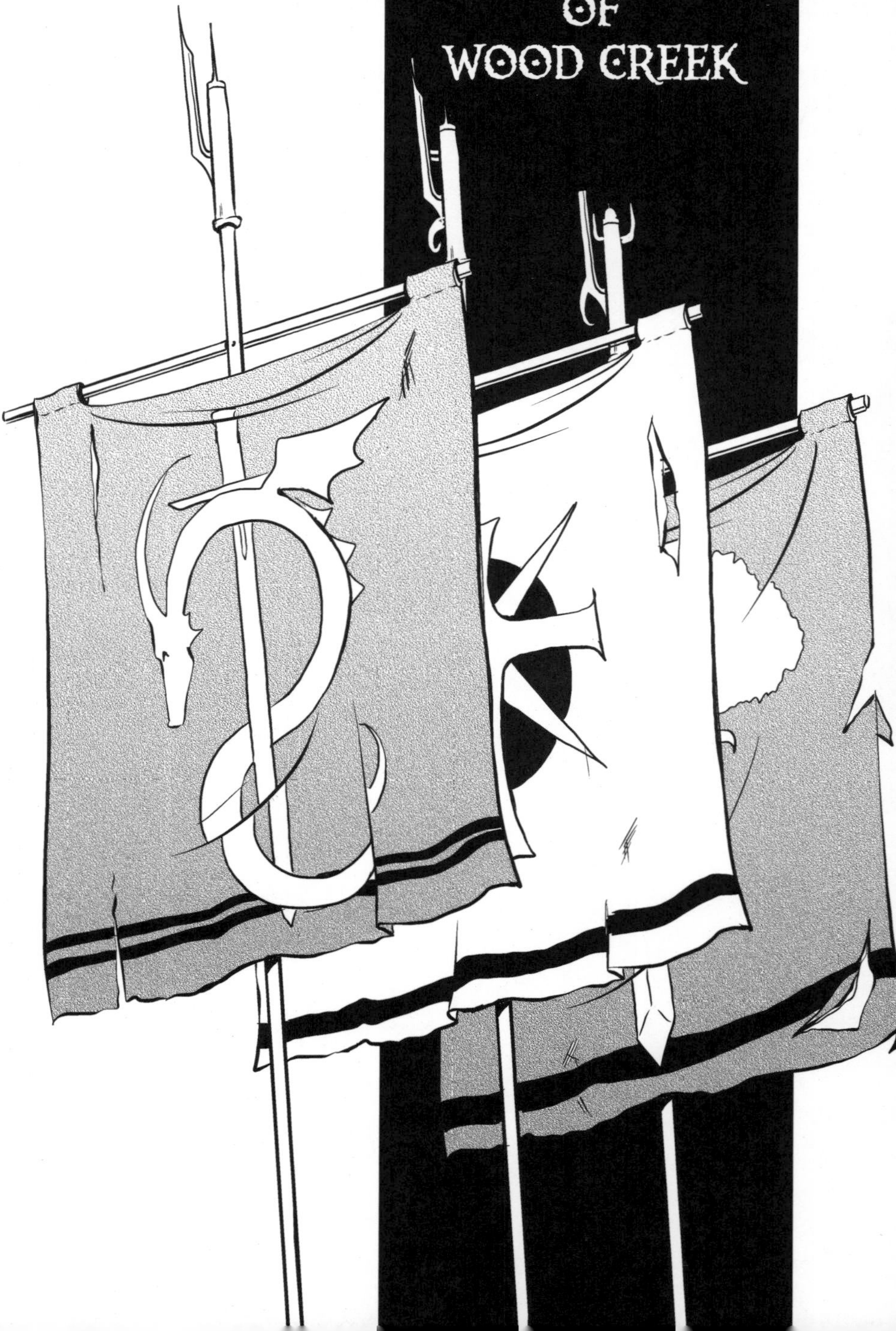

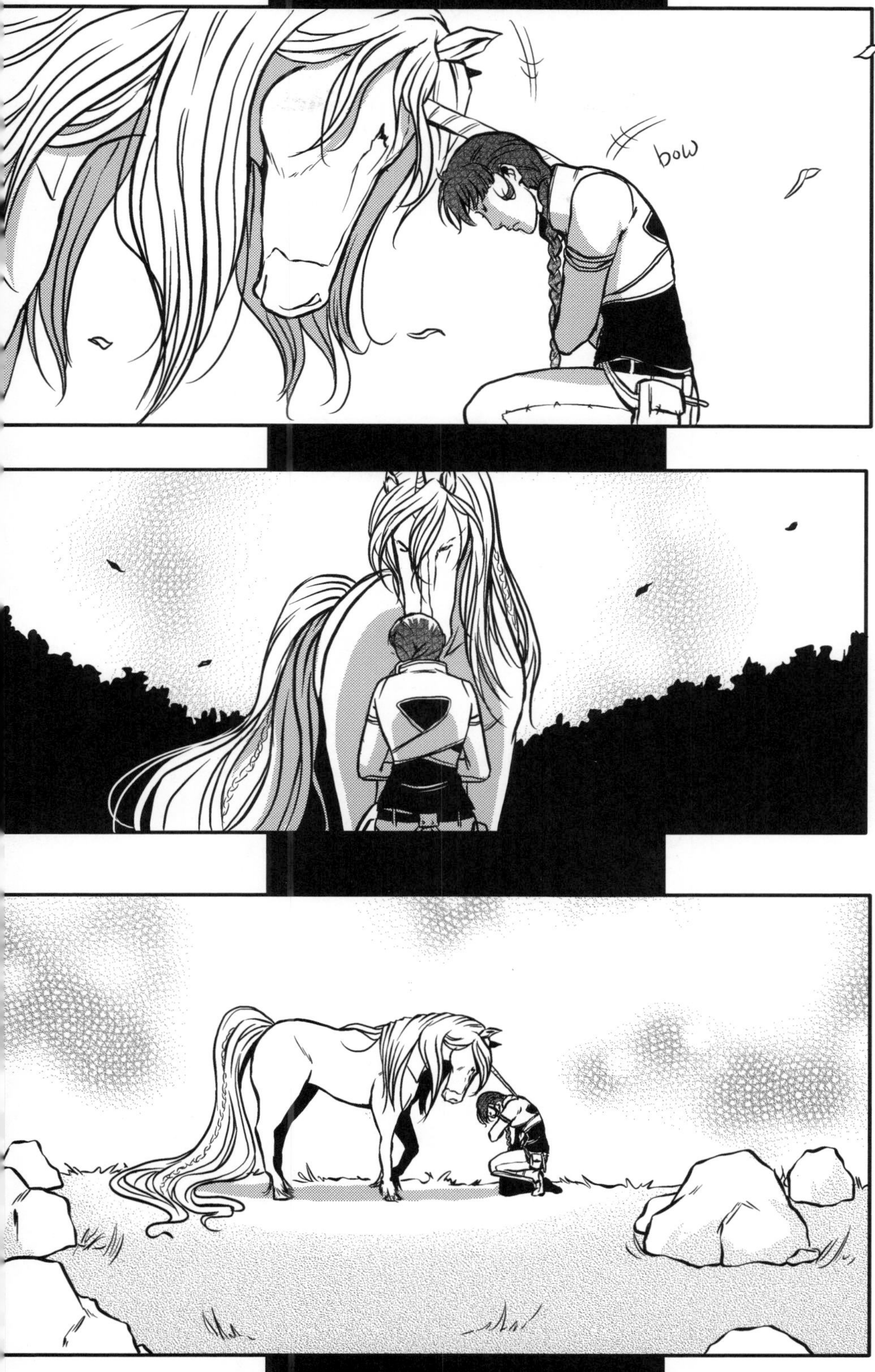
bow

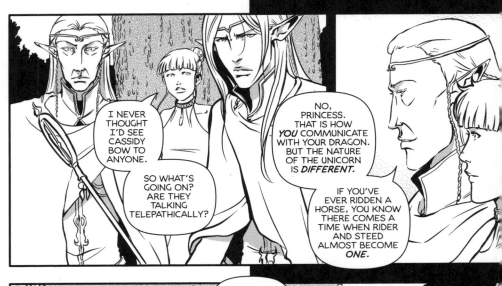

I NEVER THOUGHT I'D SEE CASSIDY BOW TO ANYONE.

SO WHAT'S GOING ON? ARE THEY TALKING TELEPATHICALLY?

NO, PRINCESS. THAT IS HOW *YOU* COMMUNICATE WITH YOUR DRAGON. BUT THE NATURE OF THE UNICORN IS *DIFFERENT*.

IF YOU'VE EVER RIDDEN A HORSE, YOU KNOW THERE COMES A TIME WHEN RIDER AND STEED ALMOST BECOME *ONE*.

I'M NOT A VERY GOOD RIDER. BUT MY MOM SAID IT WOULD HAPPEN WITH BLUE MOON.

I HAVE NO DOUBT. BUT IT IS *AIDED* BY YOU BEING ABLE TO DIRECTLY COMMUNICATE.

WITH THE RAREST OF HORSES AND *ESPECIALLY* WITH A UNICORN, IT'S SIMPLY A MATTER OF EACH *FEELING* WHAT THE OTHER WANTS.

YOUR FRIEND CASSIDY AND THE SACRED TRESSELON NOW SHARE THIS *BOND*.

BLASPHEMY*!*

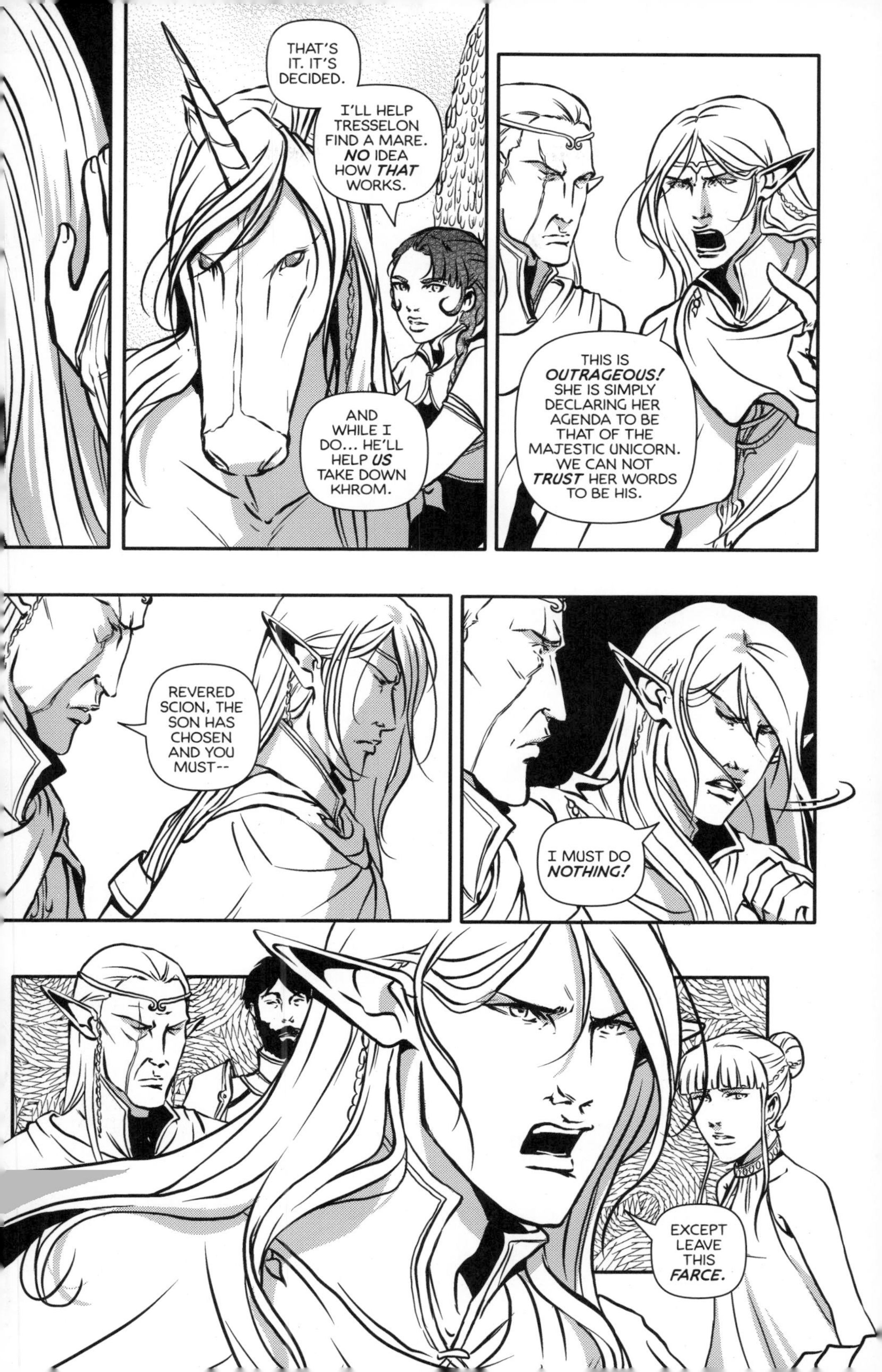
THAT'S IT. IT'S DECIDED.
I'LL HELP TRESSELON FIND A MARE. NO IDEA HOW THAT WORKS.
AND WHILE I DO... HE'LL HELP US TAKE DOWN KHROM.
THIS IS OUTRAGEOUS! SHE IS SIMPLY DECLARING HER AGENDA TO BE THAT OF THE MAJESTIC UNICORN. WE CAN NOT TRUST HER WORDS TO BE HIS.
REVERED SCION, THE SON HAS CHOSEN AND YOU MUST--
I MUST DO NOTHING!
EXCEPT LEAVE THIS FARCE.

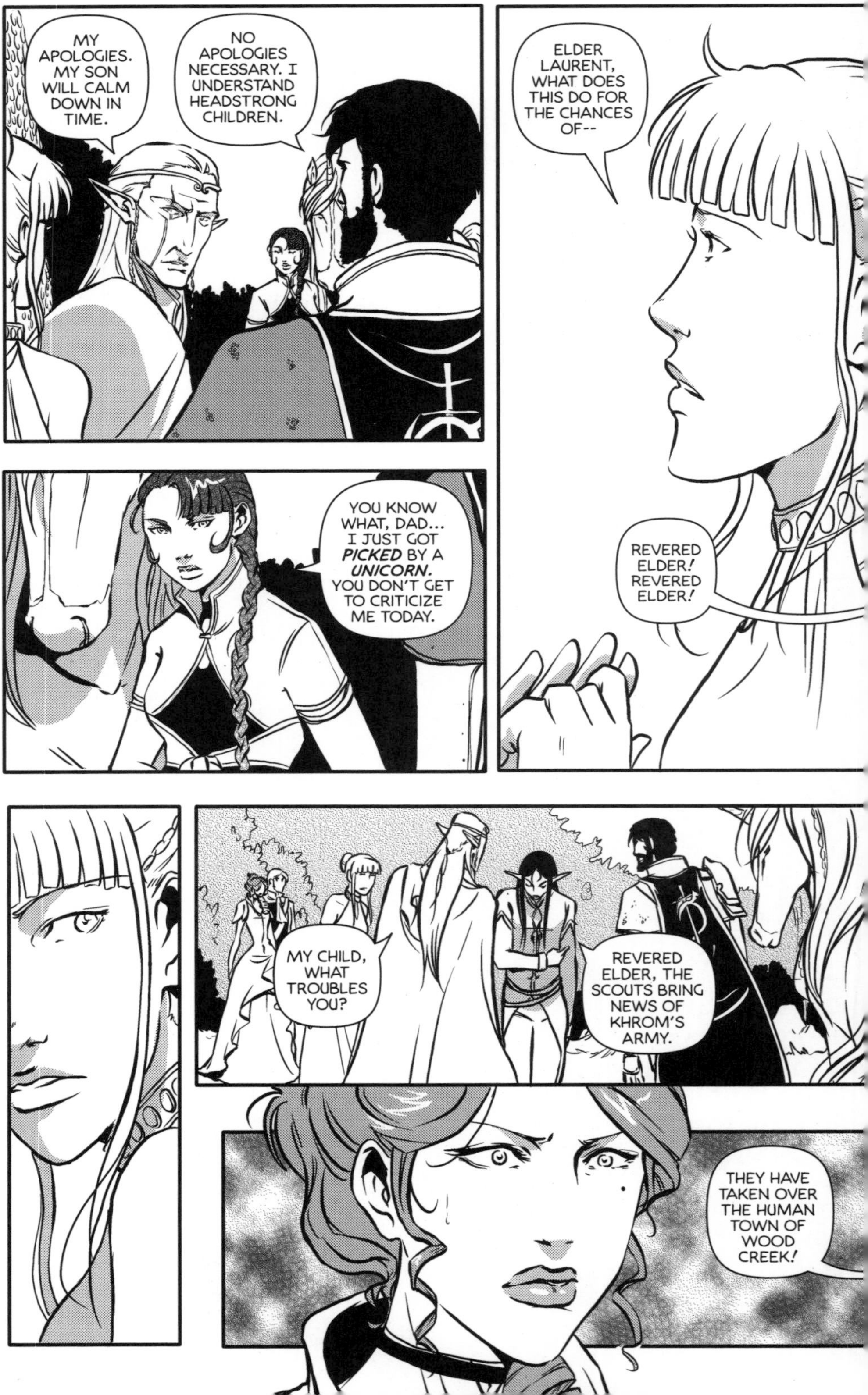

MY APOLOGIES. MY SON WILL CALM DOWN IN TIME.
NO APOLOGIES NECESSARY. I UNDERSTAND HEADSTRONG CHILDREN.
YOU KNOW WHAT, DAD... I JUST GOT *PICKED* BY A *UNICORN.* YOU DON'T GET TO CRITICIZE ME TODAY.
ELDER LAURENT, WHAT DOES THIS DO FOR THE CHANCES OF--
REVERED ELDER! REVERED ELDER!
MY CHILD, WHAT TROUBLES YOU?
REVERED ELDER, THE SCOUTS BRING NEWS OF KHROM'S ARMY.
THEY HAVE TAKEN OVER THE HUMAN TOWN OF WOOD CREEK!

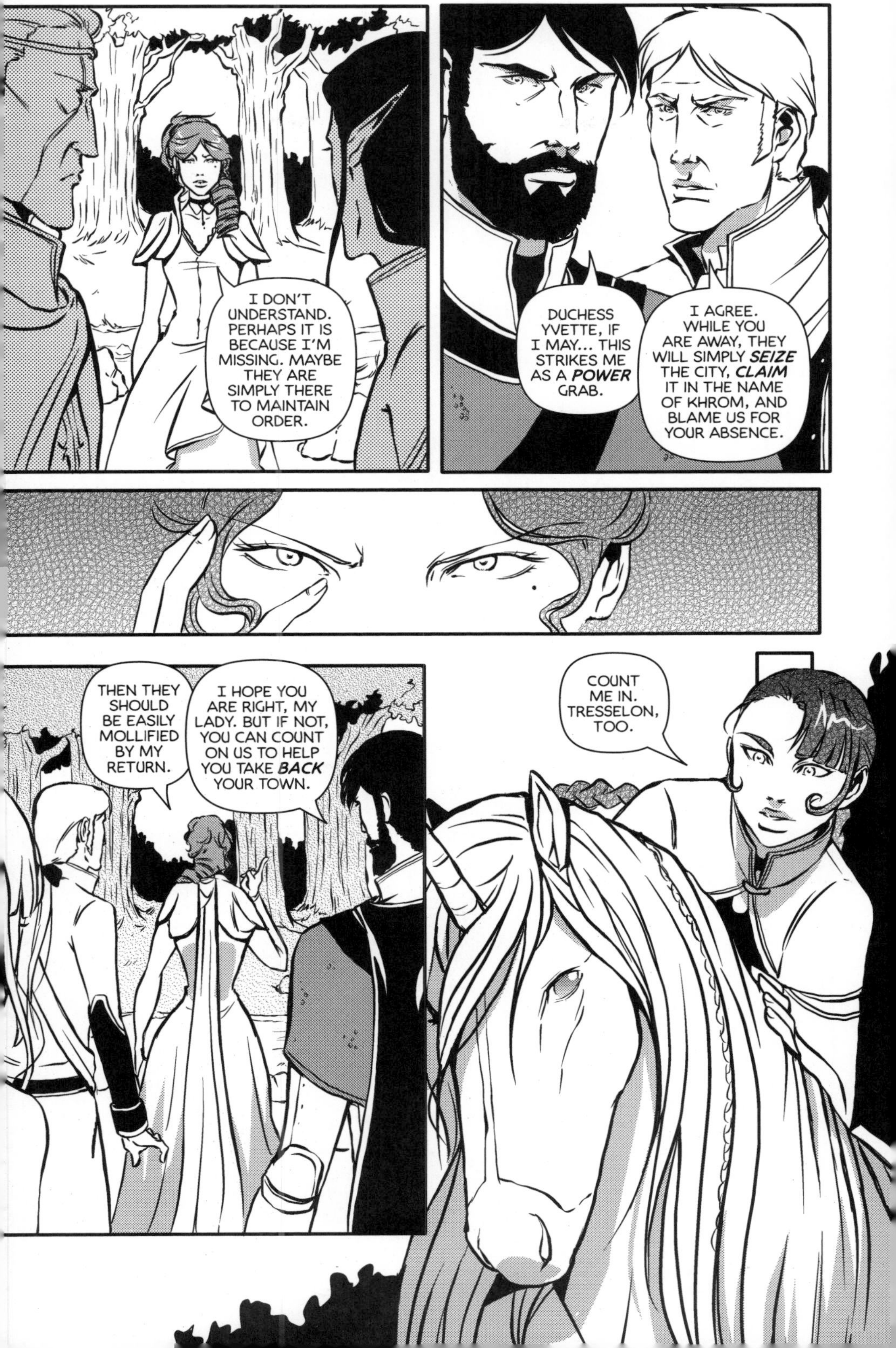
I DON'T UNDERSTAND. PERHAPS IT IS BECAUSE I'M MISSING. MAYBE THEY ARE SIMPLY THERE TO MAINTAIN ORDER.
DUCHESS YVETTE, IF I MAY... THIS STRIKES ME AS A POWER GRAB.
I AGREE. WHILE YOU ARE AWAY, THEY WILL SIMPLY SEIZE THE CITY, CLAIM IT IN THE NAME OF KHROM, AND BLAME US FOR YOUR ABSENCE.
THEN THEY SHOULD BE EASILY MOLLIFIED BY MY RETURN.
I HOPE YOU ARE RIGHT, MY LADY. BUT IF NOT, YOU CAN COUNT ON US TO HELP YOU TAKE BACK YOUR TOWN.
COUNT ME IN. TRESSELON, TOO.

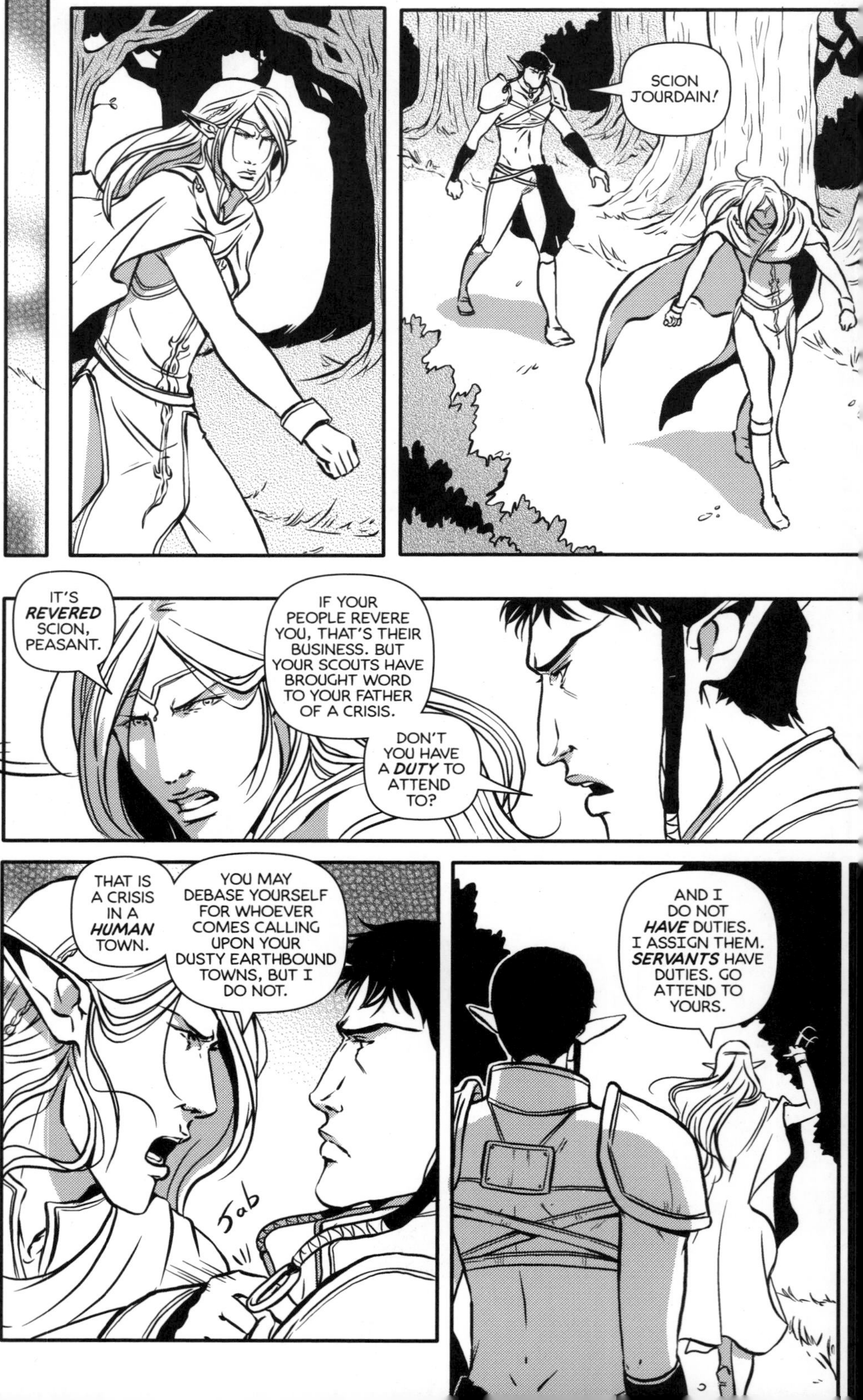
SCION JOURDAIN!
IT'S REVERED SCION, PEASANT.
IF YOUR PEOPLE REVERE YOU, THAT'S THEIR BUSINESS. BUT YOUR SCOUTS HAVE BROUGHT WORD TO YOUR FATHER OF A CRISIS.
DON'T YOU HAVE A DUTY TO ATTEND TO?
THAT IS A CRISIS IN A HUMAN TOWN.
YOU MAY DEBASE YOURSELF FOR WHOEVER COMES CALLING UPON YOUR DUSTY EARTHBOUND TOWNS, BUT I DO NOT.
JAB
AND I DO NOT HAVE DUTIES. I ASSIGN THEM. SERVANTS HAVE DUTIES. GO ATTEND TO YOURS.

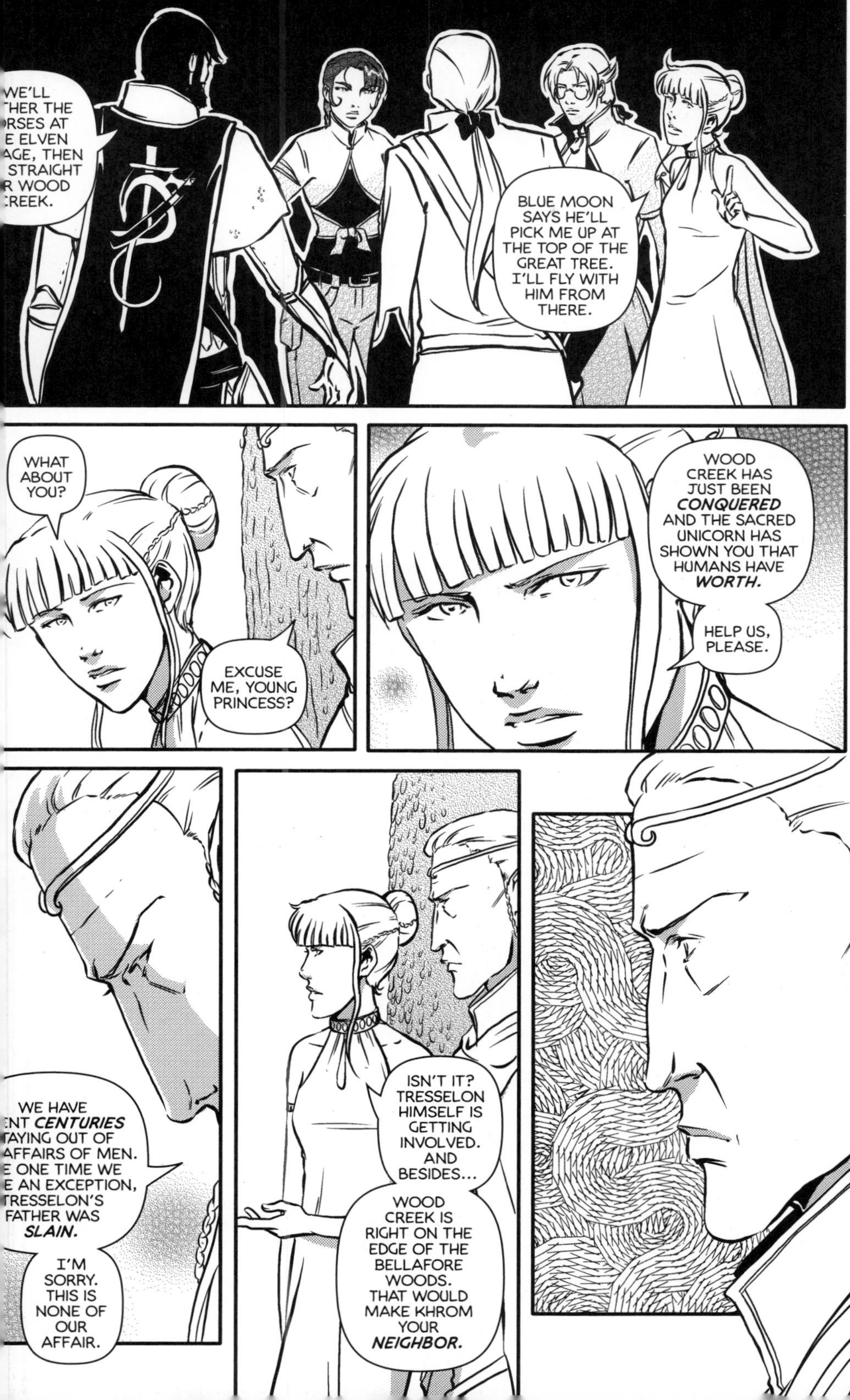
WE'LL THER THE ORSES AT E ELVEN AGE, THEN STRAIGHT R WOOD CREEK.
BLUE MOON SAYS HE'LL PICK ME UP AT THE TOP OF THE GREAT TREE. I'LL FLY WITH HIM FROM THERE.
WHAT ABOUT YOU?
EXCUSE ME, YOUNG PRINCESS?
WOOD CREEK HAS JUST BEEN ***CONQUERED*** AND THE SACRED UNICORN HAS SHOWN YOU THAT HUMANS HAVE ***WORTH.***
HELP US, PLEASE.
WE HAVE ENT ***CENTURIES*** TAYING OUT OF AFFAIRS OF MEN. E ONE TIME WE E AN EXCEPTION, TRESSELON'S FATHER WAS ***SLAIN.***
I'M SORRY. THIS IS NONE OF OUR AFFAIR.
ISN'T IT? TRESSELON HIMSELF IS GETTING INVOLVED. AND BESIDES...
WOOD CREEK IS RIGHT ON THE EDGE OF THE BELLAFORE WOODS. THAT WOULD MAKE KHROM YOUR ***NEIGHBOR.***

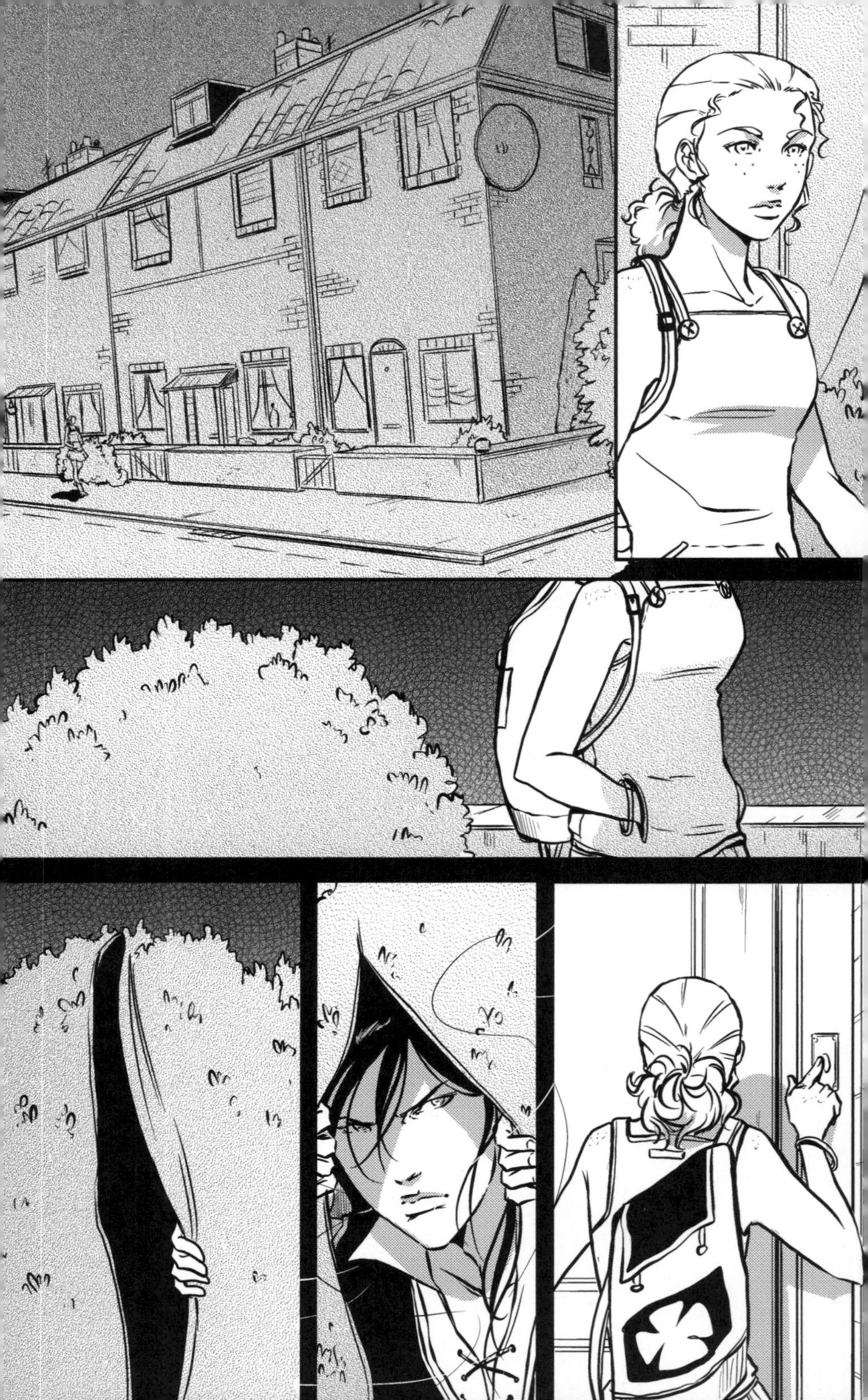

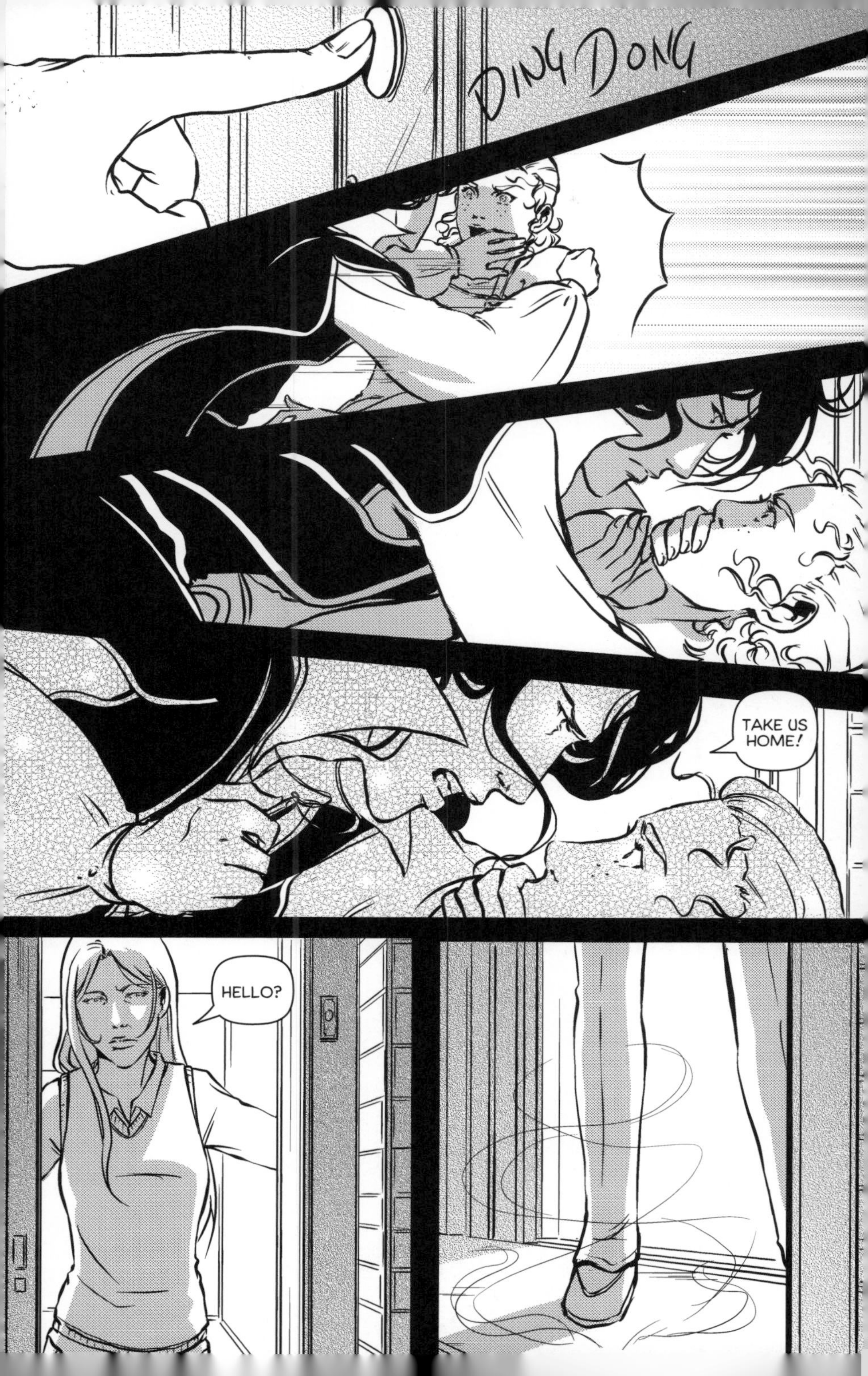
DING DONG
TAKE US HOME!
HELLO?

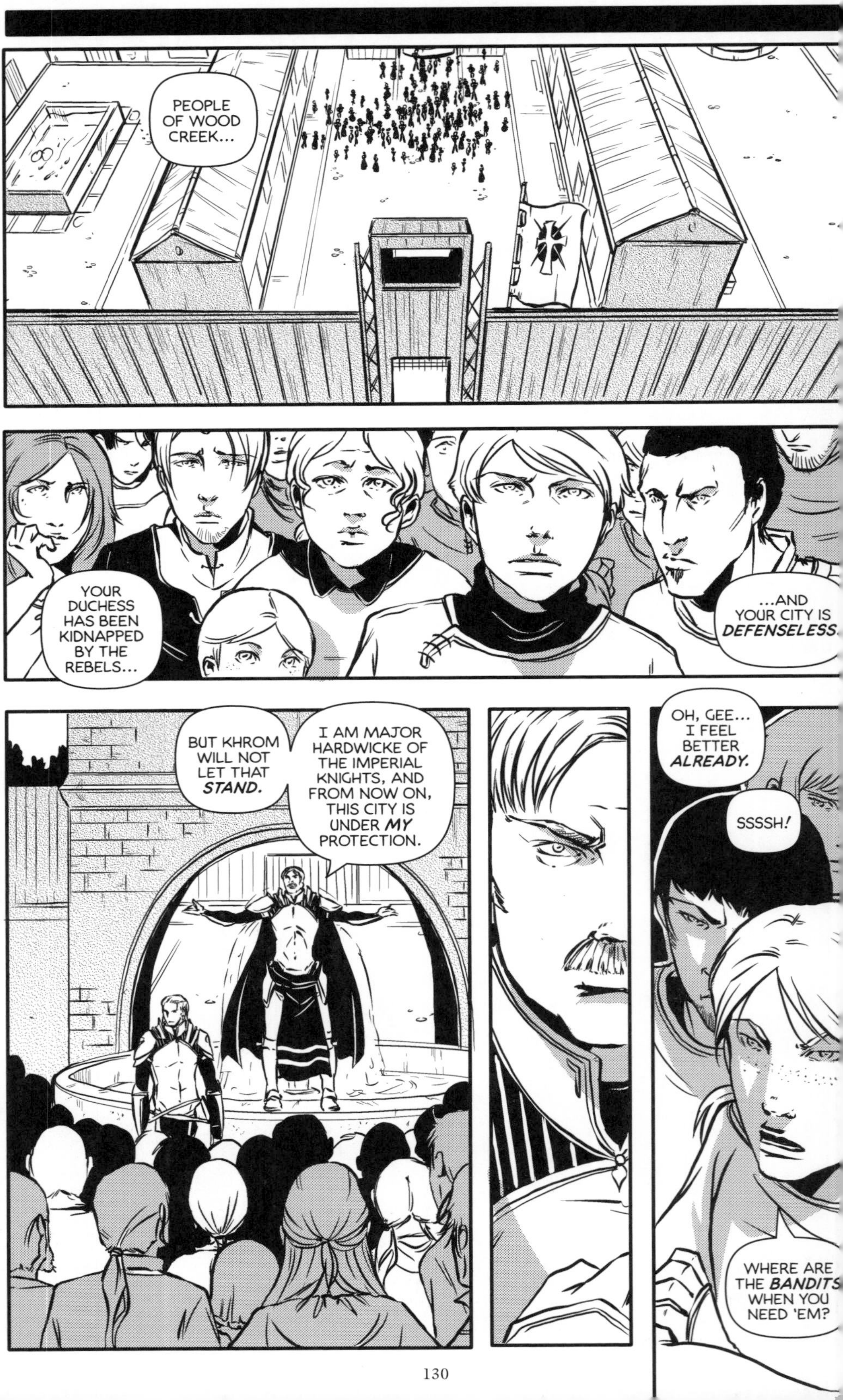
PEOPLE OF WOOD CREEK...
YOUR DUCHESS HAS BEEN KIDNAPPED BY THE REBELS...
...AND YOUR CITY IS DEFENSELESS.
BUT KHROM WILL NOT LET THAT STAND.
I AM MAJOR HARDWICKE OF THE IMPERIAL KNIGHTS, AND FROM NOW ON, THIS CITY IS UNDER MY PROTECTION.
OH, GEE... I FEEL BETTER ALREADY.
SSSSH!
WHERE ARE THE BANDITS WHEN YOU NEED 'EM?

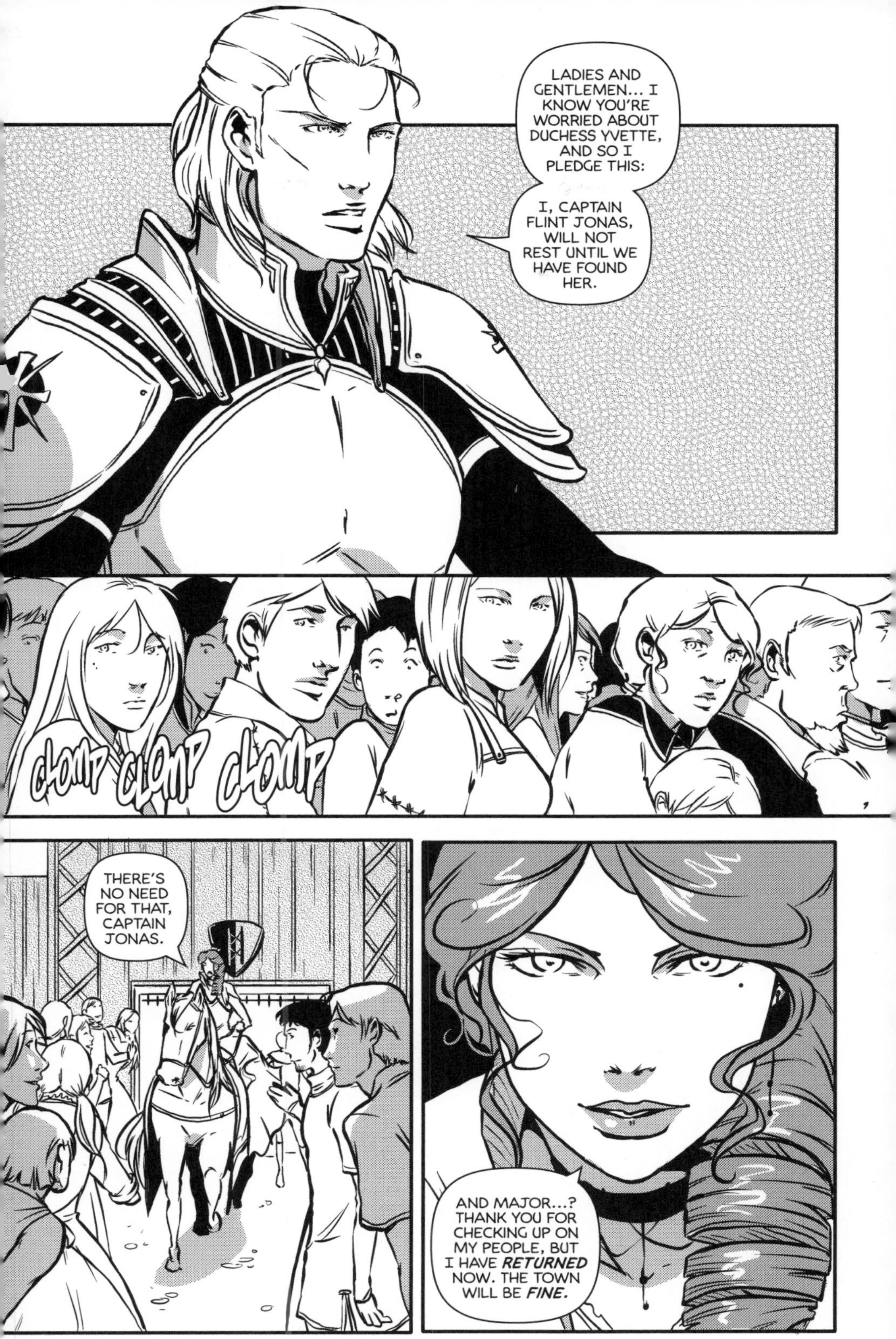
LADIES AND GENTLEMEN... I KNOW YOU'RE WORRIED ABOUT DUCHESS YVETTE, AND SO I PLEDGE THIS:
I, CAPTAIN FLINT JONAS, WILL NOT REST UNTIL WE HAVE FOUND HER.
CLOMP CLOMP CLOMP
THERE'S NO NEED FOR THAT, CAPTAIN JONAS.
AND MAJOR...? THANK YOU FOR CHECKING UP ON MY PEOPLE, BUT I HAVE ***RETURNED*** NOW. THE TOWN WILL BE ***FINE.***

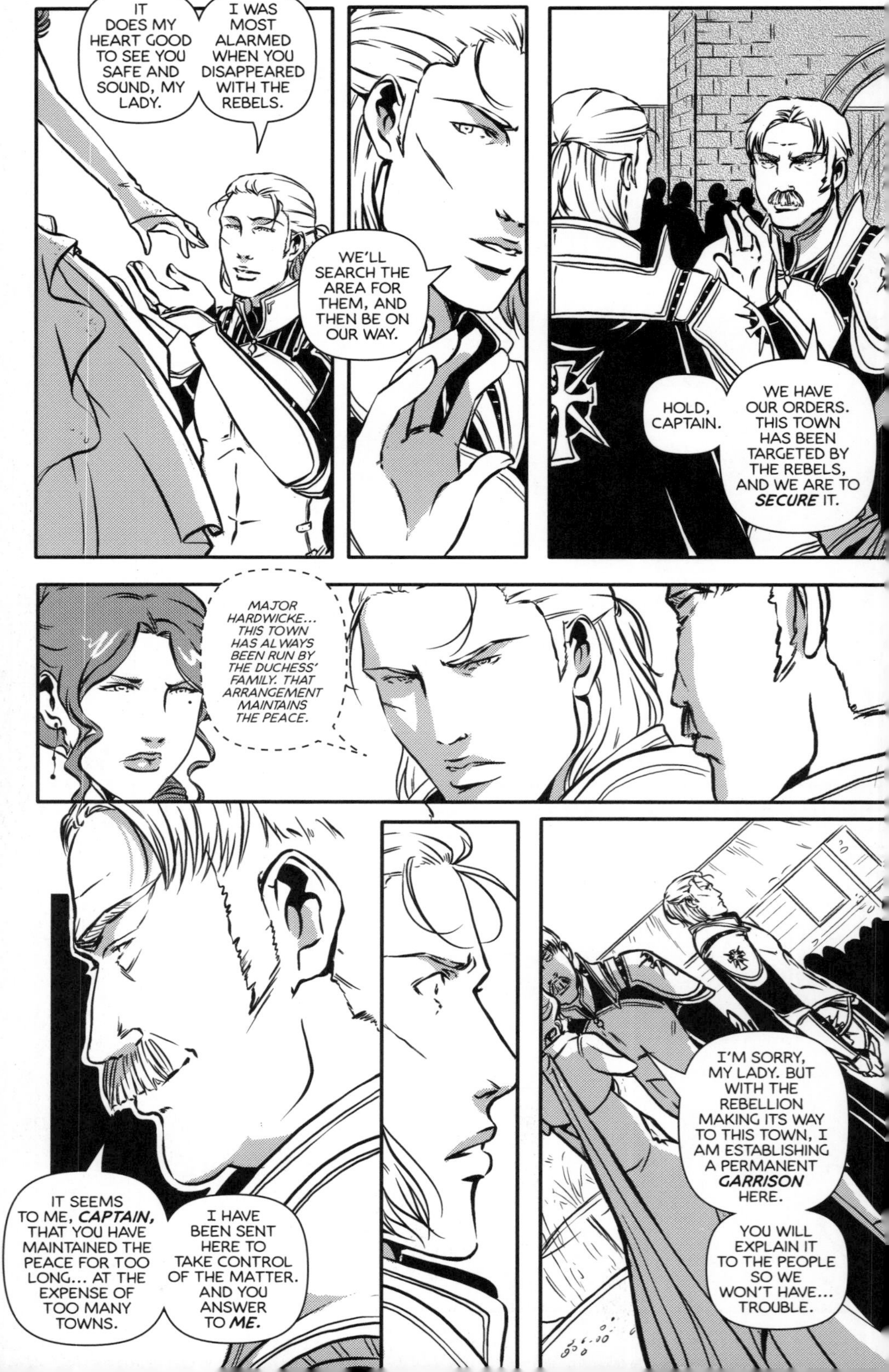
IT DOES MY HEART GOOD TO SEE YOU SAFE AND SOUND, MY LADY.
I WAS MOST ALARMED WHEN YOU DISAPPEARED WITH THE REBELS.
WE'LL SEARCH THE AREA FOR THEM, AND THEN BE ON OUR WAY.
HOLD, CAPTAIN.
WE HAVE OUR ORDERS. THIS TOWN HAS BEEN TARGETED BY THE REBELS, AND WE ARE TO *SECURE* IT.
MAJOR HARDWICKE... THIS TOWN HAS ALWAYS BEEN RUN BY THE DUCHESS' FAMILY. THAT ARRANGEMENT MAINTAINS THE PEACE.
IT SEEMS TO ME, ***CAPTAIN,*** THAT YOU HAVE MAINTAINED THE PEACE FOR TOO LONG... AT THE EXPENSE OF TOO MANY TOWNS.
I HAVE BEEN SENT HERE TO TAKE CONTROL OF THE MATTER. AND YOU ANSWER TO ***ME.***
I'M SORRY, MY LADY. BUT WITH THE REBELLION MAKING ITS WAY TO THIS TOWN, I AM ESTABLISHING A PERMANENT ***GARRISON*** HERE.
YOU WILL EXPLAIN IT TO THE PEOPLE SO WE WON'T HAVE... TROUBLE.

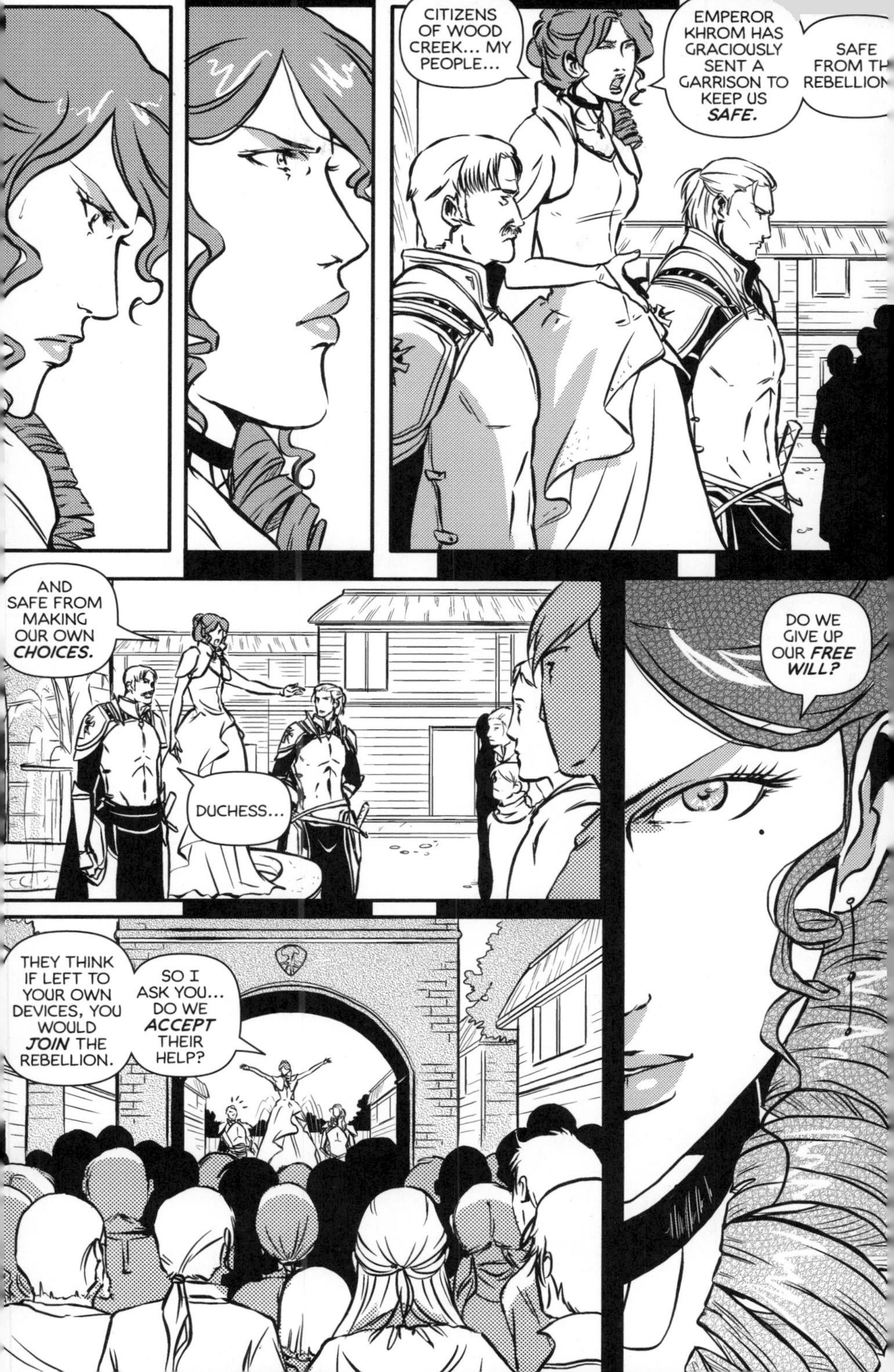
CITIZENS OF WOOD CREEK... MY PEOPLE...
EMPEROR KHROM HAS GRACIOUSLY SENT A GARRISON TO KEEP US SAFE.
SAFE FROM TH REBELLION
AND SAFE FROM MAKING OUR OWN CHOICES.
DUCHESS...
DO WE GIVE UP OUR FREE WILL?
THEY THINK IF LEFT TO YOUR OWN DEVICES, YOU WOULD JOIN THE REBELLION.
SO I ASK YOU... DO WE ACCEPT THEIR HELP?

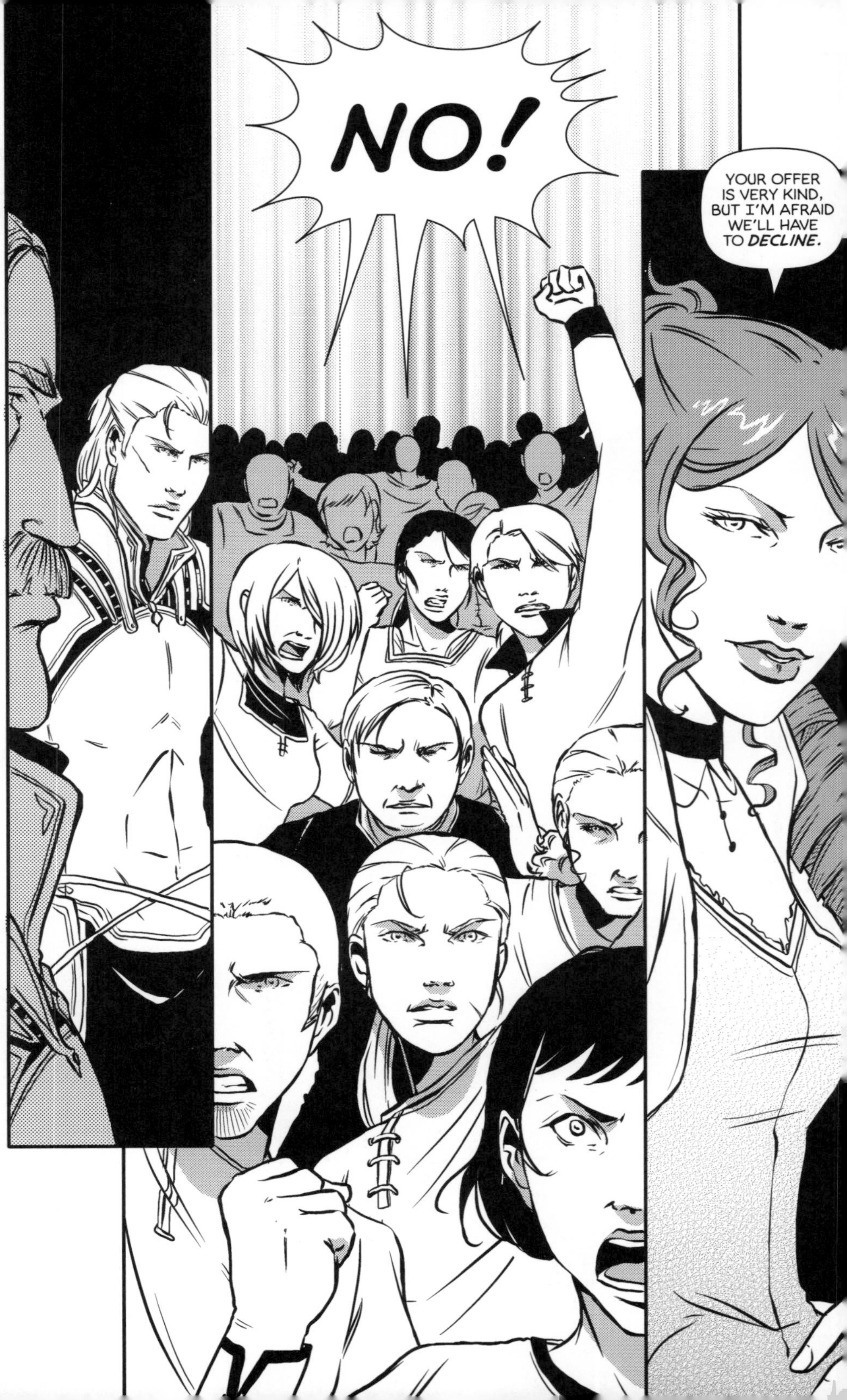
NO!
YOUR OFFER IS VERY KIND, BUT I'M AFRAID WE'LL HAVE TO DECLINE.

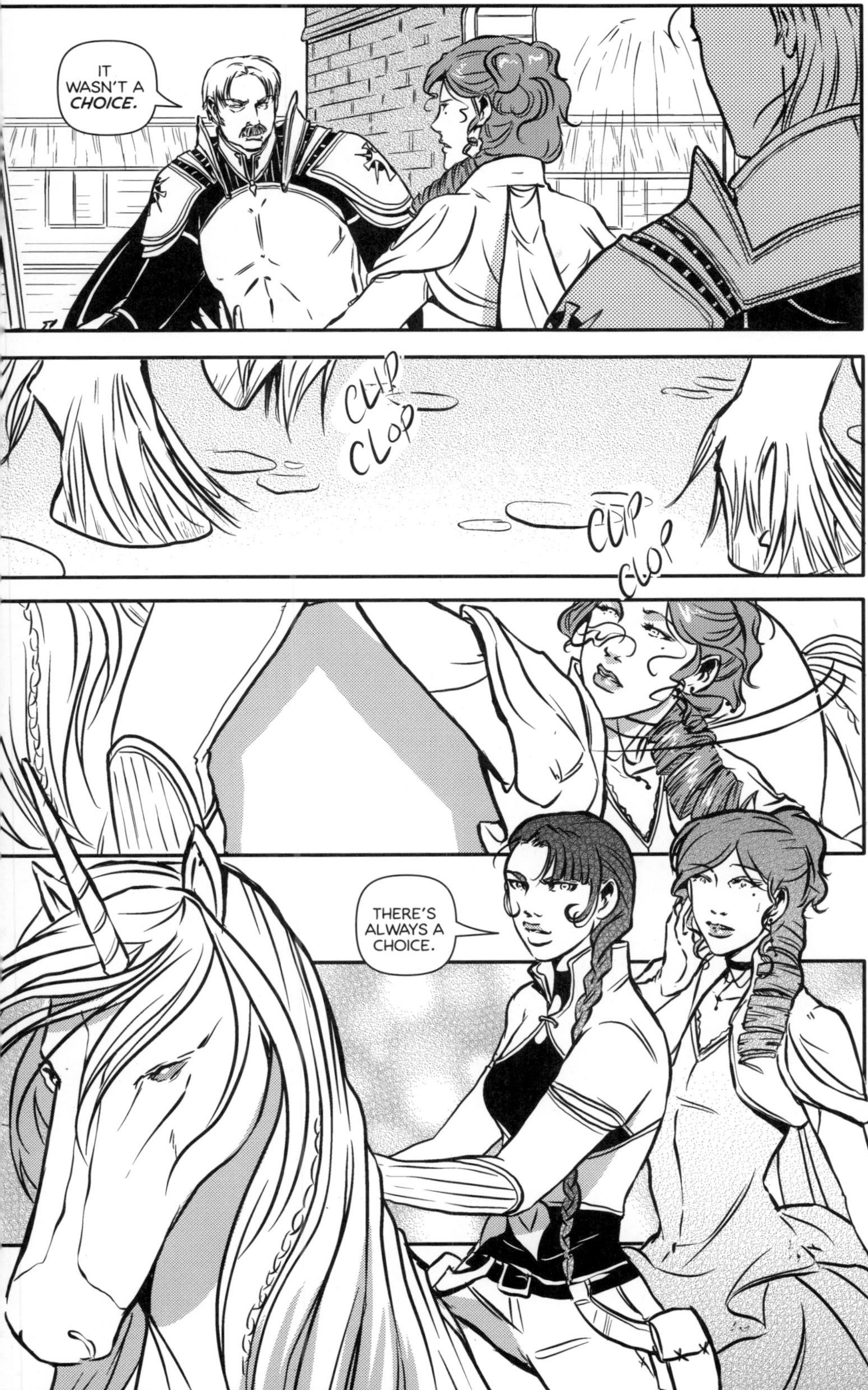
IT WASN'T A *CHOICE.*
CLIP CLOP
CLIP CLOP
THERE'S ALWAYS A CHOICE.

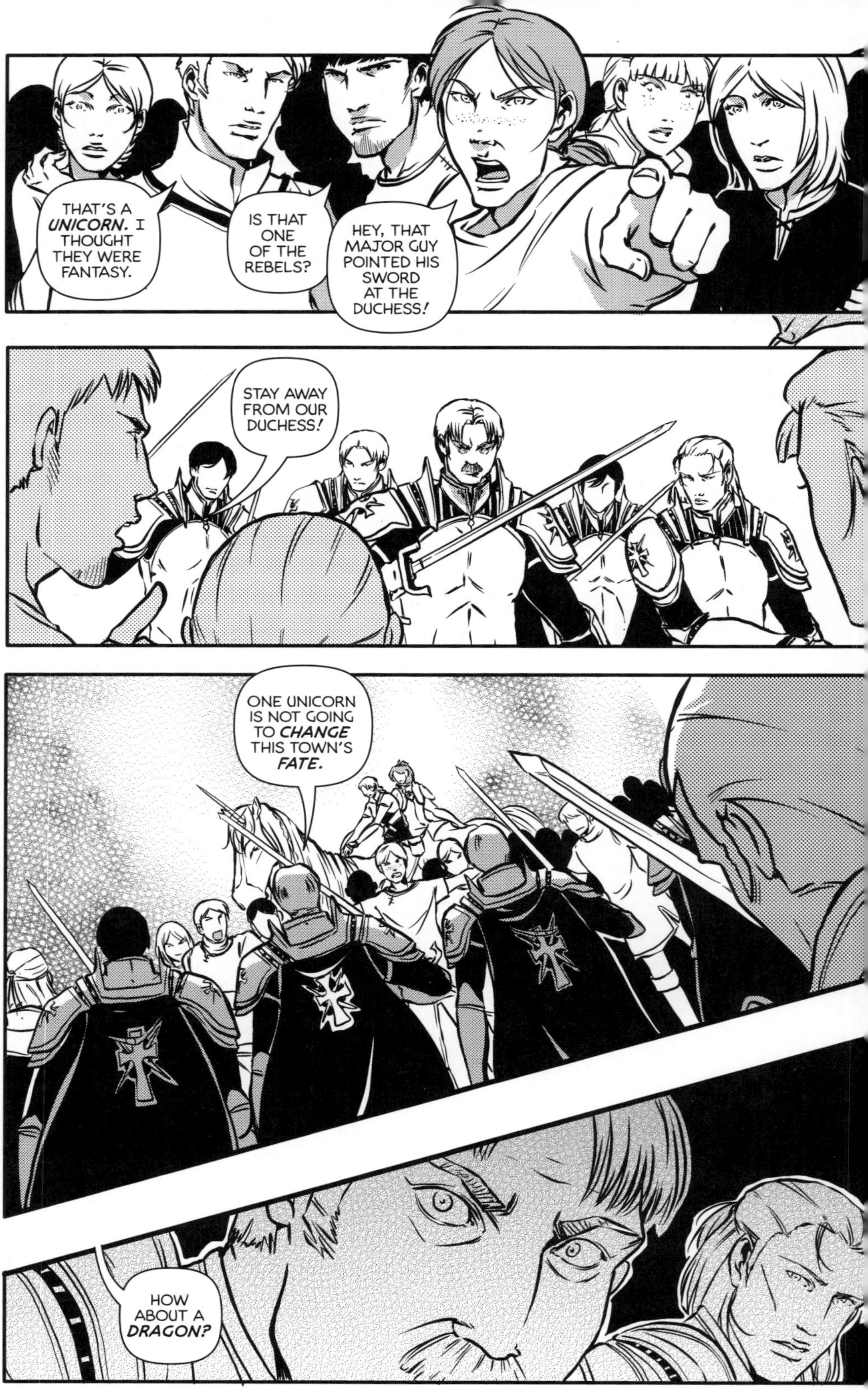
THAT'S A UNICORN. I THOUGHT THEY WERE FANTASY.
IS THAT ONE OF THE REBELS?
HEY, THAT MAJOR GUY POINTED HIS SWORD AT THE DUCHESS!
STAY AWAY FROM OUR DUCHESS!
ONE UNICORN IS NOT GOING TO CHANGE THIS TOWN'S FATE.
HOW ABOUT A DRAGON?

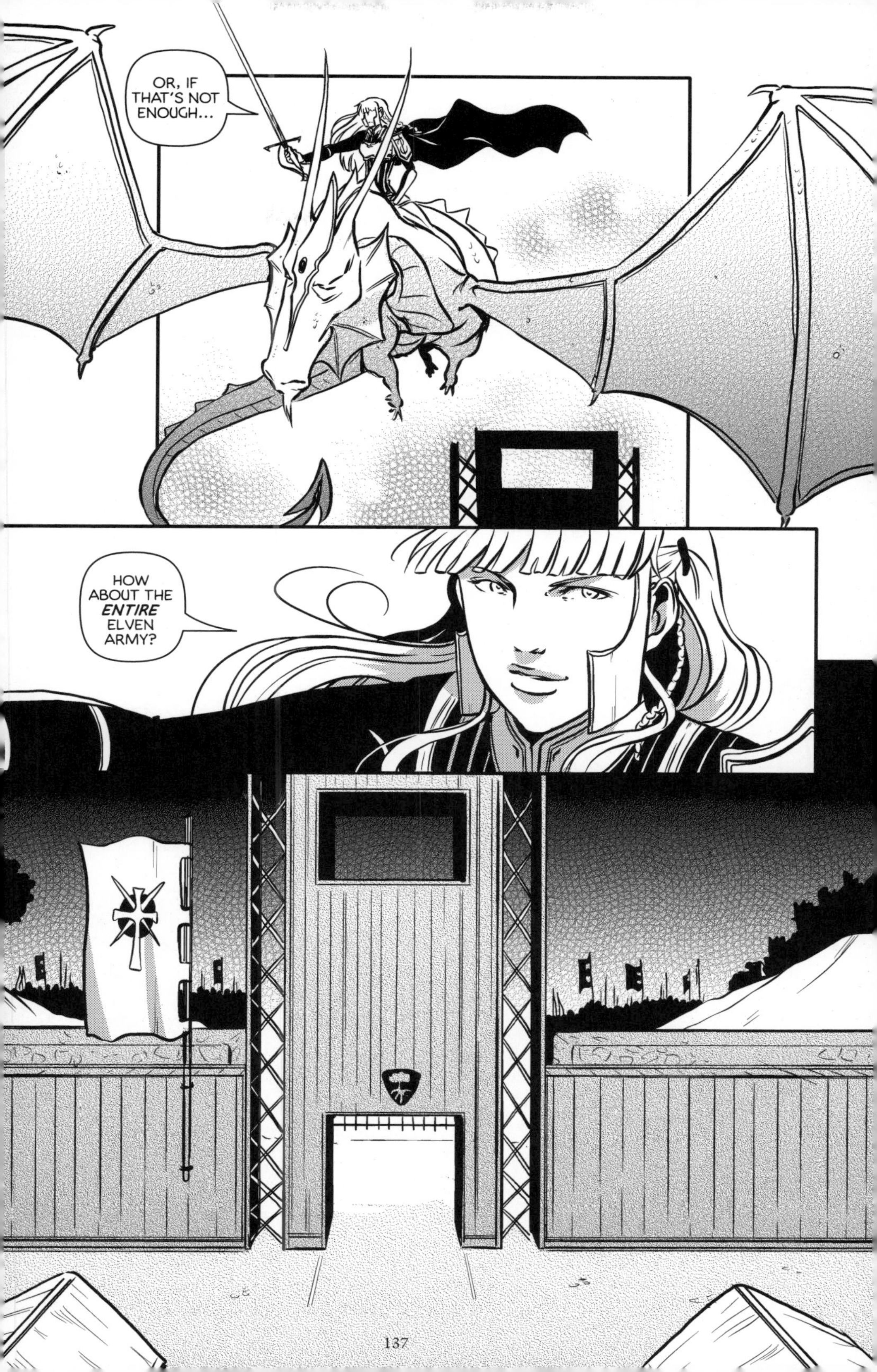
OR, IF THAT'S NOT ENOUGH...
HOW ABOUT THE ***ENTIRE*** ELVEN ARMY?

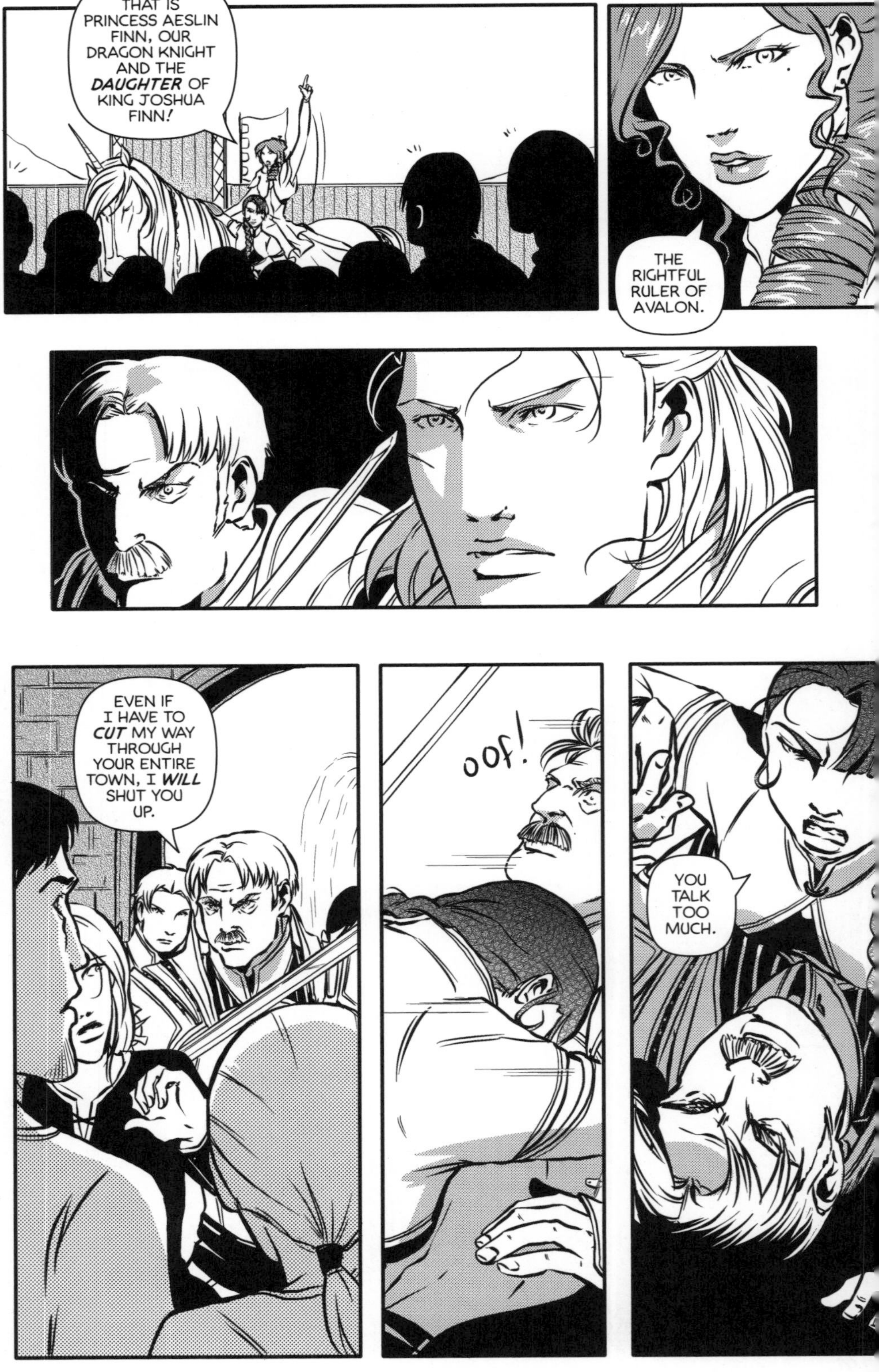
THAT IS PRINCESS AESLIN FINN, OUR DRAGON KNIGHT AND THE *DAUGHTER* OF KING JOSHUA FINN!
THE RIGHTFUL RULER OF AVALON.
EVEN IF I HAVE TO *CUT* MY WAY THROUGH YOUR ENTIRE TOWN, I *WILL* SHUT YOU UP.
oof!
YOU TALK TOO MUCH.

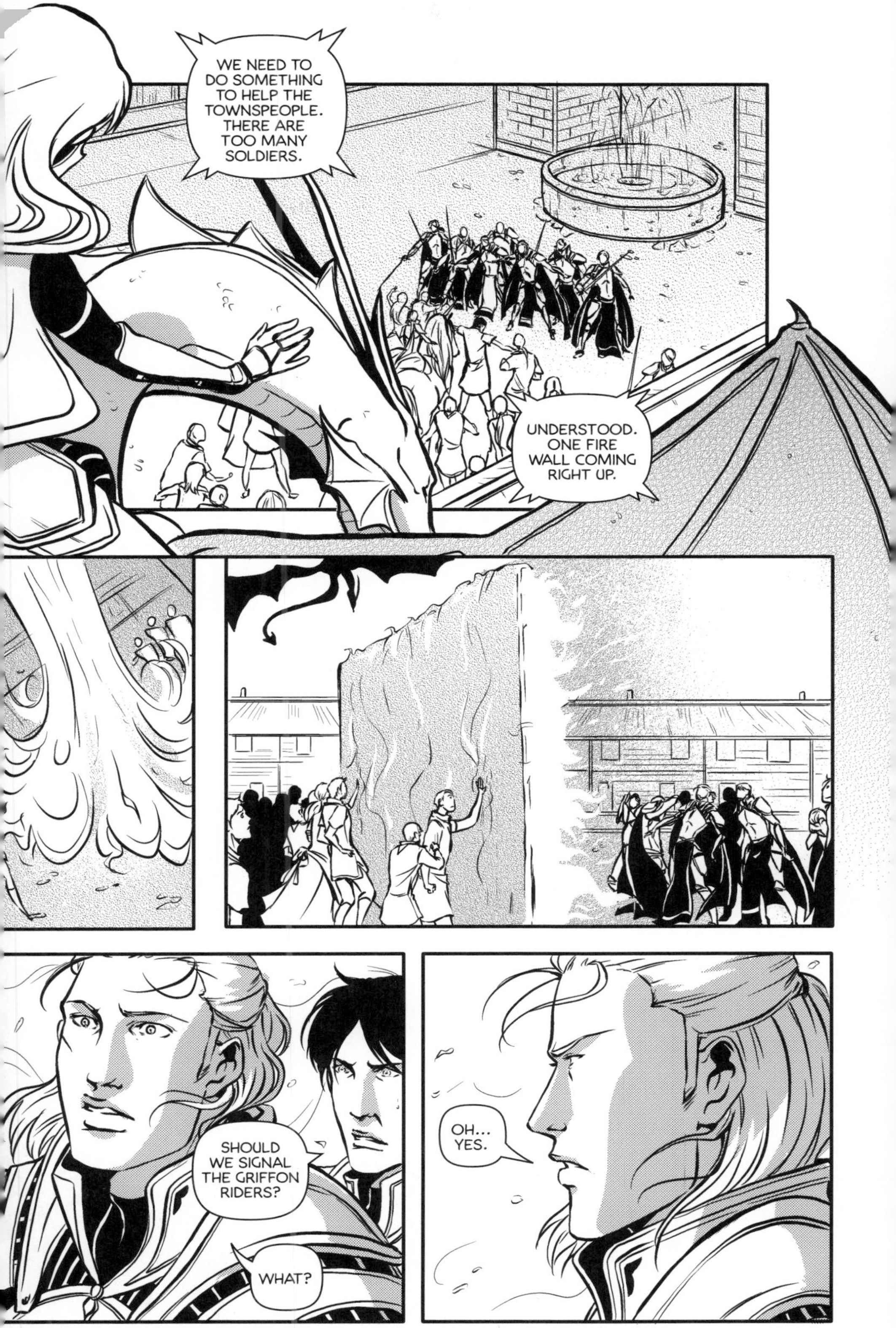
WE NEED TO DO SOMETHING TO HELP THE TOWNSPEOPLE. THERE ARE TOO MANY SOLDIERS.
UNDERSTOOD. ONE FIRE WALL COMING RIGHT UP.
SHOULD WE SIGNAL THE GRIFFON RIDERS?
WHAT?
OH... YES.

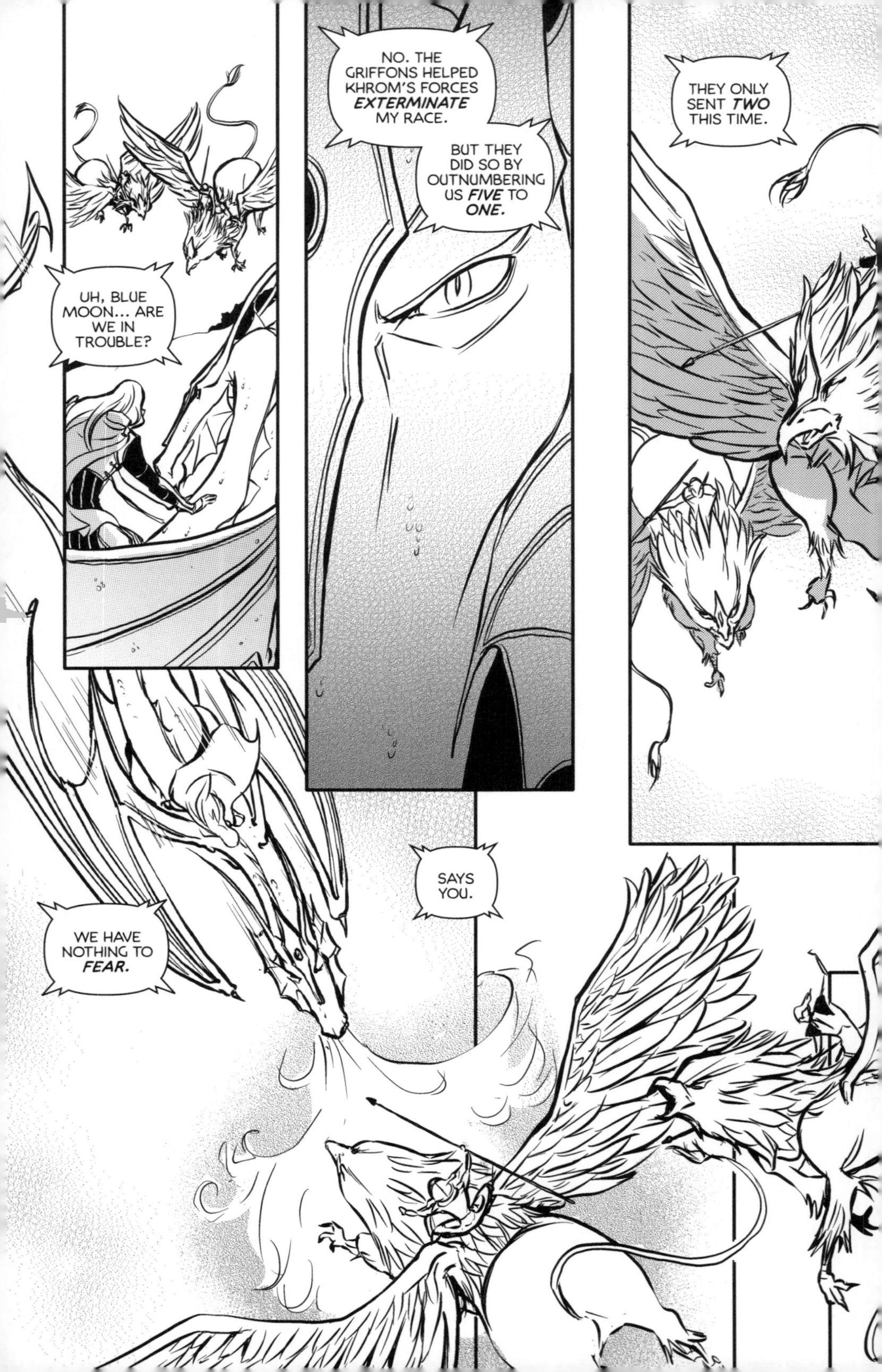
UH, BLUE MOON... ARE WE IN TROUBLE?
NO. THE GRIFFONS HELPED KHROM'S FORCES *EXTERMINATE* MY RACE.
BUT THEY DID SO BY OUTNUMBERING US *FIVE* TO *ONE.*
THEY ONLY SENT *TWO* THIS TIME.
SAYS YOU.
WE HAVE NOTHING TO *FEAR.*

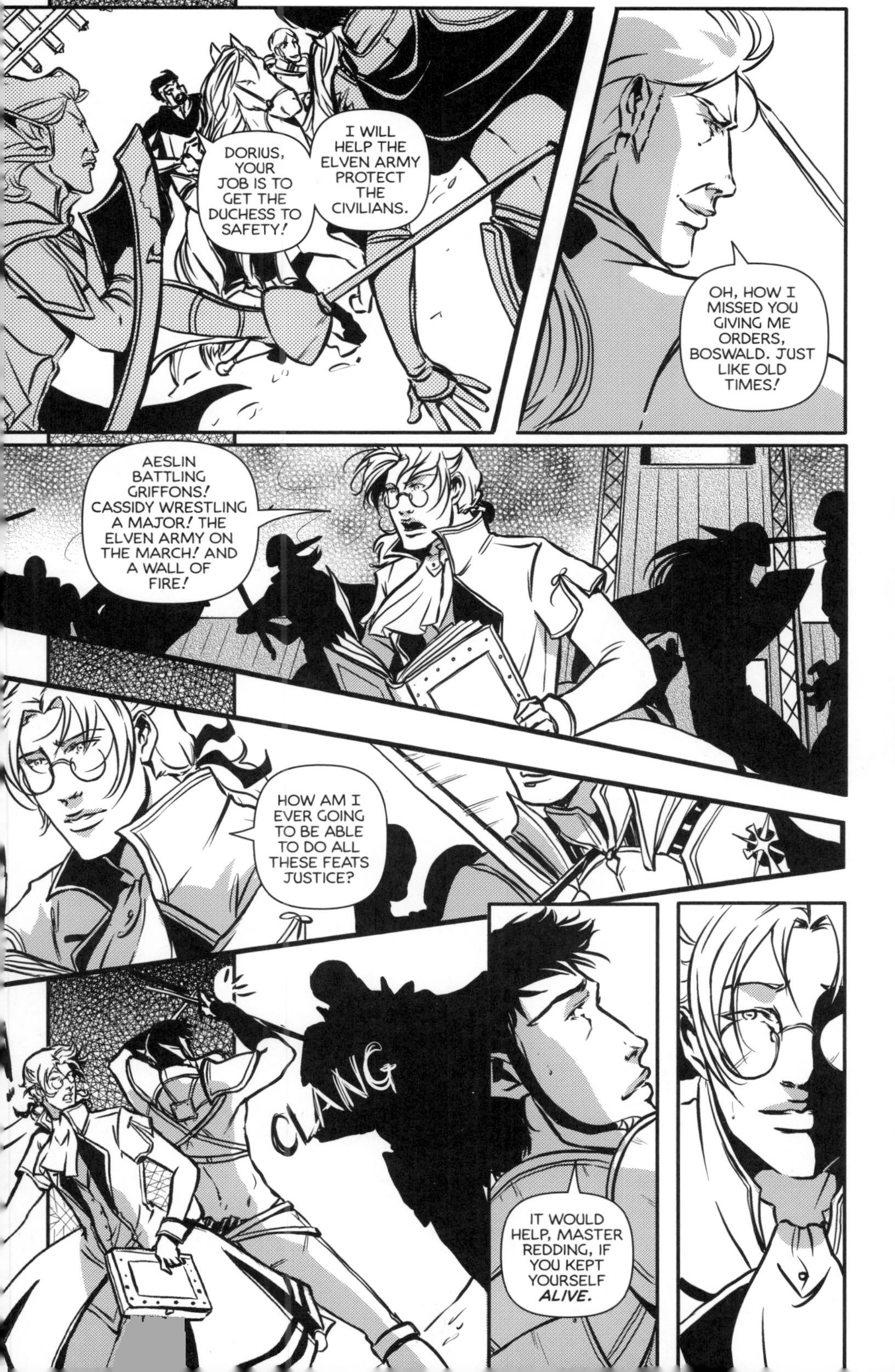
DORIUS, YOUR JOB IS TO GET THE DUCHESS TO SAFETY!
I WILL HELP THE ELVEN ARMY PROTECT THE CIVILIANS.
OH, HOW I MISSED YOU GIVING ME ORDERS, BOSWALD. JUST LIKE OLD TIMES!
AESLIN BATTLING GRIFFONS! CASSIDY WRESTLING A MAJOR! THE ELVEN ARMY ON THE MARCH! AND A WALL OF FIRE!
HOW AM I EVER GOING TO BE ABLE TO DO ALL THESE FEATS JUSTICE?
CLANG
IT WOULD HELP, MASTER REDDING, IF YOU KEPT YOURSELF ***ALIVE.***

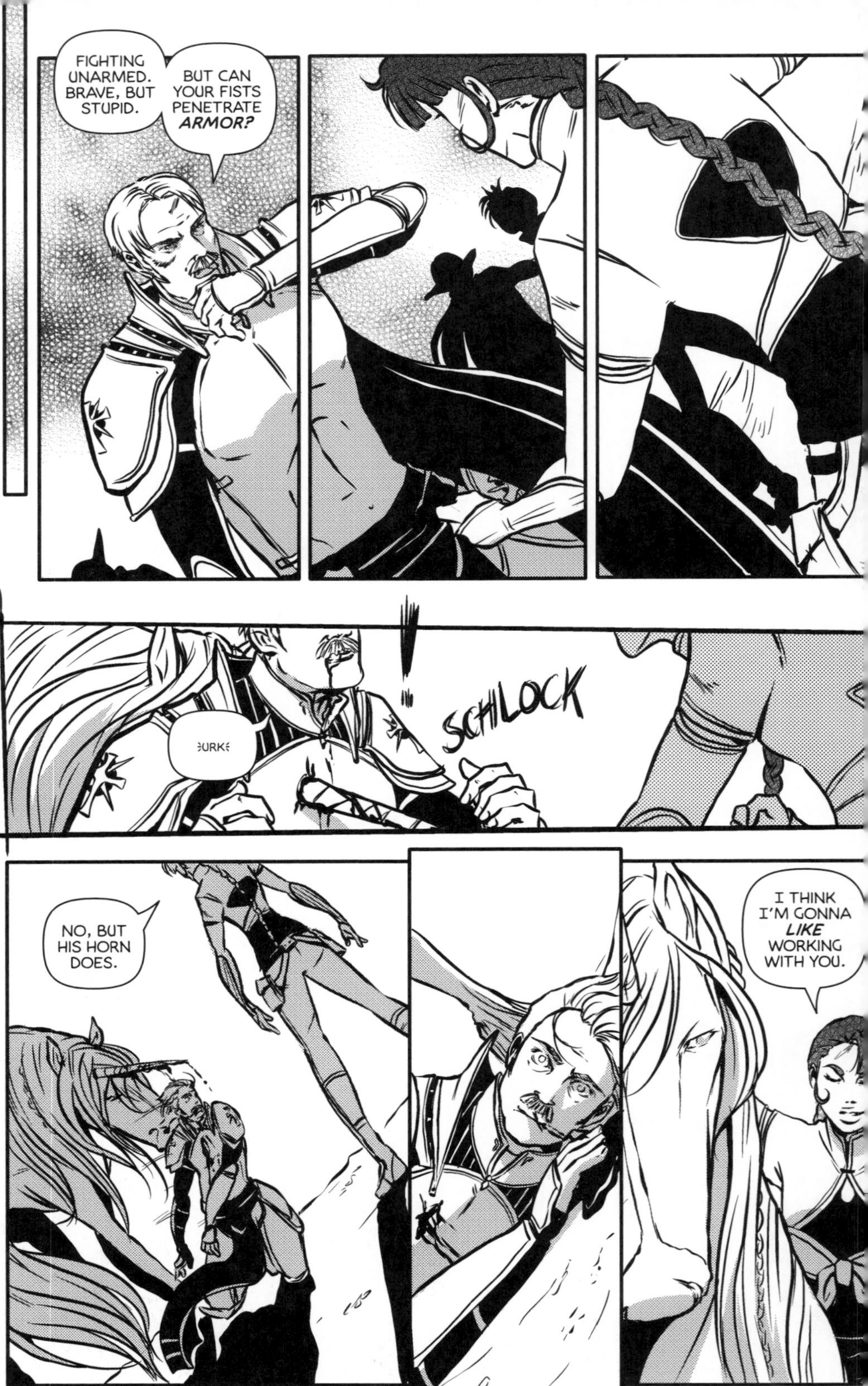
FIGHTING UNARMED. BRAVE, BUT STUPID.
BUT CAN YOUR FISTS PENETRATE *ARMOR?*
URK
SCHLOCK
NO, BUT HIS HORN DOES.
I THINK I'M GONNA *LIKE* WORKING WITH YOU.

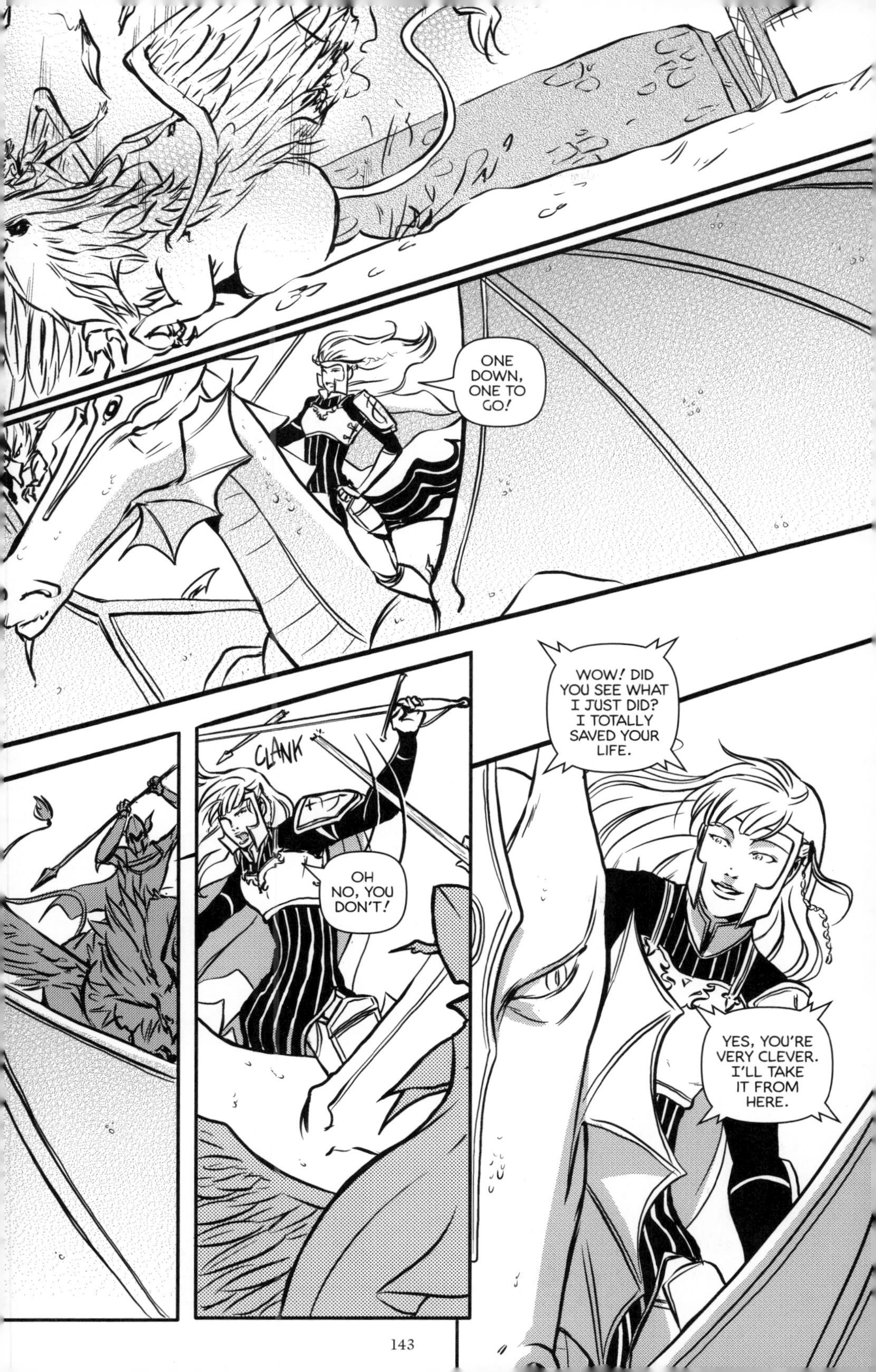
ONE DOWN, ONE TO GO!
CLANK
OH NO, YOU DON'T!
WOW! DID YOU SEE WHAT I JUST DID? I TOTALLY SAVED YOUR LIFE.
YES, YOU'RE VERY CLEVER. I'LL TAKE IT FROM HERE.

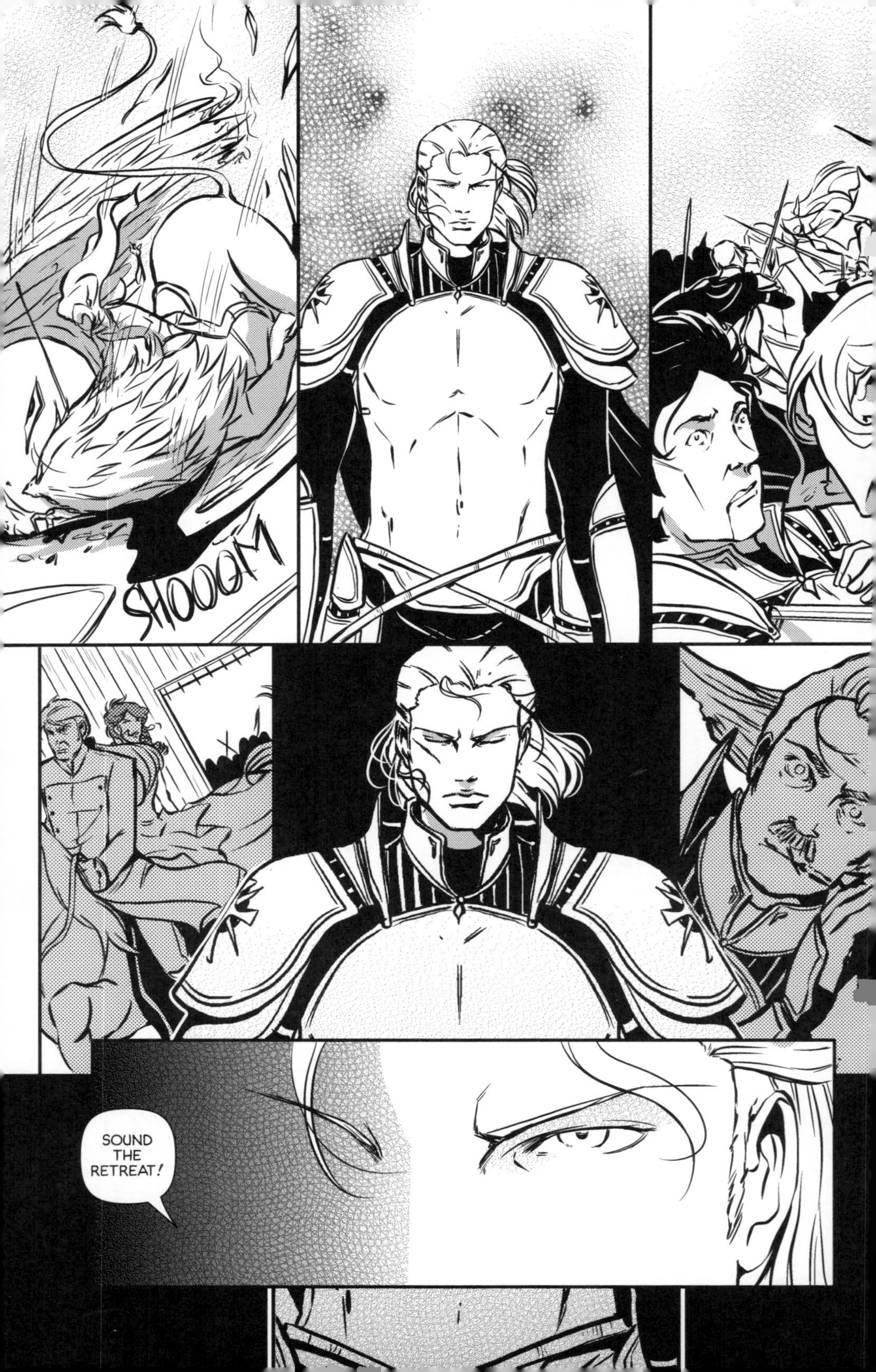
SHOOOM
SOUND THE RETREAT!

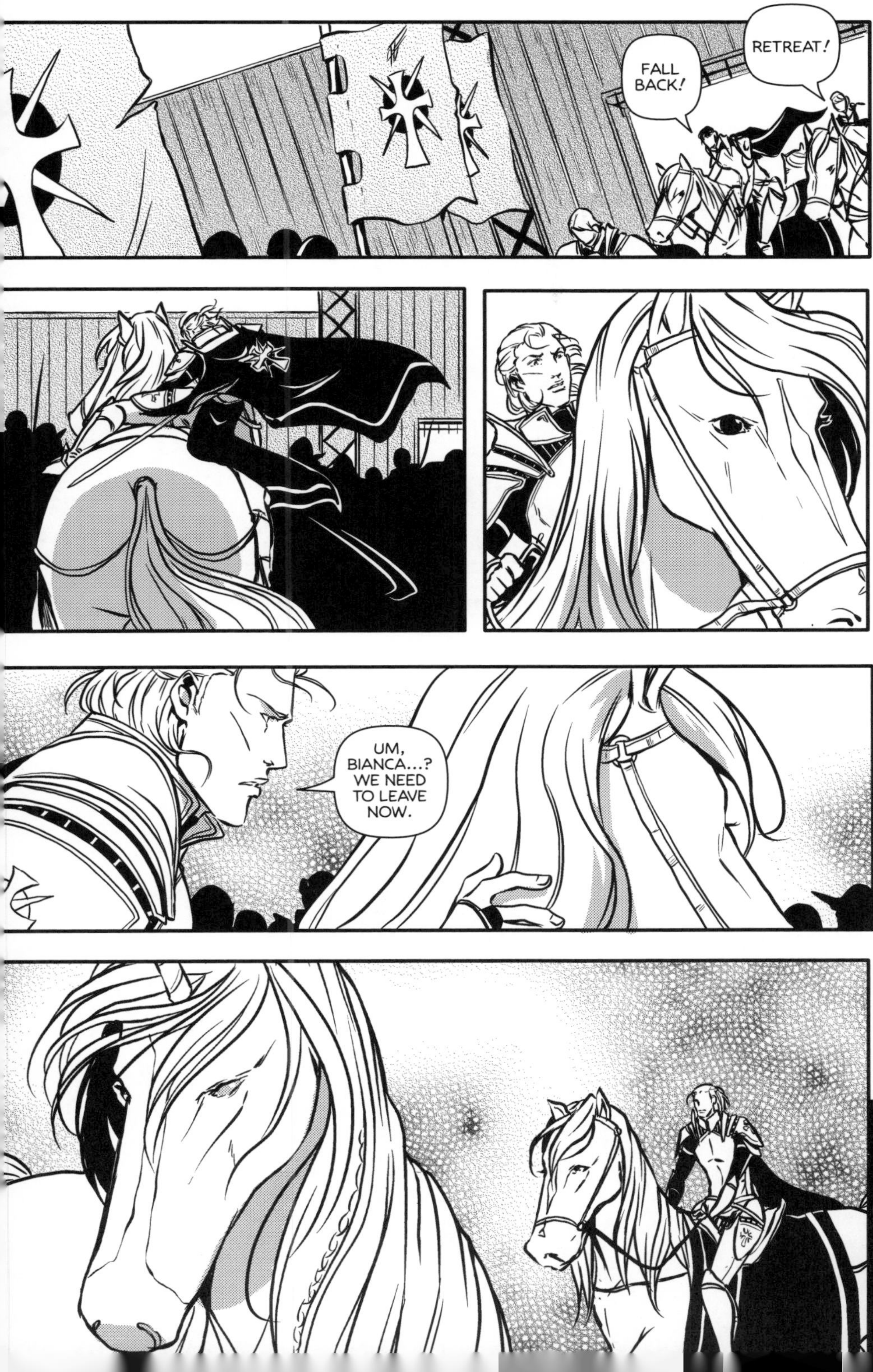

FALL BACK!
RETREAT!
UM, BIANCA...? WE NEED TO LEAVE NOW.

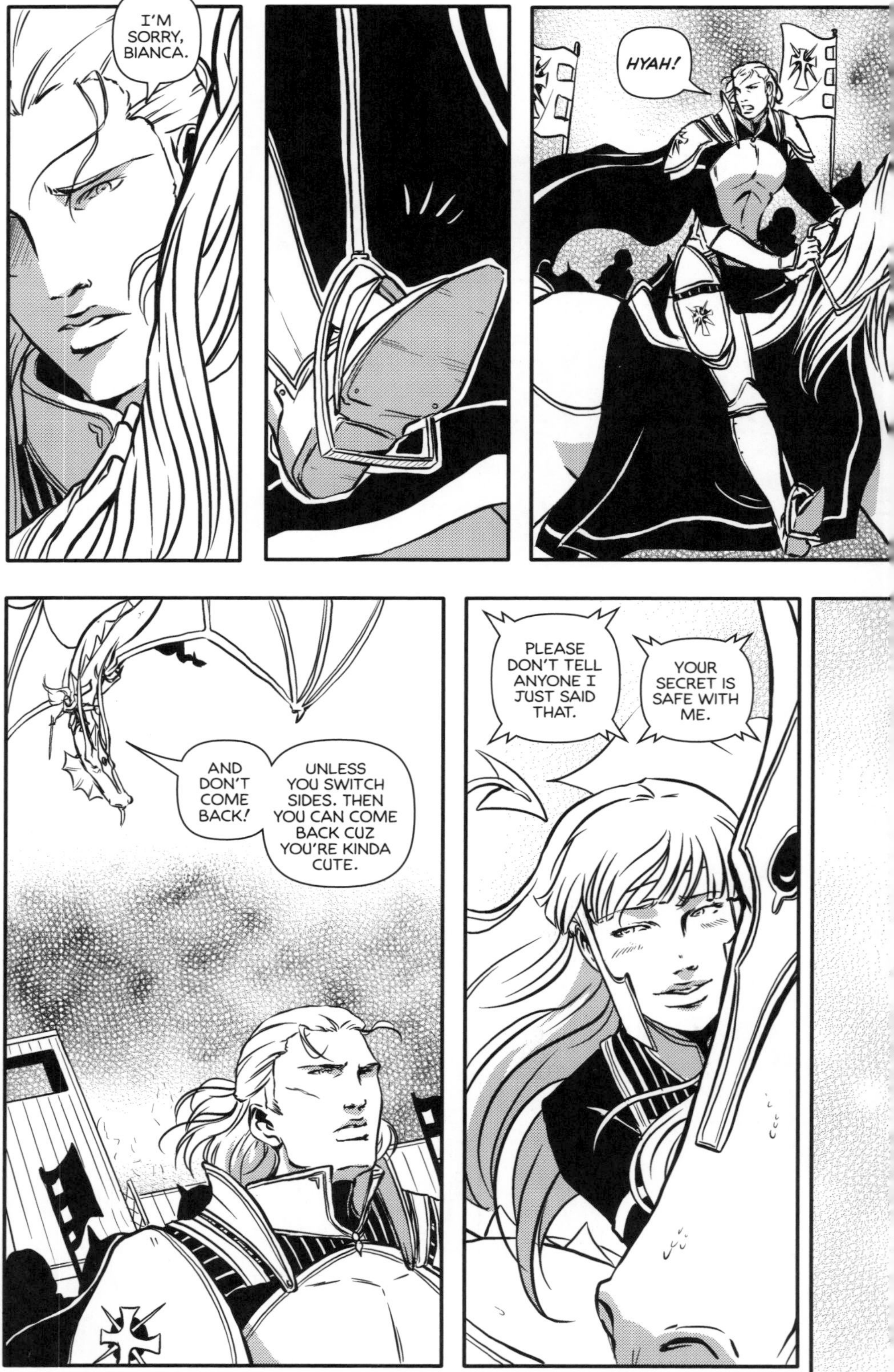
I'M SORRY, BIANCA.
HYAH!
AND DON'T COME BACK!
UNLESS YOU SWITCH SIDES. THEN YOU CAN COME BACK CUZ YOU'RE KINDA CUTE.
PLEASE DON'T TELL ANYONE I JUST SAID THAT.
YOUR SECRET IS SAFE WITH ME.

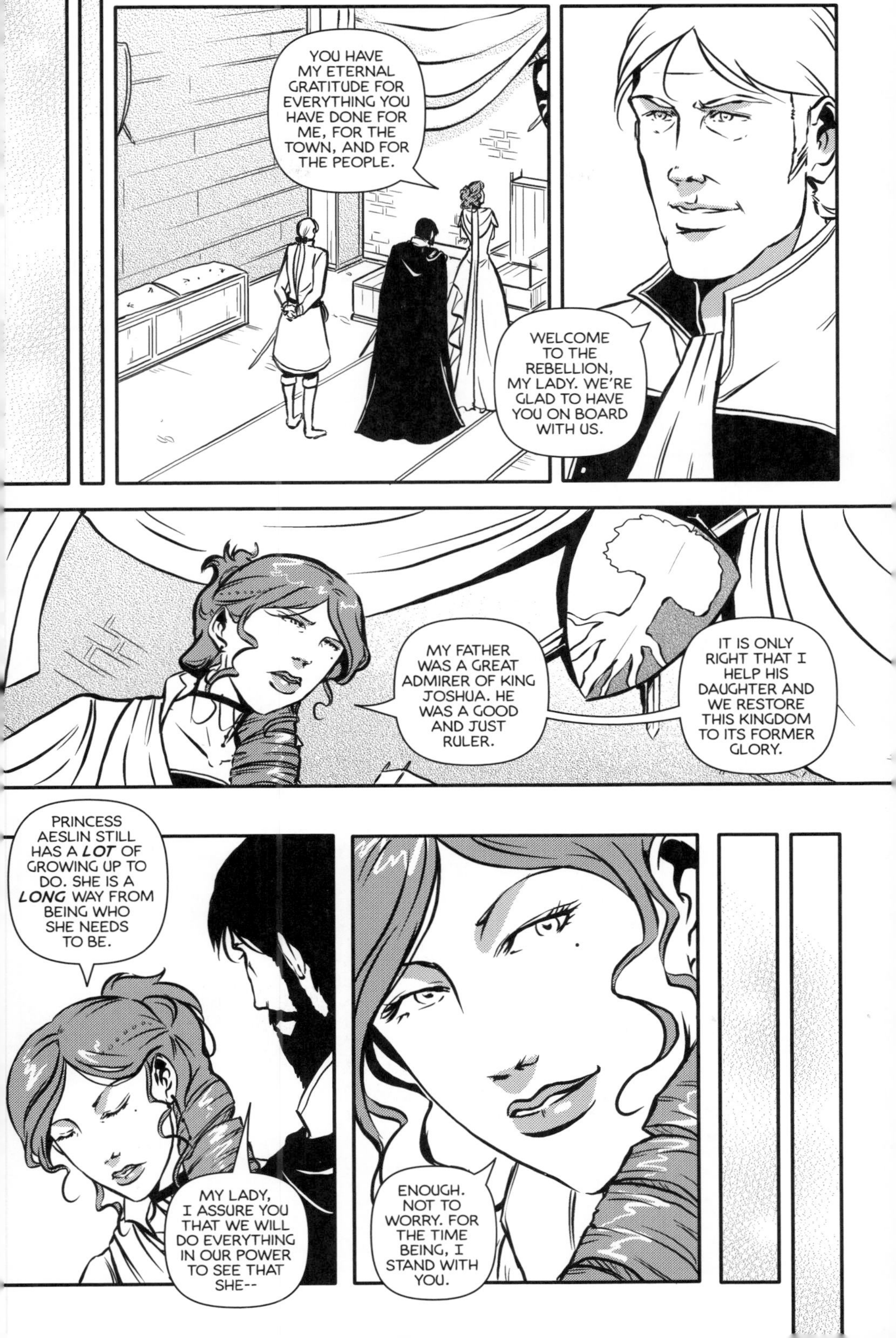
YOU HAVE MY ETERNAL GRATITUDE FOR EVERYTHING YOU HAVE DONE FOR ME, FOR THE TOWN, AND FOR THE PEOPLE.
WELCOME TO THE REBELLION, MY LADY. WE'RE GLAD TO HAVE YOU ON BOARD WITH US.
MY FATHER WAS A GREAT ADMIRER OF KING JOSHUA. HE WAS A GOOD AND JUST RULER.
IT IS ONLY RIGHT THAT I HELP HIS DAUGHTER AND WE RESTORE THIS KINGDOM TO ITS FORMER GLORY.
PRINCESS AESLIN STILL HAS A *LOT* OF GROWING UP TO DO. SHE IS A *LONG* WAY FROM BEING WHO SHE NEEDS TO BE.
MY LADY, I ASSURE YOU THAT WE WILL DO EVERYTHING IN OUR POWER TO SEE THAT SHE--
ENOUGH. NOT TO WORRY. FOR THE TIME BEING, I STAND WITH YOU.

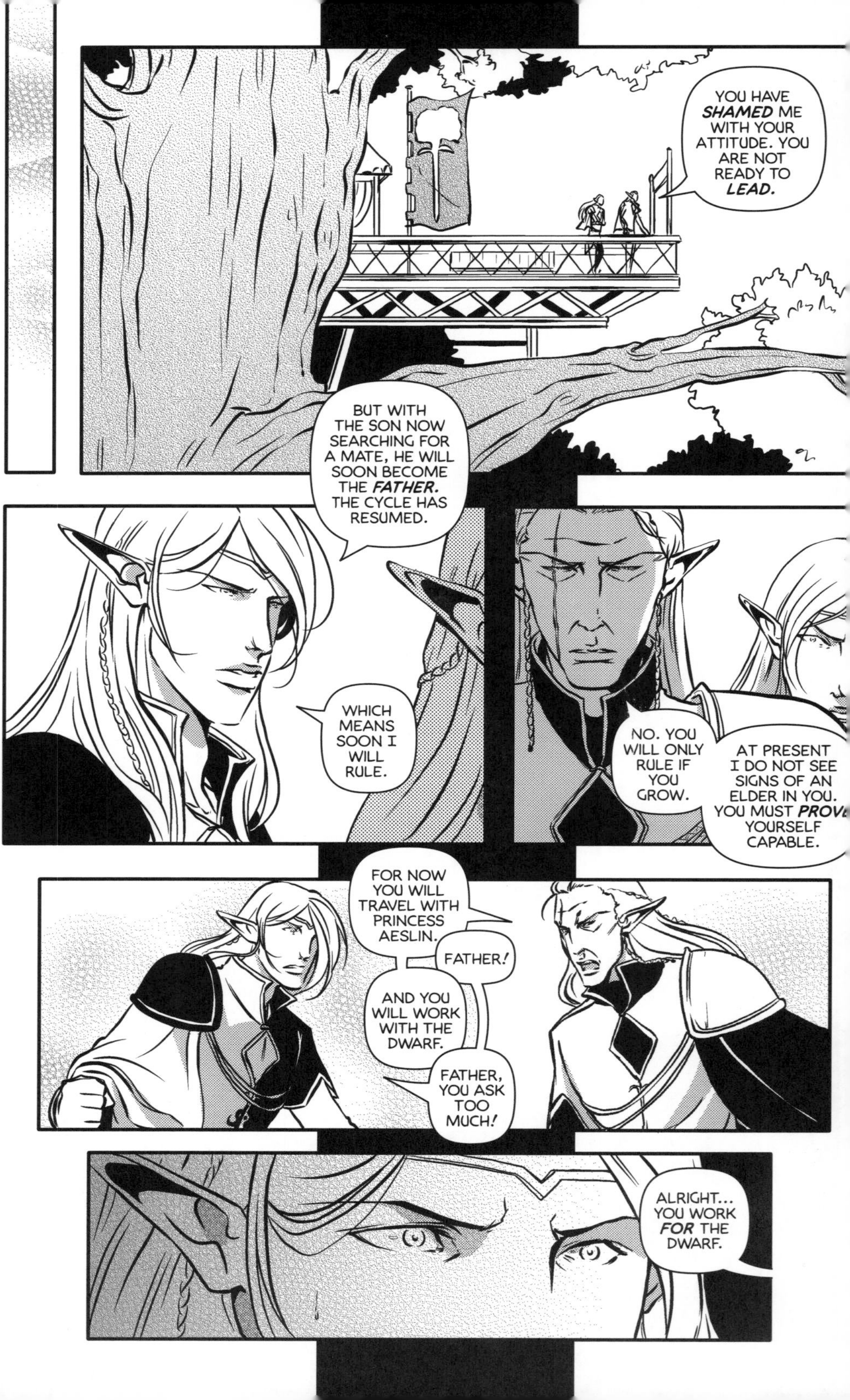
YOU HAVE **SHAMED** ME WITH YOUR ATTITUDE. YOU ARE NOT READY TO **LEAD.**
BUT WITH THE SON NOW SEARCHING FOR A MATE, HE WILL SOON BECOME THE **FATHER.** THE CYCLE HAS RESUMED.
WHICH MEANS SOON I WILL RULE.
NO. YOU WILL ONLY RULE IF YOU GROW.
AT PRESENT I DO NOT SEE SIGNS OF AN ELDER IN YOU. YOU MUST **PROVE** YOURSELF CAPABLE.
FOR NOW YOU WILL TRAVEL WITH PRINCESS AESLIN.
FATHER!
AND YOU WILL WORK WITH THE DWARF.
FATHER, YOU ASK TOO MUCH!
ALRIGHT... YOU WORK **FOR** THE DWARF.

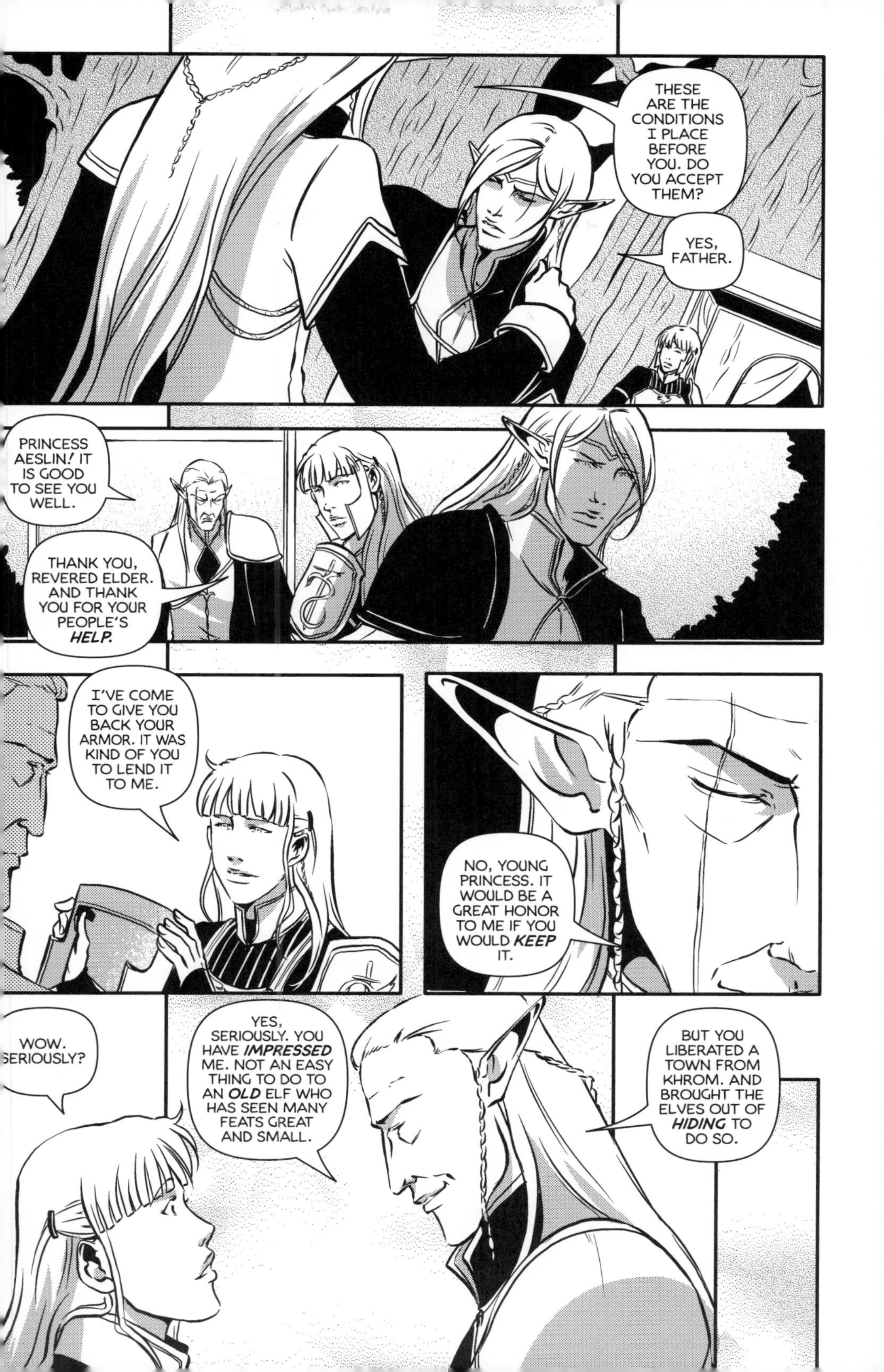
THESE ARE THE CONDITIONS I PLACE BEFORE YOU. DO YOU ACCEPT THEM?
YES, FATHER.
PRINCESS AESLIN! IT IS GOOD TO SEE YOU WELL.
THANK YOU, REVERED ELDER. AND THANK YOU FOR YOUR PEOPLE'S HELP.
I'VE COME TO GIVE YOU BACK YOUR ARMOR. IT WAS KIND OF YOU TO LEND IT TO ME.
NO, YOUNG PRINCESS. IT WOULD BE A GREAT HONOR TO ME IF YOU WOULD KEEP IT.
WOW. SERIOUSLY?
YES, SERIOUSLY. YOU HAVE IMPRESSED ME. NOT AN EASY THING TO DO TO AN OLD ELF WHO HAS SEEN MANY FEATS GREAT AND SMALL.
BUT YOU LIBERATED A TOWN FROM KHROM. AND BROUGHT THE ELVES OUT OF HIDING TO DO SO.

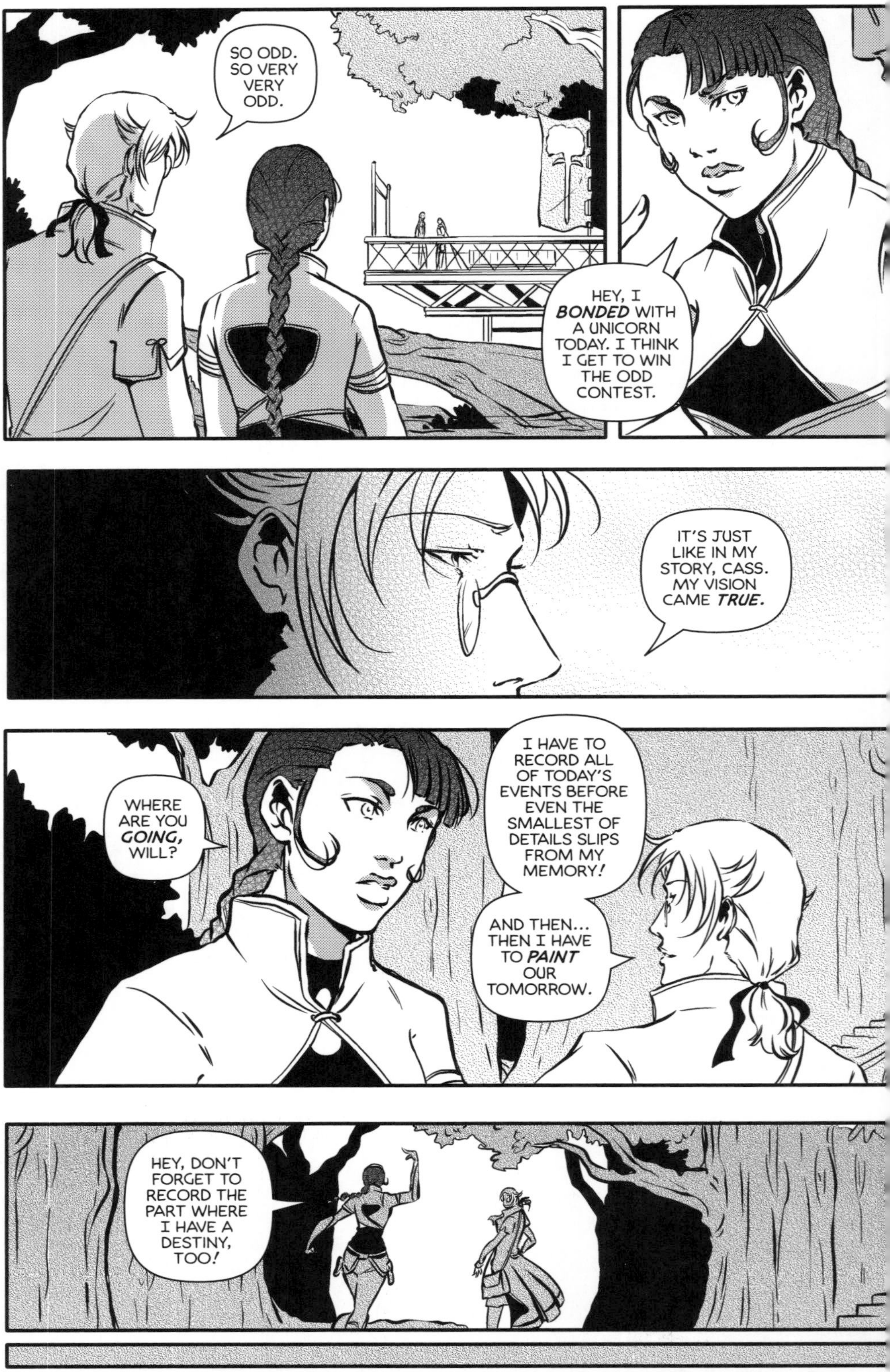
SO ODD. SO VERY VERY ODD.
HEY, I BONDED WITH A UNICORN TODAY. I THINK I GET TO WIN THE ODD CONTEST.
IT'S JUST LIKE IN MY STORY, CASS. MY VISION CAME TRUE.
WHERE ARE YOU GOING, WILL?
I HAVE TO RECORD ALL OF TODAY'S EVENTS BEFORE EVEN THE SMALLEST OF DETAILS SLIPS FROM MY MEMORY!
AND THEN... THEN I HAVE TO PAINT OUR TOMORROW.
HEY, DON'T FORGET TO RECORD THE PART WHERE I HAVE A DESTINY, TOO!

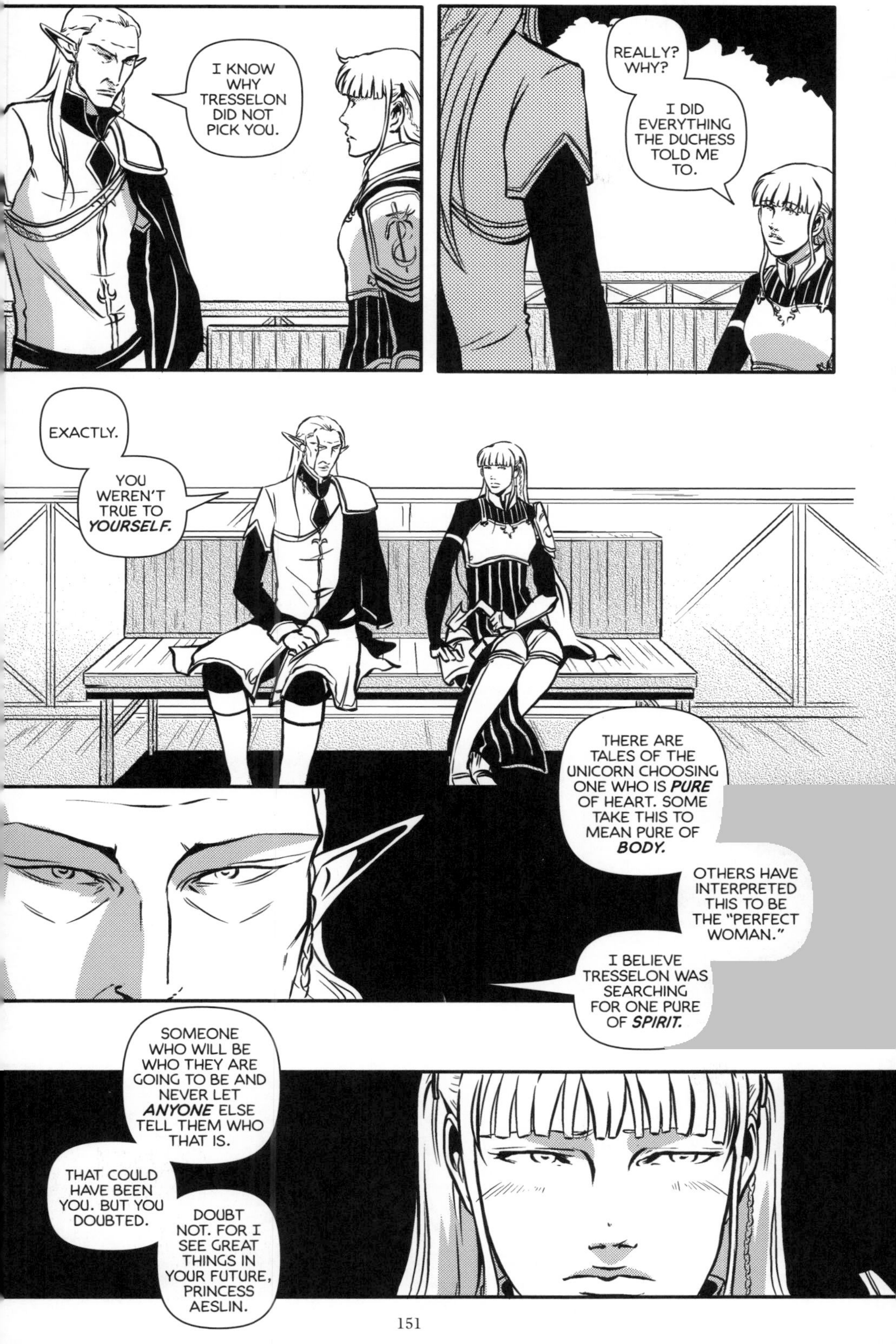
I KNOW WHY TRESSELON DID NOT PICK YOU.
REALLY? WHY?
I DID EVERYTHING THE DUCHESS TOLD ME TO.
EXACTLY.
YOU WEREN'T TRUE TO *YOURSELF.*
THERE ARE TALES OF THE UNICORN CHOOSING ONE WHO IS *PURE* OF HEART. SOME TAKE THIS TO MEAN PURE OF *BODY.*
OTHERS HAVE INTERPRETED THIS TO BE THE "PERFECT WOMAN."
I BELIEVE TRESSELON WAS SEARCHING FOR ONE PURE OF *SPIRIT.*
SOMEONE WHO WILL BE WHO THEY ARE GOING TO BE AND NEVER LET *ANYONE* ELSE TELL THEM WHO THAT IS.
THAT COULD HAVE BEEN YOU. BUT YOU DOUBTED.
DOUBT NOT. FOR I SEE GREAT THINGS IN YOUR FUTURE, PRINCESS AESLIN.

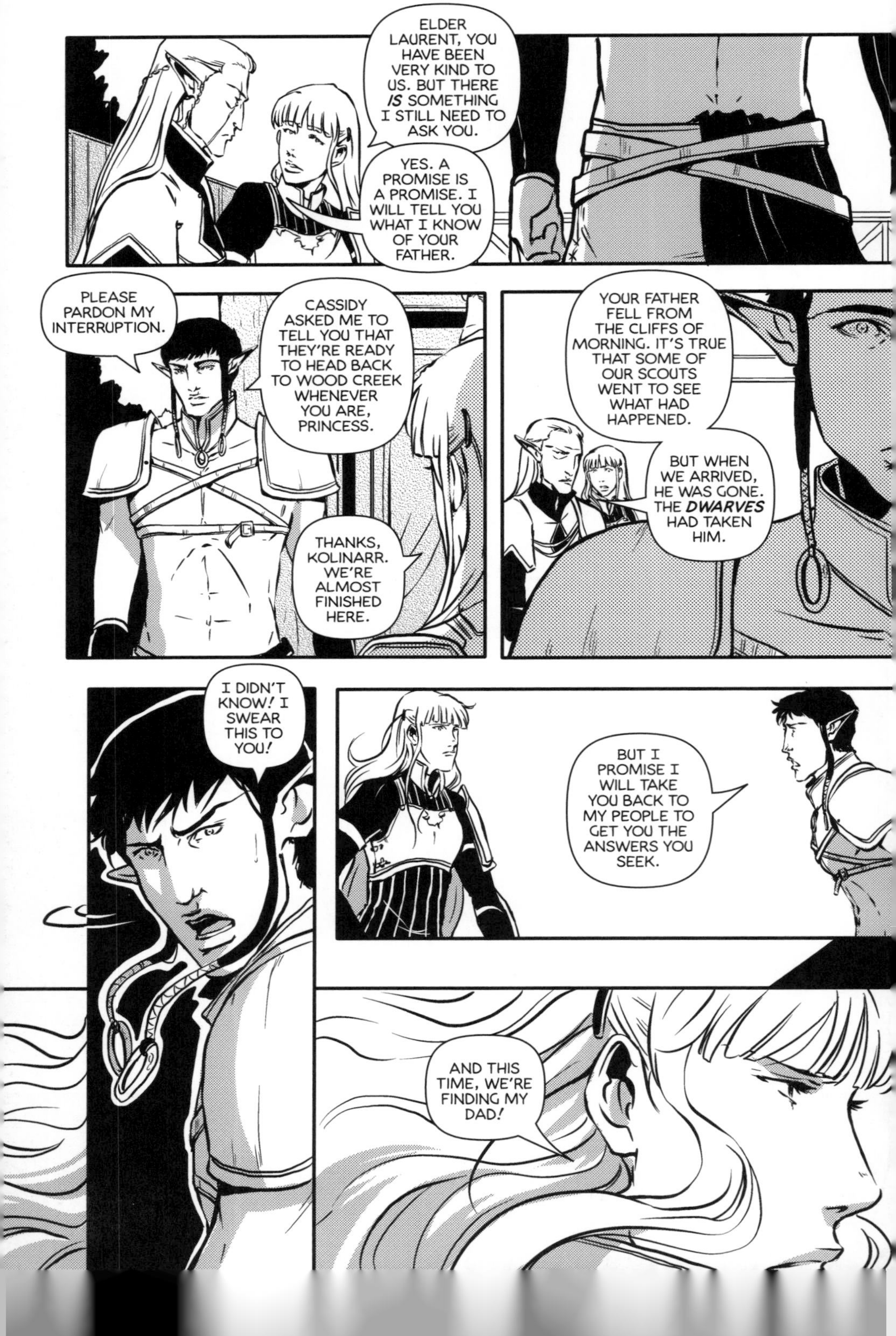
ELDER LAURENT, YOU HAVE BEEN VERY KIND TO US. BUT THERE *IS* SOMETHING I STILL NEED TO ASK YOU.
YES. A PROMISE IS A PROMISE. I WILL TELL YOU WHAT I KNOW OF YOUR FATHER.
PLEASE PARDON MY INTERRUPTION.
CASSIDY ASKED ME TO TELL YOU THAT THEY'RE READY TO HEAD BACK TO WOOD CREEK WHENEVER YOU ARE, PRINCESS.
THANKS, KOLINARR. WE'RE ALMOST FINISHED HERE.
YOUR FATHER FELL FROM THE CLIFFS OF MORNING. IT'S TRUE THAT SOME OF OUR SCOUTS WENT TO SEE WHAT HAD HAPPENED.
BUT WHEN WE ARRIVED, HE WAS GONE. THE ***DWARVES*** HAD TAKEN HIM.
I DIDN'T KNOW*!* I SWEAR THIS TO YOU*!*
BUT I PROMISE I WILL TAKE YOU BACK TO MY PEOPLE TO GET YOU THE ANSWERS YOU SEEK.
AND THIS TIME, WE'RE FINDING MY DAD*!*

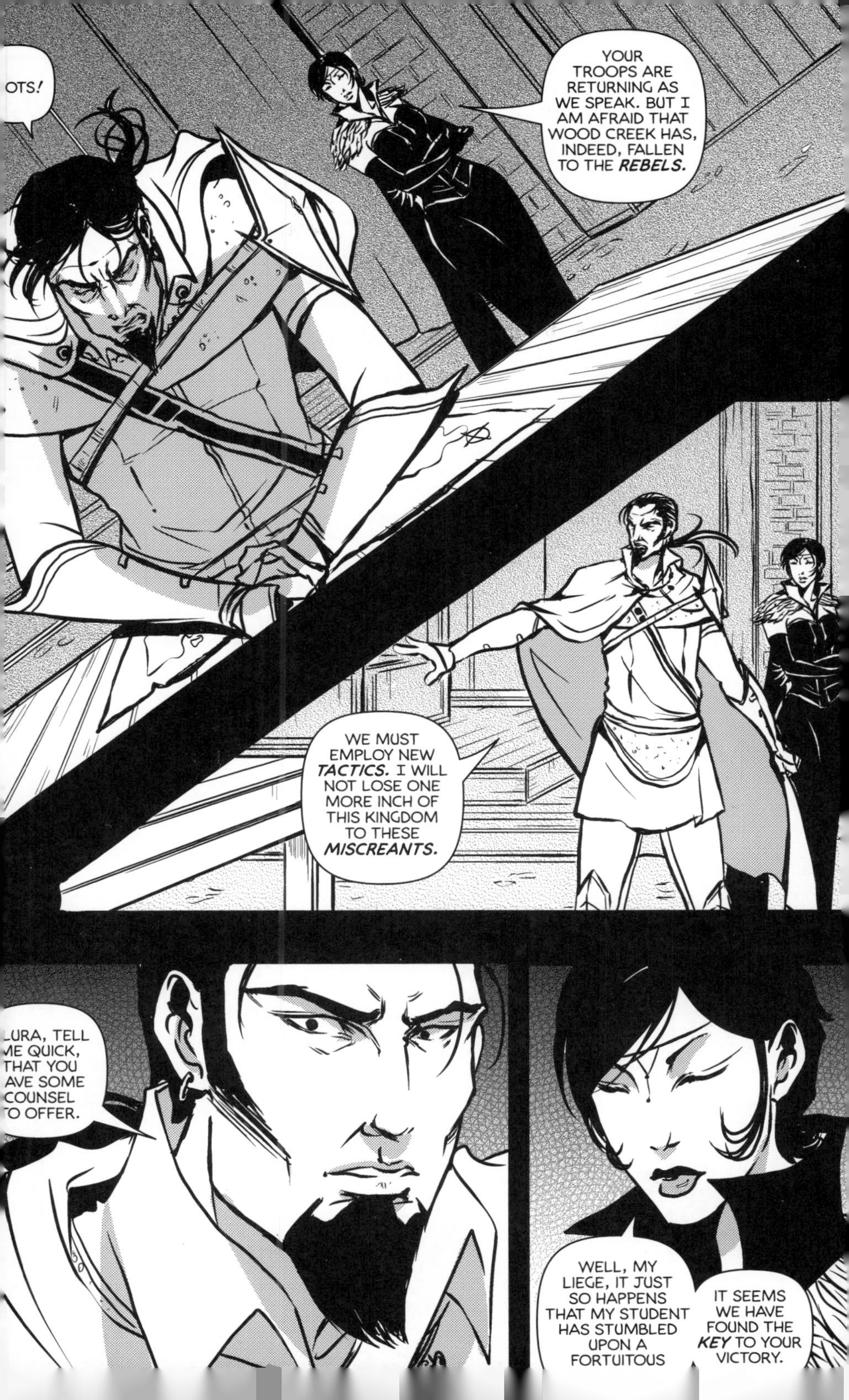
OTS!
YOUR TROOPS ARE RETURNING AS WE SPEAK. BUT I AM AFRAID THAT WOOD CREEK HAS, INDEED, FALLEN TO THE *REBELS.*
WE MUST EMPLOY NEW *TACTICS.* I WILL NOT LOSE ONE MORE INCH OF THIS KINGDOM TO THESE *MISCREANTS.*
LURA, TELL ME QUICK, THAT YOU AVE SOME COUNSEL TO OFFER.
WELL, MY LIEGE, IT JUST SO HAPPENS THAT MY STUDENT HAS STUMBLED UPON A FORTUITOUS
IT SEEMS WE HAVE FOUND THE *KEY* TO YOUR VICTORY.

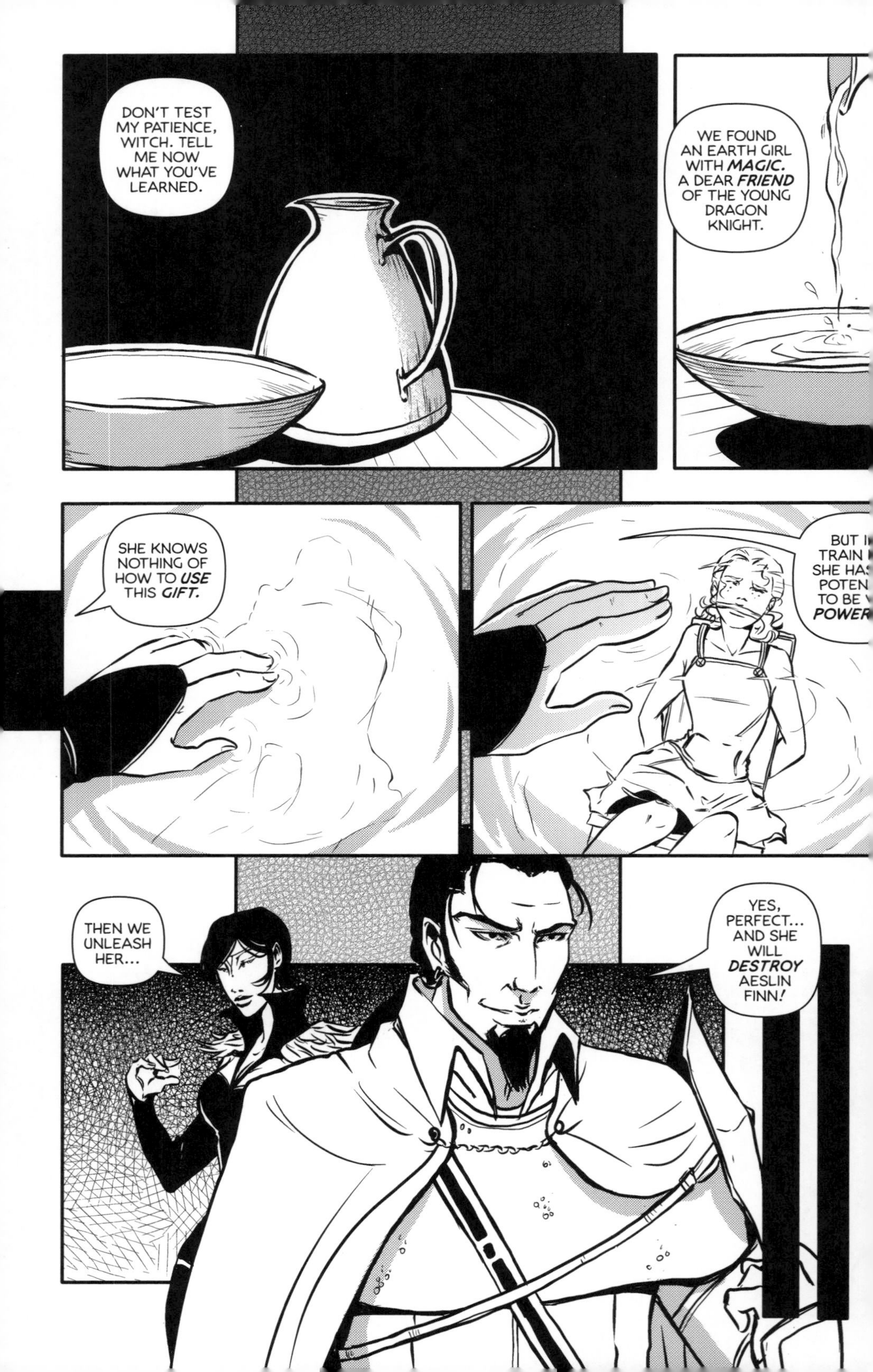
DON'T TEST MY PATIENCE, WITCH. TELL ME NOW WHAT YOU'VE LEARNED.
WE FOUND AN EARTH GIRL WITH *MAGIC.* A DEAR *FRIEND* OF THE YOUNG DRAGON KNIGHT.
SHE KNOWS NOTHING OF HOW TO *USE* THIS *GIFT.*
BUT I
TRAIN
SHE HAS
POTEN
TO BE
POWER
THEN WE UNLEASH HER...
YES, PERFECT... AND SHE WILL *DESTROY* AESLIN FINN!

ABOUT THE AUTHORS

Nunzio DeFilippis and Christina Weir are a writing team trained as screenwriters. They have worked in television, on and off, for the last fifteen years. They were on the writing staff of HBO's *Arliss* for two seasons, and worked on Disney's *Kim Possible*. They have also written an independent film called *Paradise Springs* that is in development.

In comics, they have primarily made their home at Oni Press, who have let them write books in a wide array of genres, including *Skinwalker*, *Three Strikes*, *Maria's Wedding*, *The Tomb*, *Frenemy Of The State*, and *The Amy Devlin Mysteries*.

They have also written superhero comics like *New Mutants*, *New X-Men*, *Adventures Of Superman*, and *Batman Confidential*, and have worked in the field of manga, adapting numerous series for Del Rey. They created three Original English Language Manga series for Seven Seas Entertainment: *Amazing Agent Luna*, *Dracula Everlasting*, and *Destiny's Hand*, as well as a two-volume Luna spinoff called *Amazing Agent Jennifer*.

In 2012, Nunzio and Christina released a graphic novel called *Play Ball* with Jackie Lewis, as well as *Bad Medicine*, with Christopher Mitten. Both projects are with Oni Press. They also just completed their first prose novel, a young adult thriller called *Mind Dance*, and are at work writing a second novel and a new screenplay.

www.weirdefilippis.com

Emma Vieceli is a comic artist and writer based just outside Cambridge, United Kingdom. When she's not making comics, she's thinking about making comics. Her credits include work on the *Manga Shakespeare* series (Amulet Books), *Girl Comics* (Marvel), *Dragon Heir: Reborn* (Sweatdrop Studios) and she is the artist for the graphic novel adaptations of Richelle Mead's *Vampire Academy* (Penguin Razorbill). She is over the (blue) moon to be working with Oni Press.

www.emmavieceli.com

ALSO BY DEFILIPPIS, WEIR, AND ONI PRESS:

THE AVALON CHRONICLES
VOLUME ONE
ONCE IN A BLUE MOON
NUNZIO DEFILIPPIS · CHRISTINA WEIR
EMMA VIECELI

THE AVALON CHRONICLES, VOL 1
ONCE IN A BLUE MOON
By Nunzio DeFilippis, Christina Weir & Emma Vieceli
160 Pages · B&W
ISBN: 978-1-93464-75-0

PAST LIES
AN AMY DEVLIN MYSTERY CHRISTINA WEIR / NUNZIO DEFILIPPIS / CHRISTOPHER MITTEN

THE AMY DEVLIN MYSTERIES:
PAST LIES
By Nunzio DeFilippis, Christina Weir & Christopher Mitten
160 pages · B&W
ISBN 978-1-934964-39-2

ALL SAINTS DAY
AN AMY DEVLIN MYSTERY CHRISTINA WEIR / NUNZIO DEFILIPPIS / DOVE MCHARGUE / KATE KASENOW

THE AMY DEVLIN MYSTERIES:
ALL SAINTS DAY
By Nunzio DeFilippis, Christina Weir, Dove McHargue & Kate Kasenow
168 pages · B&W
ISBN: 978-1-934964-23-1

PLAY BALL
NUNZIO DEFILIPPIS · CHRISTINA WEIR
JACKIE LEWIS

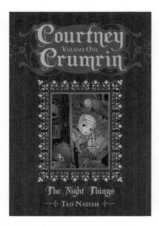

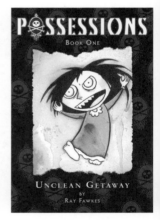

PLAY BALL
By Nunzio DeFilippis, Christina Weir & Jackie Lewis
152 pages · B&W
ISBN: 978-1-934964-79-8

Courtney
VOLUME ONE
Crumrin
The Night Things
TED NAIFEH

COURTNEY CRUMRIN, VOL. 1:
THE NIGHT THINGS
By Ted Naifeh
136 pages · Color
ISBN: 978-1-934964-77-4

POSSESSIONS
BOOK ONE
UNCLEAN GETAWAY
BY
RAY FAWKES

POSSESSIONS, BOOK ONE:
UNCLEAN GETAWAY
By Ray Fawkes
88 Pages · 2-Color
ISBN: 978-1-934964-36-1

ONI PRESS
REVOLUTIONIZE COMICS
www.onipress.com

For more information on these and other fine Oni Press graphic novels, visit www.onipress.com.
To find a comic specialty store in your area, call 1-888-COMICBOOK or visit www.comicshops.us.